DECODING ESL

International Students
in the American College Classroom

D1292372

DECODING ESL

International Students in the American College Classroom

Amy Tucker

Queens College
The City University of New York

Boynton/Cook Publishers Inc.
Heinemann
Portsmouth, NH

Boynton/Cook Publishers, Inc.
A subsidiary of Reed Elsevier Inc.
361 Hanover Street
Portsmouth, NH 03801-3912
Offices and agents throughout the world

First published by McGraw-Hill, Inc. in 1991.

Every effort has been made to contact copyright holders for
permission to reprint borrowed material. We regret any oversights
that may have occurred and would be happy to rectify them in
future printings of this work.

The authors/editors and publisher wish to thank those who have
generously given permission to reprint borrowed material:

Selected poems © 1981 by Leslie Marmon Silko. Reprinted from
STORYTELLER by Leslie Marmon Silko, published by Seaver Books,
New York, New York.

"Good Advice is Rarer Than Rubies" © by Salman Rushdie,
reprinted with the permission of Wylie, Aitken & Stone, Inc. First
published in The New Yorker.

Library of Congress Cataloging-in-Publication Data

Tucker, Amy.
    Decoding ESL : international students in the American college
classroom / Amy Tucker.
       p. cm.
    Includes bibliographical references and index.
    ISBN 0-86709-359-5
    1. English philology–Study and teaching (Higher)–United
States. 2. English language–Study and teaching–
Foreign speakers. 3. Language and education–United States.
4. Students, Foreign–United States. I. Title.
PE68.U5T83 1995
428'.007–dc20
                                  95–5137
                                  CIP

Editor: William Varner
Production: Elizabeth Valway
Cover design: Phillip Augusta

Printed in the United States of America on acid-free paper
99 98 97 96 95 EB 5 4 3 2 1

About the Author

AMY TUCKER is Associate Professor of English at Queens College of the City University of New York, where she teaches writing and American literature. Co-author of *The Random House Writing Course for ESL Students* and *Forms of Literature: A Writer's Collection* (Random House), she has also published articles on composition, literature, and art history.

For Steve

Contents

PREFACE   xi

Introduction: "Trying to Handle Two Languages at
Once": ESL Students in the College Classroom   1

**PART I   CROSS-CULTURAL LITERACY: WHAT DO
          READERS NEED TO KNOW?**   17

1 On First Reading   19
2 Rereading Chapter 1   36

PART II   IN THE COMPOSITION CLASSROOM   65

3 How to Do Things with Function Words: A Russian
       Student's Acquisition of English Articles   67
4 A Greek Writer's Idiolect: What Is Not an ESL Error?   93
5 "What Changed Me":
       Mimi Soo and the Question of Motivation   114
6 Some "Japanese" and "American"
       Rhetorical Preferences   149
7 In Which the Emphasis of Chapter 6 Is Shifted:
       Some "American" and "Japanese" Rhetorical Preferences   172

PART III   IN THE LITERATURE CLASSROOM   197

8 Breaking Literary Codes, or Reading Students' Notebooks   199
9 Notes for an American Studies Course   229

BIBLIOGRAPHY   279
INDEX   295

Preface to the First Edition

This book is intended primarily for teachers of writing. Yet on many campuses around the country, faculty members in every discipline are starting to assess the implications of two significant events of recent years: the increased enrollment of English as a Second Language (ESL) speakers and the reinstitution of core curricula of liberal arts and sciences requirements.

In the early 1980s, we began to see evidence of the far-ranging consequences of these two events on the Queens College campus of the City University of New York. In February of 1984 a questionnaire was sent to those instructors who had taught Liberal Arts and Sciences Requirements (LASAR) courses during the previous semester, asking them for their thoughts about the effects of the newly instituted distribution requirements on faculty and students, particularly nonnative students. Their responses raised many of the questions I have since tried to take up in the present study. Following are some of their observations.

Many respondents were quick to point out the relative strengths of their ESL students. As you might imagine, instructors of mathematics and science courses regularly noted that these students were often among the most accomplished in the class. One math instructor explained, "In my experience, the better foreign students, even when they have a language problem, are able to do mathematics on an advanced level. I have had students who could not pass the English requirements yet performed excellently in my honors calculus class." A number of teachers of humanities courses, as well, wrote to this effect: "The increase of foreign students—particularly Orientals—in recent years has substantially improved the quality of the classes" (Art History); "Many nonnatives are the best, most receptive, most reliable in class" (Introduction to Music); "If anything, the ESL students I had were more sensitive to literature and better equipped to handle difficult concepts than many of the native speakers. They brought to the class a broad cultural perspective that native speakers often lack" (Introduction to Poetry).

When asked what types of assignments posed greatest difficulty for nonnative students in LASAR courses, a psychology professor observed, "They need help with lab reports and other technical writing." A geology professor added that ESL students predictably have trouble with "spelling and scientific terminology." This from the Math Department: "Some ESL students resisted writing explanatory arguments and tried to use only math-

ematical symbols"; another math professor corroborated: "They have difficulty understanding verbal problems and following instructions for nontyp-
ical problems. Also, very often they understand the logic of the statement but
the grammatical errors of their answers make the logic seem faulty." An
instructor of French literature wrote, "The class was frustrating for me because I felt I was teaching masterpieces at their lowest level. However, I think
that my class did help nonnative students to understand Western culture a
little better. The main problem was that the class had very few common
points of reference. The novels were read and understood at their anecdotal
level, where students could identify with the main characters and say can-
didly, 'The same thing happened to me.' "

Of the contrasts between native and nonnative students with respect to
classroom behavior and performance, the instructor of an education course
noted, "Most of them are shy and won't ask questions; they usually believe
they should be silent and take notes." Perhaps most tellingly, an anthropology
teacher remarked, "When I announced I was giving papers rather than exams,
about 15 students (mainly Oriental) dropped the course. They were probably
the least prepared—or the most frightened. Many come to class having
passed basic courses, but without any knowledge of cultural expectations."

Some instructors said they modified various aspects of their teaching for
ESL students—slowing down lectures, defining terms and idioms in context,
simplifying instructions on exams, and so on. A few others spoke against
such practices. The following two responses, both from members of the
English Department, suggest the range of reactions to the delicate question of
accommodating nonnative speakers in courses that require extensive reading
and writing:

"I have tried to explain more carefully the cultural background of the
19th-century literature we read this term. I would like to see American
studies or American literature classes reaching out to nonnative speakers.
How could we make our courses more appealing? Perhaps a course in three
central American texts might provide cultural context, reading experience,
and vocabulary, through ample discussion of the life and background of the
books: *The Scarlet Letter, Moby-Dick,* and *The Adventures of Huckleberry Finn.*
There's no condescension in this, and possibly a good deal of cross-cultural
commentary where the students could inform the teacher. I have marked that
many of my nonnative 110 students are well educated in the literature of their
own cultures. This [would be] a way for them to draw on that experience and
develop skills in reading and writing English."

"No, nor do I intend to. Any such step would mean a further reduction
in standards at a college whose standards are already debased."

Both respondents, while describing decidedly different approaches to
the issue of nonnatives' performance in upper-level courses, express a growing concern with ESL matters that cuts across the boundaries of academic
disciplines. At the very least, further research on international students at the
college level should encourage dialogue between these voices.

Preface to the Revised Edition

In the years since this book was researched and written, the dialogue on multiculturalism has long since gone beyond the college campus and become a matter of international debate. Nevertheless, for this revised edition of the text I have chosen to let most of the original manuscript stand, inscribing as it does the tentative conclusions, enthusiasms, and occasional missteps of the decade of personal teaching history it chronicles.

ACKNOWLEDGMENTS

This book owes its existence to the students who so generously permitted me to reprint the conversations and papers that are the heart of the project. To each of them I'd like to offer my deepest gratitude and admiration.

I'm indebted to Diane Menna and Anna Brady for research assistance at various stages in this project; to my friends Nancy Comley, Jackie Costello, Susan Harris, Howard Kleinmann, Don McQuade, and David Richter for reading early versions of some of these chapters; and to many other colleagues and friends in the Queens College English Department who have freely given ideas and encouragement over the years—here I want to single out Rosemary Deen, Eric Mendelsohn, Janice Peritz, Marie Ponsot, Sandra Schor, Sue Shanker, Donald Stone, Bette Weidman, and William Wilson.

Kudos to the team at Boynton Cook/Heinemann. Like so many other teachers and writers, I owe more than I can say to Bob Boynton, who rescued this book when it had languished at another publisher. My thanks, too, to Bill Varner, who met all exigencies with intelligence and grace.

Love and gratitude, finally, to my family for their support. To my dear husband, Stephen Tanzer, who listened, spurred, and proofread, and to Nick, who loved unstintingly, this book is affectionately dedicated.

Amy Tucker
New York City 1990, 1994

DECODING ESL
International Students
in the American College Classroom

Introduction

"Trying to Handle Two Languages at Once": ESL Students in the College Classroom

A few years back I came across a provocative little item in *The New York Post* and filed it away with the rest of my linguistics research. The article featured Michel Thomas, language teacher to the stars—a man who, according to the *Post*, "whispered in Candice Bergen's ear, helped Yves Montand order breakfast, and taught Princess Grace to communicate with her fiancé," among other accomplishments. Mr. Thomas said he could teach anyone to speak a foreign language fluently—with no textbooks, no drills, no memorization, and absolutely no homework—within 10 days. He guaranteed it. "I have just one ground rule for my students," he explained. "Never try to remember anything. The responsibility for the learning and remembering is with the teacher, not the learner."

I am not a convert to this way of thinking. But I believe Mr. Thomas has tapped into a couple of important concepts in language instruction. He recognizes the importance of relieving the anxiety students inevitably associate with the task of expressing themselves in a foreign language. And while no one I know would agree that the burden of learning and remembering rests solely with the teacher, those of us who have begun to teach nonnative students after having taught native speakers have found that we do have more to remember, more variables to juggle, than formerly.

In recent years, at public and private schools around the U.S., English as a Second Language students have been enrolling in unprecedented numbers. Who are these nontraditional students, and how does their presence in the classroom affect the ways we teach? Obviously, ESL is a broad rubric. Nonnative speakers come to us with extraordinarily diverse linguistic back-

---

[1]Queens College of the City University of New York presents an extreme example of the growing phenomenon of internationalism in our schools: roughly one-third of our students are nonnative speakers, the majority of them non-Western. Represented on our campus at last count are natives of 40 countries, speaking a total of 28 languages.

1

grounds,[1] varying degrees of schooling in their own countries, and very different levels of preparation in English. Some are designated by visa status as foreign students, and plan to stay in the United States for a few years to finish their education; some have become American citizens; a number have lived in this country for a good part of their lives. Consider the following student, who emigrated to the U.S. from Korea when he was in the second grade. He speaks little English at home, and so makes occasional second-language errors, despite an idiomatic fluency beyond the abilities of most of our ESL students. His wry journal entry witnesses the frustration of a writer who speaks two languages well, lives in two cultures, but seems not to feel entirely at home in either:

> The major reason for studying English is to communicate with each other. The minor reasons include; this is the United States, and everyone speaks English. The text books are written in English. If you want a good education you better understand English. I have the word English growing out of my ears.
>
> There are two basic types of English. The proper English and your everyday colloquial English. It is commonly known to us as the term slang. Learning the English properly depends on the environment. I, for example was raised in New York City. I speak your everyday New Yorker, "you know like what I mean." This is a slang pharas commonly spoken among many of my friends. I have no trouble surviving the oral test of English. The difficulty of English is expressing your ideas on paper.
>
> The mechanics of grammar plays a major role in writing. You have to account for spelling, punctuation, verb tenses, paragraph structure, clauses, subjunctions, conjunctions and much more. It is hard enough trying not to forget my own language. But trying to handle two languages at once, it is very hard task to accomplish.
>
> I think the word English is very deceiving. They might say I speak English but I do not write in English. I have not been thought properly when I was very young. It is very hard for me to change now.

As in the case of the influx of basic writers in American colleges during the early 1970s, this demographic change requires a slight shift in pedagogical models. We suddenly find ourselves dealing with a spectrum of discourse communities that may have differing rhetorical and classroom protocols, aesthetic principles, systems of valuation, ways of perceiving and representing the world. While research of the past few decades has profoundly increased our understanding of language acquisition, fainter light has been shed on the complex processes involved in the adult bilingual's attainment of postsecondary academic skills. Limited experience with an international population of this scale and diversity tells us, however, that the bilingual's study of advanced coursework in English often demands cognitive and communicative skills different from those required of native speakers.

The result is that "ESL Composition" has evolved as a hybrid discipline, drawing—as I want to illustrate in the course of this brief introduction—on research in second-language acquisition, sociolinguistics, cognitive psychology, ethnography, and current literary and composition theory. Recent studies in these fields of inquiry share an interest in the ways we organize the world, create it, through language. Reading, writing, and speech are shaped by the cultural orientation as much as by the psychological predisposition of the language learner. Thomas Kuhn tells us that scientific knowledge is a social construct, Richard Rorty that *all* knowledge is a social construct; so rhetoricians have shown how thoughts, facts, discourses, and selves are generated by culture-specific communities. Thus for ESL students in college, even more than for native-speaking basic writers, writing papers or exams is very often a matter of figuring out just what it is English-speaking readers expect of them.

All the same, I do not wish to carry the notion of cultural relativity too far. This is a book about teaching writing and literature to native speakers of other languages, not about teaching English as a second language. Basic writers and readers share many of the same problems regardless of nationality.[2] Although we shall consider matters of linguistic and rhetorical variation in the chapters to come, the overriding concerns of this book are those of current composition theory: issues of learner motivation, syllabus design, collaborative classroom techniques, revision strategies, reading and writing connections, and communicative contexts of discourse. What I have tried to do, though, is to locate these issues in the context of the international college classroom. In a recent article reviewing the growing body of literature on multiethnic education in the United States for grades K–12, Christine Sleeter and Carl Grant note that, surprisingly, "No one . . . discusses connections between models of curriculum and multiculturalism [or] examines the hidden curriculum from a multicultural perspective . . ." (434). These are some of the considerations I had in mind when putting together the chapters of this book.

The Methods of This Study

Case histories mediate cultural generalizations. In these pages I would like to convey something of the experience of a few of the ESL students I have encountered—of their progress as language learners, speakers, writers, readers. The objective is to examine how individual students function

[2]At Queens College we offer separate basic composition courses for international students, having found that a semester or two spent in our preparatory program (College English as a Second Language, or CESL) of intensive language instruction may not be sufficient groundwork for some learners. We have also found that these students are apt to speak and write more freely in ESL composition classes. We have tried to make these sections as much like the native speakers' classes as possible. Teachers are recruited from our more experienced composition staff, more for their skill in the teaching of writing than for prior training in teaching ESL; they are encouraged to use the same syllabi and materials as for native speakers, while taking into account the special strengths and problems of bilingual students.

over a period of time—semesters, even years—given a range of communicative tasks: interviews, class discussions, journal writing, exams, various
essay and revision assignments, and so on. Each chapter investigates successive stages in the attainment of college skills in a second language, from the
absorption of grammatical structures to the incorporation of typical organizing patterns of English exposition to the encounter with American literature.

As in the case of most inexperienced writers, the ESL student's work
is frequently an admixture of incorrect and felicitous choices. The real trick
to assessing and improving the performance of nonnative students is to
address one set of phenomena without losing sight of the other—a palimp-
sest rather like the visual conundrum of a Victorian puzzle picture or an
Escher print. It would be a serious underestimation of our international
students, many of whom have had some college education in their own
countries, to limit our reading of their work to error analysis that arrests our
sights at the level of grammatical competency. Still, in an effort to make sense
of what often seems at first glance a bewildering thicket of problems in our
students' writing, I have begun several of the following chapters with an
overview of the common ESL errors and key features of a particular linguistic
system. The point of these brief surveys (the more superficial since I speak
none of the other languages discussed in this book, but have tried to learn
what I could of them, ad hoc, in the course of teaching composition to
nonnative speakers over the past ten years or so) is to recognize the individual's errors not as random mistakes[3] but as part of certain comprehensible
patterns that are both inevitable and necessary in language learning. Then
too, students who share in this process of investigating patterns of error are
more likely to rethink the incorrect or inappropriate strategies on which they
have come to rely.

By way of introducing some of the methods of error analysis touched on
in the following chapters, let me quickly summarize the history of various
approaches to the study of ESL, and then move on to matters more relevant
to the larger concerns of this book.

Early research on second-language acquisition tended to focus on explanation and correction of errors in spoken sentences. Contrastive analysis
(CA), formulated during the 1940s and '50s using methods drawn from
structural linguistics, posited that many second-language errors were attributable to interference from the bilingual's mother tongue. Contrastive analyses thus compared parallel descriptions of the learner's native and target
languages and then examined the way individuals tended to transfer
sounds, word forms, syntactical patterns, and concepts from first to second
language.

Subsequent empirical studies revealed that learners made a number of
errors not explained by contrastive analysis. Many of these errors were
common to second-language performers of very different linguistic back-

---

[3]Except, of course, for the unsystematic slips recognized as "performance mistakes,"
occurring as a result of memory lapse, fatigue, confusion, strong emotion, and the like.

grounds. Moreover, learners did not make all the errors predicted by CA: second-language students who were aware of a potential pitfall tended to skirt it, to practice "avoidance strategies." The distinction was eventually drawn between a "strong" version of CA that predicted errors and a "weak" version that explained certain errors after they occurred. It is in this "weak" form that CA survives today.

Contrastive analysis has been subsumed under the more general approach of error analysis, which analyzes all systematic errors a speaker or writer makes in the target language. A large number of language-learning errors are termed "developmental," having to do not with the differences between first and second language but with the intrinsically difficult features of the target language. Research conducted during the 1960s and '70s showed how second-language learners are likely to make many of the same errors as children acquiring their native tongue. Often they simplify a particular rule (as in "many student write composition")[4] or overgeneralize from a rule they have learned (e.g., conjugate an irregular verb as if it were regular: "I teared the paper"). It became clear that regardless of first language, adult ESL learners, like children learning English as a first language, have trouble with articles, prepositions, -s endings for plural nouns and third-person singular verbs, and other such inherently problematic features of the language. Theorists hypothesized that language learners develop an "interlanguage" or "approximative system"—a language system that differs from both the mother tongue (in the case of second-language learners) and the target language. This transitional linguistic system, really a series of "intermediate" grammars, is continually modified as new elements are incorporated during the learning process.[5]

More recently, studies in ESL have tried to determine how linguistic forms are derived by considering the way they are used in extended discourse, whether in conversations or in whole pieces of writing. Here, perhaps in part as a result of the growing presence of advanced nonnative learners in college, research on ESL students begins to branch out from applied linguistics and to borrow from other fields of scholarship. Discourse analysis and comparative rhetoric seek to show how different languages map pragmatic functions onto linguistic and rhetorical forms. From cognitive psychology derives research on the schema theory of reading (discussed in Chapter 8 of this book), showing how culturally determined viewpoint, background knowledge, and expectations affect the learner's encoding, stor-

---

[4]In a series of articles written in the 1970s, John Schumann points out that in the very early stages of second-language acquisition a learner's interlanguage is apt to reflect some of the simplifications and reductions found in the formation of pidgin languages. For example, "no" is used for most negative utterances; questions are not inverted; auxiliaries, possessive inflections, and subject pronouns are deleted; verbs are unmarked. By the same token, Schumann suggests that later stages of second-language acquisition resemble the process of decreolization, or the restructuring and expansion of grammatical forms to conform with the target language—a process fostered by social and psychological integration with the target-language group.

[5]There is the additional possibility that during this process the learner may make "induced errors," the result of faulty training and teaching techniques.

age, and retrieval of information. Current studies in literary theory have also demonstrated how rhetoric expresses the shared conventions and (occasionally conflicting) values of a given group of speakers. Whether practitioners of speech act theory, reader response, or deconstruction, literary critics have come to agree on this point: a reader's comprehension of any text partly depends on his or her familiarity with other culturally derived expectations, texts, references.

As for our *students'* recognition of such cultural variations in rhetoric, persuasive evidence comes from an experiment conducted at Syracuse University. One hundred nonnative students were asked to write compositions comparing academic writing in their first language and in English. The students, native speakers of Japanese, Chinese, Spanish, Portuguese, Farsi, and Arabic, agreed that native- and English-speaking cultures alike emphasize the three-part expository essay consisting of introduction, support for the main idea, and conclusion. Most of them added, however, that in their own countries, lengthy introductions, digressions, and extraneous details are essential elements of discourse. The students characterized their native essays as more reader-focused, more flowery and expressive than English discourse, which they perceived to be systematic, logical, direct, and cold (Martin).

To flesh out these findings, my colleague Norman Lewis recently conducted a similar experiment at the outset of one of his composition courses. Here are excerpts from three typical responses written by his students:

> My native country is China. . . . The similarity in writing is that in China and US. the idea should be clear, and grammar corrected strictly. The difference is in the structure: English writing is more direct and Chinese writing is indirect.

> [Korea] Similarity: a good essay is one in which your ideas and feelings are honestly expressed. Difference: I think Westerners are more logical in describing things, whereas we Eastern people are more speculative in writing.

> In my country [Peru] a good essay is the one that is clear making the point. We use a lot of metaphors and descriptive sentences. Compound sentences are used regularly.
> I find different in US essays that the sentences must be short. One idea, one sentence. Also that the argument must be restricted to one point of view (or one side of the story); we are not so strict in that sense. We might be more flexible to leave some questions about the real statement (to let reader "read in between lines"). Spanish language uses longer sentences with many adjectives and adverbs. Also the punctuation may differ in that we may use quotation marks more freely.
> I find it hard here in the USA because you must just fallow the rules. First comes the introduction = objective. Then the argu-

ment: 1, 2, or 3 specific points in one direccion (no way to make just one point with a very strong meaning), and third a conclusion. Sometimes it sounds like a math equation: $1 + 2 = 3$. There is less consideration of the meaning than the form.

These writers raise two related implications for composition pedagogy. To begin with, they describe alternative ways of perceiving and of organizing experience on paper. They suggest the strong possibility that nonnative students who habitually resist our injunctions to "Be Specific" and "Be Concise" and "Stray Not From the Point" are not necessarily being wayward but merely carrying over linguistic and rhetorical traditions of an academic discourse that is, say, more abstract, speculative, and elliptical. Just as important, these students indicate ways in which our own thinking about composition might have become mummified over the years. Judging from their notes, they seem to have been given a rather exaggerated formula for the expository essay in English, to wit: a topic—announced in a thesis statement at the opening of the essay—is pursued in linear and single-minded fashion and broken down into a series of subdivisions, each supported by numerous concrete examples and illustrations.

Students' comments such as those quoted above thus expose certain underlying assumptions and prejudices of our own academic discourse. Once we recognize other rhetorical conventions, and try to explain our cultural habits to others, our native customs suddenly appear denaturalized. An apt analogy for the reciprocal process of discovery in the ESL composition classroom is provided by Keith Basso at the outset of his ethnographic study, *Portraits of "The Whiteman": Linguistic Play and Cultural Symbols Among the Western Apache* (1979). Here Basso describes the mutual effects of observation in the meeting of two cultures, in this case "Indian" and "Whiteman":

> This essay rests on the premise that Indian models of 'the Whiteman' constitute what Clyde Kluckhohn once described as 'cultural portraits of ourselves,' and that by learning to appreciate these portraits—by analyzing their symbolic content and attending to what they communicate about aspects of the generic *us*— we who are Whitemen can develop a sharper and more sensitive awareness of the impressions we make upon persons whose practices for organizing and interpreting social experience differ from our own (5).

Accordingly, in addition to inquiring into other cultures, the chapters that follow will examine some of the implicit content of native English speakers' academic preferences and pedagogical strategies. We will consider how methods of reading, writing, and teaching might be opened up through encounters with nonnative traditions—or, as Basso suggests, with marginalized cultures native to the United States.

To make these observations is not necessarily to jettison time-honored preferences of the North American academy. A colleague recently mentioned to me that two Greek students in her advanced composition course informed her, "Don't expect us to write the way you do. Greeks tend to write in abstract terms, you know." I know of no formal studies to prove or disprove the students' contention, but their observation is, in any case, beside the point. Part of our job as teachers of writing is to help nonnative speakers succeed in the college curricula of their adopted home. Since they have chosen for whatever reasons to continue their education in this country, they can expect to be trained according to our native rhetorical patterns, the merits of their own traditions notwithstanding.

I am suggesting, though, that it behooves American-born observers to question preconceptions and allow for the salutary influence of other epistemologies. A few further examples, drawn from the social and quantitative sciences, should suffice to underscore the culture-specific nature of certain basic assumptions in U.S. college classrooms. Current cross-cultural research in psychology, for instance, points to the ineffectiveness of Western psychotherapy in the treatment of non-Western patients. Books such as *Naikan Psychotherapy* and *In Search of the Self in India and Japan* point to fundamental differences in child-rearing in Asia and the United States, contrasting a Western emphasis on independence, individualism, and self-assertion with an Eastern focus on cultivating closeness, dependency, gratitude, and obligation to others.[6] These differing concepts of the individual point up the ways typical composition classes in the U.S. — which frequently emphasize autobiography, nurture the writer's distinctive voice, and encourage emphatic defense of the individual's beliefs — may make greater demands on members of cultures that do not prize such expressive modes and behaviors.

By the same token, research in the quantitative sciences tells us that symbolic equations by no means constitute a universal language independent of mother tongue. One Chinese speaker maintains that while Chinese is more precise than English in depicting human relationships, most notably in the wealth of its terms for expressing kinship, English tends to be more precise in the hard sciences. For balancing chemical equations, symbols in English have to be used; the Chinese student has to make a mental shift

---

[6]Two articles on Indian psychotherapy, from the White and Pollack collection listed in the bibliography for this chapter, similarly illustrate the conflict between Western ideals of autonomy and individuation and the concept of the individual in Hindu society as part of a large social "network which determines his goals and shares his destiny" (B. K. Ramanujam in White and Pollack 65).

I cite such studies with this caveat: as you can see, this sort of research entails a certain amount of generalization that is inevitably distorting. In the same way, I realize, "the West" or "the Americans" as represented in the following chapters may tend to become homogenizing stereotypes as much as "the East" or "the Japanese." Examination of cultural and linguistic differences runs the risk not only of reifying cultures, but of setting them in contrived and misleading opposition. As I have noted, to offset the tendency toward essentialism, these chapters will focus on stories and particulars, on longitudinal studies of individual learners.

from Chinese characters to alphabetic symbols, and this shift in turn may have some bearing on the thought processes (Cheong). Similarly, as Yasuteru Otani observes, translation of many common mathematical operations into Japanese requires that the order of the symbols be reversed:

> In other words, the structure of mathematical expressions is utterly foreign to Japanese, and it can be inferred from this that mathematical expressions are not independent of nor neutral among natural languages. This is easily understood if we recall the fact that current mathematical expressions were modeled in Europe on European languages in the sixteenth to the eighteenth centuries. As the expressions become more complicated, this discrepancy between Japanese and the expressions is aggravated, and it constitutes a serious obstacle for Japanese students in the way of learning advanced mathematics (70).

And Carlos E. Vasco, having taught math in Colombian grade schools, concludes of his experience:

> [I]t revealed that making mathematics one's own can be as culturally dependent as learning literature or history, and not only at the linguistic or symbolic level. The apparent ahistoricity and aculturality of mathematics is a fiction of an adult mind that has reached the plateau of formal thought and has repressed the historically conditioned, culturally dependent reasoning of all children and most adults . . . (in White and Pollack 170).

It should be clear by now that whatever discipline we're teaching, we're not simply offering training in an isolated technical skill: we're teaching a way of experiencing the world. Even the most proficient nonnative speakers, more than their native counterparts, require training to see how language and culture dictate analysis and exposition. Yet often such matters are subordinated to more concrete and pressing linguistic concerns in our basic ESL courses and taken for granted in our upper-level humanities and science courses. If our colleges are to accommodate an increasingly international population without compromising scholastic standards, a logical starting point is our reading of ESL texts as "holistically"—to recall a buzz-word of the 1970s—as we have been trained to do with native speakers' essays. What we learn from these texts might lead to a more comprehensive method of evaluating and improving the performances of native and nonnative students alike.

Muted Groups: "Some People Think You Are Dumb When You Cannot Speak"

Let me invoke one more concept, borrowed this time from studies in cultural anthropology, that has bearing on the teaching of composition and literature. Shirley and Edwin Ardener have used the term "muted groups" in their analyses of women's cultures, and the phrase has since been taken up by feminist writers. I would like to appropriate the term for a different context if I might. ESL students often constitute a muted group, the boundaries of whose cultures overlap, but are not wholly contained by, the dominant indigenous group.

This model of containment and its frequent result, the silencing or muting of the subgroup, is useful to our understanding of how persons subsumed under the rubric of "nonnatives" are perceived from the outside and how they in turn perceive themselves and others in the host country. The concept holds important implications for the international student's ability to participate in his adopted culture while maintaining important affiliations with his home culture. We are all aware of the reticence of nonnative students in class and of the segregation of linguistic communities on campus, whether in the lecture hall or the student cafeteria. Most of us would like these students to feel comfortable enough in our classrooms to break out of the linguistic ghetto and their own sense of disenfranchisement. Held back by pronunciation difficulties, limited English proficiency, and lack of familiarity with certain rhetorical protocols, ESL students often describe experiences such as those related by the following two writers, the first Iranian and the second Korean:

> Some people think you are dumb when you cannot speak. I remember in my math class I used to afraid to ask questions or answer questions because I thought other students will laugh or make fun of me.

> Even though I have been in this country for four years, I still have a big problem speaking English with Americans. I seldom have a chance to speak English in my daily life, and I think my ability is diminishing day by day. I'm writing about this because speaking English is quite important in the classroom, and it changes my role in classroom participation.
>
> I am taking sociology courses which demand a great deal of discussion. Since I have a terrible problem in English, I have to be passive all the time; I am always a good listener, but not a good speaker. Sometimes there is something I really want to say, but I am afraid that I will make fool out of myself in front of classmates. They must think I am someone who has never thought anything.
>
> But these things would be drastically different if the classes were filled with Korean students. Then I would say whatever I perceived. In my opinion, language is the key reason why I might behave differently in Korean and American classrooms. I hope I get over this in the future.

It stands to reason that the student's cultural background may affect not only her communicative skills and comprehension but her performance in class and on homework assignments as well. The American-born student who has from the first grade been encouraged to speak out in class may be regarded as a show-off by Asians, who have been taught to maintain a respectful silence and not to question the instructor or volunteer comments in the classroom. In the same vein, to take a matter discussed at length in Chapter 7, for many Asian students, whose native cultures encourage consensus, the kind of debate valued in American classes goes against the behavioral norm. These students often express discomfiture with the argumentative essays required in many composition courses—and, for that matter, generally elicited by the Writing Assessment Test that all students in the City University of New York must pass. Consider the cranky ruminations that cropped up in a practice Assessment Test written by Ku Chien-Chung, a Taiwanese student whose progress in English will be charted at several junctures in the course of this book:

> CUNY Assessment doesn't have a clue for a student to prepare for it. Although I have only taken it twice, I discovered that there are many different topics for the test ranging from the deterioration of the American society to Reagan's economics to the meaning of life and the future world. Some of the topics are interesting; some are boring; some are not familiar to foreign students. If a student knows nothing about the topic, how can he write about something from nothing? . . .
>
> I just wrote three practice Assessment tests which were asked by my tutor in the Workshop. My mind is fed up with those topics. They are "money means everything in the U.S.A.," "fast food restraunts serves plastic dishes, plastic plates, and plastic atmosphere," and "job security is more important than career development." I wish that I could make out something suitable for the topic "The Assessment test is an abomination" from those three topic. How about that the Assessment test serves plastic atmosphere when I sit on a plastic chair, hold a plastic pen, and write about a plastic topic? It comes to me that the topics of "fast food restraunt" and "Assessment test" do have some connection, which is they are all plastic and impersonal.

Of course much of this is standard, though wonderfully eloquent freshman grousing. But I also interpret these sidetracked paragraphs with the knowledge that the writer, who had submitted highly accomplished narratives, descriptions, and analyses in his composition courses, mightily resisted assignments calling for argument. Until recently, in the school systems of Mainland China and Taiwan the latter types of discourse have largely been ignored. In place of debate, Chinese rhetorical tradition emphasizes narration as a means of introducing information, giving advice, and arousing interest. Ku and I repeatedly discussed the problem of his missing persuasive essays, so that at length it probably became clear to him that I couldn't fathom his obstinacy. One day he appeared in my office. "I once knew this Chinese boy," he began, and proceeded to narrate, in the third person, the history of his performance in my class. He made a convincing case for himself, persuading obliquely, through storytelling, as he had been trained.

In considering the diverse rhetorical options offered by the students quoted in the foregoing pages, as well as the findings of the various academic disciplines cited in this chapter, I suppose what I have really been talking about are alternative ways of empowering muted groups. I have been speaking, first of all, of expanded opportunities for our international population. As it stands now, ESL students in liberal arts colleges typically wind up doing what they can rather than what they might if given the right tools. One Chinese student from the Mainland, Xuya Chen, recently wrote a research paper for her English class in which she polled 14 other Chinese students[7] about their reasons for choosing their majors. She found that seven had chosen computer science, six accounting, and one mechanical engineering; when asked their reasons, most gave equal weight to employment opportunities and avoidance of language problems. "As to personal interests," Xuya observed, "they neglected them" (Chen 4).

This needn't be the case. Take the example of Ku Chien-Chung, the writer quoted a moment ago. Like many ESL students at Queens College, Ku originally chose to be a computer science major because of the job opportunities—and also, by his own admission, because a science major obviously has fewer demands made on his written English than a humanities major. Ku enjoyed writing, and wanted to make time for English electives, but was hesitant to do so because of his then-limited language skills. The turning point for him came somewhere in the middle of his first composition course—in the middle of a description he was writing, to be precise. He began the description ("If there is one word to describe my room, it is 'untidiness' "), proceeded to record his impressions in a lackluster paragraph or two, then started to narrate what happened when he entered his bedroom to work on his writing assignment, and finally found his real topic in a digression:

> When I read through my English composition, I often can come up with a new idea to reorganize the original one, and the teacher's compliments will also come to my mind. They stimulate me and make me keep on thinking and writing. Yet, English is so profound and still a mystery to me: there is no way for me to manipulate it right now, but express my feelings in its form. Sometimes I really think I should be like every other foreign student: study some basic English courses, learn a technical skill, find a job, get married. . . . And these two extreme feelings puzzle me.

[7]Xuya's description of her informants is as follows: four graduate students, ten undergraduates; eight female, six male; seven from China, five from Taiwan, two from Hong Kong; five had been in the United States three to six years, and nine had been here eight months to two years. As it happens, all of these informants spoke Mandarin, and requested that the interviews be conducted in that language so that they might speak their minds more freely.

I light up a cigarette and put the composition away. However, the puzzle is still around and around in my head. I wish I could solve the puzzle by applying a math formula; for example, one plus one must be equal to two. But this puzzle is always in a trade-off manner: on one end, I want to devote myself to computer and get a job fast; on the other end, there are a self-accomplishment, that I can express my thoughts in writing from which I have sort of discovered myself, and a happiness that my English writing has been recognized. I then light up another cigarette.

I will clean up my room tomorrow; I will smoke less tomorrow; I will think about what to write on the composition "A Description of My Room" tomorrow; and I will fix up my computer programs tomorrow.

To this essay Ku appended a message to his instructor:

A Short Note to Dear Dr. _____

I have found the solution for the puzzle in the composition, "A Description of My Room," and a formula applying for the solution is the following:

ENGLISH + COMPUTER = ENGLISHANDCOMPUTER

If I want to find a word to describe my room now, it is "neatness."

In Ku's formula, two elements can successfully be combined into one unit. Ku later explained, "In math, one plus one must always be equal to two. But in my equation, I broke the rules. You can do things like that in English." Ku elected to make time for English as well as computers. Examples of his subsequent coursework appear in Chapter 5 of this guidebook. Further word on Ku's progress in English can be found in Chapter 8, which concludes with a sestina Ku composed for his poetry workshop.

This growing international population can provide expanded educational opportunities for our native-born students as well. I can give you a very literal example of the American-born student's propensity for reading through cultural blinders. Recently a colleague told me he had assigned to his students Nadine Gordimer's short story "Six Feet of the Country." This widely anthologized story deals with apartheid in South Africa, and its setting, just outside Johannesburg, is stated on page one. Yet when the class was asked on a quiz where the story was set, 8 out of 30 native-born students answered "America," one specifically naming "Georgia" as the locale. How to overcome cultural provinciality? Many other teachers in our department (a number of them quoted in Chapter 8) have attested to the ways in which the participation of nonnatives in the classroom encourages the native speakers who have never left Queens—and I speak of Queens as a state of mind as well as a geographic region—to venture out of their borough and into the world.

I have wanted to indicate, finally, the options ESL students present for their teachers. As on many U.S. campuses, composition courses at Queens are most often taught by part-time faculty, who have always been called upon to respond most immediately and imaginatively to changing demographics on campus, whether to the legacy of open admissions in the seventies or to the new internationalism of the eighties. In one of our composition workshops a few years ago, these faculty members spoke persuasively about their experiences teaching nonnative students, and subsequently wrote up their comments for distribution in the English department. Here is what one colleague, Anita Soloway, had to say about the pedagogical opportunities afforded by this population:

> . . . Why do I request ESL sections in preference to regular 105s? I prefer teaching ESL students because their papers, for all their technical problems, are generally much richer than those of their American counterparts. And this is so because their experiences have been more complicated, more difficult, and often far more painful. Whereas the average American freshman is preoccupied with the move from high school to college as one of the major changes in his life so far, the ESL student is absorbed in the difficulties of adjusting to a different country and culture.
>
> For the [average] American student, freedom will mean the liberty to devise his class schedule; for the ESL student who has left his family in Greece in order to study in the United States, freedom will mean the burdens and benefits of supporting himself. And for Phan Luong, whose family were among the boat people of Vietnam, freedom has yet another, more profound meaning. In response to an assignment to write about any aspect of one's native city, Phan chronicled her family's ordeal after the Communist takeover of Saigon. The pain and fear of those years filled 10 pages whose coherence was weak but whose contents were riveting. And I find it far more exciting to help Phan or Tassos reorganize their material than to work on yet another paper about high school or college. The papers of a "regular" 105 are usually written by adolescents; those of an ESL 105 are more often written by adults discussing the very experiences that made them adults. . . . Their rare power to interest and to move more than compensates for their linguistic deficiencies.

The Outline of This Book

Let me indicate how the issues and methods mentioned in the preceding pages will be treated in chapters to come. Chapters 1 and 2 form a unit I have called "Cross-Cultural Literacy." In Chapter 1 you will find reprinted a draft of a speech I wrote in 1987, analyzing the work of two Persian-speaking students. In Chapter 2, written a year later, I reread and reinterpret the cultural artifacts discussed in Chapter 1. Taken together, these two chapters provide a prolegomenon for the book, exploring questions of how we read, represent, and inscribe other cultures—considerations that shape succeeding chapters.

The remaining chapters then roughly follow the chronology of my experiences teaching writing and literature to international students. The second unit of the book, comprising five chapters, concerns the teaching of writing to nonnative speakers of English. Chapter 3, the earliest written of these discussions, is, I regret to report, almost exclusively concerned with error. The study follows a Russian-born student through a semester of composition in 1981, picks up his progress two semesters later, and ends with an interview conducted with him in 1984. I have called this chapter a case study in interlanguage: the emphasis is on how an ESL learner acquires a basic grammatical unit of the language—in this instance, English articles, which cause troubles for most ESL students.

Moving out of this small grammatical compass, Chapter 4 surveys the range of a Greek student's written responses to a series of assignments over the course of a semester, and concludes that certain problems that initially appear to be ESL-related actually derive from this basic writer's idiosyncratic approach to a specific writing task. The chapter begins with a general outline of the kinds of methods and assignments I use in an introductory composition course, and proceeds to examine how the Greek-born subject of the study rather comically turned the glare of inquiry back on the observer, questioning the pedagogy my colleagues and I have come to hold dear. Chapter 5, which follows the remarkable progress of a Taiwan-born woman who had returned to college after a long hiatus, elaborates on a theme introduced in the preceding chapter, namely the relationship between affective and motivational variables and writing proficiency. Chapters 6 and 7 approach the much-debated question of cultural variation in rhetoric from two different perspectives. Chapter 6 examines Japanese linguistic and social forms and their relation to certain characteristic rhetorical preferences among Japanese speakers and writers. Chapter 7 reverses this process by focusing on the domestic manners of the Americans, particularly with regard to habits of argumentation, and speculates as to how the Japanese rhetorical conventions discussed in Chapter 6 might influence these students' production of argument in the American classroom.

The third and final section of the book looks at both native and nonnative students' encounters with literature written in English. Chapter 8 recounts the findings of an experimental Writing and Literature class conducted in 1984, composed of 10 native and 10 nonnative students and founded on the collaborative classroom methods discussed in the foregoing chapters on writing. My students' responses to various reading selections are analyzed in light of schema-theory research on reading. These responses, drawn chiefly from the students' journals, in turn suggest ways in which the methods and conclusions of schema research might be modified in terms of what we have learned from reception theory and poststructuralist literary criticism. The results of this experimental class subsequently influenced the design of a grant-sponsored American Studies class for nonnative students I taught in 1988, a course described in Chapter 9. In examining the American literary canon in this last chapter, I want to consider some of the broader political questions currently being raised in the process of curriculum revision on college campuses around the country. With this discussion the book comes full circle, earlier chapters on "reading" other cultures having led us back to a reassessment of our own complex national heritage.

The increasing internationalism of campuses throughout the United States has changed our notions of what constitutes the "mainstream" in our college curricula in ways we are just beginning to sort out. The following chapters are offered as a kind of foray into the hermeneutics of reading ESL texts; or rather say rereading them, since these texts on second glance may tell us as much about ourselves as they do about foreign-born others.

PART ONE

Cross-Cultural Literacy: What Do Readers Need to Know?

1

On First Reading

This chapter is really a fragment, and should be read in tandem with the one that follows. The chapter I thought I wanted to write appears in rough form in the next 10 pages or so. In those pages, delivered as a speech at a writing conference in November of 1987, I examined a pair of essays by two nonnative students, émigrés from Afghanistan to the United States via Pakistan. By way of reinforcing my thesis about the problematics of a Westerner's approach to texts by Easterners, I casually called up a few examples from the cultural apparatus available to me at the time of writing: concurrent exhibitions of the treasures of the Ottoman Empire and of Matisse's "Oriental" canvases from the Nice period, as well as a short story by Salman Rushdie that had recently appeared in *The New Yorker* magazine.

Please note that in the pre-*Satanic Verses* era when I wrote this chapter and the next, Salman Rushdie was hardly a household name, much less a political red flag. As a result, some of the observations in these pages may seem in retrospect ingenuous, and a few weirdly prescient—particularly my brief attempts toward the end of this discussion to make sense of several Indian-born students' discomfort with the Rushdie story, which, I must point out, does *not* overtly deal with religious issues. I ask the reader to try to recall a time when Westerners were less familiar with Muslim terms, and when writers of fiction need not have feared for their lives to engage those terms.

Chapter 2 is a revision of Chapter 1, written a year later. By pairing Chapters 1 and 2 I wanted to introduce the approach to reading and rereading international texts that imbricates the chapters of this book. In the process I hoped to underscore certain considerations in teaching nonnative speakers—indeed, in teaching students from any group outside the mainstream of the dominant culture: most important, that it is an unavoidably political enterprise to engage, to read, to "write" other cultures. For that matter, ESL teachers soon discover, it is equally an ideologically charged endeavor to teach one's own culture to others. But back in 1987, when my colleagues and I were busy designing special American Studies courses for nonnatives, and other faculty members were initiating a Global Studies program on campus, few of us could have imagined the ramifications of these claims.

Ironically, one of my immediate goals in the present chapter was to illustrate "teacher error," in this case the inevitable—and, I wanted to argue, useful—mistakes we make when we attempt to read and teach multicultural texts, whether the work of students or professional writers. This notion of teacher error seemed to me a likely starting place for a book about international students in American colleges. If a portion of the book were to be devoted to understanding foreign-born students' errors, why not begin by showing how teachers learn from their own initial mistakes in their encounters with foreign material?

The chapter I ended up with makes this last point more emphatically than I had intended. It is at least in one instance an account of unforeseen misreading, a howler, for all the care I had taken to avoid the absolutes of Orientalist thinking. As you will see, in Chapter 2 I go on to reexamine the material discussed here—the student essays as well as the artifacts and the short story—with various corroborations, revisions, and a few more divagations thrown into the bargain. I hope the reader will forgive me these recursions, for I have included them all to suggest the processes of reevaluation percolating during the months between writing and rewriting. Books on composition theory customarily take for their keynote a topic like revision in student writing, and that is indeed my opening text. In this case, though, the work of revision takes place not in the student's head but in the teacher's.

"Cross-Cultural Literacy": Reading Two Students' Texts, November, 1987

I've entitled my remarks with a backward glance at E. D. Hirsch, Jr.'s book, *Cultural Literacy: What Every American Needs to Know*, which caused such a stir earlier this year.[1] Hirsch defines cultural literacy as "the network of information that all competent readers possess" (2). Leaving aside for the moment my questions concerning the term "competent" in this context, let me simply observe that Hirsch evidently has a different set of readers in mind from those who make up a good part of my college community. At Queens College, and at a number of other branches of the City University of New York, at least one-third of these readers are ESL students—that is, even if they were born in this country, they might well have grown up speaking a language other than English at home. Since the majority of our international students at Queens are non-Western, it is all the more likely that they represent a variety of interpretive communities.

Naturally, one of our goals as educators is to give our students a vocabulary for discussing American texts and for writing in ways sanctioned by our own academic discourse community. But I believe that to become something like "competent readers"—to recast Hirsch's term—American-

---

[1] As the 1987 date of the piece indicates, this chapter is reprinted in the "historical present" of the speech as it was originally delivered.

born teachers and students also need to understand patterns of thinking and writing authorized by other cultures, and thus to see a Eurocentric approach to textual analysis as one among many local definitions of competency. In other words, acculturation should work both ways.

Much of our curriculum and classroom methodology is founded on the premise that we and our students agree on certain conventions of discourse—that when we look at a text together, or set out to write essays, we share many of the same underlying assumptions, goals, and values. I'd like to give you a few examples of how misguided this premise can be. I offer these illustrations for the questions they provoke about how we read our nonnative students' work, the protocol we observe in the multicultural classroom, the way ESL students read American literature, and the way we read the literature of other nations. Finally, I'd like to show how these issues do, and should, enter our classrooms regardless of whether foreign names appear on the roster.

I take as the centerpiece of this discussion a fairly innocuous student paper on an uncontroversial subject. The essay is a reasonably accomplished response to a standard introductory composition exercise: the description of a person. It was written by Najla Afzali in an English 105 class for ESL students.[2] Najla's teacher, Diane Menna, informs me that Najla is Afghani; Najla's first language is Dari, a dialect of Persian which, along with Pashto, is one of the two official languages of Afghanistan. As you read Najla's untitled essay (reprinted below in its entirety), I ask you to consider the kinds of assumptions the author seems to be making about her reader:

> When I entered the big and crowded room, I realized that his black eyes never stopped following me. He was about 6'3" tall with narrow shoulders. His bony face and prominent cheeks made him look like a sixteenth century prince. Because his big black eyes and his thick eye brows were very distinct, he stood out in the crowd. He had short black hair that was brushed to the right.
>
> He wore a three-piece black suit with a silk lapel. His white shirt and narrow silky scraf matched very well. The little black bowtie showed that he was very proper. His elegante gold bracelet and diamond ring on his left hand were shining every time as he danced. When he stepped to the front and to the back, his black shoes were shining like a piece of iron under the sun. The coordination of his clothes made him more attractive than anybody else at the party.
>
> We sat with a huge group of his family and friends in front of my table. He was sitting straight on the chair with his head up like a prince who was very proud of himself. Sometimes, the re-

---

[2]In our composition sequence at Queens, we offer English 105, for those who did not pass the CUNY-mandated Writing Assessment Test, as well as Introduction to College Writing (110) and Writing and Literature (120), both of which are required of all our students. Each semester we run an average of 10 special sections of 105 for ESL students.

flection of the red tablecloth made him glow. Whenever the lights went on and off, his black eyes and his glowing cheeks attracted my eyes toward him. His hands were almost all the time on the table and played with his golden cigarette case. Sometimes, he was gossiping with his friends, but he never stopped staring at me.

The way he was sitting, talking, and even looking was very polite and gentle. He seemed neither happy nor sad. He seldom smiled, but his smile was meaningful.

I was waiting alone for my father to bring dinner for me. As I listened to the music I started dreaming. Suddenly I saw that a shadow was coming toward my table. That was him, I couldn't believe it. His soft steps were getting closer to my table. In a very polite voice, he asked to sit at my table. I said, "yes, yes please." His black eyes at closer look were more attractive than before.

His eyes were kind of wet that you would think he was cry- ing; but those were the kind of eyes that could attract a person at the first moment. He introduced himself in a very competent way. Then he asked my name and gave me a compliment. He was talk- ing so softly and slowly. He often used words that poets use. He usually used poetical comparisons. For example, he told me, "Your perfume smells like the best spring flowers from the flower country Ireland." His words were so lovely and romantic that I even remember them.

When he seemed ready say something to me, my father came with dinner. He politly stood up and shook my father's hand. Then he looked at me in a way which I thought he meant, he couldn't finish what he wanted to say. He wanted to leave, but my father asked him to stay and eat at our table. During dinner time, his eyes looked down, which I thought he was respecting my father. He only said yes or no to my father's questions.

When he wanted to leave our table; he gently kissed my hand and said, "I hope to see you again as soon as possible." He went back to his table, but he hadn't finished what he wanted to say. His eyes were still anxious about something. They were talk- ing to me, but I never knew what they meant. While we were standing to leave the party, his eyes came out from their sockets. Surprisingly, he was looking for the second chance to talk. But he never succeeded. He was waiting outside of the hotel until our car moved and disappeared. Our car was followed by his black eyes. . . .

I'm interested in this essay for the way it subtextually propounds an aesthetic ideal, a mode of social behavior, and a rhetorical tradition, all of which differ from their American counterparts. The subject of the piece is a tall, formally attired and elaborately bejeweled stranger with narrow shoul- ders, a bony face, black hair, dark wet-looking eyes and thick eyebrows. Twice the writer tells us that he resembles and carries himself with the hauteur of a sixteenth-century prince. Granted he is not the fair, broad- shouldered, rugged WASP hero that Anglos call up from central casting—

but how many of us are? A good number of Najla's Western readers will recognize in him a Middle- or Near-Eastern ideal of beauty, and many of us share this aesthetic.

At the same time, we should note that the subject may in fact be the opposite of a native-born American student's notion of a sixteenth-century prince: here I speak of the royal line that descends through the Grimms' nineteenth-century tales and is colored and animated in the twentieth century by Disney. Actually the dark stranger of whom Najla writes might have been cast as the villain in the stories I grew up with. Yet it is Najla's evident assumption that her reader will recognize this fellow not only as the most attractive man at the party but as the embodiment of a classic and aristocratic ideal. He bears little resemblance to Prince Charming, but is clearly a cousin of the noblemen, for instance, who people the sixteenth-century manuscripts currently on view at the Metropolitan Museum in the "Age of Suleyman" exhibition of treasures of the Ottoman Empire. I cite this particular illustration not only because it provides at present the nearest available geographical and cultural analogue I can come up with for Najla's prince, but because reactions to the Suleyman show itself encapsulate, for me, the way many Westerners are apt to approach Eastern art, particularly the arts of southwestern and central Asia. This encounter may in turn suggest something of the way Westerners respond to the literary arts of the East as well.

Perhaps predictably, the Suleyman show, the first comprehensive display of Ottoman treasures brought to the United States, has not had quite the same impact, neither on the media nor on the viewers with whom I've spoken, as other major concurrent exhibitions of Western art. For example, the Matisse show at Washington's National Gallery, where the Suleyman show was originally mounted, has been hyped to a far greater extent. The oeuvre of one artist, produced within a limited period of his career, has garnered more attention than various works produced by schools of artists during the efflorescence of Turkish culture. Ironically enough, interest in the Matisse show seems to center on his numerous odalisque paintings, with their exotic subject material, intricate Eastern arabesques, and resplendently colored and patterned surfaces. Why then didn't the museum visitors of my acquaintance value in quite the same way the Eastern designs, not long ago on display in an adjacent gallery of the National, that Matisse had taken for his models?

One obvious reason is that Matisse comes to us with the authority of having been accorded the status of master. As our contemporary and fellow Westerner, he corroborates our notions of what constitutes great art, in this century at least, as well as our conviction that a painting on canvas more properly constitutes a work of art than the miniatures, vases, rugs, and embroidered garments that make up a good part of the Suleyman show. In countries such as Afghanistan, Iran, and Turkey, much artistic production continues to take the form of what Westerners might call handicrafts. Perhaps this is why the friends with whom I chatted were full of the Matisse show but had little to say of the Suleyman, if they had visited the show at all.

Another colleague, a knowledgeable and inveterate gallery-goer, character-ized the Ottoman display as "a glorious collection of *schmattas*."

The point I'm embroidering here is that Najla and her Western readers, whether teachers or classmates, may proceed from divergent ideas about what is admirable or desirable or beautiful—or about what constitutes a work of art. And while none of these differences appears to affect our comprehension or enjoyment of this particular essay, it is possible to imagine Najla's oral and written performance, and our assessment of it, being affected by such differences when she approaches other classroom activities, or homework assignments requiring her to address social and political issues that are emotionally charged for her if not for her American coevals. Perhaps the implications of these cultural variations will become more apparent as we turn to other features of Najla's description.

Najla describes a code of behavior in her essay, and here again the code contrasts with social norms in her adopted country. The young man in question is restrained—but for his disconcerting habit of staring. He is "polite and gentle." During dinner he casts his eyes down, which gesture, along with his simple yes or no answers to her father's questions, Najla interprets as signs of respect. Anyone who has had Asian-born students in the classroom will recognize such behavior not as rudeness but diffidence, though it is in direct contrast to the kind of eye contact and verbal engage-ment that Westerners customarily take for signs of respectful attentiveness. No doubt you have at times been unsuccessful in cajoling Western-style freewheeling class participation, or even "freewriting," from these students.

This much of the social code is overt in Najla's paper, but there is as well a subtext that may have further bearing on her performance, namely the matter of acceptable male and female roles in her part of the world. Najla is at all times the object of this fellow's attentions; she is the passive recipient who never initiates, neither approaches the stranger nor fetches her own dinner. The invitation to sit at her table is solicited by the younger man and acquiesced to by the young woman; the invitation to dine together is ex-tended by her father, who then takes the reins of conversation from the younger man.

Obviously this behavior, although exaggerated in form in Najla's essay, is not foreign to our shores. It is still the norm in this country for men to make the first move socially. But unlike many of our nonnative students, native-born Americans are less apt to be shocked by a reversal of this norm. It goes without saying that Christian, Judaic, and Islamic cultures hold similar prin-ciples concerning the secondary status of women. But in predominantly Muslim countries, the outward signs of change in gender roles have come more slowly and have met with greater resistance. As we know, for example, the Shah's efforts to institutionalize Western ways in Iran, as in the "libera-tion"—the literal unveiling—of women, were opposed by much of the population and eventually reversed by Khomeini and his supporters. Be-cause Islam is the pervasive cultural context in this part of the world, its adherents are often antagonistic, understandably so, to Western ideas, products, and influences, which are perceived as threats to Islamic religious and social institutions.

No wonder, then, that students from non-Western countries are nonplused by free and easy American social relationships—and that Najla, in another essay on culture shock, wrote that what most surprised her about American life was the practice of couples living together out of wedlock. By now, of course, such cultural contrasts are commonplaces among educators. But I don't know that they have been adequately factored into reading lists, discussions, and assignments in our composition and literature classes. I certainly don't mean to imply that we eliminate from our syllabi those reading or writing assignments that might cause cultural confusion among our ESL students. On the contrary, I wish to argue that this circumscription of reading and writing is neither desirable nor possible.

I simply suggest we think more carefully about the ways, for instance, nonnative readers might receive American works, and so prepare them more thoroughly for texts likely to turn up on college syllabi—texts like Tillie Olsen's "I Stand Here Ironing" or Gwendolyn Brooks's poem "The Mother" or Kate Chopin's "The Story of an Hour," to take just three selections that put a spin on traditional conceptions of motherhood and marriage, and, by virtue of their authorship, on the male-dominated canon itself. We can't gloss every word or concept, but once we are alive to potential misunderstandings we can provide richer context. In any event, as we know from our own reading of literature in foreign languages, a work need not be completely intelligible to be meaningful to the reader. As Reed Way Dasenbrock points out in a recent article on multicultural literature written in English, the experience of reading an international text, of working (and occasionally failing) to make sense of it, is in itself part of the meaning of the text (18). This experience should demonstrate most palpably to teachers and students, whether native- or foreign-born, the ways in which patterns of thinking and writing are culture-bound.

I believe it can be argued that we can't really attain "cultural literacy" without being able to view our native culture from the outside, as it were, as an artifact, and that this perspective is achieved only through reading and discussing the literature of other cultures as well as one's own. Indeed, the revealed differences between our students' native and second cultures seems to me a useful theme to explore in our writing and literature courses. We might take advantage of the international mix on our campuses, rather than bewail the further disintegration of the canon or the English language with each new generation of immigrants. The result is what I refer to as "cross-cultural literacy."

I have come to what may be another culture-specific feature of Najla's essay: her characterization of the young man's discourse. It is this feature that holds the greatest significance for our writing classes, for it appears to underscore certain rhetorical values in Najla's culture. Najla tells us that the suitor introduces himself "in a very competent way," that he immediately compliments her, uses poetical words and comparisons, and winds up with a flowery comment on her perfume and a kiss on the hand. His words were so lovely and romantic, she says, that she recalls them even now.

I read Najla's paper with a group of team teachers at Queens last week (we have a team-teaching program of about 20 undergraduates who are paired with writing instructors to assist in the classroom and in tutoring sessions). When we got to this paragraph, there was good-natured laughter all around. "If some guy came on to me with that line," one woman said, "I'd tell him to get lost." I single out this incident less for its demonstration of contrasting courtship patterns than for its illustration of contrasting verbal systems. We have all seen or heard examples of the more formal etiquette of social and economic interactions in the Far and Middle East. Among Persian speakers in Iran, to take just one example, this system may take the form of *ta'arof*—that is, of "presenting," as in giving a gift—in other words, of speaking deferentially and respectfully, offering elaborate compliments and invitations. According to custom, the speaker expresses verbally his lack of self-importance, while indicating the greater stature of the person being addressed, through exceedingly formal greetings, praise, and flattery (Tylor and Taylor 80–81). Politesse extends to public behavior even toward those one dislikes, and to a certain restraint in written judgments as well. This social etiquette serves to keep people at a distance and to reflect mutual respect. Without such amenities, communication seems blunt, brusque, uncivil.

The cultural context I've tried to provide for Najla's essay is simply by way of background; it augments but is not crucial to our understanding of her work. Neither do these cultural differences seem to have affected her comprehension of the form or content demanded by this typical English composition assignment. In the second student's paper I want to show you, however, the cultural contrasts glimpsed in the background of the first essay now come to the fore.

The essay was written in response to an in-class assignment in a special section of English 152, Great Works of American Literature. In the fall of 1986, several members of the English department at Queens applied for and received a grant from the Fund for the Improvement of Post-Secondary Education (FIPSE) to design and implement such a course for nonnative students. I won't rehearse for you here the many ardent debates among our faculty seminar members regarding our varying definitions of words like Great, Works, American, and Literature. That is ample material for another discussion.[3] Suffice it here to point out that the project grew out of the need we perceived for helping foreign-born students with their more advanced coursework in the humanities, especially since the institution of the liberal arts and sciences core curriculum at Queens College in 1981. We felt we had done what we could to help ESL students in their composition courses— although as the foregoing discussion is meant to show, there is much we have yet to consider in formulating a pedagogy for this changing population.

---

[3]Which I have saved for the final chapter of this book.

Our attention turned to the plight of ESL students who were clearly foundering in their required upper-level literature courses.

The following student text was written as a 50-minute diagnostic essay during the first week of the FIPSE course, in answer to a quotation from Tocqueville's *Democracy in America*. This is the quotation and the question framed by the teacher:

> "Americans acquire the habit of always considering themselves as standing alone, and they are apt to imagine that their whole destiny is in their hands. Thus not only does democracy make every man forget his ancestors, but it hides his descendents, and separates his contemporaries from him; it throws him back upon himself alone, and threatens in the end to confine him entirely within the solitude of his own heart."

> This passage was written by a foreign observer of American culture. What are the most important statements in the passage? You may agree or disagree with what the writer says, but please describe and then respond to each statement as fully as you can.

And here is the response written by Mohammad Amin, who, his teacher later told us, is a Russian Islamic student:

> This passage is pointing a very bitter and true fact about American people. As a forigner I observed most of the Americans and I think this passage can be very true about Americans.
>
> Being a self confidence is one of the good qualities of a human-being, but for living a good and meaning full life every one need a guide line. The guide line which can be used as a protector in the situation in which one finds himself alone and helpless. And this guid line is provided by the lives and examples of our ancestors. If we examine their way of life, then we will find out that whatever they said and whatever they did were just to set forth an example for their future generation. Every word of their sayings contains a massage, every steps of them tells us to follow it. This is the duty of the comming generation to follow every step of their ancestors. But as it is mentioned in the passage that Americans are not following the steps of their ancestors, which is leading them to the state of lonelyness and helplessness.
>
> Right now probably Americans are not realising the results of forgetting the massages of their forfathers. They were good and brave. They were the followers of truth. They had belive on their faith. That is why they are named in the history. How today's generation is going to be named in the history is a big question for the history writers and scholar. Are they going to name them as punks, or they will call them as those who forgot their selves and pull the vail of momatory joys on their faces.
>
> Well, the future history is not my concern. The only thing I want to say even Americans have full freedom of every thing, but

they should not forget their historical heros and their ancestors in
this freedom. The history shows that those nations who did not
remember their history, destroyed by their own mistakes.

Our reception of Mohammad's essay is chiefly determined by the writer's problems with English, which are far too basic and profound for this
level, even allowing for the exigencies of in-class writing. According to his
transcript, this student squeaked through English 105, having taken it twice,
and somehow through 110; we have no record of his having taken English
120, the prerequisite for this course. But I want to forgo consideration of the
author's pressing linguistic difficulties for now. I have reprinted his paper
because its *argument*, and our reading of it, I assume to be affected in part by
interference from the student's native culture, in this case the culture of one
of the nations of Islam.

I don't think, when the Tocqueville question was proposed by a member of our seminar group, any of us realized how culture-bound it was; we
didn't anticipate students' misconstruing the question except at the level of
vocabulary or syntax. Although written by "a foreign observer," the passage
seems neutral enough. If democracy makes Americans forget their ancestors
and take their destiny into their own hands, this is not necessarily an evil,
merely an observation, and it is the validity of this assertion that the students
are called upon to assess. Yet Mohammad goes several steps farther, into
censure. It is "a bitter truth" that Americans forget their ancestors, whose
every step, every saying, provides a message for the present generation.

Even in our initial "blind" reading of this paper in our seminar, the
writer's insistence seemed something more than a manifestation of the deep
regard for ancestors often seen in essays by Asian students. His response
forced us as readers to reflect on the nature of the American version of
democracy, founded on myths of self-determination and individualism, on
personal advancement and *progress* and futurity rather than reverence for
one's roots, which are in any case obscured in this land of immigrants.
Mohammad's response runs smack up against the weltanschauung implied
by this concept of democracy. The prevalent Western notion of time as the
lockstep march of history conflicts with certain aspects of Islamic ontology.
Muslim instantaneism, observers have argued, conceives of time less as a
linear progression than as a galaxy of moments or flashes, which, viewed in
succession, merely give the illusion of continuity (Merriam 17). Of course,
contrary to Western folklore about Islam, Muslim doctrine allows considerable room for debate on the subject of free will versus determinism. Yet it is
commonly held among believers that humans cannot take their destiny into
their own hands in quite the same way as, for example, we Americans,
according to our own prevailing mythology, feel ourselves capable of doing.

Perhaps for this reason Mohammad writes that "the future history is
not my concern." One thing is certain, however: he has interpreted Tocqueville's comments as criticism, and is compelled to preach respect for one's
ancestors as the antidote, although this response was uncalled for by the

essay question. I do not wish to give way to Western clichés, of the kind Edward Said has documented so thoroughly in *Covering Islam*, about Muslim fatalism, passive resignation, resistance to the "logic" of causality, and the like. I merely wish to suggest that Muslim believers, taking for their model the Qu'ran as dictated by God to Mohammad, along with the *sunna* or practices of the Prophet and the *hadiths* or traditions of Mohammad and his companions, are embued with what has been called "a general sense of practical readiness for whatever the power of God disposes" (Gilsenan 17). For Muslims, the deeds of great men of the past, particularly of Mohammad and his companions, are normative: reliance upon tradition is a formal principle of the religion. This resort to the authority of tradition is as pervasive in Muslim law as it is in theology, as interpreted and codified and occasionally modified over the centuries by religious and legal scholars, or *'ulama*.

My point is that the in-class assignment devised in the FIPSE seminar inadvertently elicits an "inappropriate" response, not predictably, of course, nor necessarily from all Muslims. We are talking about over 90 million individuals dispersed throughout nations as politically and geographically divergent as—just to enumerate the countries mentioned in the present discussion—Afganistan, Turkey, Iran, India, east and west Pakistan, the Soviet Islamic nations, and the United States. But at any rate the question draws such a response from this particular writer, whose family (so his teacher informed our seminar group after we had read the essay) had lived as Muslims in the Soviet Union, and whose religious identity may therefore have become all the more fierce for being embattled. Ultimately the seminar group agreed that the writer, while held accountable at this stage of his academic career for his serious second-language problems, should not lose points for the nature of his argument, which seemed logical enough once we looked into its cause. Call this, in a post-Borkian age, our consideration of the writer's "original intent."

I have tried to point out a few of the pedagogical issues raised by the growing population of non-Western students in our colleges, issues concerning their understanding of reading and writing assignments and our assessment of their essays. By way of analogy, I'd like to bring up one last point, the matter of our approach to literature written by professional authors from other cultures. This question has surfaced more frequently of late, since we've become more conscious of the desirability of expanding the literary canon to include the growing body of multicultural material written in English. I don't propose to delve very deeply at this point into the ways "cross-cultural literacy" might enrich our reception of texts by professional authors, for my focus in this discussion is the work of student writers. Instead I offer an anecdote that seems to me to take the form of a parable about cross-cultural illiteracy.

A colleague of mine at Queens, a very smart and experienced professor of writing and literature, taught Great Works of English Literature during the summer session of 1987. He found that a number of foreign-born students had enrolled in his class, and decided to address this international population by tailoring part of the reading list to their areas of expertise. When a three-page story by Salman Rushdie appeared in *The New Yorker* one week in June, he photocopied the piece for class discussion, and told the three Indian students enrolled in the course that he should be very grateful for their help in examining the text in class the following day.

The story, entitled "Good Advice Is Rarer Than Rubies" (appended to this chapter), concerns Miss Rehana, who has traveled to the British Embassy to apply for a visa to join her fiancé in England. She is soon accosted by Muhammad Ali, a professional advice expert and something of a shyster, who is so entranced by her beauty and bearing that he finds himself offering her advice, and finally an illegally acquired British passport, for free. He warns her that the British sahibs in the embassy will humiliate her by quizzing her on the most intimate facts of her engagement, only to deny her the visa if she slips up in the slightest detail. The young woman thanks the advice giver but declines his services. Muhammad Ali waits for her at the embassy gates, and when she emerges smiling, congratulates her on her triumph. But Rehana tells him that the visa has not been granted, for she has given her inquisitors all the wrong answers. She reveals that her engagement had been arranged by her parents when she was a child, and that her fiancé is 20 years her senior. She has a good job, in a great house, as ayah to three boys who would be very sorry to see her leave, and so, boarding the bus, she tells Muhammad Ali with her most radiant smile, "I truly do not think you should be sad."

On the first day of the fall semester I chanced to meet my colleague in the mailroom and asked him how the discussion of the story had proceeded. He replied that the three Indian students, for the first and only time in the term, had not shown up for the class in question. When he mentioned to them the next day how much he had missed their participation, one of the three smiled knowingly and said, "Oh, *we* haven't read that story yet, if you know what I mean." The professor speculated that the students, who had clearly acted in concert, might have been offended by the depiction of the lower-caste trickster figure Muhammad Ali, or perhaps by the suggestion of guile on the part of the liberated young woman in the story, or even by the subservience of the other women waiting by the embassy to be grilled by their formal colonial rulers.

A few weeks had passed when my friend provided a coda to this story. He had narrated the incident to a colleague from India, and she had re-minded him that Salman Rushdie is Pakistani, not Indian. (In fact Rushdie considers himself Anglo-Indian-Pakistani; our colleague's characterization of the Indian-born Rushdie as Pakistani alone may reflect the fact that she regards him primarily as Muslim.) A rush of new possibilities presented themselves to my friend. Had the Indian students perhaps been responding not only to caste differences or stereotypes represented in the story, but to nationalistic considerations as well? For we see on second glance that the characters in the story indeed mention cities—Lahore, Multan, Bahawalpur, Sargodha—placing the story squarely in Pakistan.

The two stories—Rushdie's and my colleague's—unpacked themselves further when my friend recalled that the three Indian students were Christian, for they had written and spoken of their religion in another context in class. And when a visiting Indian dance troop had come up in classroom conversation, one of the students had "spat out"—thus my colleague characterized the fellow's vehemence—"They're Hindus." One need only glance at today's paper to witness the tension that lives on in India among the Hindu majority and the British colonials, Christian missionaries, and Muslim and Sikh minorities. So perhaps, in light of the Muslim names and ironic cultural implications that inform the Rushdie story—as when Muhammad Ali's feet and voice act of their "own volition," or he tells Rehana it is "fated" that he be "drawn" to her—the students' silent protest might have grown out of religious nationalism to which they, but not their American-born peers, would have been sensitive.

Or maybe, just possibly, these three Indian students foresaw the American classroom on the day of the discussion to be the scene of yet another colonial encounter, where they, like the supplicants at the embassy gates, would be lumped together in the subset of Natives of the Subcontinent and asked personal and potentially embarrassing questions by people who didn't quite fathom their differences.

My friend and I cannot explain with any certainty the silence of these students. Still, the failed experiment signified powerfully for both of us. It showed us yet again how many venues there are for misunderstanding in the multicultural classroom—and how many venues for discovery.

As I indicated at the opening of this chapter, the preceding discussion was written at the end of 1987, centuries ago. The draft has been reprinted here in all its radiant harmony by way of a saunter down one of those "venues for misunderstanding" alluded to in the paragraph above. I'd like to retrace some of the same steps now, since time and circumstance have led me to rethink a few of my original conclusions, or at least the routes by which I arrived at them.

APPENDIX FOR CHAPTER 1

Good Advice Is Rarer Than Rubies
by Salman Rushdie

On the last Tuesday of the month, the dawn bus brought Miss Rehana to the gates of the British Embassy. It arrived pushing a cloud of dust, veiling her beauty from the eyes of strangers until she descended. The bus was brightly painted in multicolored arabesques, and on the front it said "MOVE OVER DARLING" in green and gold letters; on the back it added "TATA-BATA" and also "O.K. GOOD-LIFE." Miss Rehana told the driver it was a beautiful bus, and he jumped down and held the door open for her.

Miss Rehana's eyes were large and black and shiny enough not to need the help of antimony, and when the advice expert Muhammad Ali saw them he felt himself becoming young again. He watched her approach the embassy gates and heard her ask the lala who guarded them when they would open. The lala usually enjoyed insulting the embassy's Tuesday-women, but he spoke to Miss Rehana with something approaching courtesy. "Half an hour," he said gruffly. "Maybe two hours. Who knows? The sahibs are eating their breakfast."

The dusty compound between the bus stop and the embassy was already full of Tuesday-women, some veiled, a few barefaced like Miss Rehana. They all looked frightened, and leaned heavily on the arms of uncles or brothers, who were trying to look confident. But Miss Rehana had come on her own, and did not seem at all alarmed. Muhammad Ali, who specialized in advising the most vulnerable-looking of these weekly supplicants, found his feet leading him toward the strange, big-eyed, independent girl.

"Miss," he began. "You have come for permit to London, I think so?" She was standing at a hot-snack stall in the little shantytown by the edge of the compound munching chili-pakoras contentedly. She turned to look at him, and at close range those eyes did bad things to his digestive tract.

"Yes, I have."

"Then please, you allow me to give some advice? Small cost only."

Miss Rehana smiled. "Good advice is rarer than rubies," she said. "But I cannot pay. I am an orphan, not one of your wealthy ladies."

"Trust my gray hairs," Muhammad Ali told her. "My advice is well tempered by experience. You will certainly find it good."

She shook her head. "I tell you I am poor. There are women here with male relatives, all earning good wages. Go to them. Good advice should find good money."

I am going crazy, Muhammad Ali thought, because he heard his voice telling her of its own volition, "Miss, I have been drawn to you. This is fated. I too am a poor man only, but for you my advice comes free."

She smiled again. "Then I must surely listen. When fate sends a gift, one receives good fortune."

He led her to the low wooden desk in his own special corner of the shantytown. She followed, still smiling, eating pakoras from a little newspaper packet. She did not offer him any. He put a cushion on the dusty ground. "Please to sit." She did as he asked. He sat cross-legged across the desk from her, conscious that two or three dozen male eyes were watching him enviously, that all the other shantytown men were ogling the latest young lovely to be charmed by the old grayhair Muhammad Ali. He took a deep breath to settle himself.

"Name, please."

"Miss Rehana," she told him. "Fiancée of Mustafa Dar of Bradford, London."

"Bradford, England," he corrected her gently. "London is a city only, like Multan or Bahawalpur. England is a great nation full of the coldest fish in the world."

"I see," she responded gravely, so that he was unsure if she was making fun of him.

"You have filled application form? Then let me see, please."

She passed him a neatly folded document in a brown envelope.

"Is it O.K.?" For the first time there was a note of anxiety in her voice.

He patted the desk quite near the place where her hand rested. "I am certain," he said. "Wait on and I will check."

She finished her pakoras while he scanned her papers.

"Tip-top," he pronounced finally, "All in order."

"Thank you for your advice," she said. "I'll go now and wait by the gate."

"What are you thinking?" he cried loudly, smiting his forehead. "You consider this is easy business? Just give the form and poof, with a big smile they hand over the permit? Miss Rehana, I tell you you are entering a worse place than any police station."

"Is it so, truly?" His oratory had done the trick. She was a captive audience now, and he would be able to look at her for a few moments longer. Drawing another calming breath, he launched into his speech. He told her that the sahibs thought all the women who came on Tuesdays, claiming to be dependents of bus drivers in Luton or chartered accountants in Manchester, were crooks and liars and thieves.

She protested, "But then I will simply tell them that I, for one, am no such thing!"

Her innocence made him shiver with fear for her. She was a sparrow, he told her, and they were men with hooded eyes, like eagles. He explained that they would ask her questions, personal questions, questions such as a lady's own brother would be shy to ask. They would ask if she was virgin, and, if not, what her fiancé's lovemaking habits were, and what secret nicknames they had invented for one another. Muhammad Ali spoke brutally, on purpose, to lessen the shock she would feel when it actually happened. Her eyes remained steady, but her hands began to flutter at the edges of the desk.

He went on. "They will ask you how many rooms in your family home, and what color are the walls, and what days do you empty the rubbish; they will ask your man's mother's third cousin's aunt's stepdaughter's middle name. And all these things they have already asked your Mustafa Dar in his Bradford. And if you make one mistake, you are finished."

"Yes," she said, and he could hear her disciplining her voice. "And what is your advice, wise old man?"

It was at this point that Muhammad Ali usually began to whisper, to mention that he knew a man, a very good type, who worked in the embassy, and for a fee all the necessary papers could be delivered, with all the proper authentic seals. It was a good business, because the women would often pay him five hundred rupees or give him a gold bracelet for his pains and go away happy. They came from hundreds of miles away—he always checked this before he tricked them—so even when they discovered how they had been swindled they were very unlikely to return. They went away to Sargodha or Lalu Khet and began to pack, and who knows at what point they found out they had been gulled, but it was at a too late point anyway. Life is hard, and an old man must live by his wits. It was not up to Muhammad Ali to have compassion for these Tuesday-women.

But once again his voice betrayed him, and instead of starting his customary speech it began to reveal to her his greatest secret. "Miss Rehana," his voice said, and he listened to it in amazement, "you are a rare person, a jewel, and for you I will do what I would not do for my own daughter, perhaps. One document has come into my possession that can solve your worries at a stroke."

"And what is this sorcerer's paper?" she asked, her eyes unquestionably laughing at him now.

His voice fell low-as-low. "Miss Rehana, it is a British passport. Completely genuine and pukka goods. I have a good friend who will put your name into it and then, hey-presto, England there you come!"

He had said it! Anything was possible now, on this day of his insanity. Probably he would give her the thing free-gratis, and then kick himself for a year afterward. Old fool, he told himself, the oldest fools are bewitched by the youngest girls.

"Let me understand you," she was saying. "You are proposing I should commit a crime, and go to Bradford, London, illegally, and so justify the low opinion the embassy sahibs have of us all. Old babuji, this is not good advice."

"Bradford, *England*," he corrected her mournfully. "You should not take my gift in such a spirit. I am a poor fellow and I have offered this prize because you are so beautiful. Do not spit on my generosity. Take the thing. Or else don't take, go home, forget England, only do not go in that building and lose your dignity."

But she was on her feet, turning, walking away toward the gates, where the women had begun to cluster and the lala was swearing at them to be patient or none of them would be admitted.

"Be a fool," Muhammad Ali shouted after her. "It is the curse of our people. We are poor, we are ignorant, and we refuse completely to learn."

"Hey, Muhammad Ali," the woman at the betel-nut stall shouted to him. "Too bad, she likes them young."

That day Muhammad Ali did nothing but stand around the embassy gates. Many times he told himself, Go from here, fool, the lady does not wish to speak with you any further. But when she came out, she found him waiting.

She seemed calm, and at peace with him again, and he thought, My God, she has pulled it off. The British sahibs have also been drowning in her eyes, and she has got her passage to England. He smiled at her; she smiled back with no trouble at all.

"Miss Rehana Begum," he said, "felicitations, daughter, on what is obviously your hour of triumph."

Impulsively, she took his forearm in her hand. "Come," she said. "Let me buy you a pakora to thank you for your advice and to apologize for my rudeness, too."

They stood in the dust of the afternoon compound near the bus, which was getting ready to leave. Coolies were tying bedding rolls to the roof. A hawker shouted at the passengers, trying to sell them love stories and green medicines. Miss Rehana and happy Muhammad Ali ate their pakoras sitting on the front bumper.

"It was an arranged engagement," Miss Rehana said suddenly. "I was nine years old when my parents fixed it. Mustafa Dar was already thirty then, but my parents knew they were dying and wanted someone who could look after me. Then two months after they died he went to England and said he would send for me. That was many years ago. I have his photo, but I do not know what his voice sounds like. He is like a stranger to me."

The confession took Muhammad Ali by surprise, but he nodded with what he hoped looked like wisdom. "Still and all," he said, "one's parents act in one's best interests. They found you a good honest man who has kept his word and sent for you. And now you have a lifetime to get to know him, and to love."

He was puzzled, now, by the bitterness that had infected her smile.

"But, old man," she asked him, "why have you already packed me and posted me off to England?"

He stood up, shocked. "You looked happy, so I just assumed . . . They turned you down?"

"I got all their questions wrong," she replied. "Distinguishing marks, bathroom décor, all. Now I will go back to Lahore and my job. I work in a great house, as ayah to three good boys. They would be sad to see me leave."

"But this is tragedy!" Muhammad Ali lamented. "Oh, how I pray that you had taken up my offer! Now it is not possible. They have your form on file, cross-check can be made, even the passport will not suffice. It is spoilt, all spoilt, and it could have been so easy."

"I do not think," she told him as she climbed aboard the bus and gave a wave to the driver, "I truly do not think you should be sad."

Her last smile, which he watched from the compound until the bus concealed it in a dust cloud, was the happiest thing he had ever seen in his long, hot, hard, unloving life.

2

Rereading Chapter 1

We were speaking of revision.

You will recall that neither Mohammad Amin nor Najla Afzali, the students discussed in Chapter 1, had been members of my classes. Their papers were shown to me by their teachers. So I came to their work as a disinterested party, one whose reading wouldn't be affected by extraliterary variables such as knowledge about the students' backgrounds, classroom performance, previous written work, and the like. What should it matter that I didn't know these writers?

As it happens, it mattered a good deal, at least as far as my interpretation of one student's work was concerned. My subsequent interviews with the two students, conducted in December 1987 and June 1988, showed me how Eastern writers' foreign status in the Western classroom, and their assumptions about an American audience, might influence in unforeseen ways their selection of topics and methods. In addition, the interviews suggested to me ways in which my own cultural assumptions had dictated my response as a "blind" reader of their work.

To see more clearly how "the East" is traditionally represented by Westerners, I'd like to have a second look, in turn, at *each* of the cultural artifacts discussed in the preceding chapter. Hence the exploratory and discursive nature of the present chapter. The goal of each of the following reexaminations is to arrive at a closer reading of the two students' papers, and by extension of the work of the nonnative students discussed in future chapters. I want to begin by expanding at length an offhand reference made in Chapter 1 to differences in the critical receptions of the Matisse and Suleyman art exhibitions of 1987. I will then move on to interviews conducted with the two students in question during the intervening months, and to my subsequent rereading of their essays. Finally, I will return to a consideration of the Salman Rushdie short story, to see what it too can tell us about the way we read other cultures.

The Critic, the Artist, the Artifact

When I invoked Matisse's work in my earlier remarks, it was to offer some explanation for the way American audiences seemed to favor Matisse's

Orientalized paintings over his point of inspiration, represented by the concurrent exhibition of treasures from the Ottoman Empire. A year later,[1] several new questions interpose themselves between me and the Matisse canvases, questions regarding interpretation and representation. Doubtless my resurrection of such matters will seem to the reader an unconscionably lengthy digression in a book about the work of inter-national students in American colleges. But I would like this discussion to suggest by analogy how our readings of international texts—paintings, short stories, essays by students—are prefigured in ways we may not rec-ognize.

I cannot say whether Orientalism inevitably marks a Westerner's ap-proach to non-Western texts. But certainly this perspective informed Western critical reception of the two art exhibitions discussed in Chapter 1, as I have since discovered in digging up last year's reviews of these two shows. It is scarcely surprising that critical appraisals of the Matisse show in popular American periodicals of 1986–1987 outnumber those of the Suleyman exhi-bition, roughly 14 to 7. What is more striking is that the rhetoric used to describe the exhibition of Eastern art is politicized to an unusual degree—or, if you prefer, discussion of the political subtext of Matisse's work is utterly absent from the reviews of his show.

In these reviews several themes recur. The Matisse appreciations typi-cally emphasize the promethean struggle and triumph of the maestro over his bourgeois material. The reviews of the Ottoman show, on the other hand, tend to focus on the figure of the rapacious emperor. In the process of extending his empire and looting his enemies' coffers, Suleyman sponsored artisans' guilds that produced artifacts glittering with "enough gold and precious-stone work," in Kay Larson's pointed analogy, "to ransom an aya-tollah." A comparison of Larson's two commentaries in *New York Magazine* illustrates the differences that generally distinguish the critics' views of the two exhibitions. Whereas Larson lauds "the ferocity of Matisse's intelli-gence" (November 17, 1986), in her brief paragraph on the Ottoman exhibi-tion the same word takes on an ominous cast: "A ferocity lies just under the sensual surface of this show—beneath the gilding, the face of absolutism is haunting and troublesome" (October 26, 1987).[2]

The reviewers for both *Newsweek* and *U.S. News & World Report* dwell on the political and corporate sponsorship of the Suleyman show, and here again the emphasis is on the gilding more than the art. Cathleen McGuigan of *Newsweek* spends a prefatory paragraph on the exhibition's diplomatic underpinnings (Turkey's strengthening of bonds with the United States, a NATO ally) and financial arrangement. In its coverage of the Suleyman show, *U.S. News & World Report* (which a month later would review the

---

[1]This chapter was written in November–December 1988.

[2] Similarly, Jed Perl, writing for *Vogue*, celebrates the "voraciousness" of Matisse's appro-priation of "the exotic East" in his odalisques of the 1920s (December 1986). The same reviewer reports leaving the Suleyman show "rather relieved that art is no longer all pomp and circum-stance, and that artists can now let their own personalities shine through" (April 1987).

Matisse exhibition as one of a group of shows revealing "The Masters Behind the Masterpieces") focuses exclusively on the public relations angle: Turkey's $10 million campaign to enhance its global reputation and court foreign investors. Both magazine articles make much of the Philip Morris company's funding of the show. Miriam Horn and Charles Fenyvesi of *U.S. News & World Report* point out that the company is "the world's largest exporter of Turkish tobacco and the largest importer of cigarettes into Turkey—transactions valued at nearly $200 million a year." McGuigan adds that "plans are underway to build a plant in Turkey as soon as the state-controlled tobacco industry is deregulated."

The effect of all this background for an art exhibition is to suggest some covert operation of political and commercial spin control. In contrast, the mounting of the Matisse show comes off as something of a religious "quest" —the word is a direct quotation—and its organizers as positively saintly, their apotheosis occurring in Philip Hamburger's appreciation in *The New Yorker*. Hamburger interviews those responsible for the show, chief among them Jack Cowart and Dominique Fourcade, who detail their exhaustive two-year efforts to track down obscure canvases with apparently selfless zeal. Cowart says his and Fourcade's only goal "was to serve [Matisse's] art. . . . I have no Matisse stock. That's not my line of work." *U.S. News & World Report* quotes Cowart's delighted response in watching the pilgrims who move through his display: "A little spontaneous conversion takes place in the galleries."

To throw into relief the cultural politics informing the critical receptions of these two exhibitions, let me simply reverse the terms of the reviews. Mightn't one just as easily remark that the pleasure of excavating and writing about some of the Matisse canvases of this period—a hitherto-overlooked body of work—offers one or two earthly rewards for the curator and catalogue author? That private lenders to the Matisse show indeed have "Matisse stock"? That a show and catalogue with the "polemical objective" (Nicholas Watkins's phrase in the British *Burlington Magazine*) of presenting Matisse's Nice period not as a slacking-off but as a rethinking of modernism do wield a certain measure of control over public perception and critical revisionism? (Witness Robert Hughes's overheated syntax in *Time* magazine's coverage: "the overwhelming impression is of struggle and synthesis, of a mature artist who, having achieved a monumental diction before 1916, set out to reinvest it with immediate impressions before it congealed.") And while we're on the subject of the growing phenomenon of blockbuster exhibitions underwritten by large private corporations: Is this kind of funding ever disinterested? Is it worth mentioning that the GTE corporation, a company with falling earnings that lagged behind its telecommunications competitors in the 1980s, underwrote the Matisse show and three earlier shows at the National Gallery during this period, at a time when deregulation of the industry made good PR and high visibility all the more important for companies no longer protected by fixed rates? At a time when similarly high-profile exhibitions, like this year's [1988] Gaughin show at the National Gallery, were being sponsored by GTE's arch-rival, AT&T ("The Right Choice")? Evidently not.

I have hoped to indicate how critical analysis may be mediated by prevailing ideology in ways that often go unremarked. There is, of course, another level of cultural interpretation in this fable of the maestro and the sultan, namely Matisse's reading and inscription of his Eastern sources.

I am suggesting we attend more carefully to the significance of Matisse's odalisques within their historical and political context, especially since the reviewers cited above did not do so. For in a sense, both exhibitions, the French as well as the Ottoman, celebrate empire—its accumulation of riches, its influence, its exercise of power. As Suleyman extended his empire by taking the strategically situated city of Algiers, so France strengthened its empire centuries later by annexing territories in North Africa and by tightening its hold on these colonies during World War I. Matisse visited Morocco in 1911, within weeks of its becoming a French protectorate, and painted his odalisques during the postwar decade, at the height of France's neocolonial period. Matisse's artistic preferences of this period seem to have been consonant with the desires and tastes of a booming postwar art market in France whose collectors were hungry for luxury and eager to exploit the treasures and labor of the colonies (Silver 121–122). Since imperialism dictated the nature of European contact with the Eastern Other, how could it fail to reinforce certain myths of difference—the mystery and indolence of the East, the rightness of the Westerner's cultural and political dominion over other races?[3]

I'd like to consider the artist's translation of his Islamic sources, especially for what this process of incorporation reveals about features of his paintings that may be taken for granted or accorded privileged status by Western observers. Take the example of Matisse's use of two-dimensional, brilliantly colorful arabesque patterning. As Pierre Schneider points out, the decentralized and endless repetition in the designs adorning the walls of Islamic mosques or the illuminated pages of the Qu'ran signify the artist's submission—the meaning of "Islam"—to a divine presence that cannot be limited or represented. Matisse's paintings, conversely, highlight the conflict

---

[3] Perhaps Matisse's statements to the critic Teriade regarding his travels to Tahiti in the spring of 1930, just after the Nice period, will shed light on his stance as a Westerner in the East, and tell us something more about his depiction of the odalisques he had been inspired to paint after his trip to Morocco: "[in Tahiti] Laziness is stronger than everything else. That is what lies behind the amiable amorality in the customs of the islanders. Tahitians are like children. They have no sense of anything being prohibited, nor any notion of good and evil. . . . Take the next fellow's wife? Nothing wrong with that. And if you are white, it's an honour for the family and its future descendants" (quoted in Flam 1978, 61).

Such sentiments are standard topoi of travel literature written by Westerners in the nineteenth century (Nochlin 119) and of colonialist propaganda in the twentieth century. It is worth examining, in the next few pages, how these topoi are perpetuated in the paintings of the odalisque.

between a universalized abstraction and a unique composition contrived and framed by the individual artist (170–172). As we have seen, it is this spirit of the "creative genius," the imprimatur of the masterwork, that is most revered by Westerners, and that has determined the course—and discourse—of "art history" in the West. In the following definition of "art history," Jon Bird highlights the contrasts we have noted above in the reviews of the two art exhibitions:

> . . . I would here take "bourgeois art history" to signify the historical development of a discipline of connoisseurship which in its distinctive forms valorizes the individual (male) artist, the masterpiece, and the idealized Nation-State, as the dominant and appropriate objects of study. As such, art history reproduces the category of the subject as the possessor and producer of him/herself, and the democratic ideal of the free individual and the consensus society. Fundamental to this process is that most crucial hegemonic apparatus for the experience of citizenship—the museum (39).

Perhaps most revealing of the Western artist's perspective is Matisse's favored choice of subject material after his trip to Morocco, the odalisque. That is to say: an "Eastern" woman (most often a Western model posing as one), partially nude, always idle, seductively recumbent with hips invariably turned toward the viewer, occasionally veiled, theatrically costumed in the exotica of Eastern fantasy, and surrounded by Eastern artifacts such as checkerboards, samovars, "Persian" carpets, "Moorish" screens, "Turkish" chairs.

"I do odalisques," Matisse was later to explain, "in order to do nudes." But if figural representation in the art of Islam, as in Judaic art, is generally forsworn as blasphemous presumption on the part of the artist, depiction of the nude figure is anathema, as might be guessed from the strictures of purdah and chador. It can be argued that Matisse's odalisques refer less to actual Eastern subjects than to earlier masters of the odalisque: Ingres, Delacroix, Renoir, Manet. The convergence in the nineteenth-century French salon of two female images, European courtesan and Eastern woman, suggests not only the woman's sexual availability to the viewer, but also the access of the Western artist, spectator, collector, to what is ordinarily hidden from view in Eastern cultures.

How else does the image of the odalisque signify? The incremental message on the walls of the National Gallery's exhibition is that Matisse's models of the period, all these Henriettes and Zitas and their sisters, are virtually indistinguishable. Matisse plays on this feature by making his seriatim canvases self-referential, repeating not just the trappings of Eastern exoticism but the figures themselves, who are at times paired with other odalisques or with their own mirrored reflections. As Norman Bryson has commented of Ingres's odalisques, the artist's repetition of versions of the subject highlights an important element of the Orientalist fantasy, namely the *interchangeability* of the women in the seraglio (144).[4]

Let me note one last residual effect of Matisse's displacement of Eastern motifs within a recognizably Western mise-en-scène. The lush interior landscape in which these female figures lounge is obviously artificial, denoted by the same souvenirs and costumes in canvas after canvas. In his conversations with the poet Louis Aragon in 1943, Matisse spoke of his concept of signs, of the artist's need to formulate a "personal language" of plastic signs or representational methods that viewers come to recognize and absorb over a period of time (quoted in Flam 1978, 94–95). During the Nice period the repeated props and poses of the odalisques become in themselves recognizable signs. In this case, they serve as changeless cultural signifiers. Taken together, I would venture, these Eastern canvases form the static and reified landscape of the "ethnographic present."

Matisse's odalisques, then, raise questions not just about iconic representation of the Other, which is always ideologically freighted, but about the equally biased acts of definition and classification, and of perception itself. Later in his life Matisse used his earlier travels in North Africa as validation of the "realist" basis of these works. But how much of what he saw was determined by what he had been led to expect by his compatriots, how much filtered through the veil of traditional artistic representation?

Matisse repeatedly claimed, "I know that odalisques exist, I was in Morocco. I have seen some." What are we to make of the relationship between the French term and its referent? *Odalisque* is a French corruption of the Turkish word for female slave or concubine in a Muslim harem, especially the seraglio of the sultan of Turkey. The harem [Arabic: "sacred, forbidden place"] was off-limits to any male save the sultan and the Christian eunuchs who attended the inhabitants. Even Delacroix, whose *Women of Algiers* (1834) so influenced Matisse and Picasso, admitted never having set foot in a harem. Jack Flam speculates that Matisse might have solved the problem of finding models in North Africa much as Delacroix had done 80 years earlier, by painting the only women exempted from the veil: prostitutes and Jews (1986, 327). On the other hand, about the time of Matisse's travels in North Africa, official harems were being abolished, and odalisques in their

---

[4] The "Western" female models Matisse painted in the early 1920s are at least minimally individuated and often shown in more active or at least contemplative roles—perhaps turned away from the viewer and gazing out the window, reading, playing the violin or piano, even painting. In contrast, the "Eastern" subjects executed during the same period are invariably indolent. Prone, smiling dreamily or staring vaguely at some indeterminate object, they are usually set against a screen or decorative backdrop that pushes the figures nearer the picture plane or threatens to swallow them up altogether. The horizontal lassitude of the models, as well as the radically circumscribed space they inhabit, further underscores the passivity of the odalisques before the controlling fantasy of their creator. (Laura Mulvey provides a useful analogue in her important article on visual pleasure and the cinema, listed in the bibliography for this chapter.)

exotic garb were disappearing except on picture postcards trumped up for the foreign trade. Either way, the question arises: What did Matisse actually see on his trip to Morocco, and what did he *think* he saw?

The Teacher, the Student, the Text

As I have said, I would like the foregoing questions about representation to serve as preface to my discussion of student texts throughout this book, and in particular to my reexamination of the work of the two students discussed in the previous chapter. The rereading process began with my interviews with these two students, both of whom expressed eagerness to discuss their cultural beliefs and readily consented to having their discussions recorded. Here again I want to emphasize the reciprocity of the cultural encounter. Ethnographic accounts such as the conversations and texts transcribed in these pages are never transparent, but rather reflective of the interaction of informant and audience.

My meeting with Mohammad Amin in December of 1987, a month after I had first written about his essay, confirmed and clarified much of what I had seen in his in-class writing. Still, our talk worked on me in subtle ways over the next few months, particularly as it made me more aware of my perceptions about Islam. Just as important, my discussion with Mohammad, taken together with my subsequent talk with Najla Afzali, underscored the differences in belief among individuals within the same culture.

Mohammad was born in Afghanistan and moved with his family to Pakistan when he was very young. As it turns out, contrary to what his teacher had thought, Mohammad has only visited Islamic Russia once. Yet because his father was born in Turkestan, Mohammad asserts this as his strongest identity; although he grew up in Pakistan speaking Urdu, he says he feels most comfortable speaking Uzbeki, the language of his father. Like many of our international students, Mohammad is somewhat older, more politically aware and more educated than his American-born counterparts (he had two years of college in Pakistan), and speaks several languages and dialects, although as we have noted, his English falls far short of his other linguistic accomplishments.

I was particularly curious to hear Mohammad's explanation of phrases in his in-class essay such as the idea of Americans "pull[ing] the vail of momatory joys on their faces," and, more important, of his argument that "this is the duty of the comming generation to follow every step of their ancestors." In our conversation, I sought out Mohammad's explanations of Islamic teaching, including any personal interpretations of Muslim doctrine, for these privately held beliefs as well would shape his oral and written performance.

As I had speculated, Mohammad's essay was in large measure influenced by his Muslim beliefs, which seem in keeping with the Sunni sect to which he belongs. He accepts the *hadith* books (the sayings of the Prophet) as historically authentic, and takes them to be as important to religious practice as the revealed word of God in the Qu'ran. In the following portion of our conversation, Mohammad explains how an Islamic community adapts to change; at the same time he advocates close adherence to the laws set down by the tradition of one's ancestors:

AT: When they interpreted the word of God, the word of Moham-mad, and so forth, do you think that according to these 'ulama cer-tain ideas can change in Islam, or there really isn't room for change?

MA: Yes, there is room for change, like God said that when times change, situations change too, and probably you're going to face some problem that you don't find in sunnah, in hadiths, whatever our prophet said, whatever our prophet did. And what the *Qu'ran* says, probably you can't find those things . . . then, there is this thing that couple of 'ulamas, they will sit together, and they will see that what the situation is, and after that they will find . . . ac-cording to situations, they will find a way, "Yeah, we like this and this and this."

AT: Ah, so they apply the law. And those are the people you would look to ultimately for how to live your life, so that there is room for change . . .

MA: Change what, the principles? . . . Not principles. Those new things come in, like . . . there's a big controversy in Muslim coun-tries, like interest—I mean in the bank, when you put the money. We can't accept interest, because if you accept interest you go to hell.

AT: Oh, it's like money lending.

MA: Yes, we call this *sud*. So, in Muslim countries they have the banks, and if you keep your money over there, they going to give you interest, money on money, so there's this big controversy that is this sud or not? So if 'ulama says that this is sud, then the gov-ernment is kaput.

AT: But did they say that?

MA: No, they're still trying to like, yes and no, yes and no, like this. But I think this is sud, yes, 100 percent this is sud.

AT: . . . Well, now how about the controversy of free will? I mean, doesn't man have free will in this life, or has much of his life, have many of the rules of life been predetermined by ancestors, by the way things have been before this? (I know I'm asking you a huge question.)

MA: No, no, I think you can follow your ancestors too, whatever you are do, like you see our ancestor, like our Prophet, or the caliphs, like those big followers, they did, and then if you must do like those people, then it's OK. . . .

AT: And so when you speak of your ancestors, you're not talking necessarily about your grandfather, or your great-grandfather, you're talking about ancestors way back in history. . . the great caliphs, the great legal minds as well as the great spiritual leaders, the great 'ulama, going all the way back to Mohammad.

MA: Yes. . . .

AT: . . . You went to school chiefly with Muslims. And you would say that Islamic doctrine was taught in the schools. The two were very close, law and religion, the state and God.

MA: Yes. Religion is a law. The law should be our religion. Whatever is wrong, we have to check the religion, and decide how to do this. . . .

Mohammad's comments thus clarify his repeated insistence in the in-class essay that every generation must follow in the steps of its ancestors, as well as his criticism of Americans for not doing so. In view of Mohammad's testimony in the interview, his in-class essay might be seen in part as a reaction to the threat of Westernization. In this regard I think it significant, too, that Mohammad took great care—perhaps more so for his American listener—to distance himself from Khomeini and the Twelver sect of Shi'ism. He characterized Khomeini as "crazy" and Shi'ite Muslims as "too fanatic; they think that 'we are fighting for our religion' but they are not. This is the politics. . . . He [Khomeini] wants to be enemy of American, and by keeping himself behind the ideas as a Muslim, that a Muslim in America is not a Muslim." Mohammad's invective against Western ideals in the essay might have been exaggerated in response, first of all, to criticisms leveled by Khomeini and his supporters against "Americanized" Muslims. He might also have been responding to Westerners' questions about his way of life, the Islamic revolution, Arab oil, the hostage crisis, Khomeini, fanaticism, terrorism, and other similarly charged catch phrases that have crystallized Western reactions to Islam in the 1980s.

The same might be said of Mohammad's explanation of the Islamic veil in our interview, and of his use of the metaphor of the veil in his essay. In fact, during our meeting we both seemed to seize on the image as a way to talk about cultural difference in interpretation. The Qu'ran is widely supposed in the West to have first imposed the veil upon women, although actually it was a Biblical injunction that Eve cover her head and body in shame for her corrupt nature. The Qu'ran enjoins believing women "to cover their adornments (except such as are normally displayed); to draw their veils over their bosoms and not to reveal their finery . . . " (24:31). This command urges modesty of dress, not necessarily the covering of the face or hands. As you will see, Mohammad strongly advocates the veiling of Muslim women, even attributing the injunction to "cover up completely" to the

Qu'ran rather than to the 'ulama who interpret God's word. Mohammad's comments on the subject have bearing on the issues considered in this chapter, so I will quote them at length:

AT: And so in Persian, some form of Persian expression you would say, for that moment, you "pull the veil of joy over your face." Veil is an interesting choice there, because I only think of women . . .

MA: Everybody asks me this question.

AT: (laughs) Well, it's a popular question, because for Westerners, you know, a veil is a very interesting symbol; we don't have anything like that over here. Sometimes you'll see women from the 1940s wearing a little thin veil. But the whole point is it's an illusion; you can see right through it, whereas you mean, with this kind of veil . . .

MA: Yes, you just hide yourself behind this, whatever it is.

AT: All right, what does everybody ask you?

MA: They ask why they wear veils; it must look funny.

AT: It doesn't look funny, it really doesn't. It may to some people . . .

MA: We call this, I don't know in Arabic but in Persian or in Urdu or in Turkey they have a similar word, we call it chador.

AT: . . . Now, there's something in the Qu'ran about "modest dress," right? Or, you tell me, why do the women wear veils?

MA: God said that a woman got to be in veil; they don't have to show their self to the men. Because God said that a woman—excuse me—

AT: That's all right, that's all right . . .

MA: That a woman is like, a woman can bring a fight, and a controversy with two men, it's in the history, I've seen that a woman become the cause of a fight.

AT: Well, of course it can be true anywhere.

MA: All right, so they said a woman got to keep herself in the veil. First of all, doesn't have to leave home.

AT: She shouldn't leave home? She should stay at home.

MA: Yes, at home. OK, if she wants to go outside, then she has to cover her face, OK, she can keep her eyes open, this is in the Qu'ran (covers rest of face) like this.

AT: All right, just the eyes.

MA: Not the hair (covering gesture). I think Jewish people have this too. They don't show their hair.

AT: They don't show their hair, for similar reasons: you're only supposed to be attractive to your husband, not to another man. Now is this in the Qu'ran, or is this interpretation of the 'ulama?

MA: No, this is in the Qu'ran.

AT: That women should cover up completely.

MA: Yeah, that's in the Qu'ran.

AT: Now, when you say, "pull the veil" here [in your essay], you're talking about a different kind of veil?

MA: No, no, this is the veil: I'm using like, what do you call them? . . .

AT: Metaphor, simile? A comparison?

MA: Yes.

AT: In other words, you hide yourself with momentary joy, but it's really just a distraction from your right path in life.

MA: That's right. I mean, as a woman hides herself behind those veil, so men hide themselves behind those joy. But the thing is, the joy or whatever come between the man and the right way, so this is like a wall.

As our dialogue suggests, the veil is a complex semiotic web within Islam and for outside observers as well. Mohammad's metaphor recalls for me this utterance in the Qu'ran: "When you recite the Qu'ran, We place between you and those who deny the life to come a hidden barrier. We cast a veil upon their hearts and make them hard of hearing, lest they understand it" (17:45). The Qu'ran thus depicts the separation of believers and nonbelievers in terms of the veil. And indeed the veil worn by orthodox Islamic women has become, as Mohammad points out here and later in the interview, a symbol of Eastern difference, the focus of outsiders' often bemused, even derisive questions about his culture.

Since the image of the veil is a kind of leitmotif in this chapter on reading, recurring briefly as it does in the preceding discussion of Matisse, in the comments of Mohammad and Najla, and in the short story by Salman Rushdie, I would like to take our examination of the image a few steps further. I shall do so by continuing our contrast of Western and Eastern responses to a cultural phenomenon. The issue of veiling or modest dress—sometimes called "Islamic dress"—has become more complicated and politically volatile in recent years. Westerners who applauded the Shah's campaign for "modernization" of Iran during the Pahlavi reign now look upon the reveiling of Islamic women since the revolution under Khomeini as a huge step backward for the Middle East, a symbol of women's oppression under Islam and of the widening rift between East and West. In fact, though, many Islamic women who resented the Shah's program of Westernization have themselves chosen to return to "Islamic" or at least more conservative dress. Within Islamic societies, the veil has thus assumed different political, religious, and social values than formerly, and new alliances have been drawn.

Let me cite two examples that suggest the range of responses to this question among Muslim women, in this case two women of the same nationality and profession. Nawal el Sa'adawi, the Egyptian writer and physician who was jailed by Anwar el Sadat in 1981 for her political activism and feminist treatises, and who is outspoken in her resistance to symbols of Western imperialism, has often portrayed the veil as an emblem of the submission of Muslim women to the patriarchal system. In works as various as her novel *Two Women in One*, her study of women in the Arab world, *The Hidden Face of Eve*, the autobiographical *Memoirs from the Women's Prison*, and the short story "The Veil," Sa'adawi depicts *fate* as the father, lover, husband who controls the woman behind the veil. The *higaabs* or head-wraps, the *"niqaabs*—all-enveloping face-veils with small holes through which I could perceive the steady gaze of human eyes," suggest to the writer a return "to the age of slaves and harems" (*Prison* 28). On the other hand, for advocates of Islamic dress, principally educated working women, the veil represents participation as much as confinement. As one Egyptian medical student puts it, "[Islamic dress] means I am serious about myself and my religion but also about my studies. I can sit in class with men and there is no question of attraction and so on—we are all involved in the same business of learning, and these garments make that clear" (quoted in Fernea 220).

These modern forms of the veil, then, when they are worn by choice, have paradoxically come to signify within Islamic countries new opportunities for women. At the same time, they imply an ostentatious turning away from Western influences and values. This tendency has been explained as "a demand for a more 'moral' economic, political and social life, as prescribed by Islam" (Minces 51). Leila Ahmed suggests a more complicated explanation of the conflict between feminism and dominant ideology in the East: "Western women can be . . . radically critical of their cultures and prevalent ideologies. . . . For the Islamic woman however there is a whole further dimension to the pressures that bear down on her urging her to silence her criticism, remain loyal, reconcile herself to, even find virtue in the central formulations of her culture that normally she would rebel against: the pressure that comes into being as a result of the relationship in which Islamic society now stands with the West" (162).

I have been working toward a consideration of the veil as a rather literal-minded metaphor for the cultural scrim that intervenes between the viewer and other subjects or objects, something akin to what Kenneth Burke has called the "terministic screen." The veil is that most complex of cultural signifiers: symbolic of difference, while at the same time effacing the difference, the individual features, of the wearer.

I summon up these notions of the veil, of difference, of culture-specific expressions of gender, in returning now to Najla Afzali's essay. I originally reprinted her paper in Chapter 1 to illustrate how familiarity with this particular writer's native culture might enrich our reading but was not really essential to our understanding of her essay. Yet it gradually became clear during the course of our interview in June of 1988 that Najla's essay had been influenced by her home culture in different ways than the reader—this reader, at any rate—might have guessed on first reading. I began my original discussion of her essay by asking what assumptions Najla had made about her reader. I see now that I was positing a different kind of writer from the one Najla turned out to be, and a different reader from the one she evidently had in mind.

Rereading Najla's paper in light of my talk with Mohammad, it seemed to me that the pieces of her description didn't quite add up. Her essay had struck me on first reading as competent and comprehensible, despite certain internal contradictions in the piece which became apparent only when one moved outside the text itself to the cultural and social codes I was prepared to overlook. For example, I had not imagined the author to be Muslim, owing to a certain liberality in the event she describes in her paper—though in any case the incident would have seemed incongruous for most young women from southwestern or central Asia, if my other students were any indication. If even male students from this part of the world admitted they were bound by social strictures, what was a nice young woman like Najla doing in an interlude like the one she describes, replete with fulsome compliments and handkissing?

So I determined to interview the author of the essay. I started revising Najla's essay when, during our telephone chat to set up the interview, Najla told me she was an observant Muslim. And I began the process all over again when Najla walked into my office. As you read these comments, I ask you to imagine Najla entering my tastefully decorated room in the Temporary II building, a corrugated tin affair on the Queens College campus. Now, I hope you will allow me this observation of her appearance, as I have had and shall have further occasion to resort to fashion as a trope, in several of its analogic guises: the subject is wearing a short black skirt, a man-tailored houndstooth jacket, black stockings, and a low-cut black T-shirt with lace trim. For the purposes of the present discussion, please imagine her also wearing a neon necklace flashing the words "floating signifier." What had I expected her to wear? After years of teaching in the City University I can report that most of our Asian students wear uniforms such as the jeans-and-Reeboks that have become the lingua franca of the international campus. Yet I was taken aback by Najla's extremely Western attire: I now suppose because I had read her work before meeting her, and was trying to tailor her text to my cultural expectations.

In going over my rather comic initial impressions as I write this, I find myself recalling other Westerners' efforts to bring non-Westerners into line with their notions of cultural difference. I'm thinking first of all of Matisse, of course, painting odalisques in a series of hotel rooms in Nice, his bare-breasted French models got up in turbans, tattoos, veils, "harem pants." Of Gaughin, traveling all the way to Polynesia to paint the naked native nymphs he'd read about in Pierre Loti's novels, only to find that French missionaries and other colonial functionaries had already despoiled paradise and dressed up the locals; on canvas he would create the mythic, impassive, provocatively saronged Eves and Marys of his Pacific fantasy. And, closer to home, of Edward Curtis motoring around the southwestern United States at the turn of the century with a carload of "Indian" costumes and props so he could photograph the denim-clad Native Americans in loincloths befitting the members of an idealized "vanishing race."

All of which is to say in italics that I began to sense, as I sat talking with Najla, how much I had unconsciously typed her, and how much that type-casting might have overdetermined my reading of her work. Najla told me she had spent most of her life in Kabul, where she had lived with her father, who owned a sports equipment store, her mother, two sisters, and two brothers. In 1982, the Russian invasion of Afghanistan having destroyed her neighbors' homes and disrupted schooling in her city, Najla and her family left for Pakistan. They spent six months in Peshawar and then Islamabad, where Najla indeed had to wear chadri, the full veil of the orthodox Muslim woman, a practice to which she very reluctantly submitted.[5]

Najla recalled that the move to the United States was a huge adjustment for her and the members of her family; at first she was terrified to speak the little English she knew. Before me now I saw a woman assertive in her beliefs, her conversational style, and, I assume, her dealings with the world outside school—she works as a teller at Chase Manhattan Bank. She told me her relatives are shocked at the change she has undergone (in her appearance, at any rate) since coming to the United States. She explained the change by saying "life is easier this way." Lest I attribute any evidence of feminism solely to her schooling in America, Najla was quick to point out that she has always been a feminist, and that her family has consistently maintained a very liberal attitude toward women's education and careers (she mentioned her aunt, a doctor, and her sister, who works for an insurance company). After these preliminaries Najla and I began to consider the ways she has preserved cultural tradition, outward appearances aside:

AT: . . . So [you say] you will probably have an arranged marriage. Do you feel ambivalent about it?

NA: It's very hard—I don't like that; sometimes, if you don't like the person, you have to suffer.

AT: So how do you feel about that? I see a woman who looks very Westernized, but who has certain traditional beliefs.

NA: I get so confused, I don't know what to do. I don't date. But the guys understand, you never go out with them.

---

[5]According to Robert D. Kaplan, writing in *Atlantic* magazine in September 1988, Islamic beliefs in Afghanistan have amplified since the Soviet invasion of the country. About five million Afghans have escaped into Iran and Pakistan; the exiles view Pakistan as less conservative and therefore a corrupting influence, and Afghan women who went about unveiled in their own country must assume the veil in exile among strangers (18).

Similarly, during our interview Najla commented that she and her compatriots "become more religious" when they migrate to the United States, their beliefs having become a way to hold onto their culture in a land of strangers. I have heard comments to this effect from other Pakistani students, among them Fauzia Subhani, whose essay is quoted at the end of this chapter.

AT: When you were living in Kabul, did you question the idea of arranged marriage as much as you do now?

NA: When I was a kid, my parents said, this is the life, it's gonna be
like that. And I accept this idea, because right now even though I
live in this society still I have this idea. Right now, even if my parents don't care, I still couldn't go out.

AT: . . . Even though you can't, do you find yourself asking, "other
American girls can go out, why is it that I am constrained like
this?"

NA: Yeah, I'm always asking that.

AT: And how do you answer yourself? (both laugh)

NA: I have to answer myself, if I'm married and have children I will
leave them to have open minds, to go out—I don't want to be
strict, to keep them at home.

AT: Ok, so it's not for your generation, but for the next—

NA: Yes, because my cousins here are like six, seven years old, and
they're completely different.

We soon turned to a discussion of her essay, and Najla began to
elaborate on some of the influences operating in the piece. In referring to the
subject of her description as "a sixteenth-century prince," Najla had indeed
had in mind the Persian leaders (albeit from the seventh century) she had
grown up hearing about:

AT: Now let's take a look at this description of this young man—I
don't know if you remember the circumstances of this meeting—or
perhaps you made it up, I don't know, it just sounded very real
(begins to read).
. . . Were you thinking of a particular prince there . . . do you
remember a sixteenth-century prince?

NA: Yeah, I remember some stories, like a very famous fellow, a religious man, Ali? [Mohammad's nephew and son-in-law, the first
male convert to Islam; one of Mohammad's successors as leader of
Muslim community (A.D. 600?–661).] A lot of people they have an
image about him. Also Parvez? [Khosrau II, called Khosrau Parvez,
"the Victorious"; d. 628; King of the Sassanidae of Persia; made
war on the Eastern Roman Empire.]

Najla went on to show that the motifs in her essay of the hero's piercing
black eyes and the heroine's demure response were similarly influenced by
her home culture. (Of course, the Western tradition of female reticence in the
glare of the masculine gaze is merely a paler version of this social and literary
convention.):

AT: Were your brothers allowed more freedom [in Kabul]?

NA: Yes, and it's true here too—they could go out, they could go to discoteque, any place they want, they could date girls; it's not a big shame. If I dated guys, my parents gonna get mad.

AT: Well, I notice in your paper you had a motif, this fellow was staring at you, made eye contact. When you were a kid, were you told that it wasn't appropriate perhaps for a girl . . .

NA: To contact guys?

AT: Yes, with the eyes, not even speech.

NA: Yes. My grandmother told me, don't look at guys; always when we were go to school we have to look down (laughs). Still people say to me, "you didn't even see me on the street!"

AT: Of course, I don't make eye contact with people on the street either. But I can't say that it was ever told to me—it's just easier for me, in the same way that it's easier for women to dress more conservatively in New York so guys won't make cracks. But my parents never said to me, lower your eyes. I notice that this fellow here in the paper lowers his eyes when he meets your father, as a sign of respect. Doesn't it say in the Qu'ran that men and women should avert their eyes? [I am referring to Qu'ran 24:31]

NA: Not in the Qu'ran. It's the culture. Like most of Qu'ran seems . . . for man's benefit.[6]

So much, as I say, corroborated my earlier guesswork. Yet I saw that in the course of our chat Najla grew increasingly uneasy when pinned down to the particulars of her narrative, even though I had tried to suggest at the outset that the event might be "made up," and that this was acceptable and even laudable practice for a writer. Her replies to my questions—most of which still presumed an actual incident—were couched in speculative or vague terms, in conditional tenses and hypothetical examples, in qualifiers like "I think," and so on. Around the middle of the interview, the conflict between what happens in the culture and on the page became too apparent to ignore:

AT: (Reads, "He introduced himself in a very competent way.") That's a fascinating sentence for me—I'd like you to tell me about how a man introduces himself to a woman—are there certain unspoken rules?

NA: He might say, "this is my name and I come from this family." And I say, "I can't talk with you." And he says, "OK, I understand."

AT: But this fellow came right up and talked to you , so is the difference that he knew your family? You say, now maybe you're em-

[6]Note here the contrast between Najla's and Mohammad's views of the Qu'ran, though they are both of the Sunni sect.

> broidering here, I don't know if this really happened (laughs), he
> used poetic expressions and so on . . . it sounds like he's really
> moving quickly here. . . . In your country, is it a convention for a
> young man to use such poetic language, or are you making this
> up? . . .
>
> NA: I think I'm just making this up. Like in my culture, they never
> talk about love. One of my shocks when I came here was when my
> aunt said to my cousins, "I love you." You never use love like this
> in my country.

The hero of Najla's story might have been someone she had once
glimpsed, or the image of her ideal suitor, but in any case the meeting Najla
describes was, given the terms of her culture, quite impossible. Now, the fact
that she pulled an essay out of her imagination rather than reporting an
actual incident would hardly be news for teachers or any other readers, come
to that. What is more significant is Najla's explanation of how she came to
represent the impossible on paper:

> AT: So when a boy comes up to you, even a boy you know, could he
> have said these things to you? In other words, did you write it
> because it was kind of fun to make it up, it's the way you imagine
> you'd like a man to come up to you . . . or were you writing for
> an American audience?
>
> NA: Yes, I think so.
>
> AT: If he had used poetic comparisons, would you have liked that?
>
> NA: I might be shocked.
>
> AT: In other words, it would have been impossible in reality, [but] it
> was a nice idea to think about in a paper. Now if you were writing
> this for a teacher in Afghanistan, you never would have written
> . . .
>
> NA: No! I wouldn't even write that I met this guy, that I look at him.
>
> AT: So when your teacher[7] asked you to write a paper on anyone,
> you picked kind of a romantic . . .
>
> NA: No, not romantic, never, we never talked about guys. Like when
> I go out with my friends, I never say a guy is good-looking; they
> say, "What's wrong with you!" You have to keep it inside.
>
> AT: . . . So you really are writing this for an American audience.
>
> NA: Yes.

It is by now a commonplace that the writer's audience is always a fiction. But I'd like to investigate how a nonnative's fabrication of an American audience might differ from a native speaker's assumptions about her readers.

---

[7]I was referring here to her American teacher, but Najla seems to have taken this to mean
a teacher in her native country.

I'm intrigued by the problem of representation in Najla's verbal description because I believe her essay shows, in graphic form, the kind of tension implied
during our interview in her dress and words, in her cultural and individual
beliefs, and in the questions she had been asking herself about acceptable
social behavior in her native and adopted countries. Let me continue with the
interview:

> AT: OK, so it was out of your imagination, which is wonderful, I
> mean that's why we write—if we had to write everything that was
> true, it would be a very boring world indeed. Were you reading
> anything at the time, like novels?
> NA: Yeah, I used to read a lot of books, novels, like love stories. One
> of my friends is American, and she reads books and then she gives
> them to me.
> AT: Are they like those Harlequin romances? The kind of book where
> the girl at the end marries the guy, but nothing has gone on be-
> fore, they just kiss at the end. He looks into her eyes, and she's
> very shy, and then at the end of the book he says, "I love you."
> NA: Yeah (laughs). And it sometimes happens that the girl she
> doesn't like him, and that guy follows her, and then something
> happens and they get married (laughs).
> AT: Like written by Barbara Cartland?
> NA: Yeah, that was one of them.
> AT: What do your parents say when they see you reading these
> books?
> NA: Oh, they don't want me to read them; like in Afghanistan, my
> grandfather—my mother she don't mind, she says that reading
> doesn't affect your mind, but my grandfather says it affects you.
> AT: And does it affect you?
> NA: Yes.

Yes. Hence the handkissing. And the flowery effusions, which I had earlier been so willing to attribute exclusively to rhetorical traditions in Najla's
native culture. Far from a naive reader, Najla was able to characterize with a certain irony—at least in retrospect, more than a year after she had written her
paper—the conventions of the romances she had been fed by her American
friend. I asked her to describe the features of these books, beginning with the
hero:

> NA: . . . Strong, he could deal with everything around him. Rich.
> AT: The girl? . . .
> NA: Pretty. (both laugh)
> AT: That's it. Does she have any brains?
> NA: I think people like pretty girls, they don't like educated girls,
> because educated girl is not a good girl.

AT: Is she rich, this girl—or does she need the fellow's protection?
NA: Yes [she does], and the fellow knows all about her. . . .

Najla's insights into the genre correspond in several ways to the guide-line "tipsheets" that publishers like Harlequin and Silhouette distribute to potential authors of romances. But for all her literary acuity, Najla had trans-muted several features of the Western romance in telling ways. True, native speakers might be just as apt to look to models such as popular romances to shape their discourse, but it seems unlikely they would extrapolate these same features, or translate them in quite the same manner as Najla has done. For example, as I mentioned in Chapter 1, when I read Najla's paper with a group of our team teachers, the bit about the flower country Ireland did get laughs, which I effectively squelched by explaining patiently that the author was most likely translating the spirit if not the letter of her native culture. It strikes me now that in this case Najla's writing might have profited more from her American coevals' less "tolerant," which is to say less condescend-ing reception.

Let's look more closely at Najla's adaptation of the romances she had read. The heroine of her description scarcely meets the job specifications of the folks at Silhouette, whose tipsheets portray the ideal heroine as above all "independent, intelligent, and strong-willed." In the numerous romances—gothic, historical, contemporary[8]—I read after speaking with Najla, books by Barbara Cartland as well as by Marion Chesney who is also Jennie Tremaine, and Victoria Holt who is also Philippa Carr who is also Jean Plaidy, one thing is clear: the heroine of the story is forever mouthy. In each book, courtship proceeds by means of a series of verbal skirmishes in which the heroine invariably outtalks the hero.

To cite just two representative cases: the hero of Virginia Holt's *The Time of the Hunter's Moon* is a swashbuckling land baron, a lady-killer and a hand-kisser if ever there was one, but all the same the heroine remarks, "I was able to stand up to him in our verbal battles and that was because I had always found it easy to express myself lucidly. After all, wasn't I teaching English?" And the eponymous heroine of *Ginny*, by Marion Chesney, or should I say Jennie Tremaine, actually toys with the conventions of the genre

---

[8]As described in *Reading the Romance* and *The Female Gothic* (listed in the bibliography for this chapter), these subgenres—readily identifiable to fans by imprint, book cover, author's pseudonym, and the like—differ slightly. The Silhouette books are contemporary romances, but like the historical romances are less "conservative" than the Harlequins or the gothics. That is, sexual descriptions are somewhat more explicit, and the heroines more independent, even defiant. The contemporary heroine is more likely to have a career, which she expects to keep even after the inevitable denouement: marriage.

Still, Barbara Bowman points out in her structuralist description of Holt's gothic romances (in *The Female Gothic* 69–81), Holt's heroine usually has a profession, and through the initiation process of the novel gradually becomes self-sufficient even as she ultimately assumes the role of Caring Wife. Most important for the purposes of our discussion here, the heroines of the gothics (even though, Jane Eyre-like, they may initially be more quiet and submissive), and of the Cartland romances as well, soon enough become assertive and verbal.

in which she stars: in this metaromance the pragmatic middle-class heroine assumes the role of demure ingenue so as to make fools of every upper-class twit in the book and trick dashing Lord Gerald into a prenuptial tryst. In marked contrast to this bevy of fictional models, the most notable feature of Najla's heroine, as we have seen, is her passivity, her silence and downcast gaze, for *this* protagonist, as we have discovered through extraliterary means, is an observant Muslim, and in any case Romance can take a real-life heroine just so far.

I have mentioned that the hero of Najla's description is decidedly Eastern in looks and nearly Western in manner. Yet we can begin to see how Najla's young man, too, has been silenced to some degree. Throughout the essay Najla has alluded to some question implied in the hero's eyes, a question he cannot utter. No wonder: When I asked Najla what the young man would say to her father if this were an actual encounter, she told me, "The first thing he'd say is 'I want to marry your daughter'; he couldn't say, 'I want to go out.' "

Several cultural myths and protocols are in conflict here, with the result that Najla is at times as burlesque in her impression of a Western-style hero as her mentor Barbara Cartland is at imagining villains from Afghanistan, which feat, not incidentally, Cartland attempts in one of her latest (Jove edition postmarked "June 1988"), entitled *Love Is Invincible*. This book is set during the so-called Great Game between England and Russia for dominance over India and its most vulnerable frontier along the border of Afghanistan. The following excerpt from Cartland's preface should give you some of the flavor of the book, articulating as it does the rhetoric of Orientalism in its rabid tertiary stage:

> Afghanistan was a very unreliable neighbour and the frontier area was inhabited by lawless Muslim tribes owing no definite allegiance to anybody. . . .
>
> The legend of the British arms in India, written about so brilliantly by Kipling, was born out of the rocks and wadis of the North-West, where savage tribesmen lay in ambush behind the next rock.
>
> The Afghans brooded behind the tribes, and behind them all stood the Russians.

Obviously, unlike her comparatively literate and entertaining competitors in all their various noms d'amour, Cartland is too easy a mark. But I quote her for two reasons. First, she so neatly underscores a premise of my earlier reading of Najla's essay, namely that Najla's work is informed by a difference in aesthetic values, most clearly with regard to human physiognomy. In Cartland's Invincible romance, here is how the housemaid, in the broadest of music-hall dialects, says she knows the villains of the plot are foreigners: " 'No mistake 'bout that!' Flo replied, 'Black hair, black eyes, an' a swarthy skin. They 'as high cheek-bones, an', if ye asks me, they come from some Eastern country we've never 'eard of!' " You will note that these physical features are precisely those Najla has claimed for her hero.

My second reason for perpetrating Cartland at length is that the Great Game of which she speaks so glowingly is of course an earlier version of the war of Russian intervention resumed in Afghanistan in 1979 and only recently conceded. It has been remarked that in the contemporary version of the Game the United States took up the role of the British Raj, waging its most elaborate and expensive covert war since Cambodia and bringing tens of thousands of Afghani refugees like Najla to our shores, many of them to our classrooms. And I have wanted to show that however respectful my motives might have been, my earlier reading of Najla's text suffered by partaking of the same emphatic demarcation between East and West that empowers hegemony, in discourse as in war—and that countenances "lawless Muslim tribes," but only when they owe allegiance to the West.

The question of a responsible reading of Najla's paper has become rather more nettlesome than when first posed, because of an alteration in the extraliterary assumptions on which this reading, like all readings, depends. Moreover, for all the light shed by Najla's testimony, the wellspring of origin —as poststructuralist theory and the Heisenberg effect have conspired to warn us—must remain turbid. Since Najla's young man is situated somewhere between Kabul and Cart-land, his come-on, so charmingly formal when read months ago, seems now, in light of our interview, awkward and implausible. If we accept a feature of Najla's paper such as the suitor's speech, it is because we think his speech appropriately stilted and foreign sounding, as befits a conversation translated from Dari. Yet once we sense that the author is writing what she thinks will be appropriate for a Western audience, and whence that notion of audience derives, the speech becomes merely risible.

What then constitutes a responsible reading of the work produced by a nonnative student who has achieved a measure of competency in English? Critical theories of the last few years have urged far greater attention to the social field in which practices of writing and reading are located. As a result, professional readers and writers have become so self-reflexive that the process recalls one of those painted self-portraits in which the artist holds a mirror in one hand, a brush in the other, and turns away from the "inner" canvas, the portrait-within-the-portrait, to stare back out at the viewer.

Jonathan Culler once remarked that "For a woman to read as a woman is not to repeat an identity or an experience that is given but to play a role she constructs with reference to her identity as a woman, which is also a construct, so that the series can continue: a woman reading as a woman reading as a woman" (64). My point in the foregoing discussion is that reading across cultures, particularly when the scene of cultural encounter is a classroom assignment, introduces a few more distorting mirrors into the series. In the present discussion of fashion and self-fashioning I have been suggesting that Najla's audience, whether I or her teacher, Diane Menna, might be reading according to a construct of an American female teacher who is reading the work of an Eastern-born woman who is writing according to some construct of a Western female audience as posited by the folks at Harlequin Books, and so on and on. At this point if you are still trying to picture Najla, you might imagine her holding hands with her reader; now they are both wearing those flashing neon necklaces, and they are standing in the Port Authority Bus Terminal under a sign marked "THIS WAY MADNESS."

So let me rephrase my question: what might constitute a sane and practical response to some of the conceptual difficulties one is apt to encounter in an ESL student's papers, specifically when the student is not Western? Despite my wrong turns in this paper chase, or perhaps because of them, I have been arguing that the study of cultural differences is in fact a worthy and useful enterprise, even though the act of definition itself is insidious in its urge to objectify and thus presuppose superiority over the Other. I have mentioned that Edward Said among other observers has inveighed persuasively against the perils of Orientalist thinking, of reducing the non-Occidental to an essentialist abstraction. Yet it has been pointed out that Said himself falls into the same trap, invoking a construct called "the Orient" when it suits him, and comparing this presumably more authentic structure to its representation in what Said characterizes rather reductively as a monolithic Western discourse on the East (Clifford 259ff.).

The trap seems unavoidable. But while I cannot come up with a satisfactory theory of this expressive ensemble we call culture, I am no less mindful that there are variations between as well as within cultures, and that these differences affect our thinking, writing, reading, and evaluating in profound and complex ways. The catch, as Najla's essay so amply demonstrates, is that it is difficult to discern precisely where one collection of customs and assumptions leaves off and another begins, culture being a living and changeable thing. Increasingly I find myself invoking ethnographer James Clifford's remark that "Culture is a deeply compromised idea I cannot yet do without" (10).

Still, the focus of my investigation of the work of students such as Mohammad and Najla has gradually shifted to the ways in which culture is created, in some measure, by the individual. I think it worth considering the ways in which English as a Second Language students, as their rubric implies, must inevitably invent their home culture in opposition to the adoptive culture, as well as to other cultures they encounter in the American classroom. To what extent might an Eastern student's work embody a dialectic between acceptance of Western beliefs and reaction against them—especially when that student is a political and religious exile like Mohammad, or like Najla, living amid the infidels and writing in the alien corn?

Like most nonnative students, Najla is no longer a member of her country of origin; neither is she American. She speaks and writes an interlanguage on its way to becoming English. She talked to me of returning to Afghanistan if the Russian troops were to pull out. But I wonder whether, practically, she can now return to the political black hole the Russians have left in their wake, and if she does return, whether ideologically she will be able to live there as she did before her neocolonial experience in America. After our interview

Najla sent me an essay she had produced for her English 120 (Composition II) class, a response to Kate Chopin's *The Awakening*, in which she writes, "We all experience some awakenings . . . which change the direction of our lives. Sometimes these changes take us too far that we cannot come back to where we belonged first. . . . " Of Chopin's heroine Najla observes, "She could not go back to where she belonged first and she did not have the strength and guts to go farther. She was caught up in the middle of no-where." I believe this in-betweenness to be the subtext of the descriptive essay Najla produced in her 105 class. Indeed it seems to me an implicit theme in the work of most nonnative writers, professionals as well as students.

In his novel *Shame*, Salman Rushdie says, "I, too, know something of this immigrant business." An emigrant from India to Pakistan, where his family moved against his will, to England, where he now lives,[9] Rushdie is the product of several cultures. And those cultures, Rushdie would argue, are in turn produced by him:

> I, too, like all migrants, am a fantasist. I build imaginary
> countries and try to impose them on the ones that exist. I, too,
> face the problem of history: what to retain, what to dump, how
> to hold on to what memory insists on relinquishing, how to deal
> with change.

The ethnographic shift in our college population over the past decade or so has meant a number of revisions in our line of work: not just in the way we acknowledge these newcomers in our reading lists or classroom discussions, but in the way we look at American culture—or better say, the multiplicity of American cultures—and how we represent this variety of cultures in our classes. In her 120 class, for instance, Najla read works that have hitherto been marginalized in traditional syllabi; during our interview she singled out two books, Chopin's *The Awakening* and Hurston's *Their Eyes Were Watching God*, which, significantly enough, depict "arranged marriages," American style. These books provided her with means to discuss her own experience on paper, to articulate a social code and to criticize it. Marginalized works, read alongside canonically sanctioned selections, help natives and nonnatives alike to locate the ideological agenda in the literary text.

In these ways, it seems to me, a minority nonnative population has already given rise to the kind of academic program Gayatri Spivak advocates:

---

[9]And most recently, persecuted, to regions unknown. Adumbrated by that now most famous of exiles, Rushdie's words here ring all the more mournfully. I completed this chapter, including the final section on the Rushdie short story, just before the publicity broke surrounding the publication of *The Satanic Verses*. I have chosen to let the discussion stand unchanged, however ingenuous some parts may seem in light of subsequent nightmarish events. Indeed, those events seem to have rendered the issues of cross-cultural literacy even more pressing matters for consideration, just as they will doubtless color the reader's reception of the analysis in the following section.

"the pedagogy of the humanities as the arena of cultural explanations that question the explanations of culture" (117). Najla's progress through our college composition sequence suggests a student who is alive to all the possibilities we can provide. At the end of our interview this summer, I asked Najla, "Are you still reading those gothic romances?"

> NA: No. I like books about women—like *Awakening*. I really like 120 class so much, [Najla took the course with Virginia Johnson of our department] and would like to talk about women's problems.
>
> AT: Really, you've turned around 180 degrees! Because in the gothic romance as I understand it . . .
>
> NA: It's not reality (laughs). Now I like books about reality.
>
> AT: . . . Now the opposite would be something like *The Awakening*, where the woman is married, and unhappy . . .
>
> NA: . . . She changes. Do you know . . . *Pygmalion?* I love this book.
>
> AT: Did you read it in English 120?
>
> NA: Yeah, and still I have it and sometimes I read it again.

I asked Najla why she liked *Pygmalion*, the drama of another "ESL" speaker, enough to reread it. As you will have gathered by now, she said because "It's about change."

Re: Reading "Culture"

In light of the foregoing sets of original and revised readings of cross-cultural material, I find that a similar reconsideration of the "parable" of Rushdie's short story and my friend's teaching of it, recounted at the end of Chapter 1, discloses further significance. For Rushdie's "Good Advice Is Rarer Than Rubies," like the classroom incident it occasioned, represents a scene of cultural inscription.

I want to be clear about the rationale behind the following expanded analysis of the story. By including various rereadings throughout this chapter, I have not meant to suggest that the validity of an interpretation is always contingent on some arbitrary choice of method or point of view. Rather I want to show that, as Louis Marin has commented,

> . . . *meaning is plural*, that the possible, the latent, and the divergent enter into its very definition—not just into its speculative definition, but also into its concrete production, be it that of the writer or that of the reader, of the emitter or the receiver of the message at different moments of history and at different places in the world and in culture (239).

As I have hoped to demonstrate, interpretation is deepened by consideration of the social and political context of a piece of discourse. My own experience of rereading Najla's paper, of having misread it in the first place and of having subsequently interviewed her, to her occasional discomfiture, about the meaning of her work, leads me back to the implied confrontation between Easterner and Westerner that lies at the core of Rushdie's story.

Further impetus toward re-vision of the story as a metatext, setting up its own literary dialogue with colonialist history and literature, comes from locating the story in the context of Rushdie's previous work. I refer particularly to his two novels of subcontinental partition and exile, *Midnight's Children* and *Shame*. Narrative in both novels is reader-conscious and self-referential in the extreme, loaded with both historical "fact" and implausible coincidence; doubling back on itself, "falling apart" like the subcontinent itself, the book undercuts Western classical realism at every turn. The sense Rushdie imparts of the illusory nature of the phenomenal world carries over into the noetics of perception, the deceit of fiction, and the creative (or destructive) act of recording history itself. Pakistan is described in *Midnight's Children* as "a country where the truth is what it is instructed to be" (389) and in *Shame* as a land founded on a rewritten past, on the necessary covering over of centuries of Indian history (87).

This background points the way to our reconsideration of "Good Advice Is Rarer Than Rubies," a story on the face of it fairly "realistic" in narrative technique, in terms of the concerns of Rushdie's previous projects: the tale of the reluctant exile, the shaping role of the reader in apprehending the verbal process of a text, the impossibility of a disinterested history, whether told by British colonialists or subaltern nationalists. If we take our cue for rereading from these concerns, as well as from the agenda of poststructuralist theory to examine what a work of art omits as much as what it includes, the central and heuristic scene of the story may in fact be the "missing" scene in which Miss Rehana meets her British inquisitors.

The narrative of the story, as well as the setting itself, inscribes the legacy of colonialism on the subcontinent. Events unfold before the gates of the British Embassy, whose inhabitants hold, or withhold, the passport to cultural migration. The encounter between Rehana and the sahibs inside the gates is an off-stage occurrence. What we *do* have are two partial versions of the confrontation: Muhammad Ali's mock interrogation of Rehana before she enters the embassy, and Rehana's summary recounting of it, after the fact, to Muhammad Ali. Both informants mimic, satirize, appropriate the Westerners' words. Using what we learn from these *Eastern* observers' versions, we are asked, as Rushdie invites his readers in *Shame*, to "join in" the reconstruction of the missing scene.

In this way the strategies of the narrative expose the limitations of representation, whether in art or literature or history. These limitations are particularly evident with regard to events in the East, which Westerners traditionally receive from other Westerners, and which are shown, as in the instances examined earlier in this chapter, to be skewed by the outsider's overdetermined vantage point. As Mohammad Amin remarked during our interview when I asked him if he resented Anglo law in his country, "Which country are you talking about? . . . Because the amazing thing, that British are in all those countries I've been—It's history!"

As the Subaltern Studies Group has shown in its examination of Indian and Pakistani historiography, the "sanctioned ignorance" of rational expectation theory is the mainstay of neocolonialism (cited in Spivak 199ff.). And it is this same cognitive failure on the part of the British that the heroine of Rushdie's short story is able to exploit for her own purposes. As Muhammad Ali explains, the sahibs think all the Tuesday-women claiming to be dependents of residents in England are "crooks and liars and thieves." Rehana protests, "But then I will simply tell them that I, for one, am no such thing!" Yet she discovers, ironically through Ali's "good advice," that the view from within the embassy walls does not admit differences among supplicants. If she tells the truth, the sahibs will not believe her. Eventually she triumphs and resists migration to England by withholding from her inquisitors whatever information she has, thus conforming to the British sahibs' misapprehension of members of her culture. She gives them what they expect. Playing the "Easterner," the dependent "Tuesday-woman," she conforms to type.

In her subsequent reconstruction of the confrontational scene, when she reveals to Ali information she has concealed from her questioners, Rehana literally displaces the site of domination in discourse. This strategy of subversion, as Homi K. Bhabha has remarked in another context, turns the gaze of the subordinate back on those in power (173). Ultimately Rehana remains something of a cipher, not just to the sahibs who believe they "see through" her but to the advice giver and the reader alike. The liberated, orphaned heroine refuses one form of colonization while resuming her subservient status as ayah—an Anglo-Indian term for retainer or nurse—to someone else's children. At the story's ending as at its opening, she is glimpsed in a "veiling" cloud of dust: barefaced but nevertheless "concealed," like the other veiled Tuesday-women who hang back on the arms of their male protectors, at the gates of the embassy, at the margins of the story.

In these ways the story provides a paradigm of reading and interpretation by suggesting the exclusive and contradictory nature of historical and cultural truths. History, literature, literary and art criticism, pedagogy, are irreducibly written in the language of ideology. Catherine Belsey characterizes traditional Anglo-American critical practice this way: the commentator appropriates the text by "closing" it, smoothing out its inconsistencies. "Having created a canon of acceptable texts," Belsey continues, "criticism then provides them with acceptable interpretations, thus effectively censoring any elements in them which come into collision with the dominant ideology" (109).

In the process of examining and revising my own interpretive practices in this and the preceding chapter, I have not been arguing for an exclusive reading of Rushdie's story or Najla's essay or Matisse's odalisques, but rather for the ways in which the significance of a text resides in the reader's apprehension of the multiplicity of interpretive processes for that text. In this spirit I offer one more reading of "Good Advice Is Rarer Than Rubies," this one by Fauzia Subhani, a Pakistani student in my team-teaching seminar. In November of 1988 we discussed this story in seminar. As in the case of the English literature class described in Chapter 1, the American-born students in the class all assumed the story took place in India, and all appeared to accept the cultural givens of the story as naturalistic representations. Fauzia was thus prompted to write the response reprinted below.

The daughter of two journalists, Fauzia lived in Karachi until her family was forced to flee Zia's regime. Like Najla Afzali, she is Western in dress and deportment and traditionally Muslim in her religious beliefs and social mores. I reprint Fauzia's response as a final commentary—though by no means the last word—on Rushdie's story. As you might have predicted, this Urdu speaker's reading in some ways conflicts with and supersedes my own interpretations. Her criticism ironically brings into focus the reactions of the Indian-born students about whom I speculated in the preceding chapter, and, just as important, glosses a certain amount of *new* presuppositional cultural material to which most Western readers would otherwise have no access, no matter how many times they reread the story. Her comments—which Fauzia urges me to tell you are "really notes"—deepen our apprehension of the already vexed relationship between writers and readers, even among individuals who share the same culture. Finally, Fauzia illustrates how the context in which a foreign-born writer's work appears may affect its reception—and possibly its inception.[10]

Rushdie and His Pakistan

There are profound universal themes in Rushdie's story, but not enough to support the artificiality of the setting and voice. Muhammad Ali is the embodiment of midlife crises. He is portrayed by Rushdie as an elderly man charmed, beyond reason, by the young woman before him. ". . . the oldest fools are bewitched by the youngest girls," he explains. The rusted chains of bureaucracy evident in the story are present today even in the most developed nations. Rushdie tells of the half-hour or perhaps two-hour breakfasts which are common in the East. I felt he captured the relaxed mood of Pakistani life well. Beyond this point though, Rushdie enters into a story that lacks temporal reality.

Rushdie is describing the attitudes and views that existed in Pakistan 20 years ago. Perhaps it is my Pakistani nationality that demands a more basic, more critical look at these details. His details in this story are of a place I don't recognize. The voice is of a

[10]Fauzia's commentary, like my own, was written before *The Satanic Verses* was released. But her impassioned reaction to the *New Yorker* story, in fact, illuminates the controversy attending publication of the novel.

stranger. I wouldn't call Rushdie indifferent, but certainly absent. A person who takes the responsibility of representing a culture to a foreign audience has an obligation to accuracy. I realize that this is a cumbersome task, but a necessary one. If Rushdie wrote this story for a Pakistani audience, I would have no quarrels with him. That audience would have the information to refute or accept the plausibility of the story. But his New York audience cannot be expected to have the same information. Thus, the responsibility falls on the author.

Rushdie denies this option. He is describing the Pakistan of an era when London was the Holy Land. Twenty years ago, London was known as "walaiat," an Urdu word for *abroad*. That word is only a source of humor among Pakistanis now. Rushdie refers to this mistake, which Miss Rehana makes twice: she calls England "London." A couple of decades ago this was a common mistake, because people thought of all the West as London. This is no longer the case. Even Pakistanis realize the corruption that infests England. It is no longer the Land of Opportunity. America is the Pakistani dream now; England is just a summer vacation. Besides, the spread of world communication makes it impossible to believe that London could represent "the West" to anyone. The appreciation for culture in both the East and the West has enhanced world relations. An example of this effort can be seen in Bloomingdale's of New York, of all places: their theme for this year is called "The Year of the Dragon." And on the Eastern front, Pakistanis crave their American heroes in "The Cosby Show" and "Family Ties." Due to these efforts, the concept of West has changed for Pakistanis.

I appreciate Rushdie's detail, though (as outdated as it is). More disturbing to me is his female character. "Miss Rehana" is not a real woman. This upsets me because finally I saw portrayed in fiction a strong Pakistani woman who insists upon her identity. The major problem is she has no identity. A woman who is beautiful and young would not be satisfied by being an ayah in Pakistan. An ayah is a servant who looks after the children and does housekeeping. It is a loving woman but not necessarily a respected one. Rushdie's Rehana would not let herself be placed in that position. Well, let us suppose the woman has an undying love for children; she would never be hired anyway. Pakistani Muslim men are allowed to marry four wives simultaneously. Thus the possibility of losing one's husband is a very big fear there. No woman would hire a live-in ayah whose eyes did bad things to the digestive tracts of men, as our Miss Rehana's do.

She is also portrayed as a woman committed to a man she has not seen in many years. Arranged marriages still take place in Pakistan, but not like this. Twenty years ago this was common, because of the harsh travel conditions. Now it is very uncommon that a couple would be engaged without even seeing each other. The spread of communication has encouraged intercontinental marriages, though. They often take place between strangers, but now the couple is given a chance to visit and to know each other. Most of the time both have the option to refuse the marriage.

Pakistan has charm. It has centuries of culture just waiting to be discovered. (I take full responsibility for my bias.) Salman Rushdie has failed to capture the essence of that Pakistan. As an exile living in Britain, he is the foreigner, the other, but "Good Advice Is Rarer Than Rubies" lacks even the excitement of the foreigner.

Through the work of observers such as Foucault and Said, we have come to think of literature as a cultural force that is shaped by its sociopolitical milieu and in turn has the power to reshape our vision of the world. I believe the increasing body of work produced by our international students constitutes such a reshaping text within the academy, weaning us from certain ethnocentric canonical and critical beliefs. These students have challenged dominant value systems by pointing to differing modes of thought and expression, and so decolonizing our processes of interpretation. The resulting interaction of cultures, which I have earlier dubbed "cross-cultural literacy," seems to me a revitalizing force in the academy.

I embarked on the preceding chapter, in part, with the intention of illustrating "teacher error." The theory of error analysis in linguistics tells us that the student of a foreign language must make mistakes in order to learn. Errors are evidence of the student creating his or her own interlanguage, which partakes a little of the native language and still more of the adopted tongue, and which should be viewed as an "approximate system" on its way to becoming a true second language. I think we should allow teachers the same latitude. I cannot say what new blunders I have committed in my rereading of the texts discussed in this chapter. But I believe the errors we make when we expand our reading to include foreign texts have to be made, if we are to discover how we can best engage our nonnative students, and if we are to hear what they have to tell us.

PART TWO

In the Composition Classroom

3

How to Do Things
with Function Words
A Russian Student's
Acquisition of English Articles

The following study, the earliest and most rudimentary undertaken in this book, was begun in 1981 in the aftermath of one of my composition classes into which a nonnative student had been placed. In a postmortem of puzzlement, I tried to make sense of this student's struggle to learn English, of what that might entail on the level of grammar alone. At this stage in my career I had not yet decided how I wanted to go about teaching writing at all, much less how or whether I could effectively teach grammar, still less how I should approach such matters with native speakers of other languages. These questions I am still trying to sort out. But the following exercise, though more narrow in scope than my subsequent investigations, taught me several things about the complexity of even the most basic of enterprises in language learning. Just as important, the exercise forced me to find rules and formulate explanations for what I, as a native speaker, had told my first ESL students were "idiomatic" constructions.

The question of how a Russian student acquires knowledge of the rules governing English article usage will be discussed in detail in this chapter. The result is a case study in the logic of one learner's interlanguage. Let me explain. It has been suggested that first-language interference partly results from the learner being called upon to perform before he or she has acquired sufficient knowledge of the second language (Krashen 67). Several observers (e.g., Wode; Kellerman) hypothesize that for this linguistic transfer to take place, the learner must *perceive* a similarity between a particular item in the first language and in the target language. When there is no comparable item in the native language, however, the learner's interlanguage — reflecting the half-digested grammar of the target language — takes over. This Russian speaker, for instance, writing in her journal, describes and illustrates her overriding grammatical problem:

> My biggest problem is articles. Sometimes I leave them out, sometimes I put a wrong ones.

The point I want to underscore in this chapter is that linguistic phenomena such as articles or plural markers must be examined in terms of both the native language of the learner and the target language in which they occur. Thus the above student's difficulty isn't simply a question of Russian not having grammatical morphemes that correspond to the English *a(n)* and *the*. Russian speakers, like the Chinese and Japanese speakers whose work will be discussed in chapters to follow, aren't used to thinking quite the way native English speakers do in terms of mass or countable nouns, any more than English speakers are accustomed to thinking about the gender of nouns—which is why English speakers are apt to have difficulty memorizing the sex of inanimate objects when learning Russian or Romance languages.

Thus ESL students are bound to be baffled by certain grammatical signals, like those regulating articles, that native speakers rarely get wrong. My reason for undertaking this brief investigation years ago was to attempt to explain a set of phenomena regarding function words that native speakers absorb "naturally," never setting out to learn them nor having to explain their use. I wanted to see how a nonnative speaker might make sense of these function words when left to his own devices, for my student, so far as I can tell, during the three years traced in this chapter received no formal instruction in the matter of English article usage.[1]

This history begins with a worst-case scenario. Oleg Gokhman emigrated to the United States from Russia at the age of 17, speaking very little English. He entered Queens College in September of 1980, scored 3 out of 12

---

[1] As for the verdict on how or even whether such instruction is of more than perfunctory use for language learners, the jury is still out. The question is particularly vexed when it comes to teaching rules governing function words like prepositions and articles. Beyond the rudimentary principles of definite versus indefinite, article usage is often, as we shall see in these pages, a matter of idiom memorization and stylistic choice—matters difficult if not impossible to teach.

In his fine review article on the controversy surrounding formal grammar instruction (1985), Patrick Hartwell sifts through the evidence of some 75 years of experimental research. He concludes that as the two sides of the debate have been unable to agree on how to interpret their findings, research has "for all practical purposes told us nothing" (106).

A couple of articles cited by Hartwell, however, are relevant for our present purposes. Ellen Bialystock's study (1981) of English speakers learning French suggests that learners first make an intuitive judgment of grammaticality, using implicit grammar rules they have unconsciously absorbed, and only then search for formal explanations to justify their judgments. An experiment devised by a colleague at Queens, Herbert Seliger (1979), leads to a related if more complicated conclusion. Native and nonnative speakers of English were tested for their ability to use the correct form of the indefinite articles *a* and *an*; the speakers were then asked to state the rule governing their choices. No correlation was found, for either native or nonnative speakers, between the ability to state the rule and the ability to apply it correctly. Seliger concludes from these data that grammar rules are of little use, *except* for those learners who think they are of use, for the rules help them to access information they have *already* internalized.

Finally, as Hartwell points out, the one assumption that unites many composition theorists is that one learns to control language not so much by learning rules or definitions in isolation as by manipulating language in meaningful contexts. Attention to surface form develops tacitly as an adjunct to rhetorical competency. The intertwining of these developing language skills is the subject of subsequent chapters in this book.

points on the CUNY Writing Assessment Test, and was enrolled in the college's CESL preparatory program. At the end of the semester he scored—by some fluke—a 6 on the Test, and was placed in a native-speaker basic writing course (now called 105), for which, as you will see from the essay reprinted below, he was ill-equipped. At the end of the course, he scored another 6 on the WAT. The following semester he again began the English department's composition sequence and went on to complete these requirements without further interruption.

An English 110 essay reprinted at the end of this chapter shows that Oleg's performance improved somewhat over the semesters, although this change was by no means as sudden or striking as in the case of the students whose work is examined in later chapters. Oleg's prose gained minimal linguistic competency but lost a lot of blood in the process.

Oleg's first effort in his English composition class, an autobiographical narrative, is far less proficient than the average ESL student's 105 work, yet it is fairly typical of ESL compositions in that the writer's ideas dramatically outdistance his ability to express them grammatically. The writer manages his narrative adroitly, incisively illustrating his thesis concerning the Russian immigrant's disillusionment at the inequities of capitalism. At the sentence level, though, his paper is a resounding failure. I'd like to go through the essay, first, to examine some instances of interference from the student's native language, as well as of the kinds of developmental problems encountered by beginning ESL students regardless of first language. Afterwards, I'll focus on specific errors in article usage that crop up in this and subsequent essays Oleg produced in 105, since the work of a Russian speaker at this introductory level of English is especially suited to an inquiry into how a learner might acquire over time the most basic of English grammatical morphemes.

First Impression Is Sometimes Deceptive

I came to the United States more than a year ago. At that time my impressions about this country were great. I! (as all new immigrants) couldn't understand how people had built such beautiful life for themselves. Everything here admired me: plantiful in food, variaties in clothes, TV programs, sea of cars on the streets, skyscrapers swinging in the clouds. It was America as such, how I imagined it in Russia by viewes, which I saw in American movies and by oure relatives' letters, who lived in America. I couldn't see anything bad in this country.

But there is truth in somebody's words, who said that one moment can chang our life, and such moment changed my opinion about life in America.

It was a beautiful, sunny, spring day. I was at home and didn't know what to do. Suddenly great idea came to my mind. I desided to go for a walk and watch the city. I'd never gone out just for viewing the life in New York.

I took the subway near my house and making myself comfortable I tried to read the paper, but I don't like to read in the
subway, and I began looking at the people around me. There
weren't many of them. Everybody was thinking about something.
"What can worry them in this rich country, where people don't
have to think how to buy a good piece of meat for the next day?"
I asked myself. But I really wasn't interested, what they were
thinking, I just felt cheerful and sang a song to myself.

Bright rays of spring sun dazzled me when I came out from
the dark moist subway. I walked in the beauty, majesty and
wealth of Fifth Avenue. On my left side were tenant's buildings,
not much of what you can see in other places. I walked down the
street. There were stores of some of the richest in the world, richest hotels, richest jewelry shops. Sometimes horses and carrages,
riding by cabmans, wearing old fashion suits, bow ties, and top
hats, pass by. It was very interesting, just like in the old movies.

Rockefeller Plaza and Linkoln Centre amazed. People were
so cheerful and happy. They were smiling and it seemed they
had no problemes. Very often I rised my head to look up at the
majesticy and mighty skyscrapers. I felt such delight. Only one
think couldn't appropriate in my mind: "How is it possible that
one, and sometimes few of such buildings could belong to one
man?"

The more I walked the more I surprised, and suddenly . . . I almost run about something big and warm. At first I
couldn't realize that it was alive object. Then I saw that it can
move, but I was afraid the fact that it was human, but unfortu-
natly it was so. It was something that people ussially call "hard to
discribe." This man (or woman) was sitting right on the sidewalk,
coiled up. His hair didn't look really like hair—it remained me
strings. His face . . . Don't think that I want to discribe expression on his face. If I could only compare expression on it and expression of the stone wall, probably the last could tell me more.
His mouth, eyes and nose fused together and I couldn't distinguish them. Saliva was dripping out his mouth. There is much to
tell about his clothes (if I only can call it so). First of all he was
barefooted. All holes on his pants was more than material. Something what remained me jacket was over his sholders. Nothing
more disgusting I've ever seen in my life . . .

It was almost sunset. I turned away and very fast, almost
running I went home. It was getting colder. I passed again
through all places, which I saw befor, but they couldn't impress
me any more. I came down again to the moist, dark subway. All
the way home I have been thought: "What country is this which
make slaves of money from the people, for who money is higher
than human felling?"

I have chosen this from among Oleg's other essays for the power of its
observations. In light of the mournful conclusion drawn by this outside

observer of American culture, it seems all the more trivializing to limit our sights in the present discussion to grammatical considerations, much less to niggling matters like article usage. But such is the project that occupies us in this preliminary study; we shall have to leave more pressing questions raised by nonnative speakers in our composition classrooms for subsequent chapters.

I'd like to begin by discussing errors that seem to provide clearest evidence of first-language interference: those concerning orthography. The Russian writer's spelling is naturally influenced by his pronunciation. Most Russian sounds can be considered allophones, positional variants, corresponding but not identical to English sounds. (" 'Gaw-gol,' not 'Go-gall,' " Vladimir Nabokov waspishly corrects the English reader of his book on Gogol. "The final 'l' is a soft dissolving 'l' which does not exist in English. One cannot hope to understand an author if one cannot even pronounce his name" [150].) While the slight variations in these phonemes are generally acceptable in speech (except to Nabokov in his professorial disguise), they may account for occasional misspellings in the student's written production of the language.

A number of spelling errors in this essay, such as the addition or subtraction of a silent *e* (*oure, befor*) and the substitution of *k* for *c* (*Linkoln*) or *s* for *c* (*desided*), are common to many beginners, since there is no audible distinction in these words between the two letter choices. But several other misspellings may be attributable to first-language interference. For example, Oleg writes *plantiful* and *variaties*, presumably because for a Russian speaker the difference between "open" and "closed" vowels is difficult to discern: The relative tenseness of vowels is an important characteristic of English but in Russian has no phonemic value (Mentcher 48). So besides missing the /æ/ versus /ɛ/ contrast in the above-mentioned words, Oleg mistakes /ɛ/ for /i/, writing *felling* for *feeling*—an error that persists semesters later, as we'll see in the paper quoted at the end of this chapter.

Native Russian speakers also tend to have trouble pronouncing the English semivowels *w* and *j*, which perhaps explains Oleg's reference in a later essay to that famous scientist, Charles Darving. In addition, a common mistake among both Russian and German speakers is the "devoicing" of a final voiced obstruent (voiced obstruents, i.e., those consonants produced with an obstruction of airflow and a vibration of the vocal cords, include *b, d, g, v,* δ [as in *this*], and *z*; the unvoiced counterparts of these phonemes are *p, t, k, f,* θ [as in *thin*], and *s*). This error leads to confusions such as bad/bat and tab/tap, and probably to Oleg's substitution of *think* for *thing*.

Far more serious errors in this essay are those having to do with the agreement, tense, and voice of English verbs, and here, as in the case of the misspellings, the problems can be traced to features of both the learner's first and second languages. Rarely can an error be locked into a single category such as transfer, overgeneralization, or simplification; what we most often witness in second-language error analysis is the dynamic interplay between two languages. For instance, a conceptual difference between languages may lead to a pronoun-referent agreement error, as when Oleg writes, "There is much to tell about his clothes (if I only can call it so)." In an interview conducted in December of 1984,[2] during which Oleg was able to correct the majority of the errors he had made three years earlier in his first essay, this problem of agreement was broached:

> TEACHER: [You wrote] "There is much to tell about his clothes if I only can call it so."
>
> OLEG: By "it" I mean clothes.
>
> TEACHER: Well, clothes is plural.
>
> OLEG: Is it?
>
> TEACHER: Yeah. So you would say, instead of "it," "them." *Clothing* is singular but *clothes* is plural.
>
> OLEG: It's curious, because in English you say "it" for non-alive objects but if it comes in plural it's same as for live objects— "them." In Russian, you would say it in singular—in Russian there is no *clothes* in plural.
>
> TEACHER: What about *hair?* "Your hair is long"; in English we say it in singular.
>
> OLEG: Plural—in Russian it's always plural.

Conceptual differences may account for other verb errors in Oleg's work. I don't mean the kinds of irregularities that often appear in the writing of beginners in English regardless of first language—for example, agreement mistakes involving the third-person singular *-s* (. . . "What country is this which *make* slaves . . . "), or the mix-up of two different verbs ("Something what remained [=reminded] me . . . "), or the confusion between the transitive verb *to raise* and the intransitive *to rise* ("Very often I rised my head . . . "). Rather I refer to errors like these:

> Everything here admired me . . .
> The more I walked, the more I surprised . . .

and this, from Oleg's revision of his essay:

> The more I walked, the more I was admired. . . .

The problem in these examples stems from the student's misunderstanding of English passive verb constructions. Passive constructions are much more frequently used in English than in Russian. Moreover, English passive constructions are very rarely rendered into Russian by means of corresponding Russian passive forms of the verb. In English, both transitive and intransitive verbs can be used to create passive-voice transformations,

---

[2]The transcript of this interview is reprinted at the end of this chapter, along with the transcript of a conference with the same student held in May, 1981.

whereas in Russian, only transitive verbs are characterized by the category of voice. Russian most often translates English passive constructions through syntactic means, and occasionally by means of the finite form of a corresponding reflexive verb (Akhmanova et al. 30–32). It seems logical to view the verb errors in the foregoing sentences as arising from misconceptions about a grammatical category used far less frequently, and expressed very differently, in the ESL learner's mother tongue.

Additional verb tense errors found toward the end of Oleg's essay may similarly be viewed in terms of differences between Russian and English verb systems. Oleg's use of the past tense instead of the past perfect ("I passed again through all places which I *saw* befor, but they couldn't impress me any more") is common enough practice even among native speakers of English. Still, in explaining English verbs to Russian students it is useful to remember that Russian has no relative tenses such as past perfect or future perfect. The "sequence of tenses" rule dictating a shift in tenses is unknown in Russian, which relies less heavily on auxiliary verbs than English does. As Oleg noted during our December 1984 interview, it is perfectly acceptable in Russian to use the past tense in the sentence quoted above. Further, a native Russian speaker may initially have difficulty differentiating between the simple and continuous tenses, because the continuous aspect is not a category in Russian (Mentcher 50). In his first paper Oleg writes, "All the way home I have been thought . . . "; in the 1984 interview he was able to unscramble the verb phrases by using the past continuous tense: "All the way home I was thinking. . . . "

The most prevalent errors in Oleg's paper concern English articles. In view of more substantial ESL problems such as those just discussed, teachers understandably tend to assign relatively low priority to errors in article usage. The rules and exceptions governing English articles are so bewildering in number and utter whimsicality that these morphemes are among the last to be acquired completely, by first- as well as second-language learners. Indeed, Dulay and Burt, in a study of children's acquisition of English as a first language, classified article errors as *intralingual*—that is, arising from the properties of the target language. On the other hand, Dušková, studying the errors made by adult Czechoslovakians writing English compositions, maintained that article omission is an *interlingual* or interference error, in this case the result of the fact that Czech has no equivalent for this part of speech. It seems reasonable to assume that second-language learning is influenced by both the learner's native language *and* by the degree of complexity of the grammatical form being learned. Thus English article rules, which bear a high degree of semantic complexity, will present greater difficulty for native speakers of languages such as Russian, Chinese, and Japanese, which have no morphemic equivalent for articles, than for speakers of languages that have articles. As Zobl (172) points out, the latter group is likely to achieve control of the form more rapidly than the former.

This observation is the starting point from which we may engage in some linguistic detective work by studying in rather exhaustive detail one student's use of articles in writing and speech—a longitudinal study of performance involving the rudiments of contrastive, error, discourse, and speech act analysis. We will be comparing sentences from Oleg's first essay with sample sentences from his later written work as well as from transcriptions of the two interviews with him conducted 3½ years apart. (The 105 assignments from which I will quote are a revision of an autobiographical narrative, a "modern fable," and a response to a newspaper editorial.) The discussion that follows will doubtless tell you more than native speakers care or have to know about article usage. But this kind of investigation, which is finicking to the point of tedium and therefore, mercifully, need not be repeated in the remaining chapters of this book, is meant to demonstrate that seemingly haphazard mistakes often prove to have a logic all their own: the logic of the learner following the rules of his own evolving interlanguage.

The Acquisition of Articles: A Case History

A brief survey of some principles of English article usage will suffice to explain why Oleg consistently misunderstands their function at this early stage of second-language acquisition, and why the problem persists to some extent in the work he produces semesters later. In English, the primary structural function of articles is as determiners that precede nouns. Their chief semantic function is to mark nouns as definite or indefinite. The indefinite article, *a(n)*, signifies an *unspecified one* among others: "*A* student wrote this paper." The indefinite article is used for an indefinite or representative member of a class. The definite article, *the*, signals a *particular* person or thing: "*The* student who wrote this paper is Russian." The definite article is required in numerous contexts; to cite just a few examples, it is used for familiar persons or objects in the environment (We hiked in *the* mountains), for persons or things particularized by the verbal context (*The* student I just mentioned), for a class as a whole (*The* bison is an endangered species), with a "ranking" adjective or ordinal (*The* middle class; *the* fifth day), with abstract nouns or gerunds + *of* phrases (*The* instruction of students; *the* instructing of students), in *of* phrases after words of quantity (Some of *the* students), with words referring to events or government (*The* Fourth of July; *the* government ruled), with certain place names (*The* United States [versus _____ America]; *the* Alps) . . . and this is not to enumerate dozens of additional idiomatic usages. More confusing still, English specifies that in a number of situations *no* article be used: before a plural countable noun that refers to persons or things in *general* (They were good _____ writers); before a *mass* noun, such as water, air, oil, and so on, when it appears in a general context (compare: *The* air in the Alps is thinner/_____ Air is thinner at higher altitudes); and before an *abstract* noun, such as beauty, life, truth, and the like, when it appears in a general context (_____ Honesty is a habit).

A Russian student of English is bound to be undone by all these rules, to say nothing of idiomatic distinctions native speakers make in a sentence such as "I went to *the* library after I came home from _____ school." As the grammar books tell us, Russian has neither definite nor indefinite articles; "a student" and "the student" are both translated as **СТЧ ДЕНТ**. If it is necessary to state that a given student is spoken of, Russian speakers say "this student." If just any student is meant, as in "a student told me," Russians say *"one* student told me."

Of course this explanation greatly oversimplifies the matter. Russian does express definiteness versus indefiniteness despite the lack of articles, chiefly through word order. In a language like Russian, where grammatical relationships are expressed by morphological markers, word order is freed for the purpose of guiding the listener through the message, as opposed to English, where the relatively fixed word order serves to mark grammatical relationships (Thompson 88). In English, subject normally precedes predicate, and it is this prescribed order that often identifies the parts of a sentence. The Russian plethora of inflectional endings obviates this syntactic function, so word order may serve other functions.

By the relative positions of the subject and predicate, the Russian speaker can indicate definiteness or indefiniteness. The rule governing this subject-predicate inversion in Russian states that *what is presupposed* is usually stated first—in other words, the *given* (= "theme") must precede the *new* (= "rheme"). New information, the element that characteristically appears at the end of the sentence, roughly corresponds to the English use of *a(n)*, whereas the information that is taken as already known by the listener corresponds to the English *the*. It has been pointed out that historically, precisely when languages (such as English and Bulgarian) have lost case, they have tended to develop articles: articles partially assume the semantic and grammatical function of word order (Lake 48).

It comes as no surprise, then, that American students of Russian tend to have difficulty learning appropriate Russian word order, which is extremely and perplexingly "context sensitive" (Launer 61–69). Conversely, we can expect that native speakers of Russian or of other languages that lack articles will initially make the three kinds of English article errors discussed below. Moreover, as Hakuta and Zobl have pointed out, they will most likely take longer to acquire the proper forms than will speakers of languages possessing a corresponding grammatical category.

Omission of Articles

Discretion being the better part of valor, articles are often omitted in Oleg's early papers. As a number of linguistic studies have shown, marked structural contrast tends to promote avoidance or underrepresentation of a grammatical form (see, for example, Schachter; Hakuta). In Oleg's later essays, this particular error becomes less of a problem, presumably due to the learner's heightened awareness of articles through correction and rewriting.

The question arises: Since from the beginning the writer at times demonstrates his understanding of some basic rules governing article usage, why does he omit the required articles in similar cases? Take, for instance, four sentences that appear sequentially in Oleg's first essay:

> It was a beautiful, sunny spring day.
> I was at home and didn't know what to do.
> 1.1 Suddenly *great idea* came to my mind.
> I desided to go for a walk and watch the city.

In light of correct sentences 1, 2, and 4, the error in sentence 3 is puzzling. Yet when the examples of article omission in this essay are collated, they suggest what may be an underlying common bond. Consider the following:

> 1.2 I! (as all new immigrants) couldn't understand how people had built *such beautiful life* for themselves.
> 1.3 Everything here admired me: plantiful in food, variaties in clothes, TV programs, *sea of cars* on the streets, skyscrapers swinging in the clouds.
> 1.4 Don't think that I want to discribe *expression* on his face.
> 1.5 If I could only compare *expression* on it and *expression* of the stone wall, probably the last could tell me more.

Throughout his essay, the writer can correctly write "a day," "a year ago," "read the paper," "the stone wall," "in the subway," "down the street," and so on. These nouns are clearly singular and countable. But in sentences 1.1 through 1.5, the nouns for which Oleg has failed to supply an article—*life, idea, sea, expression*—are not concrete, but rather less tangible, less easily identifiable as singular and countable nouns.[3] Similarly, this error appears in the title of the composition: "First Impression Is Sometimes Deceptive." *Impression*, a sensation, impalpable, appears without an article—although, confusingly enough for the student, *either* the indefinite or definite article would be correct in this case. The foregoing examples suggest that Oleg might have learned (after a fashion) that the article is usually dropped with an abstract noun, and then generalized that this rule applies to nouns such as those cited above.

In example 1.2—"such beautiful life"—there seems to be a further complication, made more apparent if we compare the sentence with another farther along in the essay:

[3]There is one sentence in Oleg's essay that qualifies as an exception to his misunderstanding of the "abstract noun" rule: "I walked in the beauty, majesty and wealth of Fifth Avenue."
The exception suggests that Oleg is at least dimly aware of the rule for using the definite article with an abstract noun that is followed by a qualifying phrase. Compare these sentences:
_____ Love is an abstraction.
The love that I have for carbohydrates is overwhelming.
In similar cases of sentences with qualifying phrases, however, Oleg is just as likely to omit the definite article.

    1.6   But there is truth in somebody's words, who said that one
           moment can chang our life and *such moment* changed my
           opinion about life in America.

On first examination, this omission of the article seems odd. Unlike the nouns in the preceding examples, "moment" is more clearly a countable noun, and the writer shows his awareness of this fact by singling out "one moment" in the same sentence. (Remember that Russian speakers of English may equate the indefinite article with "one.") But what we may be seeing in example 1.6 is an amalgam of transference from the Russian speaker's native tongue (∅ article) and a developmental error in the use of an idiom. The clue here seems to be in the student's misunderstanding of the idiomatic use of *such* versus *such a(n)*. Further clues are found in examples from this essay and one written later on in the semester:

    1.7   It was America *as such,* how I imagined it in Russia by
           viewes, which I saw in American movies and by oure
           relatives' letters, who lived in America.
    1.8   He didn't rush to check the number, because he was sure
           that *such unlucky person* like him can never win. . . .

Native English speakers, of course, distinguish among *such, as such, such as,* and *such a(n)*. Depending on the meaning intended, an article may or may not occur between *such* and the noun it modifies. Oleg does not make these idiomatic distinctions: he seems to have learned the definition haphazardly, and generalized that *such* does not take an article. This hypothesis appears more plausible in light of another example from Oleg's revision of his first essay. In his rewrite, most of the article mistakes have been corrected (although unfortunately other errors abound). Yet Oleg writes in his addendum to the final paragraph:

    1.9   All the way home I was thinking about the way which
           brought that beggar on the street to *such unpleasant life.*

The learner is grappling with a noun (*life*) that is abstract ("life is often unpleasant") as often as it is countable ("many lives were taken"), a problem compounded by his misunderstanding of the phrase *such a(n)*.

    In the remaining case of article omission (1.10) in this first essay, we can discern the same sort of developmental error. For additional examples of this error, we'll turn to two related sentences from Oleg's subsequent work:

    1.10 "How is it possible that one, and sometimes *few of such*
           buildings could belong to one man?"
    1.11 Winding his scarf *few times* around the neck, Sam walked
           on.
    1.12 The prize was over *million dollars.*

The error in 1.10 and 1.11 appears frequently in the speech and writing of most ESL learners. No doubt the problem is rooted in the subtle distinction native speakers make between *few* and *a few*, a difference most native speakers would be hard pressed to articulate. The *American Heritage Dictionary*, for example, begs the issue—it offers a definition of *few* as "amounting to or consisting of a small number," followed by an ambiguous elaboration using the example of *a few*: "an indefinitely small number of persons or things; not many: *Bring me a few of your books.*" To this entry is added the second definition of *the few*, as in "the chosen few; the select." The usage note appended to this definition considers only the question of when to use *fewer* versus *less*.

Yet of course there *is* a difference between *a few*, which corresponds to "a small number, several," and the more negative connotation of *few*, meaning "not many." In other words, there is a significant semantic distinction here:

> *A few friends* will help me celebrate my birthday tonight.
> *Few friends* will help me celebrate my birthday tonight.

So in example 1.10, Oleg has written the opposite of what he intends. He has written that the man in question can possess *few* buildings, meaning "not many," whereas he wants to emphasize that "even as many as" *a few* buildings can belong to one man.

Why is this error so prevalent among ESL students, even though "a few" is used by native speakers more frequently than "few"? One probable reason is that nonnative speakers have trouble hearing many function words: according to the stress patterns of spoken English, the vowels of articles, prepositions, and so on are greatly reduced, and may be missed by the nonnative listener. In addition, and more curiously for ESL learners, "a few," though singular in form, is always used with a plural verb. Hence the ESL speaker's tendency to eradicate the indefinite article. (It would seem from the transcript of the 1984 interview that in speech, at least, Oleg had still not picked up the distinction between "few" and "a few.")

A related error appears in example 1.12. Again the student is persuaded that a collective noun (*few, million*), when it functions as an adjective and is followed by a plural count noun (*buildings, dollars*), ought not be preceded by an indefinite article. Further, he may be tempted to generalize that since one does not say "a seventy dollars," one cannot say "a million (or a hundred or a thousand) dollars."

Although these errors of omission occur far less frequently in the student's later essays, they remain the most persistent type of article error in his speech. Of the eight errors in article usage recorded in the May 1981 tutoring session transcript appended to this chapter, seven are errors of omission (examples 1.13 through 1.18 and 1.20):

1.13   On *midterm* I got 77.
1.14   See, it's *very very boring course.*

1.15   . . . all course what we been doing just . . . *one by one read
one story*, just like that, you know . . .
1.16   Mostly, must, must, eh . . . *Method* that I like is underline.
1.17   You have to read it with *group words, group of words.*
1.18   I cannot write when, *good feeling* (?)
1.19   *The sickness* [has its own virtues].
1.20   Why, because, just . . . *profession of future.*

The persistence of the error in conversation is hardly surprising: under the strain of producing spontaneous utterances, the student often reverts to a kind of "learner pidgin" of simplified grammar and syntax. This tactic may be seen as part of what has been called the learner's "communication strategy": like many nonnative speakers, Oleg pays more attention to the content of his utterances than to formal proprieties that might take time to bring forth, because he doesn't want his listener to become impatient. He may ignore the question of articles altogether, particularly when groping for a word (1.16) or feeling (1.18). (In the latter example, the learner's verbal shorthand is particularly difficult to decipher; he seems to be going for "when I am feeling good.") Alternatively, he swallows the syllable he produces before a noun (1.20), or perhaps (in the case of 1.15) translates the indefinite article before "story" into its closest Russian equivalent, "one," which he repeats with an English idiom he has picked up: hence, "one by one read one story. . . . "

Example 1.14 appears to be an instance of a speaker with limited conversational resources relying heavily on prefabricated expressions. At the opening of the interview, Oleg leans on catch phrases: "it helps if you practice," "you can't speed without practice," "every day have to practice," "it comes with practice." A similar device is to use "very very," as in "Is very very hard." And elsewhere, of course, "very" appears between the copula and the adjective: "my teacher is very lazy." Sentence 1.14 may show the student following the pattern of copula + adverb + adjective, even with the addition of the singular count noun ("course").

Finally, in sentence 1.17, the student repairs his own assertion by adding the preposition for "group *of* words," but still omits the article. This phrase may occur for the same reason as the errors in examples 1.10 through 1.12; that is, the collective noun "group," used with a plural object of the preposition ("words"), is perceived as a plural noun—which demands no article.

Supplying an Article Where None Is Required

In contrast to the previous examples, in utterance 1.19 ("*The sickness* [has its own virtues]") the student inserts an article where none is needed. This less typical speech error must be viewed in the context of the discourse:

OLEG: I read an article, that sickness have, has its own virtues.
TEACHER: That what?
OLEG: Virtues.
TEACHER: That what does?
OLEG: The sickness.

We might call this kind of performance mistake "teacher-induced." Although the student's initial response indicates that he knows the appropriate article rule in this case, an error arises when the interviewer requests clarification of the student's unintelligible utterance. The learner appears to have misinterpreted the question as a request for repair—a logical assumption on his part, since this method is frequently used by teachers to correct grammar errors. In his previous assertion, the student recognizes "sickness" as an abstract noun which (in this case) takes no article; he even goes so far as to correct the plural verb to its singular form. When questioned, however, he seems to think the interviewer is correcting him, and so mistakenly supplies the article.

In only one instance in his first essay does Oleg incorrectly supply an article where none is required:

2.1   I'd never gone out just for viewing *the life* in New York.

As in the speech error noted above, here the learner uses a definite article with an abstract noun, "life." He has not fully grasped the fact that, depending on its contextual classification, this noun may be particular or general, and may require the indefinite article, the definite article, or no article.

In the essays Oleg wrote later on, however, the balance is tipped to this type of error, as the following examples show:

2.2   Usually *an alcohol* makes people active, but it didn't work on Sam.
    2.3   It was pretty late when the persent of ~~the~~ *an alcohol* in Sam's body reached enogh high point[4] and Sam decided to go home.
    2.4   The moral of the story is: never loose *a hopness* in your life.
    2.5   This article is about *a famous people* such as. . . .
    2.6   Until the time when everybody will be aware of the fact that people must love each other we cannot have *the success* in averting war on our planet.

In these examples, the writer supplies indefinite articles for abstract and mass nouns. As we have seen, in his earlier work Oleg uses "people" correctly, both with the article ("the people around me" = plural-referential) and without ("I couldn't understand how people had built" = plural-mass). Yet later on, he makes the unlikely mistake (in this context, in which he

---

[4]Here Oleg seems to have generalized from one usage of "enough" that the article is omitted from the idiomatic usage "*a* high enough point."

means "persons" rather than "a nation") of using the indefinite article with "people" (2.5). A similarly strange usage is "an alcohol" in examples 2.2 and 2.3—all the more unexpected since, on two occasions in the same essay, he correctly uses a synonym, "whiskey," without the article:

> Every day returning from work he stopped to relax, get *some whis-key*, and forget about everything unpleasant in his life.
> He was smoking and drinking *whiskey* really slow.

But as 2.3 shows, Oleg is hyperaware of the language's demands for articles, and has even considered a possibly correct alternative—"the"—only to cross it out. At this point, then, the learner is testing the rules he has learned imperfectly; it would seem that as a result of this experimentation Oleg makes errors he wouldn't have made earlier.

In sentence 2.4, again, the writer attaches the definite article to an abstract noun, *hope* (which has been transmogrified into the neologism "hopness"—an unhappy application of a noun-producing suffix [-*ness*] Oleg has learned). In another sentence, Oleg uses the article with his synonym for *hope:*

> He didn't rush to check the [lottery] number, because he was sure that such unlucky person like him can never win, but every time *a paltry hopness* pushed him to play.

Here Oleg means *one* out of many hopes, and a paltry one at that. In this context the indefinite article seems reasonable enough; why not then, the writer might have asked, in the moral of the fable (2.4)?

Substitution of One Article for Another

In the body of writing examined here, we find only two instances of the student's confusing the indefinite and definite articles. The first comes from Oleg's modern fable:

> 3.1   Tomorrow he'll must pay *a rent* for the apartment.

The use of the definite article with "rent" is almost idiomatic in English. Oleg seems to have made the logical though incorrect assumption that rent is a countable noun: since rent is paid monthly, 12 "rents" a year, he might have deduced that the indefinite article is used.

The second example comes from a later essay:

> 3.2   Usually *an Army* of any country consists mostly people from
> *a middle class.*

There are two article errors here. First, the writer evidently doesn't realize that the "of" phrase after *army* particularizes the noun and therefore requires the definite article. In the latter half of the sentence, might Oleg have been thinking (as a result of interference from his native culture?) of "middle class" not as a specific identifying phrase formed with a so-called ranking adjective, but of "middle," "upper," and "lower" as less formulaic adjectives applied to social strata?

Errors in Subsequent Work

Having examined at length this writer's use of articles in the papers he produced during his first semester in English 105, we'll conclude with a brief look at an essay Oleg produced two semesters later for his English 110 (Introduction to College Composition) class. Oleg brought this and several other papers to our meeting in 1984. I reprint the essay here, despite its many errors of conception (the result of his attempting a too ambitious textual explication—the assignment seems unsuitable for the class level) because it is the most thoughtful and energetic work he produced in either English 110 *or* 120 (Writing and Literature), and because it shows the author facing grammar choices that dovetail with those he made in his first essay. In keeping with the limited project of this chapter, we will focus on these points of grammar, rather than on the author's interpretive difficulties, for the remainder of this discussion. (The footnote numbers in the essay refer to A. L. Rowse's edition of *Shakespeare's Sonnets*.)

> The Sonnets of Shakespeare offer us the greatest puzzle in the history of English literature. But if we speculate over the sources of the Sonnets we can conclude that they were not written as a pazzle for a reader. "They were written straightforwardly, directly, by one person for another, with an immediate and sincere impulse. They were autobiography before they became literature."[1]
>
> Out of 154 of Shakespeare's Sonnets I have shosen Sonnet number 118. I don't know exactly why I was attracted by this sonnet in particular; I think that there is a reflection of the idea of the sonnet in my own life. Like in any other sonnet Shakespeare doesn't tell what exactly he means by it; he lets our imaginations work. In my opinion, this is the nicest attribute of the poetry when a real word is presented in romantic way. Every poet has its own stile, own peculiar way of looking at the world. I am amazed by the ability of Shakespeare to reflect his own felling in such a romantic and deeply lirical way.
>
> In the Sonnet 118 Shakespeare tries to convince a reader that the people have to be very careful when they chose their pleasures. I think that the author tries to make a distinction between pleasures and pain. "Distinction? Does it have to be said in

prose, moreover in poetry? It is ridiculous trying to prove some
thing that have come to us together with life." That's what, probably, everybody thinks before they read the Sonnet. Of course, at
the first glance it seems that there cannot be two opinions about
the distinction between such two fellings as pleasant and unpleasant. But after reading the Sonnet we really get confused, "What a
joy really is? What causes unpleasant fellings?" Shakespeare says:

> Like as to make our appetites more keen
> With eager compounds we our palate urge;
> As to prevent our maladies unseen
> We sicken to shun sickness when we purge . . .

Through the power of his pen Shakespeare tells us in these four
lines that sometimes we sharpen our palates with tart contrasts in
order to increase our appetites (even though we use bitter spises).
Sometimes "to forestall illness we make ourselves ill with medicine in purging."[2] (Again we have to go through the challenge in
order to get pleasure—be healthy, in this case.)

In the rest of the Sonnet Shakespeare tells us about his own
life (though not specifically). From real history we know that
Shakespeare wasn't happy in his married life[3] and in this Sonnet
he shows that he doesn't much relish his choice:

> To bitter sauces did I frame my feeding.
> And sick of welfare found a kind of meetness
> To be deseased, ere that there was tru nedding.

Saying this Shakespeare means that for the pleasant moments that
he had when he just met his love (as he thought then) he must
pay the prise now being unhappy.

The very last two lines of this Sonnet is really the moral of
the Sonnet. Shakespeare says:

> But thence I learn, and find the lesson true,
> Drugs poison him that so fell seek of you.

I think that these two lines are the hardest to comprehend. In my
opinion in these lines Shakespeare tries to say that on his bitter
experience he had learned that if a subject of some joy doesn't
bring pleasure any more, we begin to regret that this subject ever
gave us a pleasure (and was it a pleasure?). The main point of this
Sonnet is that we don't have to defy our first sweet fellings, because these first fellings are blind.

I would like to conclude my composition with the words
that I've heard from one very old and clever man, "People are like
apples in the store. When we buy fruits, other than apples, we
can see when a fruit is rotten and we just put it away and never
touch it; but when we buy apples sometimes we don't see the rotten part that is inside of an apple. Only when we get home and
cut a nice-looking apple we can see that it is rotten."

Whatever the shortcomings of the writer's powers of literary interpretation at this point, and they are indeed considerable, his sentence errors have been reduced in the intervening semesters—although he is still performing way below par for 110. There is discernible improvement in his understanding of passives, as in the sentences with the clauses "I was attracted by . . . " and "I am amazed by. . . . " Of greater importance is his more assured handling of verb tenses, particularly sequences of verbs.

At the same time, many errors persist, some of them having apparently become "fossilized." Fossilized structures are those that tend to remain as potential performance errors, even when the student has learned—or at least has been taught—the correct form. Phonemic slips such as *pazzle* for *puzzle*, *seek* for *sick, felling* for *feeling,* are evidence of the compelling authority of the author's inner voice, which overrides what he knows to be the proper spellings. In the first instance, Oleg has spelled the word correctly elsewhere; in the second, he is copying "directly" from the sonnet itself; as to the third, he demonstrates in the interview conducted in 1984 that he knows how to spell *feeling*. In addition, the writer shows that he still has not mastered the rules for reversing word order when formulating questions in English, although he is doubtless aware of them by this point in his college career. (Oleg notes in the second interview that Russian questions are indicated through a change in intonation rather than word order.)

There are, of course, far fewer article errors in this essay than in Oleg's early narrative, although these errors still crop up occasionally, and predictably so. What is interesting, however, and surely maddening for this ESL student, is that several of the article errors in this essay involve different and even contradictory principles from those governing the examples culled from his earlier work. Why ought the author have said in line 4, "a puzzle for *the* reader," and similarly, farther down, "Shakespeare tries to convince *the* reader"? Why say "at first glance" rather than "at the first glance," especially since, as noted in the rules listed at the beginning of this discussion, *the* is used with a "ranking" adjective or ordinal? These questions should once again convey the breadth of the regulations concerning English article usage, should suggest how many rules native speakers have unconsciously absorbed and how great a distance the nonnative speaker must traverse to gain mastery of even this narrowly circumscribed province of English grammar.

As I noted at the outset, this kind of inquiry, though perhaps an appropriate starting point for decoding ESL, will not take the writing instructor very far. In the chapters to come, questions of grammar are subordinated to our consideration of whole essays and larger issues of composition.

APPENDIX 1 FOR CHAPTER 3

Transcript of May 1981 Conference

TEACHER: You're taking Reading now, as well? How's that going?

OLEG: I don't know yet. On midterm I got 77.

T: Well, that's good.

O: See, it's very very boring course.

T: Why?

O: Because . . . maybe I shouldn't say this . . .

T: No, it doesn't matter, go ahead.

O: No, because my teacher is very lazy, you know; all course what we been doing just . . . one by one read one story, just like that, you know . . .

T: Yes—Do you have homework?

O: What?

T: Do you have any homework?

O: Sometimes asks, eh, answer silly questions. Now is more interesting because we have speed reading. . . .

T: You like that . . .

O: Uh-hunh.

T: So, so you were really good at today's exercise, then, with speed reading.

O: Well, it helps if you practice, you know.

T: Well, what did he tell you that helps? What's the secret of speed reading?

O: Well, just, you can't speed without practice. Every day have to practice.

T: Would you like one of these? (offers candy)

O: I don't want.

T: So, what do you do for practice?

O: Nothing.

T: Nothing? (both laugh) You learned the secret but you don't listen to it . . .

O: Right . . .

T: So, you're supposed to practice skimming with your hand? (gestures)

O: Mostly, must, must, eh . . . Method that I like is underline. Is very very hard; it comes with practice, you know. You have to read it with group words, group of words . . .

T: Yes.

O: You can read a page, about four seconds.

T: But you don't practice.

O: I don't. Like I tell you, I'm lazy. No, I tell you, I'm lazy; thing is, I have no time to make my homework.

T: Where do you work?

O: In a nursing home.

T: That's right, you told me, you cook . . .

O: Not really cook . . .

T: (laughs) But prepare some food . . .

(Interruption)

T: So what was your schooling like in Russia?

O: Just high school.

T: Then you came here, how old are you now?

O: One year, ten months, is all.

T: OK, and you're how old?

O: Eh, nineteen.

T: So you started Queens? . . .

O: Last fall, last semester.

T: You did; and you were at the ELI [English Language Institute] . . .

O: CESL.

T: CESL. And you took how many courses there?

O: One.

T: Just the one. All right, and then you took the Assessment Test, and they placed you in 01. You got a 6 . . .

O: Um hmn.

T: Well, you're making quite an improvement, I'd say. So let's take a look at one of your papers.

O: In my native language, you know, I couldn't write . . .

T: Why not?

O: . . . good. I don't know, it depends from my mood, you know.

T: Yes.

O: I cannot write when, good feeling.

T: You can't? Only when you're depressed?

O: You see, I didn't give you one more paper, about the discussion about the news article (looks for it in notebook).

T: Yes.

O: I read an article, that sickness have, has its own virtues.

T: That what?

O: Virtues.

T: That what does?

O: The sickness.

T: Sickness has its own virtues. Ah, who wrote that?

O: I just got . . . see, before I read this article I couldn't understand; see, when I feel good I cannot write something good. When I feel bad, I do better.

T: Yeah, well then we've got to keep you unhappy.

O: So sometimes I make it, um, artificial.

T: Artificial? What do you mean, you make up something? . . .

O: I just try to remember, to remain to myself all, all, everything what happened, you know, everything wrong.

T: Yes . . . That's a good technique (student laughs); I'm going to try that.

O: It doesn't work on everybody.

T: No? (while student looks for paper): What do you think you'll major in eventually?

O: Computer science.

T: Why?

O: Why, because, just . . . profession of future.

T: Do you think that's something you'd like to do? Or is it just that it's financially a good idea?

O: Not financially; but I cannot think something better.

T: In any case, you want to stay here. Would you want to return to the U.S.S.R. if you could?

O: No.

T: Why not?

O: Why not?

T: Yeah.

O: I don't know, I just, I just don't feel like. Why did I feel better emotionally, over there?

T: Yes, yes.

O: I was educated over there and all my childhood was over there. And, it's not because I left, I came over here, you know, and every time you growing up, you feel like I miss something . . .

T: Yes.

O: Your childhood, and friends, everything, so it . . . I feel . . . emotionally not so good because something going away from me.

T: Yes. Is your family over here?

O: Yes.

T: Your whole family? Do you have brothers and sisters?

O: One brother.

T: Well, let's go over this paper . . .

APPENDIX 2 FOR CHAPTER 3

Transcript of December 1984 Conference (Discussion of Student's First 105 Paper)

O: I don't know if you know it, but that [story] wasn't true; I just made it up.

T: No? (both laugh) but it was very good—I believed you. Now the truth can come out. But it was very imaginative. OK, "Everything here admired me." What were you trying to say?

O: I was admired by everything around me.

T: What you would say in English is, "I admired everything around me." If you're admired by everybody, it means everybody around you thought you were great. What you mean is that you thought the objects and the skyscrapers and so forth were great; so you would say "I admired everything around me." "It amazed me"—it surprised you.

O: Well, I tried to find a better word for "surprise."

T: I see, amazed me. "It was America as such how I imagined it in Russia. . . ."

O: The way I imagined it. Is it all right?

T: You did beautifully. You had only been here about four or five months when you wrote this. " . . . by views which I saw in American movies and by our relatives' letters who lived in America." Can you think of another way you would have said that?

O: It was the country that I saw in the movies and I read about in letters of my relatives. . . .

T: " . . . who lived" . . . then the "who" becomes clear because it clearly refers to the relatives. That's very good. "But there is truth in somebody's words who said" . . . that's tough, that's hard.

O: You know, like sometimes you quote.

T: Yes, that's fine, that's good. . . . The "who" sort of dangles here and again like this in this sentence—it had to be a little clearer.

O: (unintelligible)

T: All right, that's a possibility, something like that. "But I really wasn't interested what they were thinking." In English that's followed by *in*—interested in: "Are you interested in computers?" It's a two-word verb. OK, "On my left side were tenants' buildings, not much of what you can see in other places."

O: Which you probably won't see in other places.

T: Good. "There were stores of some of the richest in the world" . . .

O: There were the richest stores in the world.

T: Quite right. "Only one thing couldn't appropriate in my mind." What were you trying to say there?

O: It wasn't clear for me; I just couldn't comprehend it. But in Russian you can say that.

T: What can you say?

O: It couldn't fit in my mind.

T: You could sort of say it in English. In other words, you don't have to say in Russian, "I couldn't make it fit; it didn't seem appropriate." In Russian, you can say, "One thing couldn't fit in my mind," or "one thing couldn't appropriate in my mind"?

O: I didn't find the right translation of the word.

T: All right. "How is it possible that one or sometimes few of such buildings"—are you aware of the difference between "few" and "a few"?

O: No.

T: (Explains difference.) "The more I walked, the more I surprised."

O: In Russian you can say it.

T: I'm told that in Russian, you have fewer passive constructions. How would you say this sentence in English?

O: The more I walked, the more I was surprised.

T: Yes; and "I almost run about something"?

O: Run into.

T: It shouldn't be run, though. Run is the past participle.

O: Bumped into.

T: Well, bumped into or ran into—the past tense. "But then I saw that it can move." What verb should this be?

O: It was moving.

T: All right, but what would the past tense of *can* be?

O: Could move. Because in Russian, you can say that in present tense.

T: Because Russian doesn't have the same fixed sequence of tenses— past, past perfect, and so on?

O: Yes, in this sense, Russian is easier.

T: "But I was afraid the fact that it was human."

O: Of.

T: "His hair remained me strings." What do you mean here?

O: Remind me.

T: You need the past tense here—"reminded me"—and what would come next in English?

O: (Silence)

T: "Of—reminded me of."

O: Reminded me of?

T: Yes.

O: It's just an expression.

T: Exactly.

O: See, once you write something, you see that it's incorrect, but sometimes it's hard to change once original thought is in your mind. It's hard to retrain your mind; you know it doesn't sound right, but it's hard to (unintelligible). I would write it over again. You know, I wouldn't do the same mistakes, but looking at the old writing it is hard to correct it.

T: Well, it is difficult, but you're doing pretty well, I think. All right, can we do a few more sentences? "If I could only compare expression on his face and expression of the stone wall, probably the last could tell me more."

O: This sounds for me OK.

T: The only thing you're missing is the article. In other words, "expression" is a count noun—you can say, "two expressions, three expressions"; did you know that—or did you think . . .

O: Articles—even now, sometimes it's a problem.

T: Well, that's to be expected. "There is much to tell about his clothes, if I only can call it so."

O: By "it" I mean clothes.

T: Well, clothes is plural.

O: Is it?

T: Yeah. So you would say, instead of "it," "them." *Clothing* is singular but *clothes* is plural.

O: It's curious, because in English you say "it" for non-alive objects but if it comes in plural it's same as for live objects—"them." In Russian, you would say it in singular—in Russian there is no *clothes* in plural.

T: What about *hair*? "Your hair is long"; in English we say it in singular.

O: Plural—in Russian it's always plural.

T: Yes, that's the way it is in Romance languages as well. "All holes in his pants was more than material." How would you say that?

O: I meant the area of holes on his pants was more than material.

T: Good. Now, "holes was more than"—there's another singular there even though "holes" is plural.

O: The holes were more than the material.

T: Yes, if you have "holes" you have to say "were." If you have "area," "was" is correct. Now, "something what [reminded] me jacket."

O: "What"—I think it should be "something *that*."

T: Yes!

O: *That* and *what* is the same in Russian; we have only one word for these two words. When you're showing something, then there is a difference: "that" (points).

T: But apart from what we call the demonstrative, where you are pointing to something . . .

O: Then *that* and *what* is the same.

T: "I passed through all the places which I saw . . . "

O: Seen.

T: Which I seen?

O: Had seen.

T: Yes, again, it's the past perfect. Now in Russian . . .

O: No, you could just use the past tense.

T: Now, "All the way home I have been thought."

O: Was thinking.

T: OK. . . . "What country is this that makes slaves of money from the people, for who money is higher than human fellings." Would you try to rephrase that?

O: Which turns people to slaves of money . . .

T: "For who money is higher than human felling"

O: Whom.

T: Good. "Than human fellings."

O: Than human feelings.

T: So how would you spell that?

O: Double E.

T: In questions, as I understand it, in Russian, you don't change the word order.

O: Yeah, you just change the intonation.

T: Is it a rising intonation? Ask me in Russian if I'm a teacher. (Student utters question in Russian.) So it's a high, rising intonation. That's good, you've corrected most of your errors. Some things, too, take years to learn, like two-word verbs, idioms, articles, and so on. . . . Is your family here in America?

O: My whole family is here.

T: And what, exactly, made you leave Russia?

O: Well, you know, a lot of people—you see, it was not so easy for me to realize at first. I was usually thinking it was, you know, because there was so much freedom. I tell the truth, that while you stay in Russia, you don't feel this lack of freedom over there because once you don't know what's good, you can't distinguish between good things and bad things. They don't expose you to the Western culture very much unless you, you know, find ways to do it. So once you don't know better life—they train you so that you don't really think much [garbled]. But I think the main reason was the lack of freedom for Jews—*that* I felt very much, because you could actually distinguish—inside the country there are Jews and non-Jews.

T: So when you were asked your nationality, in Russia, did you say Russian or Jewish?

O: Jewish. You had your passport which everybody could see that you are.

T: And your parents too felt the persecution, in terms of their jobs?

O: Not so much in jobs because my parents didn't take high positions. My father was a photographer; my mother was a nurse. But what happens is they don't usually let Jews take high positions, like being a manager, being in charge. . . . What they do is, they put in charge a Russian person and then make a Jew his advisor. It's like people, you know, Russians, they don't really like Jews. Russians don't know much about religion, you know, about Christianity, not because of Jews as a religion group, but because they are Jews.

T: I see.

O: In Russian literature a lot of Russian writers, like Gogol and Pushkin, were anti-Semites. And in their writings you can see few sentences—Gogol, in *Dead Souls,* you know, says "filthy as a Jew," things like that. . . .

4

A Greek Writer's Idiolect
What Is Not an ESL Error?

In the wake of the preceding discussion of second-language errors and acquisition, this chapter takes the form of a caveat. It is important to keep in mind that not all lapses in an ESL student's writing are ESL-related. Quite the contrary. As in the case of a native student's writing, linguistic difficulties are just as likely to stem from a nonnative writer's uncertainty about what she wants to say, and why and to whom she wants to say it. So forewarned, we will survey in this chapter a Greek student's performance on a variety of assignments in English 105, the basic writing course at Queens for students who have failed the Assessment Test on entering CUNY.

Like many of our foreign-born students, Koula Markantonatous demonstrated a considerable degree of cultural sophistication and a simultaneous lack of texture and development in her early work in English. As the semester progressed, she became more adept at expanding her ideas on paper, although many structural and mechanical problems persisted. The point of the present discussion is to demonstrate how some of these impediments were called forth by this particular writer's approach to a specific assignment more than by the demands of composing in a second language.

In contrast to the concerns of the preceding chapter, then, this discussion focuses on questions of underlying organization and purpose in several whole pieces of writing—even though a lack of idiomatic fluency and a number of glaring grammatical errors might be likely to sidetrack the reader. At the same time, here and in the following chapter, I want to pay attention to the process of the writer's development over the semester, since a clearer picture of the student's strengths and limitations emerges from the consideration of a sequence of writing samples in relation to one another. An overview of performance in a variety of writing activities encourages our analysis of texts as communicative events, behavioral acts. Many of the author's problems emerge as powerful indicators of the kinds of difficulties writers face in any language, and of the strategies this particular writer has devised for meeting or avoiding them.

Somewhere in the background of this discussion we shall also be looking at *teaching* as a behavioral act. Like many of my colleagues, I have come to hold dear certain principles of composition pedagogy. Chief among these are an emphasis on prolific writing; a view of thinking and composing as recursive processes of drafting and revising; the subordination of error correction to creative and communicative concerns; the encouragement of the writer's distinctive voice (as well as experimentation with other voices); the premium placed on concretion and narrative, especially narratives and exempla derived from the author's experience; the fostering of collaborative learning and peer response to student texts. Of course most of us have learned over the years that not all methods work for all students, still less for all assignments or class sessions. Even so, working with international students has pointed up for me the distinctly American bias of these shibboleths, especially with regard to the value our methodology has come to place on the personal and the particular. This does not mean I have renounced any of the above. But the experience has made me more chary of adopting one classroom approach to the exclusion of another, and perhaps less insistent in my advocacy of what has been called the "cult of self-expression." Accordingly, toward the end of this chapter I shall briefly speculate on how the foreign-born subject of the present study might have been studying me.

Let me begin by outlining the kinds of assignments and methods I might use in a typical introductory writing class. I include this very general summary to suggest how commonly used writing class techniques are adapted to the ESL composition classroom. This background is meant to pave the way not only for our discussion of Koula's work, but for the following chapter, which shows the very different responses of another ESL student to virtually the same syllabus.

To encourage the habit of writing immediately and often, I ask students in both my writing and literature classes to keep journals, in which they will be writing throughout the semester on a variety of topics—some suggested, most of their own choosing. Students may occasionally decide to expand some of their journal writings into longer papers, according to their particular interests and themes. They begin to see how writing for oneself as well as for others can be a heuristic for problem solving: that is, how the goals of personal writing dovetail with the demands of academic writing.

I assign at least seven or eight formal essays, plus substantive revisions of several of these papers, the earliest of which draw on narrative. Family stories and autobiographical anecdotes form the core of a couple of essays illustrating some general principle or moment of change in the writer's life. From my colleagues I have filched a number of structures for this assignment. Bonnie MacDougall Ray, who figures in the following chapter, asks students to describe a point in their lives that corresponds to what E. M. Forster in *Aspects of the Novel* calls "time of value" as opposed to daily time. The former, the element in which a fictional character lives, centers on a localized event that changes the character in some way. Marie Ponsot and Rosemary Deen suggest several very useful kernel sentences on the order of "Once I was ————; Now I am————," two-part coordinating structures for organizing autobiographical essays. Sandra Schor has made an excellent case for pairing autobiography-inspired assignments, having discovered that as students work on these adjacent essays, their texts become more expansive and insightful. I agree. I've found that after students write what I call the "regret" paper (tell the story of something you regret having done, and explain why you're sorry you did it), they're bothered by something left unsaid. They want to go on to analyze the reasons behind their actions. The young man who writes of a shoplifting incident wants to explain what prompted him to be "a wild and heedless boy." Pairing the "regret" paper with the "Once I was" essay allows him to do so.

From autobiography-inspired essays we may move to another form of narrative, the contemporary fable, which teaches analogically with an exemplum drawn from the imagination or events outside the author's life. We then proceed to several other approaches to problem solving in the essay form—perhaps pulling a thesis out of a quotation or a single word, debating the merits of mayoral candidates, analyzing a stereotype—and conclude the semester with a few in-class essays as practice for the CUNY Writing Assessment Test, which is used as an exit exam. By this point I hope students have learned that they may use any of the strategies practiced earlier in the semester to organize and develop their responses to the typical agree/disagree format of the Test.

Particularly in the ESL classroom, I want to emphasize the mutual dependence of discursive and grammatical choices. Each assignment is at least partly envisioned as generative of a particular linguistic skill. With description we might work on sentence combining through coordination and subordination; with narrative, the present perfect and past tenses; with fables, the conditional tenses, and so on. Let's take a pair of brief examples, in this case of the uses of parallelism in narrative. Before reading his essay about the night his friend got him drunk, a student writes this sentence from his paper on the board: "I didn't know if I should compromise my principles and keep my only friend, or keep my principles and lose my friend." The class can see how the moral choice at the heart of the paper is reinforced on the sentence level by the conditional verb and the parallel construction. A classmate, in a paper on a misconceived haircut, demonstrates how to use parallel structure for comic effect when she writes, "We know that joy is short and regret is long." The project of essay writing is thus presented as a collection of language activities, including grammatical considerations, all of which strengthen the writer's control over communicative structures. Most often, grammar errors are discussed in the context of the individual's essay during conferences with me or my team teacher. But we frequently work in class on manipulating grammatical forms as stylistic devices, all of us writing and rewriting these favorite or less successful sentences from our work on the board.

By the same token, I want students to see how the acts of reading and writing comment on and enrich each other. When I began teaching in the early 1970s, prevailing wisdom dictated the use of students' writing almost exclusively as the text for the course. Since then I've come to believe in the effectiveness of introducing a few reading selections during the semester— poems or short stories or essays by professional writers, with an emphasis on material from a variety of cultures—as prompts for writing tasks. To show a range of possible journal entries I've photocopied pages from Sei Shonagon's *Pillow Book*; for narrative I might use a poem such as Pound's "The River-Merchant's Wife"; for the regret essay Langston Hughes's two-page story, "Salvation," works well; to illustrate the possibilities of contemporary fable I've assigned Lawrence's "The Rocking-Horse Winner." These selections provide many ESL learners with their first glimpse of literature in English. Particularly since the fairly recent reintroduction of a core curriculum of humanities and sciences at our school, it seems a good idea to acquaint students, however summarily, with literary genres they will be reading and analyzing a few semesters hence. Students clearly enjoy discussing these selections as much as they do their own or their classmates' work, and come to recognize connections between acts of rereading and rewriting.

Most of the activities of the class shamelessly promote the less-than-radiant freshman composition trinity of Clarity, Wholeness, and Concrete Illustration of Thesis. Revision is emphasized as the means to achieve these goals, and is normally approached through class discussion or, occasionally, workshops in smaller groups. At the beginning of the semester, for example, a student might read aloud a story she has recounted in her journal, perhaps a tale told by a family member; her classmates then jot down why *they* think she told this particular story, or what significance they think it holds, and their constructions of the thesis are compared with the author's. The range of responses opens up possibilities for the writer when she sets out to write her introduction and conclusion, and points up places in the narrative that need emphasis or detail. Alternatively, auditors may be asked to write down questions they would like to ask the author, and this kind of close attention almost invariably results in the writer's more probing revision of a glib first draft.

Thus each writer in the class has opportunities to practice reading her own work, to hear the responses of a community of listeners, and to comment on the work of others, so that revision becomes an act of rethinking more than the mere correction of grammar based on the teacher's marginalia. The impetus, because it comes from the group, seems less arbitrary than a single reader's suggestions. The teacher here is less a purveyor of information than a participant, and often the class is further decentralized by the presence of an undergraduate team teacher, who shares the responsibility of shepherding various classroom activities and holding individual conferences.

From time to time we may approach revision by having students work on expanding at length an interlude, definition, or description from the first drafts of their papers. These exercises at best allow writers to excavate hidden moments of emphasis in their essays, and at least foster the kind of attention to local detail that American readers favor. I point out to my classes that although an essay rarely consists entirely of, for example, description, it is often an important element of the stories, explanations, and analyses they write. Commonly the problem with this sort of exercise is that it exists in a rhetorical vacuum: writers have to have a clear context and audience for describing people and places, lest viewpoint and organization falter. Using the descriptive passage as a way to sharpen the thesis of a larger essay provides the point of the drill.

As I say, much of what I've just outlined has become fairly standard procedure in many college writing classes in the United States. The remainder of the chapter will be devoted to my student Koula's responses to these methods and assignments.

My students are encouraged to write in their journals around four times a week for at least 15 minutes at a clip, and to continue this practice throughout the semester. The first of Koula's notebook entries was written in answer to the question, "How do you feel about keeping a journal?"

> Some people have the habit of keeping a journal. Sometimes these journals contain literary essays, small masterpieces.
> Van Gogh's journal is contained his whole life. It is his autobiography. Reading it we learn his work and his viewpoint about art.
> Leonardo's or Michelangelo's notes are so useful to us. They teach us. We see here their deeds and their thoughts.
> On the other hands we have journals girls keep before marriage. They contain girlish dreams.
> I have never kept so far a journal. Last night a friend told me that she keeps one since fifteen. I am thinking of starting keep one.

Despite the reluctant sentences and minimalist paragraphs, Koula displays here, and very pointedly, I think, the range of her reading. Equally noteworthy is the delaying of personal response, although this kind of reaction was called for by the assignment: the "I" is relegated to an afterthought. In Koula's estimation, journals are either the serious and instructive workbooks of artists or the repositories of girlish dreams. An art major, Koula seems to locate her purpose somewhere between the two poles: hence her wary final sentence about "thinking" of starting to keep a journal, even though this assignment was a requirement of the course. The student is sending her teacher a message.

Successive journal entries subtly reiterate the message in what amounts to the writer's own educational manifesto. In related research, Anita Wenden observes that adult ESL learners, when questioned in structured interviews, often reveal explicit beliefs about how to learn a second language, and, moreover, that these beliefs seem to influence what the speakers actually do to help themselves learn. I think Koula's journal yields a similar set of clues as to her notions about language learning. Here is Koula's response to the next journal assignment, in which the students were to describe a favorite class:

> As I recollect my life in college, it comes in my mind[1] a
> night class I had once. I will not be referred in specific details and
> how fruitful this class was to me; besides all those I really enjoyed
> this class. Tired people from a whole day's labor trying to concen-
> trate to the lecture and so willing to work. A unity was among the
> students and the teacher stayed so close to us with a continuous
> talking and force us to work. I consider that, in this class learned
> how to think.

Koula announces quite purposefully that she will not describe this wonderful class with specific details. Of course, specific details were exactly what had been requested in this bit of writing, in preparation for which we had spent the better part of several class periods practicing ways to secure an abstract concept with the ballast of concrete data. Note too that the aspect of teaching Koula singles out for admiration here and in the next entry—*lecturing*, the teacher's "continuous talking"—is at odds with the composition class tech- niques described earlier. This is a point to which I want to return at the end of the chapter.

In the following entry—the students wrote on a topic of their choice— Koula becomes somewhat more voluble on the subject of another course she was taking at the time, in ancient Greek. She measures the course against her studies in Spanish and English; what impresses her most about "this special language" is its distinguished heritage—its roots, development, and litera- ture:

> This semester I thought to have a course of ancient Greek
> language. In my previous semesters I have taken a course of
> Spanish and of course some courses of English. I have to mention
> that Greek is my native language. What impressed me by the first
> day was the difference of teaching of this language comparing to
> the others. The teacher is referred to the roots of the language,
> the development of it and very often about the spiritual men who
> spoke, thought and wrote in it. I have always been thinking that
> studying a language is a simple matter same in any of them. Now
> I can see the conseption and the inspiration of this special lan-

[1]The phrase "it comes in my mind," as well as the use of the pleonastic pronoun to anticipate the subject "a night class," seem to be translations from the Greek. As to Koula's use of "all those" where English requires either a plural noun after *those*, or the singular "all this," or a substitute noun: in Greek the plural demonstrative would be used, and need not be followed by a plural head noun (Efstathiadis and King 163).

guage. I am also surprised to see an american so enthusiastic
about it. I thought that, this was only for the Greeks.

This passage, in which Spanish and English run a poor second to Greek
in Koula's estimation, indirectly frames the question of the role psycholin-
guistic variables play in second-language study. Especially in recent years,
researchers in linguistics have engaged in rather spirited disagreement on the
issue of the relationship of learner attitudes and orientation to second-language attainment. Several of their studies focus on the inherent difficulties of
obtaining and assessing empirical data on elusive factors such as personality
and motivation. The debate will be analyzed at length in the following
chapter, where the comparatively rapid and dramatic improvement of a
Chinese ESL student—given the same assignments as Koula—will be considered in terms of the literature to date on affective variables in second-
language acquisition.

For now I simply want to underscore a point that seems obvious but in
fact has been the object of occasional dispute. The bulk of this research, for all
its contradictions, suggests that progress in second-language attainment is
influenced in some measure by aspects of the student's personality, commitment to the target language, attitude toward members of the cultural group
whose language is being studied, practical reasons for learning the language,
and so on. These attitudes in turn depend partly on the learner's feelings
about her native culture, and the extent to which she prefers her own
language and culture over the target language and culture. Much of the
research on motivation examines sentence-level tasks in the process of second-language learning itself, whereas the present inquiry concerns how
advanced ESL students acquire college-level skills like composition in their
second language. As a result, the case studies discussed here and in the next
chapter concentrate on a slightly different element in the affective equation,
namely the individual's responses to different kinds of communicative tasks
in longer pieces of written discourse.

What does Koula's writing, along with her class performance and our
conversations together, reveal about her approach to English? In her journal entries and subsequent papers Koula shows a powerful identification
with the Greek language and heritage and a concomitant distance from the
target language. In her conferences with me and my team teacher, Koula
habitually expressed doubts about her need to take several required courses
in English composition, since they were not necessary for her major in stu-
dio art, and since she intended eventually to return to Greece. Koula's
relationship with her teachers and fellow students was unfailingly cordial;
her resistance good-humored, never adversarial, but nonetheless constant.
Her indifference to the language, her reluctance to work on development
strategies and grammar in our conferences together or to revise her papers,
certainly contributed to some of the semantic and syntactic derailment in her
written performance. Perhaps too, Koula's reluctance hindered her speech

and writing in less obvious, cyclical ways: her handwriting was often il-
legible, and her accent extremely pronounced, with the result that her verbal
participation in class was limited because she was all but incomprehensible to
her fellow students.

Koula's pride and literacy in her native culture, demonstrated most
forcefully in the essays and conversation quoted farther on in this chapter,
suggest the likelihood that her writing was grounded in the precepts of that
culture. If we were reading only one of her essays in isolation, such as the
autobiographical essay I want to consider in detail in a moment, it might be
tempting to look for the source of Koula's problems in that essay in aspects of
rhetoric which are encouraged or discouraged in her native land. For example, many of our Greek and Cypriot students, who constitute a large portion
of the nonnative population at Queens College, maintain that the Greek
educational system encourages more abstract (and lengthy) development of
the thesis, and does not prize personal anecdote as illustration of a general
principle.

Needless to say, such rhetorical preferences are scarcely limited to
Greece. Over the years students from a variety of linguistic backgrounds
have remarked on the less personal or autobiographical nature of the essays
they were asked to write in high schools and colleges back home. For that
matter, I have heard other native English speakers not schooled in this
country, British and Australian colleagues, wonder aloud at the American
confessional mode and its legacy in many American composition syllabi,
which frequently take personal reflection for their Rosetta stone.

But in any case, as I've indicated, not all the writing problems of
ESL students can be traced to cultural variations in linguistic and rhetorical
systems. Far from it: a good many are common to basic writers; and some
have to do with the individual, the task, and the context. As we shall see
after looking at Koula's vague and confusing autobiographical narrative,
this same author later wrote several narratives—dealing with the experiences of others rather than with personal experiences—which show her
perfectly capable of writing specific, detailed, chronologically sophisticated
accounts. I believe that in retrospect we can see how the puzzling abstractions of Koula's autobiographical essay owe less to interference from her
native culture than to a combination of the writer's particular troubles with
her subject and her resistance to some of the cultural and pedagogical habits
of her adopted home.

I have earlier cited a study showing how through self-report an adult
learner may reveal certain beliefs about language learning, and how these
beliefs in turn may actually shape the individual's learning strategies. In a
similar vein, Jerome Bruner's 1987 study of informants telling their life
stories advances the argument that "eventually the culturally shaped cognitive and linguistic processes that guide the self-telling of life narratives
achieve the power to structure perceptual experience," so that ultimately "we
become the autobiographical narratives by which we 'tell about' our lives"
(15). That is, as Bruner observes, in our practice of the ancient and apparently

universal narrative form of the autobiographical account, the plot lines we create for ourselves become maps for laying down routes into memory and ultimately for organizing experience itself.[2]

What can the plot, structure, and fabula of Koula's autobiographical narrative, reprinted below, tell us about this learner? It is useful to view Koula's personal narrative, which though problematic has its fine moments, in light of what emerges as the author's idiosyncratic manipulation of the language of personal recollection. Many of the essay's flaws seem to derive from psychological avoidance strategies more than from second-language difficulties. I refer not to the linguistic phenomenon whereby second-language learners tend to avoid grammatical structures that pose potential problems (see Kleinmann), but to the more general meaning of avoidance, the individual's unconscious desire to evade thoughts or memories she finds unpleasant or anxiety-provoking. The most significant errors in the following essay—imprecision, repetition, disorganization, circumlocution, ellipsis—typically work to befog meaning, and to distance the author from her material. Here is Koula's autobiographical essay, in which students were asked to discuss a "turning point": recall an event that changed you in some way and discuss how and why it changed you.

Anna

Who said that childhood friends last forever? That is not true most of the times and the worst of all it is very painful. For one moment to another any relationship can end or one's life can entirely change.

We were the childhood friends, the good companions in games. Since her childhood, she has been a very selfish person, considering herself above the others. It was contemptible for her to speak or even to greet the peasants. She could not understand my enthousiasm to work in the fields. She liked to exaggerate things about herself, in a such degree, that there were times I turned my head on the other side not to listen to her. If a stranger heard her talking about her expenses might think that her father was a tycoon. It seemed that it did not bother me then; It started much later as we were growing up, I, as a very free spirit, and she, as a very conservative one; but we had never conflicts while we exposed our ideas to each other.

We came closer to each other the last years we were in New York. As we were alone in a foreign country, we needed each other more than before, so when she left I felt very intensively

---

[2]For related observations on the reconstructive nature of autobiographical memory, see Craig R. Barclay's article on "Schematization of Autobiographical Memory" (in Rubin 82–99), and the essay by Markus (see bibliography). Markus tells us that "self-schemata are cognitive generalizations about the self, derived from past experience, that organize and guide the processing of self-referenced information contained in the individual's social experiences" (64). His argument, seconded by Barclay, is that these self-schemata come to control attention and memory in the present.

her absence. When she called me from the airport for the last good-bye I asked her to come back.

As children we were together only during vacation. It seemed that it did not affect us. Every time we were together again, we seemed as we never aparted before, for one single day.

We explored together the countryside. We liked to call ourselves New Robinsons. We felt excited when we discover a new area of the country, we had not known before. In late afternoons, we loved to sit on the big rock with the two holes on the top, under the old olive tree, watching the sun changing colors on the sky. When a chameleon appeared on the weeds we liked to observe it as it changed its colors according to the colors of the weeds and of the earth. We thought how people look like chameleons in their trying to please. As night fell around and turned the colors into gray, we were still sitting on the big rock, wondering and dreaming about the future. It was the last time, we planned to leave for New York. Perhaps it was our last summer in the country.

The summer noons we liked to wear big straw hats and very large glasses, and walk around the big yards of the house, or in the streets of the village. When at last we felt very exhausted by the hot sun of the noon, we fell asleep till afternoon.

Our great enjoyment was to steal fruits from strange tree-gardens. In our afternoon promenade in the fields, we climed on the trees and caught branches with fresh ripe pears and plums. We cut them with great pleasure and ate them very hurry, because we did not want a stranger's eye to see us, so the syrups dripped from our mouth and we always returned home with dirty dresses.

Even the night could not apart us. We liked to stay late in the night, under the starry sky, sitting on the steps of the house and look at the pure summer sky, the galaxy, and the great bear; or when the night turned to cool we stayed inside, trying to see the vast future in front of us, or how the next year of school will be.

But, why don't I need her anymore? Perhaps her fault was, at our last meeting some months ago, her trial to persuade me to follow life's ruthm. "People work for money, you must understand that," she told me while we were fighting. "I have not asked you to borrow me money" I answered. Perhaps she is not any more willing to accept me as I am; even after I explained her that I believe very strongly in Sartre's statement. "People die for an idea or for nothing."

Naturally, many of the grammatical, lexical, and syntactical missteps in this essay are attributable to the process of second-language learning. As examples of the kinds of errors common to all learners of English, we might cite the non-idiomatic phrases "most of the times" and "the worst of all [it is . . .]"; the misuse of "intensively" and "apart," as well as of the preposition "on," as in "the sun changing colors on the sky" and "When a chameleon appeared on the weeds." Similar kinds of errors include the writer's difficulties with parallelism and tense sequence, as in "how the next year of school *will* be" (English mandates the conditional tense here because although the girls were speculating about the future, the story is cast in the past tense), spelling ("enthousiasm," "ruthm"), and vocabulary (using "tree gardens" for *orchards*). Among the errors we can attribute to native-language transference are the translation of the expression "I turned my head on the other side"; the missing pronoun in paragraph 2 ("If a stranger heard her talking about her expenses might think . . . "), since in Greek, the repetition of the pronoun here would be a pleonasm;[3] and the confusion in the last paragraph between *borrow* and *lend,* because both words are expressed by the same word in Greek, as they are in Chinese and a number of other languages.

But most often the writer seems to be having difficulty with *connections*—first of all, with the connection between herself and Anna. And this confusion to some extent causes Koula to obfuscate the relationships between thesis and conclusion; between the exposition and the long, lyrical, narrative portion of her paper; between paragraph blocks; even between clauses.

In fact the most troubling aspects of Koula's essay cannot rightfully be termed errors at all. Koula makes her paper superficially cohesive through reference, substitution, conjunction, and subordination. But as we know, these devices don't ensure coherence. In this essay, actually, they often create confusion, for instance by allowing the author to avoid specifying the cause of her fight with Anna. Take the repeated use of "it" in paragraph 1 ("it is very painful"), paragraph 2 ("It seemed that it did not bother me then; It started . . . "), and paragraph 4 ("It seemed that it did not affect us"). Koula's use of anaphora without clear antecedent in each case obscures the subject of the discourse. Coupled with "seemed," this "it" becomes a distancing mechanism, like Koula's repeated use of "perhaps." Each device is a way for the author to remain noncommittal about the reasons for the fight with her friend.

The same might be said of Koula's use of conjunctions. In the compound sentences of paragraph 1, the causal links between clauses suggested by "and" and "or" are unclear. Further ambiguity, concerning temporality, stems from her use of the subordinator "while," as in "we never had conflicts while we exposed our ideas to each other," and "she told me while we were fighting."

These ambiguities culminate in the dialogue the author recreates at the end of the essay. Hitherto I have been talking about sentences and paragraphs, the components of written discourse. A similar disjuncture is evident in the writer's rendition of speech acts. Koula's characteristic evasions call into question all the elements that constitute a conversation. The

---

[3] A similar error appears in the final line of the journal entry quoted on page 98: "I consider that, in this class learned how to think."

messages are obscure. Relationships—between speaker and auditor, between various past and present events, between oral and written channels—
are blurred; connections must be supplied by the reader, yet we aren't given
sufficient information to do so. When and where does the conversation take
place? How does one utterance gibe with the next? We are given an answer,
"I have not asked you to borrow me money," but what exactly is the
question? What is the nature of Anna's assertion that "people work for
money, you must understand that": Is the topic of discourse the motivation
for work, the need for money, Koula's shortage of funds? Is this a warning or
a bit of advice? Is it the cause of the discord or merely a symptom? Once
again, the unclear conjunction—"she told me *while* we were fighting"—
makes it difficult to say.

Taken together, these various distancing devices allow Koula to side-
step description and analysis of the dissolution of her friendship with Anna.
Yet this is the event that the reader is initially given to believe will be the
heart of the essay. Contrast the truncated, muzzy conclusion with the hyper-
developed idylls that take up most of the essay: the paper is top-heavy, out
of whack. The time sequence is unsettling, especially when it comes to the
period Koula and Anna spent in New York. What is the relationship between
the events mentioned in paragraph 3 and in the last paragraph of the paper?
Still more disorienting: at the end of paragraph 5, Koula seems to be moving
toward the turning point in the friendship by discussing "the last time" Anna
and she were together as playmates. Instead, she pulls back from this obviously painful prospect and proceeds to retread much of the same ground in
the next three paragraphs, so that at the end of the penultimate paragraph
we find Koula and Anna where we had left them in paragraph 5, gazing at
the night sky and wondering about the future. The confusing chronology,
the digression, the unbalanced structure of the paper, the imprecise function
words, permit Koula to avoid confronting the nature and cause of the rift she
describes. The result is vagueness, an abstraction, as I have suggested, that
appears to be a consequence of Koula's idiosyncratic writing and speaking
strategies, particularly when faced with this particular communicative task,
more than of some culture-specific notion of rhetoric.

I want to turn later on to Koula's desultory stabs at revising this essay,
an activity she undertook only at my behest, a few weeks before the end of
the semester. But first I'd like to illuminate some of the features just remarked by showing them in the light of Koula's subsequent work, an arm-
chair luxury more often granted the commentator than the teacher.

Following the autobiographical narrative assignment, the students were
asked to compose a fable, a story illustrating an abstract moral. After writing
and discussing traditional fables and parables in class and reading "The
Rocking-Horse Winner," they wrote their own contemporary moral tales.
Koula fared much better on this assignment, probably for two reasons. The
less personal nature of the assignment granted her distance from the narrative, especially since she chose to quote the story of another speaker. And
she selected a topic dear to her heart: the Greeks' stubborn refusal to be

subjugated, as demonstrated by their heroic defense of a fortification on native soil during World War II. Koula begins by announcing her thesis, which she supports by recalling at length a story she heard told by a survivor of the siege, and concludes with her own substantial commentary. Let me emphasize that here, in contrast to her earlier performance, her orchestration of the narrative sequence is assured, the connection between the frame and the tale quite clear.

The Heroic Sortie of Fortification 23

It is a fact that the Greeks fight till death. As they know how to live and how to fight, they also know how to die.

Here, I will narrate a true story, as I heard it from a neighbor, one summer night under the shadow of the grapevine. This man is an old warrior of the Second World War, a defender of the last Greek frontiers, who survived that hell.

Of course, it goes some years back, but I believe it is always new, and it teaches a good lesson to all of us, how to prefer death than captivity.

The event I will be referred to is taken from the war in 1940, and the last moments of the fortification 23 in Roupel. How it is really like the glorious Cougi in 1821!

"Very early that morning the Germans started the fight with inflammatory machineries. Two of the soldiers burnt their faces. We continued to fight with a few machine guns which had remained. They repeatedly asked us to surrender; we very proudly answered 'No.' They used all their mechanic media to capture us, without success.

"But how could we imagine that they would also use the inhuman medium of the gases? Yes, they did use gases to win Greece, those who till that day had won so many great nations, without any serious resistance.

"The Germans, after they had enclosed all the fortification's wainscots and portholes of ventilation, they established machineries in the entrance, and they started to throw gases into the fortification. Vainly we tried to renew the air, with the machines we had inside. The commander was taken by horror hearing his soldiers to ask him for help. He was going mad, when he understood that it was impossible for him to give any help. He started to run like a mad man in the porticos, and ordered everybody to wear masks. He himself did not wear, and his breathing was caught. The soldiers started to fall down. In a while the floor was covered by dying bodies. The lights had gone out, and a dense darkness convered us. We breathed very heavily.

"The wireless sent the last S.O.S. The gas-jets filled the sky. We counted the minutes which had remained to us, till that awful death. However, we were still alive. The commander shouted with his remained strength, 'No, we are not going to die in this

way. It is better to die by a bullet, breathing free air. And as you
are still alive, creep to the exit. We are going to make a sortie. We
will not die like dogs.'

"He called for a last time the fortifications 17 and Instimbei,
which were still fighting desperately, and told them that we
would make a sortie. He ordered us to blow up the remained ma-
chinery guns and he ran to overtake the others, who were fighting to reach the exit. We fired our last bullets and handgrenades
and we rushed to the exit. The Germans ran to encircle us.

"However, the Greek soldiers did not want to be surren-
dered. They prefered to die than to throw down the rifles and lift
hands. They fought breast with breast with the iron-bound Germans. 'Hitler's blond children' could not believe what they were
seeing. How was it possible, a handful of warweary, sick, hungry
men did not want to submit to their indomitable power? Was it
ever possible to prefer death than captivity? The Greeks were
fighting with a few rifles. The Germans fought with their howit-
zers, their handgrenades, their mortars, and machine guns.
Though, they had encircled us, it was not easy to catch us, to ex-
terminate us."

After all, we have to say the truth. It was the first time
throughout the war, that a nation had resisted them. For first time
they saw that these warriors were still equivalent to their ancient
ancestors.

A strange admiration came to their souls. In conclusion, I
will refer what the German General Emberhard Kesler[4] wrote in
his personal diary, which was published after the war was ended.
"Those men were not simple defenders of a fortification. They
were supermen, who fought for their country's freedom. The battle which continued was hard and implacable. However, those
short soldiers fought with their souls. They fought to show how a
race resists, when it loves its freedom. And the Greeks are a free
race. We must accept it. They showed it to us on the inaccessible
mountains of Epirous with our Italian allies. They showed it to us
in Roupel. They showed it to us later in the cities and villages
with their resistance. However, we did not respect them. We
killed thousands of them and we sent many others in prisons and
in camps. However, the truth is only one. Races may die; the
Greeks never."

The theme marching through Koula's work, whether journal notation,
personal narrative, or fable, should be evident by now. Koula's subject is the

---

[4]I have never been able to locate this name or any of its variants, neither in biographical
dictionaries nor in histories of the Greek resistance. The closest name I could find in this context
was German field marshal Albert Kesselring, leader of attacks on the Mediterranean front, who
published his memoirs after the war. No such account appears in those memoirs. Had Koula
reconstructed the historical record, as well, to fit her "self-schemata"?

importance, to the writer and to the countrymen she so admires (though not to Anna, whom she disavows), of the individual's immovable resistance to domination or conformity. By Koula's running account, this is the national bond uniting the "spiritual men" who spoke and wrote ancient Greek; the warriors at Roupel whose brave tenacity made them "equivalent to their ancient ancestors"; and the "free spirit" of Koula herself, as portrayed in her autobiographical essay and implied by analogy in the essay we shall look at in a moment. At this juncture I think it not stretching the point too far to conclude that Koula's thesis tells us something further about the source of some of her problems with written and spoken English. I am suggesting that her emphasis on this ideological stance is a thread, however tenuous, connecting Koula's repeated choice of subject matter throughout the semester with her resistance to certain demands of the course, the college curriculum, and her adopted tongue—all of which I believe she associated, not altogether unreasonably, with the forces of conformity and cultural hegemony.

Koula's theme resurfaces one last time in the final in-class 50-minute essay she wrote, in which the students were to defend or challenge a common stereotype concerning some group with which they were affiliated—say, accounting majors, or members of a particular national, linguistic, or religious group. Koula writes about her compatriots from the Greek island of Cephalonia, who, she maintains, are distinguished from other Greeks by their "open mind, free spirit, fixity, and . . . great humor." (A linguistic sidelight illustrates the independence of this group: Cephalonia and the other Ionian islands remained outside the Greek kingdom until 1864, when they were ceded by the British to Greece. The demotic tradition—the language of contemporary spoken idiom—flowered in these islands. Well into the twentieth century they were not affected by laws requiring the more formal *katharevousa* dialect—the official language of the Greek national state between 1967 and 1974—to be used in the schools [Bien 40; Joseph 2]).

The time pressures of extemporaneous writing notwithstanding, Koula makes her point effectively, humorously, by offering as proof a scene that, once again, takes place at the time of the German occupation of Greece during World War II. This context is especially significant, I think, for it makes all the more compelling the issue of asserting one's independence and difference in the face of domineering foreigners. As in her fable, Koula does not tell her own story in illustration of her thesis about her national group, but elects to tell someone else's story. Moreover, the essay unfolds through the spoken dialogue of an argument—the sort of straightforward dialogue Koula is unable or unwilling to negotiate in her autobiographical essay:

> In Western Greece there's an island named Cephallonia.
> People who come from there are distinguished from the rest of
> Greeks by their open mind, free spirit, fixity, and above all they
> are famous for their great humor.
>   A journalist once narrated a satyre taken from his own life:
>   "It was the German occupation in 1940 and traveling in
> Greece had become very harsh. I had gone to Thessaloniki for

work. On the return I had to renew my passport. In the proper office there was a so big line, which reached out to the street. When at last I reached the desk, the clerk asked:

—What's your name?

—Skouris

—Father's?

—Gerasimos

—Age?

—42

—Where you were born?

—In Cefallonia

"It was fine till here, but when he came to the last question, things changed.

—Profession?

"I turned my head and I looked at the big line behind me. The clerk, very upset by the delay, asked again:

—I asked you about your profession. Are you going to answer at last?

"Then I answered.

—Cefallonian.

—Are you crazy? I asked you about your profession. What your job is. Cefallonian is not a profession.

—Yes it is.

—Listen. I can't waste my time with you. Next, please.

"Then I started to pray to the Cefallonian god for help. It was no answer. He played with me. He had forgotten me.

"Sir," I started, "first I was a clerk in the bank. After that I became an officer, and again a clerk. I have worked in real estate. I became an advertiser, a poet, an author, a professor in an accounting school, a journalist . . . So, write Cephalonian."

"The clerk very simply accepted the situation and wrote down Cefallonian."

Do you think that he had not succeeded in all the professions he did? Yes, he had, but he had also the typical Cephalonian spirit. [Note: the various spellings of Cephalonia are Koula's.]

In parodistic form we have once more the single-minded assertion of local identity, the valorizing of imperviousness to change or modification of viewpoint despite alterations in circumstance and venue. Now, in assigning essays that allow students to choose their own topics, I expect and welcome the student's repeated though varied exploration of a personally relevant theme. So what I am remarking here is not so much that Koula elaborates on a particular idea throughout the semester, nor that the theme tells us a good deal about how Koula organized experience in life and on the page, although I have wanted to show how the theme becomes incrementally more clear and meaningful when examined in the context of an entire body of work. More important, however, I have wanted to draw a connection between Koula's choice of subject and her approach to her studies in English and to the activities of the composition classroom, not least among which is the process of learning to see one's work from different perspectives and to revise accordingly. The remaining pages of this discussion will be devoted to differing perspectives on revision: Koula's and mine.

My students are invited to rewrite any of their essays during the semester, and two or three of these revisions are required. Where most of her peers seemed pleased to have the chance to rewrite, if only for a better grade, Koula saw no need. Where some were moved to shift focus, Koula stood pat. I presume there is at least one such holdout in every writing class. How to convince the unwilling writer whose essay surely merits a second look?

As it happens, the hobbyhorse Koula rode all semester long pointed the way to a partial if less than satisfying resolution of some of the problems in her earlier autobiographical narrative. Normally, as I say, a student is prompted to review her work according to the reactions of her classmates. Since Koula curtailed her participation in the group, the revision, if indeed Koula were to vouchsafe it, would have to occur in private conference, with much prodding and a lot more *ex cathedra* intervention than either of us would have preferred.

Let me reconstruct for you the scenario of the belated conference Koula and I had toward the end of the semester concerning her revision of the autobiographical essay. The turning point of the essay seemed (at least to me) to be the elliptical conversation with Anna, the one of which Koula gives puzzling snatches in the last paragraph of the essay. I therefore took this passage for a point of departure. Before our meeting I asked Koula to try to record the entire conversation she had had with Anna. The next day I found her bivouacked in my office with a revision of her original opening, every sentence an evasive maneuver. Notice that even in this weakened version of the introduction, Koula underscores the theme of the (seemingly inevitable) severing of connections, due to some change in the other as opposed to the self:

> All the nice things finish so quickly, sometimes before they even start. Friendship, this so rare and wonderful feeling, which connects people most of times ends somewhere in time. Usually those endings cause very much pain, but sometimes it's inevitable. You can't face the fact that from one moment to the other persons so dear and so related to you become strange.

I observed that this addendum didn't really help the reader understand what went on in Koula's last meeting with Anna. "But why do I have to make that clear?" she asked. "Chekhov said the writer doesn't have to say it all, he must force the reader to think. In the *Apologia* and the *Republic* Socrates uses examples, like in his explanation of justice, but not the kind of specifics you want from me."

I saw Koula's quandary. Added to the unpleasantness of recalling a painful and complicated incident was the burden of proof to a reader whose rhetorical values and assumptions Koula *did not believe* she shared, a point of emphasis I shall return to farther on. I explained that this reader, anyway, needed a guide through the paper, and for the remainder of our conference I took the part of the inquiring and ingenuous American with a pragmatic approach to discourse—the representative reader I now wanted her to envision as she wrote. Koula took the high road, assuming the role of the highly principled teacher whose every gesture found its analogue in ancient Greece. What, exactly, were the convictions she held that Anna did not share? "I believe in friendship, like the friendship between Damon and Pythias." True to form, Koula had hit upon an analogy emphasizing not only the mutual devotion of two Greek philosophers, Damon consenting to substitute himself for his imprisoned friend, but the willingness of both to die for their beliefs.

I told Koula I still couldn't make out the relationship between the opening and closing paragraphs and the rest of the essay. Would she please take 15 minutes to write down what she had said to Anna at their last meeting? She wrote, and then read this to me:

> Anna knows pretty well that I hate others to try to tell me
> what to do. I have learned to respect people and their occupations
> and I claim the same thing for myself. I reminded her that I know
> what I want, what I seek in life, what I struggle for, and I follow
> my way. I told her the last time I saw her, "I want to work in
> spite of everything. Not to be rich, not to be famous."

Here I interrupted, "What, exactly, did Anna want you to do?" She replied, "I'm a painter, interested in art, not money. Anna wanted me to settle down like her. She works in a bank." Fine. She wrote this into her revision, and continued reading,

> I tried to explain to Anna that I am indifferent about what
> people think and do. At this point, I started telling what Socrates
> said to Critos, but Anna said, "Please stop, that's philosophy."
> "Yes, it is, but philosophy is absolutely necessary in our
> lives."

Again I remonstrated, asking Koula to refresh the memory of the reader who might have forgotten her Plato. In the *Crito* dialogue, she explained, Socrates affirmed that one person can be right while all others are wrong. Koula had discovered yet another way to invoke the example of a prisoner who refuses to compromise his principles, even at the behest of his friends, at the risk of censure, at the cost of his life.

Koula then read what became her final paragraph:

> The whole situation started from the fact that Anna knows
> that I need to support myself. So she tried to persuade me to go
> into commerce, just to earn money. Her intention was good, she
> never thought for any reason to insult me. But really she can't see

that I am struggling in life to be honest with myself. Perhaps she is no longer willing to accept me as I am; even after I explained to her that I believe very strongly in Sartre's statement, "People die for an idea or for nothing."

The reluctant second draft, pieced together in this ersatz dialogue between Socrates and Ben Franklin, brought to light important links between the original thesis and the narrative portion of the essay. Time and motivation permitting, these connections might have opened up further revision. For me, in view of the new ending, the focal point of Koula's original essay about Anna now seemed to be the chameleon that appears in the weeds in paragraph five, a negative exemplum to Koula of the way people change their colors in their desire to please.

In most ways Koula remained resolutely unchameleonlike during the course of the semester. "I follow my way" was the point to which she kept returning in her revision of her autobiographical narrative. But in the process of humoring her reader, she may have discovered a few things about the topic of her autobiographical paper, and I hope about writing for an alien and what must have seemed to her an intractable audience. The discussion and revision were preliminary at best, but served to disclose certain patterns and relationships, in life as in rhetoric. I believe that if Koula had continued working, the connections she had drawn would have made it easier for her to resolve the thematic and formalistic inconsistencies in her paper. I am equally convinced that the resulting clarification of ideas and structure could have helped her to recognize and to correct some of the attendant linguistic problems that had made her first draft the most difficult among all her essays to decipher.

I have said above that "motivation permitting," Koula might have continued with the revision process, but obviously her intransigence—or perhaps, she thought, mine—mitigated this process throughout the semester. I'd like to conclude the present discussion with a few further thoughts on why this might have been so. It would seem Koula was convinced that the agenda of the English composition classroom—not just the intermittent concern with personal anecdote, but the recognition of the reader's need for clarification of structure and thesis—was somehow different from that promulgated in her native country, and therefore arbitrary. What matters here is not whether these differences exist between the two cultures (and as I hope to show in a moment, they do not to any significant or vitiating degree) but that Koula seemed to perceive them as antithetical, and to regard the act of accommodating one system as a disloyalty to the other.

One of the goals of the composition classroom should be to highlight cultural diversity. The point is to value diversity of response (a writer may construct, as Koula did, an Assessment Test response entirely in the form of dialogue, so long as she gets her point across), but not at the expense of communicative function. Observers from various disciplines—Thomas Kuhn, Richard Rorty, Chaim Perelman, among others—have demonstrated how rhetoric is epistemic, how discourse arises from and in turn creates a community's world view and interpretive practices. The normative function of the community becomes even more important in the context of the heterogeneous ESL classroom. Our students may come from different discourse communities, but over the weeks of the semester they come to agree through dialectic on certain textual conventions, and to see that they are accountable to their peers for intelligibility and evidence. This pedagogy asks students to recognize their contributions to the meaning-making process, and to view successive essay drafts as both exploratory and productive of what they want to say. Learning to accommodate the conventions of the typical writing workshop in the American classroom is an act Kenneth Bruffee has called "a sort of reacculturation." This process Koula steadfastly resisted.

We have seen how normally, although certainly not in the circumstances of revision I have recounted here, the teacher's role in the collaborative classroom is more facilitative than prescriptive. By way of contrast, recall from Koula's early journal entries that what impressed her most was the solidarity of a class attending to the teacher's lecture. Similarly, what delighted her about her ancient Greek class was the "difference of teaching of this language" compared with her Spanish and English classes. The teacher discussed the roots, development, and history of Greek, and showed an enthusiasm for her culture that Koula found unusual among Americans. Recollect, too, Koula's foot-dragging response to keeping a journal, where she distinguished between adolescent "dreams" and the "teaching" of serious artists. We can infer from Koula's observations and subsequent performance that she remained distrustful to the end of pedagogy based on group discussion, peer collaboration, and emphasis on discourse as a means of discovery and social interaction.

No more was Koula convinced that, after all, many of the conventional purposes and modes of expository arrangement are stable enough from culture to culture in the West (though not necessarily, as we shall see in future chapters, from West to East). In Book III of his *Rhetoric*, Aristotle places great emphasis on clarity as one of the most important elements in rhetoric, and suggests that different genres must be adapted to particular situations and the expectations of the audience. One might see the prizing of concrete detail or even the personally expressive as recent local addenda to the practices Aristotle outlines of persuading through narratives, exempla, fables, descriptions, confirmations or confutations. These activities have been the mainstay of Western education.

Richard Ohmann has convincingly shown that the most common revision rule in American rhetoric books—"Use Definite, Specific, Concrete language"—stems from an ideology that focuses on the ahistorical present moment, on the fragmentary perceptions of the individual, on the empirical "verifiability" of superficial sensory data, and on the presumption of the universality of these features and values. Ohmann warns that this advice may trap students in solipsism and inhibit the relational thinking made possible by abstractions and generalizations. Koula might have raised similar objections. In this chapter I have wanted to show that rhetorical emphasis on the concrete and personal indeed springs from a characteristically American viewpoint. But I would add that the collaborative class, particularly in the case of international students, can provide a way out of this insularity of perspective. The class provides a cultural context, and collectively agrees on textual conventions, for the writing event.

"To construe philosophy as dialectic," R. E. Allen observes of Plato's teaching methods in the *Dialogues*, "is to view it primarily as an activity, not a product, as a discovering of truth rather than a set of truths discovered" (23). As James Kinneavy has pointed out, from Aristotle, Socrates, and Plato one can trace the hermeneutic tradition that regards meaning as dependent on context. Finally, then, what unites modern instructors with those "spiritual men" of antiquity Koula so admires is a belief in the power of discourse to create community, and vice versa. Many writing classes in the United States have come to privilege the heuristic procedures—the notion of rhetoric as a process of questioning, discovery, and revision—that Plato so compellingly illustrates in the *Apology*, the *Crito*, and the *Gorgias*.

In the *Gorgias*, Socrates puts forth two definitions of rhetoric. Rhetoric may be the facile power of persuasion, indifferent to truth. Or it may be the philosophical inquiry aimed at truth, carefully structured, and corresponding to certain agreed-upon (as opposed to universal) laws of logos—arguments, accounts, reasoned conclusions. One of the greatest and indeed most *concrete* illustrations of the two definitions of rhetoric occurs in the *Crito*. This is the dialogue in which Socrates purportedly says at his trial that he prefers death to exile, and which Koula herself invoked in defense of her principles during our conference on revision. The dialogue pits Crito's speech, a random and unconvincing exhortation to Socrates to escape from wrongful imprisonment, against the point-by-point refutation of Crito's argument by the personified Laws of Athens. I would have hesitated to introduce so lofty an analogy into our private colloquy, but I wonder if Koula would have been more inclined to persuasion had I reminded her that the Laws of Athens present a sequential argument organized around a single principle, that of the individual's obligation to the laws of the community. Socrates is convinced by the force of reason that without the common consent of individuals to these laws, however imperfect their applications might seem, neither community nor discourse can be sustained.

5

"What Changed Me"
Mimi Soo and the Question of Motivation

A Chinese woman from Taiwan who has lived in the United States since the age of 16 is still, two decades later, barely literate in her adopted language. At age 35 she enters college for the third time, founders for a semester, and then suddenly demonstrates stunning linguistic progress. How to explain? If we could isolate the causes, if they were constant from student to student, we would all be better instructors. But tracing an individual's learning trajectory, the relationship of causes to effects, is something like observing the behavior of subatomic particles: the path of incident must be inferred after the fact, from tracks on a photographic plate, a computer printout, a written page.

Presently you will see a lamentably substandard first essay written by our Chinese student, Mimi Soo, who was misplaced into English 105 in 1983. The paper, hardly developed enough to be termed an essay, is reprinted here for several reasons. To begin with, as in the case of the Russian student whose essay appears at the beginning of Chapter 3, the author shows only passing familiarity with written English, so that her first paper provides a representative selection of developmental and interference errors. These will be further illustrated in the following pages by comparison with similar examples drawn from the English essays of other Chinese students.[1] Along the way we shall also delve into a few of the perplexities of English grammar and usage.

More important, while Mimi's paper is neither developed nor structured nor quite English, it is charming in its detail, and because of this faint promise I determined in 1983 to monitor the author's progress over the

---

[1]I should note at the start that because I will be quoting the work of students from different Chinese-speaking countries, as well as numerous secondary sources, the systems of romanization for Chinese names and words will vary considerably throughout this chapter. Moreover, except in the case of Ku Chien-Chung, who preferred to be called by his family name, students' names are printed in the English fashion, with the given name first.

semesters. It is on account of the writer's subsequent improvement, finally, that the essay appears here, for it represents something of a success story. Possible reasons for this success will be examined in the latter portion of this chapter, which takes up the matter of motivation and affective variables in adult second-language learning. The resulting discussion should thus be read as a companion piece to the preceding chapter.

Mimi Soo moved to Long Island from Taiwan in 1964. At the time, as Mimi remembers it, there were no other Chinese families living in the town of Plainview. Since there were few foreign-born students at the local high school, Mimi received no special ESL instruction. She recalls that although her performance in most courses was dismal—she wasn't even capable of copying homework assignments from the blackboard—she was passed along for two years, chiefly because of her ability in mathematics. "They didn't know what to do with me," she says; "I wasted all those years."

Upon graduating high school Mimi took courses at Suffolk Community College, dropping out after a year to work for Northwest Airlines. She took another stab at college work in 1977–1978, completing 8 credits in accounting at Queensborough Community College. Five years later, having run a successful clothing business, her two young daughters now in school, Mimi decided to go back to college. She entered Queens in September of 1983, enrolled in English 105 but was reassigned to a lower-level writing course in our CESL (College English as a Second Language) program, then went on to 105, which she had to repeat during the summer term because she failed the CUNY Writing Assessment Test. As she later explained, "I did well in the class but when the Test came, I panicked. I didn't know what I was thinking about any more! I think when I failed my teacher was more upset than I was."

At the time of our interview in October 1984, Mimi was enrolled in English 110. A recurrent theme in our conversation was Mimi's sense of the disparity between what she wanted to say and what she was able to express in her written work in English. She was quick to point out her knowledge of four very different Chinese dialects—Mandarin, Cantonese, Shanghainese, and the local Taiwanese dialect—and expressed disappointment that her achievements in English hadn't kept pace. But she seemed pleased to look back to her first English paper, which provided tangible proof of her linguistic progress, and volunteered to discuss some of the paper's second-language-related errors in detail.

Here, then, is Mimi's first 105 essay, a description of her grandmother, or "Popo" in Chinese. (The sentences are numbered for reference in the discussion that follows):

[1] I called Grandma-Popo, she was a short, thin, little lady.
[2] Takes tiny little steps, but she walks fast. [3] Every time we shops, she disappear on me, sometimes I felt like tie a string on her so she wouldn't be lost.

[4] I remembered she nets and nets, and her perfectly polished
nails, I kapt all the little sweater she netted for my grils.
[5] I remembered when ever I was hurt or angry, she would always agrees with me, and went off to the kitchen and make soup.
[6] that was her way, and I love her.
[7] Down the basement, I still kapt her clothes, they are all so
new, she loves to buy, and bottles and bottle of perfume, she always smells good.
[8] If I can turn the times back, I like to take her to shop once
more.

When asked to develop the paper, to add further detail to the paragraphs
she'd written, Mimi submitted the following notes. If anything, the sequence
is more haphazard, the sense of sentence boundaries less secure:

Popo likes to net, but she doesn't do it well. she netted a sweater
for me one sleeve was longer than the other. I war it any way. the
scaf she netted me went around my neck three times is still too
long, and it's getting longer.
Popo always complain she has to look up to other people. even
when she wear high heels.
She love it when people refer me as her daughter. She will smile
and say the only few words she knows "No. Me Grandma"
All thoes years I known her, she only wore one heir stye. push
back all her heir with a bun in the back of her head.
She always has nail polish bright red. she always smell good. always look as if she was ready to go out.
She loves to cook for me. always tells me she was making soup.
and I will always go to have her soup. she never tells me she was
loney.

How do you help a student to locate and correct even a portion of the
errors in these papers? It's hard to know where to begin. Certainly not in
an introductory composition course: the student first has to learn the fun-
damentals of the English sentence. Mimi's instructor and I agreed that she
would more profitably begin with CESL 31, a lower-level intensive English
language and writing course, and Mimi, already adrift in a class too advanced for her, was relieved to take up our suggestion.

"Takes Tiny Little Steps": Of Grammar, Syntax, and Style

But where does the CESL 31 teacher begin? As it is our first business to
attempt an explication of this text in terms of interlingual and intralingual
problems, we'll begin with the most basic and pervasive errors, those concerning subjects and verbs, and then proceed down a rather arbitrary hier-
archy of errors to those concerning plural markers and orthography. Years

ago, in his wonderful *ars poetica* on the Chinese written character, Ernest Fenollosa celebrated the ideograph as at once concrete and metaphorical, a word picture for which our own poor alphabet offers no equivalent. He went on to excoriate those foreign grammarians who "have begun to torture this vital speech by forcing it to fit the bed of their definitions" (67). So rebuked, I embark on the following pages mindful that in the service of pedagogy I shall be, to use Fenollosa's terms, importing into my cursory reading of Chinese grammar the weaknesses of my own formalism.

One of the most striking features of Mimi's first two English papers is her uncertainty as to what constitutes a sentence. Comma splices such as one finds in sentences 1, 3, 4, and 7 are common enough in the work of native as well as nonnative beginners. A more obviously ESL-related error is the absence of the subject from sentence 2 in the first paper and from the last few sentences in the second paper. One likely reason for the omission, as Mimi herself noted during our meeting, is that the relationship between the subject and predicate is looser in Chinese sentences than in English. Most English sentences, with the exception of commands, require subjects, even when a "dummy" subject must be supplied, as in the sentence "It is raining." In spoken and written Chinese, however, many sentences lack subjects: the Chinese speaker often thinks it redundant to state the subject if it is understood, and, initially at least, may carry this way of thinking over into English. For the same reason, Chinese speakers may omit the object from the sentence, as is permissible in their own language.[2]

In fact, in several related ways Chinese is far more tolerant than English of reference omission. As in Mimi's case, Chinese learners may delete the pronominal copy in many contexts where English requires pronoun reference, a type of error noted by Chiang (1981, cited in Tsao). Moreover, although modern Chinese has an equivalent of the English *it* (*ta*), its use is more restricted than in English, being chiefly used to refer to animals. Linguists point out that when speakers of Chinese need to refer to inanimate objects, they use lexical repetition or $\emptyset$ pronoun depending on the position of the reference in the sentence.

The English verb system presents obvious problems for all learners of the language, but a few contrasting points in the Chinese verb system should bring into focus the kinds of difficulties students like Mimi are likely to encounter. For instance, Chinese verbs aren't inflected for number or person

---

[2]For the most part, throughout this chapter, I do not draw distinctions among the dialects of Chinese, the most prominent being Mandarin and Cantonese. These dialects diverge widely with respect to vocabulary and phonological detail—so much so that they are often mutually unintelligible in spoken form. But the differences are not germane to the purposes of the present discussion, since the basic grammar of these varieties of Chinese is virtually the same, as are the underlying structural characteristics of their phonology.

Unless otherwise attributed, the sources for the features of Chinese discussed on the next few pages are the *Contrastive Study* and Li and Thompson's *Mandarin Chinese: A Functional Reference Grammar*, listed in the bibliography for this chapter. I am also indebted to Feng-Fu Tsao's review of the literature of Mandarin/English contrastive analysis, particularly to his summary of several articles, cited below, which have not yet been translated into English.

to agree with their subjects. This difference, taken together with the fact that the English third-person singular -s ending trips up learners of standard English, native-speaking or otherwise, may explain why Mimi correctly inflects some of her verbs for agreement, as in "[she] takes," "she walks," and so on, but also writes, for example, "Every time we shops, she disappear on me." Of course, to Mimi, and, for that matter, to her readers, the meaning of this incorrect sentence is perfectly clear: the addition or omission of an -s on the verb is inconsequential to the sense of the statement.

Nor are Chinese verbs inflected for tense, mood, or agency. Rather, the verb is controlled with a set of temporal particles, comparable to English words such as yesterday, tomorrow, just now, and so on. Needless to say, time as it is expressed in Chinese is very different from the concept of time as it is expressed by verb tenses in Indo-European languages. One linguist, J. Charles Thompson, contrasts the English speaker's notion of time as "an ever-rolling stream" with the Chinese speaker's sense of time as a series of discontinuous units occurring in succession, like separate beads coming one after the other on a string. Actually, Thompson goes on,

> There are many of these strings, occurring concurrently and even within each other. The particular string being considered depends on the event being described and the speaker's attitude toward it. Furthermore, the size of the time units involved may vary tremendously. In the Chinese *syyle*, which might be used where an English-speaker would say "he is dead," the two time units concerned are a man's lifetime and eternity. On the other hand, the action of picking up a pair of glasses, putting them on, reading a few words, taking them off, and laying them down, may be described in terms of seven time units . . . (71).

More than this, I neither propose to explain nor profess to grasp the subtleties of the concept of time as articulated by the Chinese verb system. No more do I maintain that English tenses make sense. Let's take just a few of the whimsicalities of the "simple" present in English. This tense can be used not only for narration of action taking place at the time of the speaker's utterance, but—in the guise of the "historical present"—for narration of events that took place in the distant past. As J. L. Austin has noted, the simple present also has a performative function, as in statements like "I now pronounce you husband and wife" or "I bet you can't name the capital of Montana"—a distinctive function for which, again, words like "simple" and "present" and "indicative" are misnomers. And what do learners of English make of expressions of intention and futurity in a sentence such as "I go to Los Angeles [on Monday]"? Moreover, while it seems "logical" enough for English speakers to use the simple present for habitual actions ("I jog") and for timeless assertions such as "Two plus two is four," it has been pointed out that Chinese speakers are justifiably mystified by an English statement such as "he is dead," in which the present tense is used to describe a condition that existed in the past and will continue until the "end of time" (Henry Lee Smith, Jr., cited in Thompson).

Which brings us back to the verbs in Mimi's descriptive paper, since they ricochet between past and present, prompting the reader of the first paper—this reader, anyway—to dwell rather ghoulishly on the question of whether Popo were still with us. In our subsequent interview, Mimi told me Popo had not been alive when she had written the description. When I mentioned that this wasn't clear from the paper, Mimi laughingly explained, "I thought I *was* writing in the past tense! I figured at that time that if I begin the sentence as past, the whole thing is past tense. I didn't think that every sentence had to refer in the past tense. In Chinese you would say *tsung ch'ien* —means long ago—and then you would say whatever you want to say."

Differences in the way the two languages manipulate verbs may explain why far more advanced Chinese students of English sometimes employ the past and present tenses interchangeably in sentences that are otherwise grammatically correct. Take these sentences from Su-Chuan Tsai's journal entry on the beauty of Chinese calligraphy:

> Unlike English alphabets (letters), every Chinese character has its particular stroks. When I was small, I enjoy writing a lot, as if I were drawing.

This writer incorrectly switches from past and present in the second sentence, yet she is familiar with the subjunctive mood. Would that our native students were.

Another frequent verb error among beginners in English, whether young native speakers or foreign-born adults, is the tendency to overgeneralize by applying the past-tense rule for regular verbs (= add -*ed*) to verbs that are conjugated irregularly in English. Naturally, there may be slips of this kind even in the best of nonnative papers, as in this example from a very proficient speaker of Chinese and English, Soraya Chang:

> It was Monday afternoon: 4:30. I was on my way home from school and standing up holding onto this bar as best I could because the bus was extra-crowded. . . . On its way, the bus jumped and *winded* frequently, so I tried to move the least and stay quiet.

Because verbs aren't inflected in their native language, Chinese students will probably be further stymied by English modals and modal auxiliaries, which are in anyone's estimation a complicated matter. Beyond the lexical contrast between English and a language that has no exact equivalents for the auxiliaries *can, should, may,* and so on, there is the matter of subtle semantic gradations among modals. For example, in framing English questions, *could/might* is sometimes deemed more polite than *can/may*. Then too, English speakers often distinguish between *may* (permission) and *can* (ability). In Chinese, possibility or speculation is expressed through adverbs (roughly equivalent to *perhaps* in English) rather than through equivalents of English modals. To take a related question of usage from our student's first essay, Mimi writes "If I *can* turn the times back . . . " when she should have used *could*. The modals *would, should,* and *could* are often used as the past tenses of *will, shall,* and *can,* yet in this sentence English requires the past tense for a wish that is clearly expressed in the *present*—a conditional-tense usage that must surely puzzle the Chinese speaker.[3]

Adding to the confusion of tense formation in English is the fact that *to be* and *to have,* the most irregular verbs in English, have no exact equivalents *as function words* in Chinese. That is, there is a word in Chinese that means "to be" when occurring between two nominals, just as there is a word that means "to be in possession of"; but when these words function as progressive and perfective aspect markers in English, they have no precise translations in Chinese.[4] Consider verb constructions such as "are be able" in the following journal entry, Ko-Ping Chen's commentary on her native language:

> You may feel Chinese is easy to study. The only thing that makes you work hard is to memorize the characters, but when you have memorized more than one thousand words you are be able to communicate with Chinese. The grammer is easier than most of languages, at least I never use present perfect tense when I was in China, but I have used this tense now.

Ko-Ping might have mistaken some of the other verbs in this passage, but she's got the present perfect covered, all right. Actually, this is no minor feat: the present perfect tense is a particularly puzzling phenomenon in our language, being neither a past nor a present tense but partaking a little of both. The present perfect is used to characterize an action that began in the past, continues in the present, and may go on into the future. ESL students frequently have trouble with this tense. At the same time, I am compelled to mention that my colleagues and I have likewise noted in native speakers' papers the seeming demise of the present perfect, along with the late lamented past perfect, which disappeared from English compositions some

[3]In Chapter 1 of *The Linguistic Shaping of Thought: A Study in the Impact of Language and Thinking in China and the West,* Alfred H. Bloom takes up the larger and more volatile Whorfian question of the cognitive effects of the absence in Chinese of formal lexical or syntactic means to signal hypothetical or counterfactual premises. According to Bloom, the Chinese do appear to shun counterfactual reasoning in speech and writing, and have trouble solving deduction problems containing premises of this sort. Bloom gives evidence (some of which is effectively challenged in the Birdsong and Odlin review of the book, cited in the bibliography for the present chapter) to argue that these cognitive phenomena are causally related to the linguistic phenomenon.

[4]For an elaborate "semantico-syntactic" contrastive analysis of "be" and "have" sentences in Chinese, see the article by Chu listed in the bibliography. Chu also touches on certain "preferred structures" in Chinese, suggesting links between syntactical, semantic, and rhetorical predilections. These structures will be examined briefly further on in this chapter.

years ago. At least Ko-Ping, whatever her other difficulties, is experimenting with verb tenses, at the behest of her instructor.

Another, very different kind of verb error appears in this clause from Mimi's first essay: " . . . sometimes I felt like *tie* a string on her," and again in the final sentence of the paper: " . . . I like to take her *to shop* once more." Infelicities like these tend to arise from the caprices of idiomatic English verb chains. In English, certain verbs can only be followed by the infinitive or base form of the verb (we're going to *stay* home tonight; we have to *leave* tomorrow), while other verbs must be followed by a gerund (let's avoid *wasting* time; did you finish *painting* your house?). Chinese draws no formal distinction such as English makes in these cases between infinitives and gerunds. Since these English collocations have no basis in logic—idioms rarely do—these lists of verb chains simply have to be memorized by the student.

A kindred problem, also common to most ESL learners regardless of nationality, is the question of two-word verbs and which preposition each takes:

> When you listen Chinese, you will feel that its sound is very soft and the tempo is very slow. From the language, we can know that Chinese people loves peace.

That Chun-Hsiu Chiang omits the "to" after "listen" in this sentence is natural enough, especially since "hear," an intransitive synonym, doesn't take a preposition. This might be viewed as a developmental error, owing to the difficulty English presents with respect to prepositions, which often seem assigned arbitrarily. But the problem can also be regarded in terms of the contrast between the speaker's first and second languages. Chinese speakers have a tendency to delete prepositions in some English phrases because the intransitive verb in question is transitive in Chinese. Thus a Chinese speaker translating from his native language might say "I not afraid thunder" or "She often thinks her parents back in Taiwan." So a verb + preposition problem such as that found in the above sentence may be twofold. First, in Chinese, the English verbs *listen* and *hear* are rendered by a single word (*tīng*)—just as *look* and *see* are both translated as *kan* (*Contrastive Study* 173, 190). Second, there is nothing in the Chinese equivalents of these single words that reflects the transitive-intransitive distinctions between the English pairs of verbs.

Chinese nouns, like Chinese verbs, are not inflected for number. Notice that Mimi applies the -s plural marker intermittently, either omitting it ("all the little sweater") or using it erratically: I can only speculate that by the phrase "bottles and bottle of perfume," Mimi means "one more than a lot of bottles." Instead of changing the noun itself to show plural, Chinese uses specific words to indicate number, as in "I bought two orange and three pear." Once again, the Chinese speaker may understandably sense that an affix—in this case, the plural marker—is unnecessary in such a sentence because it adds no significant information to the statement.

Consider the following paragraph from the journal of another basic-level CESL student, Kelly Chow, who is having trouble with the singular and plural of English nouns. Kelly's knowledge of English is at best rudimentary, but a few of the singular/plural distinctions in this passage might perplex even the most advanced ESL student:

> I remember when I was in junior high school, whenever went out with friends for a movie, we always buy popcorn to add more enjoyments. Since popcorn is so cheap and so good for we those junk-food eater, everytime I eat it, I am so enjoy. When I watch TV or read papers with one quart of popcorns, I feel so relax and satisfying. My eyes on the comedy TV program or papers, my mouth is crunching the salty-buttered popcorn at the same time, my hand is taking the oily popcorn to my mouth. My mouth non stop in crunch the popcorn until I empty the cup; certainly, my mouth and hand are full of oil and salt, even my papers. My cavities is calling help too.

"Enjoyment" is an abstract noun, and so does not have a plural form—despite the fact that one can tot up different kinds of enjoyment, and that one can say "entertainments," as Graham Greene terms his lighter literary works. The rule for "popcorn" is that it is a noncountable noun, like air or coffee; yet in New York, at least, you can say, "I'll have a coffee" when what you mean is, "a cup of coffee." And popcorn, although technically a mass noun, can be counted by kernels, individual units, like M&Ms and nonpareils. No wonder Kelly hedges her bet, using both the singular and plural forms of "popcorn."[5] English is obviously arbitrary with respect to countable and noncountable nouns: if we can say "a leaf" why can't we say "a grass"?—they come in individual blades, after all. Besides, although *grass* is usually a mass noun, it does have a plural form, meaning "several members of the plant family *Gramineae*." A certain ironic slant of light on the mutability of English grammar thus licenses Emily Dickinson to note the Bird that "drank a Dew/ From a convenient Grass," and elsewhere to write, "The Grass so little has to do/ I wish I were a Hay—."

Naturally, the English noun system (to say nothing of reversals of expectation such as those on which Dickinson plays) will present problems even for speakers of languages such as French or Spanish, which have the count/noncount distinction as well as noun markers equivalent to English articles. The difficulty is clearly compounded in the case of speakers who aren't used to thinking in quite the same terms of mass and countable nouns or of articles. (Li and Thompson, cited by Tsao, observe that although in

---

[5]In her paragraph, incidentally, Kelly makes another error typical of many ESL learners when she writes, "for we those junk-food eater." In Chinese, object and subject pronouns are the same: a Chinese speaker might say, "I gave he my pencil." Moreover, there is no *spoken* gender difference for *he* and *she*, or *him* and *her*. So it is not unusual for a beginning Chinese speaker of English to have trouble distinguishing the subjective case of a pronoun from its objective counterpart, or to confuse the gender of pronouns.

Chinese definiteness or indefiniteness can be specifically marked by *zhe* (this) or *na* (that) or *yi* + classifier, this is infrequently done, the more usual way to show definiteness being through word order.)

A number of prominent, more easily explained errors in Mimi's papers concern spelling: "nets," "kapt," "scaf," "grils," and so on. Here is where we can most clearly see the interference of the writer's first language, for the problem is not just the result of the illogic of English orthography—frequently the reason for native speakers' misspellings—but of phonemes that differ from one language or dialect to the next. In our interview, Mimi maintained that she has never learned English spelling rules, but instead has had to memorize the spelling of English words. Words not committed to memory must be sounded out; but Mimi's own language, lacking certain sounds or combinations, may lead her to hear certain sounds differently or not at all. For example, the /I/ or "short" *i* sound occurs in Cantonese mainly in the combinations *ik* and *ing*, so we can anticipate that the combination *it* as in *knit* might be a problem for the Chinese speaker. Chinese does not have a phonemic contrast between the /ɛ/ and /æ/ sounds. Many Chinese students tend to hear and use /ɛ/ (as in b*e*g) for /æ/ (as in b*a*g); they have a hard time distinguishing between *hem* and *ham*, *said* and *sad*, or, in Mimi's case, between *kept* and *kapt*.

Other areas of phonemic difficulty for Chinese speakers concern the voiced-unvoiced contrast, which is not a phonemically distinctive feature of Chinese. Problem sounds include /dʒ/ (as in *judge*); the *-th* sounds—both hard (*that*) and soft (*thin*)—for which Chinese speakers may substitute /s/, /t/, or /d/; the voiced fricative /v/ (for which they tend to substitute the unvoiced consonant /f/); and of course the /l/ and /r/ sounds. The Chinese /l/ only occurs in the initial position; the /r/ is retroflex and does not occur initially. Such features might explain Mimi's "grils," a seemingly fossilized misspelling that crops up again in essays she produced much later on.

This contrast in phonological systems appears to account for the only spelling error in the passage quoted below. The excerpt comes from a paper called "New York and I," an essay I shall have occasion to quote from again, as it was written by Ku Chien-Chung, the Chinese student whose college career, you may recall from the introduction to this book, we are also following. In that chapter we looked at examples of work Ku produced in English 105. Ku's further progress may be glimpsed in this excerpt from an essay he produced in his English 110 class, and will certainly be evident in the excerpt quoted later on in the present chapter. (The 110 assignment in question was to compose a "New York Notebook" of vignettes to illustrate some characteristic quality of the city, in the manner of Joan Didion's "Los Angeles Notebook." Having read the Didion piece, the students were to illustrate their theme in four or five brief segments—through dialogue, description of a scene, or narration of an incident.) Ku's orthographical slip is obvious enough in origin and would scarcely be worth mentioning were it not for the authorial assurance of the context in which it occurs, in the last line of this minutely rendered spiel from a subway conductor on the F train:

But, this time I heard quite clear, "Good evening Ladies and Gen-
tlemen, may I have your attention please; this is your conductor
speaking."

It continued, "This is the F train to Coney Island; This stop
is Queens Blvd, the last stop in Queens; You may change E train
on the express track, N and GG trains at local track or change
number 1 and 2 but upstairs to La Guardia and Corona areas; Ely
Ave., Long Island City, will be next stop; May I remind you to
carry your personal objects and the newspapers with you when
you left your train; Thank you for the cooperation to help us
keeping your train clean; May all of you have a present evening,
thank you!"

(Lest you think this speech is merely long-winded, I should in fairness to the
writer reprint its sequel, which explains Ku's purpose in quoting the conductor at length. Ku's characteristic viewpoint is that of the outsider:

In the beginning, I couldn't even believe my ears; after a
few stop, I sat loosely on a seat and listened to it closely. During
the local stops, the conductor only made a short speech and I felt
as if I had lost something and the conductor had been replaced.)

A related error—again, whether of mishearing, misremembering, or
mistake in performance, it's difficult to say—this time of an idiom rather
than a single word, occurs in a paragraph from the "New York Notebook"
essay of another 110 student, Soraya Chang:

The disc jockey then said: "I'm going to make you work your
butts out for this one: what's the song I played after the weather
at 9:23? And don't forget to give me that phrase that pays!

Recalling this patter, again with notable fidelity, Soraya seems to be confusing the English slang expression for "to work hard" with another idiom,
"to butt out," meaning "to keep out of another person's affairs." In the same
way, when Mimi Soo leaves out the preposition in writing "down the basement" in her first paper, she may be confusing this phrase with the idiom
construction "down/up the stairs/street/block," and the like.

In the matter of how native language influences sound production,
spelling, and idiom usage, Soraya Chang presents an interesting case. Her
parents are Chinese, and she speaks Chinese at home and attends a Chinese
school in the afternoon following her classes at Queens College. Yet Soraya
grew up in Venezuela, speaking Spanish, so in the same essay we find her
making another spelling error that a Chinese speaker wouldn't be likely to
make, but that a Spanish speaker would:

Few months ago, I was on my way home from Chinatown
on the F train and saw a very *especial* girl sitting between two

men: an American and a Chinese. There was something peculiar
about her. She was wearing a knitted top, dirty old blue jeans,
Indian sandals—the ones with lots of strings and very low
heels—listening to a loud walkman and knitting another shirt
very rapidly. While she was doing so, she kept bouncing her head
back and forth, with the rhythm of the music in her walkman.
She would also sing "oh, yeah, I love you, baby; come on, baby"
and sometimes hum the melody. Both men would close their
eyes, but the american one would overlook her and seem *especially*
puzzled by the girl.
      A little while later, when the girl was about to get off, I no-
ticed that both men were bouncing their heads the same way the
girl did.

In English, *sp*, *sk*, and *st* can occur in initial positions in words, whereas
in Spanish, the same sounds occur, but are always preceded by a vowel. So
the problem is a matter of distribution, of the sequence in which consonants
are likely to appear in a given language. English has spy, school, and student, whereas Spanish has espia, escuela, and estudiante—and especial.
The problem grows knottier since in English we *do* have the word *especial*—
which in English has a narrower application than *special*, being reserved by
native speakers to signify preeminence—as well as the adverb *especially*.
Soraya is familiar with this second usage and uses the word properly toward
the end of the excerpt.
      Our discussion to this point has been limited to matters of grammar and
mechanics in the work of Chinese speakers of English, insofar as they illuminate analogous errors in Mimi's paper. But the structure of Mimi's essay,
or rather the lack of it, warrants consideration as well, not least because it
may tell us something about a beginning writer's problems with organization. As for the question of a distinctively "Chinese" approach to exposition,
I do not want to push the point too far, certainly not with regard to Mimi's
paper. Inexperienced writers regardless of national origin are likely to have
particular difficulty shaping the descriptive paper, since there is no logical
order to follow as there is, for instance, in a narrative paper of chronological
events. Besides, it's quite possible that, assuming there are different rhetorical preferences in Chinese versus English, Mimi might not have mastered
the organizational patterns of her own first language (although I've noted
that she was sufficiently versed in the *syntactic* structures of Chinese to draw
distinctions between them and English structures when we discussed her
paper a year after she had composed it). I do want to use Mimi's paper,
however, as a springboard for thinking about the methods of "indirection"
often noted by my colleagues in the essays of some of Mimi's compatriots.
      The claims for and against the existence of distinctive national forms of
exposition have been mentioned briefly in the introduction of this book, and
will be taken up again, more vigorously, I hope, in Chapters 6 and 7. For now
I will simply (and too reductively) summarize the argument by juxtaposing
Kaplan's (1966, 1972) contention that Chinese paragraph development con-

trasts with typical English paragraph structures with Mo's view (1982, cited in Tsao) that English-speaking writers often develop paragraphs by the same means as the Chinese. These elements are *Chi* (introduction), *Cheng* (literally, "hook up," or elucidation of the topic), *Juan* ("turning," as to another viewpoint), and *He* (summary or conclusion). A compromise between these two viewpoints is offered by Tsao, who speculates that Chinese writers place greater importance on the moment (*Juan*) in the paragraph when the viewpoint "turns" on a tangent. This observation, Tsao ventures, suggests Chinese speakers' dislike of structures that are too direct, in contrast to native English speakers' characteristic preferences. The findings of Chen regarding beginning-level Chinese writers in English (cited in Qu 45) support the hypothesis that rhetorical structures preferred in the mother tongue are often initially carried over into the second language. In our conversation Mimi commented on this point: "It's very true that Chinese prefer indirect method. When my husband and I listen to a piece of music together, he might read the Chinese lyrics to me, and he will tell me how beautiful it is because it does not say it directly. You have to feel it, you have to imagine it. It's very different from the American way, I mean, they'll just blurt it out: 'I love you,' rather than leading you to that feeling."

None of the above is to predict that Chinese-born students will omit transitions and causal markers from their written work in English. On the contrary, Chinese students may just as likely emphasize connectives, although this practice may be hypercorrection based on their perceptions of stylistic preferences of English speakers (especially teachers). The following paragraph comes from an autobiographical essay written by S. P. Chan, a Chinese student in an English 110 class. S. P.'s essay subsequently appeared in an ESL textbook, shorn of its supernumerary transitions. This is the original version:

> In addition to being the "tornado mouth" of the fifth grade, I talked constantly at home. I loved to tell short stories to my little brother. Reciprocally, he delighted in following me around and listening to my tales. Moreover, I always told my parents what I had done in school during the day, and what I would do tomorrow. In fact, my mouth always seemed to be open, except maybe when I went to sleep. Conclusively, talking was one of my hobbies. Chatting all day long gave me great pleasure.

And here another student, Hing-Po Leung, exhibits the same tendency in a comic narrative:

> . . . The monkey belonged to my neighbor. She called her monkey a "Boso" and loved it very much. Meanwhile, the monkey was destroying my papayas. I immediately used a bamboo to get it down. But before I could touch it, it screamed aloud.
>
> During that time, my neighbor came and told me to stop beating her monkey, that it would come down by itself. Sud-

denly, the most promising papayas dropped to the ground and
the monkey was very happy on the tree.

I tried to climb up, but it was too high for me; therefore, I
had to wait till that devil monkey to come down.

After a few minutes, the monkey was still on the tree. I
couldn't wait anymore; therefore, I picked up the bamboo to get it
down again. . . .

An interesting sidelight, perhaps a corollary of this concern with transitions in English, is that it is an acceptable feature of Chinese sentence structure to have pairs of connectives such as although/but and because/therefore in the same sentence. This construction would of course be redundant in English. Thus another Chinese student, Xiao Tian Qu, writes of his father,

He works twelve hours a day; therefore we only see him a
few hours a day. Although we only see him a little, but we love
him very much.

In general, however, it has been observed (for instance, in Wang, quoted by Tsao) that while written English exposition leans toward hypotaxis—the use of connecting words between clauses and phrases, resulting in a highly subordinated style—Chinese tends toward parataxis in use of connectives. Clausal conjunction is usually necessary in English but often nonexistent in Chinese. In Chinese classics and modern prose, causal relations are more often than not expressed without causal markers such as *because* or *if*, but rather are comprehensible through context (Qu 46). Native English speakers, on the other hand, as reported by Witte and Faigley in their modification of Halliday and Hasan's theory of cohesion, tend to rate those texts higher which show a high percentage of cohesive ties. Both languages have the same means of creating sentence cohesion—reference, substitution, ellipsis, and lexical repetition. But Chinese seems to prefer nonuse of these forms, while in English the forms are more evenly distributed, at times overused out of concern for "logic" at the expense of what Chinese would consider redundancy.

What I would like to draw together are possible links between the grammatical processes discussed hitherto and the larger processes of rhetorical expression. Proponents of the theory of contrastive rhetoric have observed that "Asian" writing is often purposefully nondirectional, in contrast to exposition as it is commonly taught in U.S. schools. And indeed it is not unusual to hear American teachers complain that a particular Chinese student's paper was lovely, but that they had to get to the end of the essay to discover what it was really about. By way of analogy we may recall that the history of Chinese art has generally been free of the Western Renaissance notion of single-point perspective—the one "right" perspective from which to regard objects and organize paintings. Then too, Chinese painting has traditionally underscored the power of delineating through the *absence* of brush and ink, through the few bold or feathery lines indicative of a mountain range or a handful of blossoms. (We shall see this affinity for allusiveness intensified in the arts of Japan, briefly discussed in the following chapter.) In the same way, some rhetoricians suggest, the Asian writer may lead by indirection.

Chapters 6 and 7, as I have indicated, will consider in detail the question of whether there are characteristic "Japanese" expository structures, as well as the more vexed question of how or whether such structures are transferred by beginning Japanese writers in English. Still, it is far less problematic to attempt generalizations about rhetorical styles in a culture as homogeneous as that of the Japanese than it is to make comparable assertions about the disparate nations of Chinese speakers. In the present chapter, therefore, I simply want to support the proposition that some rhetorical choices in Chinese students' papers—papers that, unlike Mimi's essay, have developed paragraphs and some semblance of order—may be the products of cultural styles. If these texts do not quite show different structural preferences, they may at least show a greater tendency toward allusiveness, in contrast to the average American-born student's way of looking at the world and shaping discourse.

It goes without saying that native differences in rhetorical strategies need not be liabilities. As Brown (1987, 82) has observed, it is important to remember when discussing the phenomenon of language transference that the process may be facilitative rather than error-producing. That is, aspects of the native language may be *positively* transferred to the second language. Any discussion of "difference" in the writing of Chinese ESL students must include at least an oblique look at the merits of the indirect method. Those American-born teachers of my acquaintance noted above are just as apt to observe that Asian students' papers are characterized by a subtlety that sets them apart from the essays of native speakers of English. The passage below is another of the series of vignettes that make up Ku Chien-Chung's "New York and I" piece. The thesis of this excerpt, suggested in paragraph 1 and played out with great delicacy in the rest of the passage, is the same as that of the earlier-quoted subway conductor's aria from the same essay.

> I lived in an apartment in Elmhurst, Queens, New York when I first arrived in this country. At the moment, I mentally didn't even make a clear and distinct line between New York and the whole U.S.A. for, to me, everything else other than me, my family and my apartment were not belong to me and they were foreign land.
>
> Because of the snow, I was cooped up in my apartment and spent some time watching the outside world every day during the first winter here. The large temperature gap between indoor and outdoor covered the window with a film of vapor. I loved to use my finger tip to write down some Chinese characters on the vapored window to feel the reality of New York, the cold and snow.

Then I would either wipe out those characters or write many words on the window to let the words overlap on each other until I could see it through.

The outlooking view from my window wasn't a good one. An old apartment building, same as the one I lived in, stood face to face against my window. Between the two apartments, there was a subcommercial street, Elmhurst Ave., and a sidewalk perpendicular to the building on each side of the street. The windows on the other apartment were the most direct view from me and most of them were shaded with curtains. If lucky enough, I might see some unshaded window and try to say hello to the people who lived in there. Many times, the responds I got was that witnessed the curtain being pulled down. On the right side of the building, I could see a corner of an intersection of two streets; on the other side there was a single house with the eye-catching signs, "Beware of dog" and "alarm system installed" on its door.

This passage shows how Ku's feeling of being an outsider in New York is conveyed elliptically, and tells us as well something of Ku's achievement in English during the semester that had passed since he produced the texts quoted in the introduction to this book. Ku's further adventures in English will be chronicled in Chapter 8.

But our present topic is Mimi Soo's progress, evidence of which was advertised at the outset of this chapter. So it is with Mimi's journals and essays, as well as some of the larger cognitive and pedagogical issues they call to mind, that I want to continue this discussion.

"Who Am I?": The Role of Motivation

Having spent a semester in an intensive preparatory-level writing course, Mimi once more entered English 105. At the beginning of the term she produced the following paper, a wry and detailed narrative of an early experience with English. Here Mimi uses the metaphor of the Manhattan power failure of 1965 to describe her own linguistic "blackout." I believe her essay indicates in both subject matter and execution how far the author had come, not just in the intervening years, but, more important for our purposes, in the scant few months since she had resumed her college studies:

Black Out

It was just before that long electrical black out in 1965; I had suffered an unforgettable personal black out.

That was the second month after I arrived in the United States. Mother asked me to go down the street to get her a loaf of bread, but before I went out she suggested that I should write down the word "bread," just in case I forgot how to say it. Well, I thought it was unnecessary. However, when I entered the store, the word "bread" had somehow disappeared from my mind. As I was searching for that word in my head, I was searching for the bread on each shelf.

I thought to myself that I might not know how to say it, but I surely knew what it looks like. No bread was in sight, so, I decided that I would ask the man with the white apron for help. I told him that I wanted the top and the bottom of a hamburger, thinking that buns and bread are put at the same place. He pointed buns to me, and I saw no bread next to it. Then, I tried and asked for the thing that you put hot dogs in (mother also used bread to roll hot dogs). He pointed rolls to me and that was next to the buns. I said "No" again. By then he was getting a little anxious and starting throwing words at me: "meat," "lettuce," "ketchup" . . . everything that you could think of that goes on a hamburger or a hot dog. Finally I said "Please wait, listen, I want the thing on the top and on bottom of a sandwich." "You mean bread," he shouted. I nodded my head, but before I could take another breath of air, "We ran out of bread," he said.

While I was walking out of the store and thinking of what had happened was like in a dream. At that moment all the lights went out, and I thought to myself it was not just a dream but a nightmare.

Since then not only do I write down everything I need to get, but also carry a flashlight with me at all times.

A short time later, Mimi submitted a preliminary draft of an essay that indirectly raises the question of how an individual who has lived in her adopted country for many years is suddenly able to make rapid headway in second-language acquisition. The following, I must emphasize, is an unretouched photograph:

Who Am I?

I am a girl, who is struggling to become a woman. A girl needs to be protected, needs to be told what is good for her, and a girl has no true identity or destination. On the other hand a woman is in charge of her life, and she herself is her own responsibility.

A few years ago, when I was cleaning out my drawer, I came across a picture. In the picture I saw my children, I saw my husband, and I saw myself, the perfect wife, the perfect mother, but there was something missing. I didn't see me. I felt an emptiness and a numbness exploding in my body. I couldn't breathe and started to choke, to choke untill I vomited. After that incident I wasn't the same girl anymore. I began to realize that I am not a part of anybody, but I am an individual, and being an individual is to be independent.

Since that self discovery, I quit my job; the job that I had with my husband for ten years. I opened up a boutique with my friend. It was the day we hung up our store sign, that I felt like awoman. Two years later, when I decided to sell my shares to my partner and to become a student again, I felt like a woman. Taking care of the house, the children, going to business dinners with my husband, and coming home to my desk to work on my English, made me feel like a woman. I feel like a woman with ideas, with creativeness, and with a goal to achieve.

Whence Mimi's recovery from the limbo of interlanguage? Linguists have long speculated that motivation and other affective variables such as confidence and self-esteem, while not positively correlated with innate ability, do affect the learner's acquisition of the target language. As I have noted in the preceding chapter, this is a complex and much-debated issue. Research on affective variables is necessarily speculative, however controlled the conditions of the experiment. In the above essay Mimi traces an important change in her life back to a glimpse of herself in a photograph. The relationship between that electrifying moment of "self-discovery" and its effects in time—the mass, energy, and momentum of colliding bits of charged matter, to return to the analogy with which this chapter commenced—can only be surmised from these traces on the page. Yet the matter of motivation, and, just as important, the question of how it is defined and measured, has substantial bearing on our understanding of the learning processes of Mimi Soo and the other adult ESL students discussed in this book, as well as on the development of our own teaching methods. With these considerations in mind, I propose to survey the vicissitudes of the relevant research of the past two decades and then draw from this extensive catalogue a few tentative conclusions.

Most linguists writing during the 1960s and '70s argue that motivation plays a pivotal role in language learning (e.g., Carroll 1967, 1975; Stevick 1976; Clément, Gardner, and Smythe 1977). Gardner and Lambert have identified and tried to assess the influence of two different orientations toward the learning task: "integrative motivation" (the desire to be like representative members of the target-language community) and "instrumental motivation" (the desire to achieve proficiency for practical reasons, such as getting a better job, doing well in school, and so on). Although early studies (e.g., Gardner and Lambert 1959) emphasize the importance of integrative over instrumental orientation in second-language learning, later work by Gardner and Lambert (1972) and by Lukmani (1972), in a study of Marathi-speaking students learning English in India, supports the preeminence of instrumental orientation.

Subsequent studies have repeatedly produced conflicting hypotheses about the role of these two orientations. Indeed, one measure of the contradictions inherent in such research is that the examples of "instrumental motivation" cited above might just as easily be interpreted as examples of "integrative motivation," since valued members of the community are likely to be successful in school or on the job. The cumulative hypothesis suggested by the dialectic advanced in the pages of successive issues of *Language Learning* and like publications is that the two types of motivation are not mutually exclusive. Second-language learning seems to involve both, the relative importance of each depending on the individual, the task, and the context.

Over the years observers have considered in turn the relationships between language-learning success and factors such as attitudes toward self, national group, and target language group; reasons for living in the host country and intended length of stay; expectations of motivational support from the target language group; and social or cultural distance from the target group. Here again, the results of these studies often speak at cross purposes. Oller, Hudson, and Liu (1977) discover a significant negative correlation between English proficiency and the desire of the Chinese graduate students in their test group to remain in the United States (a measure of integrative motivation). They do find, however, a substantial correlation between attained proficiency and the students' attitudes toward themselves, toward other speakers of their native language, and toward Americans. Oller, Baca, and Vigil (1977), examining the responses of a group of Mexican-American women studying English in New Mexico, find that the more positively these subjects rated Anglos on traits such as "sensitive," "kind," and "considerate," the lower their scores on an English proficiency test. Chihara and Oller (1978) assess the attitudes of Japanese students learning English in Japan toward themselves, other Japanese, English speakers, learning English, and traveling to an English-speaking country. Their results show weak or negative correlations between all attitudinal measures and attained ESL proficiency.

Genesee, Rogers, and Holobow (1983), on the other hand, argue that "social psychological models of SL [second language] learning need to consider the role of intergroup factors more seriously." In their study, adolescent English-speaking Canadian students of French were asked why they were learning French and why French-speaking Canadians wanted them to learn French. In regression analyses it was found that the respondents' expectations of motivational support from the target language group were significant and in some cases unique predictors of SL performance. Svanes (1987), evaluating the results of a questionnaire completed by foreign students studying Norwegian at the University of Bergen, comes up with a different predictor of performance (though one may posit a link between his findings and those of the aforementioned study by Genesee et al.). Svanes contends that while no positive correlation was found between grades and integrative motivation, the best predictor of variance in groups of students with differing language and cultural backgrounds is the variable of "cultural difference," which is judged greater for the Asian, Middle Eastern, and African students than for the American and European students in Bergen.

What accounts for the maze of reversals in the research on motivation? Chihara and Oller suggest two possible explanations. First, the relationship between attitude and achievement seems to be indirect—that is, attitude affects motivation, which may in turn affect language learning. Second, the researchers' means for measuring their subjects' attitudes may be unreliable. Measurement of affective variables is necessarily indirect, based on inference from the subjects' statements and behavior. Moreover, we might add, problems lie in the subjective definitions of the abstract constructs being measured. To take the example of the study by Svanes noted above: how does one define the parameters of a cognitive and affective construct like "cultural distance"? The phrase has been used by linguists like John Schumann (1976, 136) to refer to attitudes toward, and relationships (dominant, subordinate) between, target-language group and second-language group. Svanes measures the term in his study by gauging exposure to Western culture, and proficiency in English or another European language. How do we measure distance precisely, or distinguish between "actual" and "perceived" difference—and is the distinction made on the part of researcher or learner?

As to the relative merits of measurement procedures, again we have disagreement. Oller and Perkins (1978) question the validity of self-reported data, arguing that subjects would be reluctant to disagree with accepted social behavior and would tend to give answers colored by the "approval motive" and self-flattery. Pierson, Fu, and Lee (1980), analyzing the relationship between attitudes and English attainment among secondary school students in Hong Kong, find that direct measures of attitude (that is, asking subjects for their reactions toward the use and study of English) is a better predictor of ESL attainment than indirect measures such as asking the subjects to rate themselves, the Chinese people, and Westerners. Scovel (1978) maintains that ambiguous test results might be traced back to the wide range of variables researchers have lumped together under the rubric of "affect." He points out, for instance, that a sharper distinction should be drawn between "facilitating anxiety," which may heighten the student's intake of information, and "debilitating anxiety," which impedes learning. Clément and Kruidenier (1983) trace the contradictory results of previous studies to ambiguities in the definition of orientations (especially in the earlier-mentioned overlap of instrumental and integrative motivation). They say research has been further clouded by the effect of differences in ethnicity, in individual intelligence and aptitude, in educational and social milieu (e.g., Japanese studying English in Japan versus those studying English in the United States), and in target language.

Upshur, Acton, Arthur, and Guiora (1978) conclude that causal relationships between affect and proficiency cannot be proved by simple correlational and cross-sectional studies, because these relationships are dynamic and vary greatly across subjects, contexts, and learning tasks. They suggest that feedback models may be more fruitful areas for investigation. They also find it more plausible that both cognitive and noncognitive aspects of personality affect language attainment, and that language attainment in turn affects personality. In other words, high achievers may tend to acquire positive affective tendencies as a result of doing well in language learning.

The latter possibility is strongly suggested by the results of Savignon's 1972 study of English-speaking students of French in Montreal. The hypothesis also seems to be supported by the findings of Hermann (1980) that among German children learning English in Germany, those children *already fluent* in English displayed a significantly greater desire to associate with native English speakers. Additional corroboration comes from Strong's 1984 study of Spanish-speaking kindergarteners in an American classroom: the faster learners were able to progress without an overt desire to identify with Anglo children or a rejection of their own culture. Further, the children who were more inclined to befriend Anglo children seemed to derive no measurable language-learning advantage from this orientation. The fact that the children who spoke English fluently showed a greater desire to associate with Anglos indicates that integrative attitudes may follow rather than lead to second-language proficiency. But as Strong points out, this evidence may simply mean that integrative motivation does not play the same role in the second-language learning of youngsters as it does in the case of adults.

How does this ouroboros of research help us to interpret Mimi Soo's history of English study, and what implications does it hold for our own teaching practices? Mimi's own testimony, as well as the work she produced in English 105, suggests that she had gained in confidence, self-esteem, and sense of purpose when she reentered college after a long hiatus. The inconsistencies of the research outlined above, though, offer faint illumination of the causal relationship between this change in attitude and her linguistic progress. While no conclusive statistical evidence emerges from studies on the learner's self-esteem, the link between self-esteem and language learning has been suggested by Heyde (1977) and in the previously cited research by Oller, Hudson, and Liu. Brown (1977) hypothesizes that self-confident learners are more likely to take risks and make the mistakes necessary for language acquisition. Beebe (1983) expands this hypothesis by noting that fossilization, the incorporation of certain patterns of error over time, may result from the learner's unwillingness to take risks.

Another factor, we know, is essential to the learner's progress, and that is *time*—to focus on goals, to devote to study, to make use during the "incubation period" (when obvious attention is not being directed toward the task at hand) of lessons that have been unconsciously absorbed. A phonological case in point: a study of the effect of eight weeks of training on second-language learners' pronunciation revealed no significant difference in pronunciation improvement between the trained and untrained groups of students or between group and individual instruction. Yet all the students tested showed some pronunciation improvement in the course of the study, suggesting that change occurs over time more than as a result of formal training (Madden 1983).

By emphasizing the element of time I mean to suggest not simply duration but a period of heightened receptiveness on the part of the adult learner. Gardner, Lalonde, and MacPherson, in their research (1985) on social factors in second-language attrition, come up with no clear-cut interpretations of the retrospective self-report data they collected, but conclude that "no characteristic of the individual is necessarily static. It is quite possible that attitudes as well as second language skills may change during the incubation period, and future research would be well advised to consider this possibility" (539). Let me offer one more bit of research in phonology to underscore the role of fluctuating periods of motivation in the growth of an adult learner's acquisition of college skills in a second language. Flege (1987) examines the vagaries of the empirical and theoretical literature to date and finds no conclusive support for the neurologically based Critical Period Hypothesis of foreign-language learning. The critical or optimal period of language learning may thus be independent of the individual's age. Perhaps then, for an adult language learner like Mimi Soo, who began studying English as a second language at age 16, and whose errors, to judge from her first effort in English 105, seemed to have become fossilized in the 16 years she had been in this country before resuming her English studies in her thirties, psychological and emotional "ripeness is all."

Certainly, changes in Mimi's motivation and attitude toward self and education led her in 1983 to reenter the formal academic environment of the college classroom. As a result she increased her possibilities for language intake over a period of several semesters through greater exposure to English and the discipline of its usage, as well as through the opportunity for prolific writing[6] and—this last element is essential—generally supportive feedback from her teacher and peers. The variable of motivational intensity, crucial to pedagogy, must be factored into the language-learning equation. That is, variables such as personality and innate ability are mediated by the type of

---

[6]The kind of prolific production I refer to here emphasizes written practice in class and at home. But the relationship of *oral* practice in the *classroom* to proficiency is, I regret to report, yet another matter of some dispute. A study by Day (1984) of Asians in an intensive English program in Honolulu shows no significant relationship between classroom participation and scores on oral interviews and cloze tests, or between classroom participation and use of the language away from the classroom. (Even more dramatically, Busch [1982], in her study of adult Japanese learners of English in Japan, finds that "introverted" students—as measured by a standard personality test—performed significantly *better* in their English pronunciation than "extroverted" participants.) But we must remember that Busch's study is limited to a single group of learners from one culture. And as Day himself acknowledges, his findings not only contradict Seliger's (1977) evidence that use of the target language is a factor in second-language acquisition, but fly in the face of most teachers' intuitive sense of what goes on in class. Day points out that his investigation, limited to oral practice, focused only on quantitative use of the target language, not on qualitative use: a simple monosyllabic utterance received the same score as a lengthy and complex utterance.

Christopher Ely's more recent (1986) study of classroom participation may be closer to the mark. Data was gathered by means of classroom observation and audio recording, and proficiency was measured by correctness and fluency on a story-retelling task and correctness on a written final examination. The results of the causal analysis include findings that language-class discomfort negatively predicted language class risktaking, risktaking positively predicted classroom participation, and this participation positively predicted oral correctness for English-speaking college students in a beginning Spanish class.

With regard to the matter of ESL learners in the college classroom, the problems and limitations of the studies outlined above and in the preceding pages point the way to future research based on more holistic approaches to a sequence of various kinds of oral and written assignments.

cognitive activity in which the learner is engaged, and by the learner's attitude toward that specific activity. McLaughlin (1978), noting that first-language transfer errors seem to occur more frequently inside the classroom than in other settings, argues that instruction and assignments should be oriented toward communicative tasks rather than toward memorization of rules and error correction. Gardner, Lalonde, and Moorcroft (1985) find that the effects of attitudinal/motivational attributes rest on how well individuals react to a specific task. They conclude their study by remarking that if attitudes and motivation along with language aptitude can be shown to play such an important role in the artificial environment of the laboratory, "consider how much more influential they must be in the real-life classroom environment!" (226).

The foregoing observations about second-language acquisition, then, corroborate the beliefs long held by many teachers of composition that we should be encouraging all of our students to take risks in oral and written work, emphasizing inventiveness and play before grammatical precision, and concentrating on communicative function within the essay as a whole rather than on sentence-level work. This is not to say that all ESL students, even under the best of conditions, will advance so dramatically as Mimi Soo, nor even that one will find in the work of Mimi herself a steady progression toward confidence and fluency. In the following journal entry Mimi narrates an incident that must surely be common among second-language learners. She later explained during our interview that the passage was occasioned by her teacher's having reprimanded her in class for not keeping up with the other students. (I have bracketed the deletions and self-corrections Mimi made during the editing stage. These formal operations indicate to some extent the process of Mimi's conscious application of grammar rules she had learned.)

Feb. 3, 84

When I was sitting in the corner of my music class last week, I couldn't help feeling inadequate. My heart just sunk deeper and deeper. I hated that felling. I knew it's [was] going to take days before I could feel balance[d] and incontrol again. Oh! how I can understand Maxine Hong Kingston's feeling. When she says that a telephone call makes her throat bleed and takes up that day's courage, and it spoils her day with self-disgust. But she was a little girl then, and look at me, I'm a grown woman. Do I have the time that she had? Can one pain compare with the other? There are so many questions in my mind, and all waiting for some answers.

I had trouble with almost every third word that came out of the professor's mouth, and not till later [that] did I realize[d] it was names and places of some famous musicians. As I was sitting there wondering what I was doing in that class, and what [do] I

> needed this for, in a strange way I felt calmer. It may be a numb-
> ness, but I didn't care, as long as it was not a sinking feeling.

Here Mimi articulates quite movingly some of the problems confronting the adult learner in college. Before we trace Mimi's further progress in school, I hope the reader will permit me to use her journal entry as the occasion for one last excursus. In the next few pages I would like to note several more sociocultural variables that are not specifically addressed in the literature I have summarized on motivation and affective variables in language learning, but that may nevertheless affect Chinese students' progress in American colleges.

No doubt many students, native and nonnative alike, have had experiences similar to the one Mimi describes above, and some might well have reacted as strongly. But if Mimi's reaction seems to you exaggerated, keep in mind the Asian-born student's preoccupation with "acceptable forms." This is a manifestation of the cultural concern for saving face, a concept most Westerners are familiar with and probably share to a limited extent. In the Far East, perhaps the most extreme illustration of this concept, so far as education is concerned, is literally a matter of life and death: we've all read about the suicides of 12-year-olds in Korea, China, and Japan each year when the exam results are published. I need hardly point out that our students' zeal is tempered once they come to the States. Still, this idea of "face" may continue to influence our students' behavior in school here to some degree.

Another aspect of the notion of saving face has bearing on the Asian student's performance in class and on homework assignments. My colleague Jackie Costello reports that when she began teaching at Lingnan College in Hong Kong, she routinely asked her students if they understood the lesson. Everybody always did. Later she discovered that they weren't simply protecting their own faces but their Western teacher's face as well. Their admission that they didn't understand might imply that she hadn't done her job properly. A silly question would cause the student to lose face; on the other hand, a difficult question that the teacher couldn't answer would cause *her* to lose face. It stands to reason that Chinese students in America are initially loath to ask questions, probe assignments, criticize, freewrite, brainstorm, make mistakes. Yet without this experimentation, without error, as we have seen, there can be little progress in language learning or in writing.

Several more related aspects of our Chinese students' possible expectations about education should be mentioned for what they suggest about these students' approach to their work in English—an approach that, again, often stands in opposition to methods promulgated in American schools. Paul Harvey (1985) has summarized a number of papers on Chinese learning methods and their effect on the teaching and learning of English in the People's Republic of China. (The same features, according to the students I have interviewed, generally apply to classrooms in Taiwan and even in some measure to the British-influenced school system of Hong Kong [as described, for example, in Ma 1982].) Harvey's summary of these methods:

> . . . a concentration on intensive reading as a basis for language study; a preoccupation with the careful, often painstaking examination of grammatical structure and a corresponding lack of attention to more communicative skills; the use of memorization and rote learning as a basic acquisition technique; a strong emphasis on the correction of mistakes, both written and oral; a view of literature and a reverence for the printed word which tends to lead to the teaching of non-extensive skills; the use of translation as both a teaching and a learning strategy. There are also other factors, such as the monolithic examination system in China and the perceived role of the teacher, which have to be considered (183).

Harvey warns against ethnocentric Western commentators' dismissing such methods out of hand, and suggests that our own educational system may be equally rigid in some ways. Indeed I recall that my own high school lessons in French and Spanish were governed by most of the features noted above. But I do want to point out a corollary function of the Chinese system. The same respect for authority and tradition that deters students from questioning their teachers or the material they are studying may also lead them to the kind of obeisance to scholarly sources, particularly in their research papers, that Western students are routinely warned against—and often disregard!—but that the Chinese in many cases consider perfectly acceptable. (Carolyn Matalene [1985] has described the same set of phenomena, observed during the semester she spent teaching writing in China.) We might also note in this context that until very recently Taiwan, for instance, had no formal copyright laws for published material, nor was the country bound by Western laws guarding against the unlicensed reprinting of the "private property" of the author.

The Chinese method of instruction, as suggested in the preceding paragraphs, is not freewheeling participation but rather respectful copying from the model of the masters. While it is true that art students in the West have also traditionally been encouraged to copy works of the old masters, ultimately the goal of these technique-mastering exercises in the West is the fostering of individual inventiveness. Ken Haas, who taught photography at Hong Kong Polytechnic for several years, relates a story, widely circulated over there and perhaps apocryphal, illustrating the difference between the two approaches. He explains that it is not uncommon in Hong Kong for five or six young people to pool their money and send one of their number to a master photographer for lessons. The master brings his students to Repulse Bay on the south side of the island, puts his old Rolleiflex on a tripod, takes the traditional picture of the junks on the bay silhouetted against the horizon. He then removes his camera from the tripod so that each student in turn can set up his camera and take the identical photograph. The prevailing notion is that there is a proper way to take photographs, to paint—for that matter, to write—and consequently that you show your skill by how closely you can approximate a form that has been preserved for generations.

My point is not that these differences in cultural values are impasses to understanding or success, but rather that they must be examined and made clear to ESL students. Attitudes toward such matters as plagiarism, for example, cannot be assumed to be constant from culture to culture. But it is a relatively easy matter to explain the Western idea of what kind of borrowing constitutes a scholarly offense as opposed, say, to citation of data that lie within the public domain. The same acculturation must be fostered with respect to the student's notion of "appropriate" classroom behavior, risk-taking as opposed to face-saving, and inventiveness as opposed to adherence to formulae.

The foregoing comments, as I say, doubtless pertain to some of our newly arrived Chinese students. But remember that Mimi Soo had lived just as long in the United States as in Taiwan by the time she came to Queens College. As you have seen from the evidence of her earliest essay, her experiences in the American high school system and her subsequent life and work in New York had done remarkably little to disturb the hibernation of her second-language aptitude and writing ability. Yet somehow these abilities were awakened in the environment of the English composition classroom, during a period of a few months, on her third go-around in college. Why?

We can only speculate on the basis of regression analysis of Mimi's written work and subsequent oral commentary. Several powerful influences seem to have converged at this point in Mimi's life, and here I want to suggest the interaction of individual motivation and sociocultural environment. The fact that her children were of school age allowed her to resume the role of full-time student in addition to her duties as wife and mother. In the intervening years her attitude had apparently changed toward her own capabilities and toward the goals of education. Fairly recent developments in the social climate of the United States had enabled this shift in priorities among many women of her generation. Most important, having mastered some rudiments of English grammar in the obviously effective basic-level class to which she had been reassigned, Mimi was fortunate enough to land in the classroom of a teacher, Bonnie MacDougall Ray, who encouraged her students to find their own topics and to expand and revise them over the semester. Then too, Mimi (unlike her counterpart in the preceding chapter) clearly bought into the premises, purposes, and methods of journal-keeping, personal narration, and introspective analysis on which many such composition classes in the United States are founded.

Mimi herself alludes to the changing social forces around her in these notes for a revised conclusion scribbled hastily at the bottom of the "Who Am I?" paper quoted earlier:

> I am glad that I am growing in this changing world, a world
> that not only is giving women like me the awareness to be a full
> person, but it is also giving us a chance to become one.

She examines the subject of her own shift in attitude more fully in the
following essay. This is a first draft produced midway through her first 105
class, based on the two-part structure "I used to think —————/ But now I
know —————," one of the "seed sentences" suggested by Ponsot and
Deen:

> I used to think that going to school was a waste of time, but
> now I know that I was wrong.
> In those schooling years, all my elders were telling me that I
> was having the best time of my life. I didn't understand that at
> all. My feeling was how can it be the best time of my life when I
> had so many straight rules to follow. Those rules were: no
> make-up, no jewelry, no boy friend, I must wear my hair
> straight and short, I must wear a uniform at all times, and I must
> have test every month. I felt so bitter about those rules at that
> time, that I overlooked the importance of learning and enriching
> myself.
> I began to understand those rules after I left school. Those
> rules were made for us so that we didn't have to worry about
> what to wear to school, how to wear our hair, or what color
> make-up to use. Those rules were made to make sure that our full
> attention was on learning not dating.
> I am thirty-five years old now, and I am a mother of two
> children. Going back to school is a hard task for me. I alway re-
> greted those years that I had wasted. I feel that I am paying a
> debt that I owe by going back to school. I often tell my children
> that live have many stages, and that we should finish each stage
> before we go on to the next. Then, we don't have to go back to
> the unfinished business.

It takes no revisionist stretch to see how, like Koula's essays, examined
in the preceding chapter, Mimi's work consistently yields up variations on a
theme. Assigned similar writing topics and two-part analytic structures, each
of these two students works out what she wants to say and at the same time,
I think, reveals something about her distinctive approach to second-language
learning. From an oblique angle, Mimi returns in the above essay to the
themes announced in her "Who Am I?" essay, namely the process of change
and growth in the life of an individual and in society as a whole, and the way
childhood experience is both connected to and mediated by adult reflection in
writing.

By the same token, when called upon at the beginning of her first 105
semester to write a description prompted by a single word, "kitchen," Mimi
characteristically chooses a two-part structure, comparing her former attitude
to her present viewpoint. She concludes, "Now I am married, and have my

own kitchen. At first, I was very excited about it, but I found that I really don't like being in there as much as I thought I would. . . . The kitchen is a place where I do my cooking when I have to. It didn't mean more than a place to cook when I was a child, and it doesn't have to mean more than that now." And on a practice exam in preparation for the Writing Assessment Test (WAT), Mimi's response to the topic of fast food restaurants begins, "I thank God for the people who invented the fast food restaurants. Being a woman of today's fast moving world, I find these types of restaurants are life savers sometimes. Just the other day I had to study all day for a test, and also had to attend class that night. There was no dinner, and I was just about to get panic and my daughter said, 'Hey Mom, why don't we go to McDonald's for dinner?' "

I realize that in the pair of excerpts above Mimi comes off like a pitch-woman for Hamburger Helper. Please understand that in quoting these fragments I do not wish to hypothesize a correlation between women's lib and language learning. Come to that, Koula, the subject of the preceding chapter, gave every indication of being a feminist—as well as an artist, Marxist, and staunch defender of students' rights—to little visible effect in her performance in English. I merely want to point out an addition to other important differences in learner motivation noted in the previous chapter. You may recall that Koula's essays—even those assignments based on two-part structures—consistently emphasize the importance of steadfastness, fixity, resistance to change. Mimi's essays, on the other hand, focus on the subject of transition and growth, not just in terms of her becoming a woman but in terms of the cognitive processes of defining herself within that category, and of defining that category within the context of evolving gender roles in her adopted country.

Let me give you one last example of Mimi's ability to expand her theme. The following essay, based on the idea of the autobiographical "turning point," may be contrasted with Koula's response to the same assignment, reprinted in the preceding chapter, in which Koula laments the alteration of a childhood friendship. Several features should be evident from the essay, produced toward the end of Mimi's studies in English 105. Here, once again, Mimi emphasizes the necessity of change. She demonstrates a grasp of English grammar and of the typical structure of its "model" narrative essays, moving from general statement to corroborating story to "moral." She has clearly absorbed the forms of literature she had read in English class—in particular the Maxine Hong Kingston memoirs mentioned in her earlier journal entry, in which Kingston describes her attempts to overcome the muting effects of gender and cultural difference.

What Changed Me

Ever since I can remember, I walked around with the attitude that I was better then anyone. Maybe I had to feel that way
about myself, in order to protect my own vulnerability. My vul-

nerability was due to the fact that I was the only student in the whole school, whose parents were divorced. With all the pain and loneliness inside of me, I didn't know that other people had feelings too.

It was a hot afternoon in May, and school was almost finished. We were to be promoted to third grade in September. While we were just feeling great about everything, myself and two other girls decided to pick on a girl name Lee. Lee was different from us; she had white skin and reddish hair. We were making fun of her apprence. At first she just stared at us, then after a while she ran away from us, and we thought nothing of it and went for lunch.

We must had said something extremely bad to her, because she was missing for the first period after lunch, and we were getting worried. I kept hoping that she would be all right, so we wouldn't be in trouble with the teacher. My heart started to beat quikly, when she didn't show up for the second period. By now the teacher was getting upset, she started to ask around who had seen her last. I prayed so hard for her to show up, even it meant that I would be punished. Just before I was asked by the teacher, Lee came into the class with her mother, father, and her dog.

Her hair was massy, and her face, her arms, and her legs were covered with scratch marks. There were puffed up and swollen. It was awful, and it was the must painful thing that I had ever seen. Lee's mother was very angry at Lee for scratching herself and not telling why. While Lee's mother was hollering at Lee, and the teacher was pleading with Lee, to tell why she had done that to herself, I was harrify. Harrify that we had hurt her so mush that she wanted to scratch her skin off, and I was also harrify with the fact that she was just like me. Her way she was hurting herself had remained me of my own self-hatred.

From that moment on I saw people differently, I no longer drew the line between them and me. Lee and her red marks had been with me since that hot day in mid May. We never became friends, but the lesson learned will stay with me for ever.

I think Mimi shows her competence in this essay, persistent grammatical problems notwithstanding. A few errors still seem to owe something to second-language interference, chiefly in the phonological mistakes apparent in misspellings such as "apprence," "massy," "must" instead of "most," "mush" for "much," and "harrify." Others appear to be performance mistakes, as when Mimi writes "there" when she clearly means "they." Several more problems may be developmental: the two comma splices, the substitution of "then" for "than," the missed -ed ending on "harrify," the misunderstanding of the two-word subordinator "even if," the use of the past perfect instead of the present perfect in the penultimate sentence, and the verb phrase "must had." (This confusion is compounded by the fact that *must* is a highly irregular modal: the past tense of *must*, in the sense of obligation, is *had to.*) Nevertheless, the readers to whom I showed this essay agreed that its errors are of the sort that do not interfere with its comprehensibility and that can be cleared up fairly easily in revision, an activity Mimi had willingly engaged in over the semesters.

More significant is the texture and authority of the essay: the writer's sure movement between lesson and evidence; her sense of purpose, closure, and indelible detail. Mimi had once seen an image of herself in Lee, the girl who was different, who wouldn't talk. Over the course of several semesters and numerous essays, she found her voice.

In our interview in 1984, Mimi, like so many ESL students, expressed impatience with what she characterized as her slow progress in English. She talked about her current English 110 assignment, an essay on *The Elephant Man*, in terms of how differently she would approach the task in her native language. "I have to say things in a different way in English, to convince my teacher that I'm smart in spite of all my grammar errors," she explained. "My thoughts are much more complex in Chinese; in English, I just don't have enough words. And I don't like to put things so elementarily."

Postscript, January 10, 1989

Real-life chapters are untidy and open-ended. The preceding discussion was written for the most part in 1985, with an update on motivation research of the last few years. In preparing this manuscript for publication, I wanted to chat with Mimi Soo once more, to see how she was getting on and whether she could offer further comments on her former experiences in English composition class. For I had learned she had again dropped out of school, and it seemed to me that this stage of her academic career must be noted in the interests of a more realistic picture of the waxing and waning of an adult learner's motivation. Then too, I wanted to see the progress—or attrition—of her oral production of the language since our conversation in 1984, when I had noted such an extraordinary leap from her oral and written discourse the year before.

So Mimi came to tea last week, and stayed for a couple of hours, and allowed me to record our conversation, which I reproduce below with little deleted save a few repetitions and my own occasional interjected questions. I have earlier mentioned the very valid reservations some researchers have expressed concerning self-report as a means of analysis, though much of the research on affective variables depends on self-report questionnaires. As you read Mimi's comments you will be aware, as Mimi herself notes, of the ways in which retrospection blurs events, causes, and effects. The powerful motives of rationalization and self-justification or self-flattery; the rampant influence of self-help lingo in the 1980s; the effects of the observer and the uncontrolled and informal environment of the interview; the fluctuating enthusiasms and distractions of the intervening years: these are some of the mitigating circumstances of such testimonials.

Still I offer Mimi's words for their insight as well as for their amplification of many of the statistical findings reported in this chapter. Oller (1981, 24) has remarked of the research linking achievement in second language to affective variables, "the conclusions of the theorists are no more nor less empirically secure than the measures of affect are valid." In the preceding paragraph I have noted rather apologetically the uncontrolled environment of my interview with Mimi, but it might just as easily be argued that these same circumstances enabled the subject to expatiate on her own motives in ways not engendered in labs or classrooms. Obviously I have thought it important throughout this book to augment the quantitative research on record with qualitative and anecdotal data, with vertical studies of individual learners, with whole pieces of discourse and longer texts, as opposed to short answers on questionnaires. The results may be less quantifiable, but judging from the contradictions of the relevant research, not much less reliable.

About five minutes into our chat I showed Mimi the essay she had written entitled "Who Am I?" She stared at it intently for a time, and then began,

"I just broke out in a sweat, just looking at this paper. You remember that commercial, 'You've come a long way, baby?' I recall that feeling, yes; when I look back, and see something that reminds me of my past, and who I've become today, I feel very strongly about that. I don't think a person change from one characteristic to the other, I mean you don't give it up, it's in you somewhere; you choose not to be that way. You don't forget that; you're still like that somehow, but you choose not to use that as an instrument of life. So when I read this again, it was just, 'oh—that was me!'

"When I went back to school my two girls were 9 and 10. Until that time I had always debated it in my mind—should I, shouldn't I, should life be this way, should I be more daring? I had questions then, when I was looking at the photograph I describe in this essay—I think my girls were about 5 and 6 at the time—but it took me the longest time to decide what I should do, because I was always concerned about what a wife or mother should be. So you sort of deny your own feelings and desires. When I saw that picture, I knew that that's not the person I want to be. And I knew: time to change.

"To define 'wife' and 'mother' was the hardest thing for me, because I did not grow up with my mother; my parents divorced, and I grew up with my grandmother, Popo. So I don't know how a mother should be. And that's very hard for my own mother, because I always think a mother should be perfect, and that's the role I've been trying to play, when I had my own kids. It was very hard for me; I almost had to give up everything, to a point that I didn't know myself anymore. So that's why didn't have myself: I devoted myself to my husband and my children.

"These papers were written at a particular point in my life. If I would have to take the course again, would I write something like this? I probably would, because I shared this information with my own children—because I want them to understand me, I want them to know me as a person. For their early life, I tried to be a perfect mother, until one day my daughter said to me, 'Mommy, you're so perfect.' That scared the hell out of me, so from that moment on, I didn't want them to see me as a perfect person. I am not. I am experienced; if I did something right [it was] because I was experienced, I learned from my mistakes. This was a period of great change in my life.

"When I went back to school, my kids were in second and third grade. I remember Angela announced to the whole class that her Mommy's going back to school. My kids and husband were very supportive. Going back to school of course is very typical of the Western world; in Taiwan you don't have this kind of opportunity. You might go back to take a course in how to plant flowers, but you don't really go back to school to have that kind of improvement. You want to know why I went back to school. I always regretted that I did not graduate from college. Having a college degree was the biggest thing in my life at that point. I still did not graduate. But it doesn't mean as much as before. Then, I guess, I didn't have confidence in me. I didn't know who I am. I thought by having a paper or some kind of a 'visa stamp' on you, then you're OK, you are a smart girl, person, you'll be recognized. I think all my life I wanted to be recognized.

"I used to work for my husband; he published a Chinese daily newspaper. I worked in the editorial department, took advertising, that kind of thing. But I wanted to go out on my own. I started a clothing store with a partner on the Upper West Side, and then sold my shares to him. I decided that having a boutique was not enough for me, and I wanted to go back to school. At that point I was very interested in myself: I wanted to know who I am. So I thought if I were going to college, I would learn the language better, and I want to take up psychology. There are so many things I don't understand about human beings, how they act, their reasons for doing things. I wanted to understand because I don't want to be a victim any more. I feel that, I felt that I was a victim, because of my parents' situation, their separation. I felt that my life was so tough: I had to move to the States, learn a different language. I left my father in Taiwan, to come here, to have, I don't know, a better life? A better future for myself.

"When I came to Queens College, I definitely had a career in mind: I wanted to help other women. I wanted to be able to understand them; I wanted to run some kind of a social work program, so I could help other women to recognize themselves, to bring them out in the open so that they can grow, as well as how I found myself growing. That was the biggest thing on my mind at that time. I still haven't given up that goal. At some point in my life I'd like to work with battered women in Chinese society. Maybe I understand them better now. If you don't have self-esteem, you bring certain behaviors on yourself. After a while it becomes a process of conditioning, like learning to like alcohol or spicy food: maybe after a while the pain feels good."

[Looks at the journal entry about her embarrassment in her music class] "Ah! I didn't understand what he was saying in class, so I flipped through the notes in the back of the book. Maybe he thought I wasn't paying attention to his lecture, but he really embarrassed me. I had very mixed feelings about this. One was that I was a victim again—'why pick on me, I'm trying my best to learn your subject?' Maybe if he would take the time to know his student better, he would give me the benefit of the doubt. And the other feeling was that I was greater than him, because he was pitiful to act this way—to have to humiliate a student in front of the class. In Taiwan, I don't think this would happen. We're more reserved in public, which is both good and bad. For this teacher to react that way, he must be very unhappy in a certain area, but he's expressing his anger, it might be on me, or on somebody else, but it's a relief for him. But you don't see that in Taiwan, or in the ancient societies: they held back. They might be very unhappy, but they don't pick on you; instead they're beating on themselves.

"That first semester, I also took chemistry, and a basic English class [CESL 31]. I had a very strict teacher. I probably concentrated too much on a perfect sentence, rather than what I wanted to say. If you want to write an essay, of course the sentence structure is important, and you have to make people understand you're talking about the past or the future or whatever. But my own feeling is if I had stayed with just the grammar, I would not get anywhere with it. I would be a very rigid storyteller, because I want to restrict myself in a certain area. If I would just take that course, I don't think I would ever pass [the WAT], because I think English is a very imaginative subject. For you to become interested in writing or whatever, the teacher has to be able to draw things from the student. With this teacher, grammar, you know, past tense, past perfect, that was good; but with the other English teacher [Bonnie MacDougall Ray], I tell a story first, and then I go back to correct my grammar. You have to want to communicate. Dr. MacDougall brought things out from you, and that makes it interesting for you to learn. The essays . . . she would have us read something, and then we would talk about what we had read. I remember one story about a mirror in the shape of a boat, or—that symbolized something, which I don't remember! There was a story about the Chinese girl who couldn't talk [from The Woman Warrior]. There was another essay about an immigrant family live in a one-room apartment, and they were describing the tables, the furniture—it makes you think twice about things. You take a lot of things for granted, about the way a cushion is shaped, or what color it is, [but] I like things like that. It worked for me. It did not work for a lot of students—they don't care what shape this chair is, or what color—but for me it works.

"In Taiwan I was not an extraordinary student. I had never written before, not like this. In Taiwan we wrote compositions once a week on the subjects they gave us, like 'Who's your favorite person,' 'Whom do you admire,' 'What do you think of the Olympics, or a particular athlete,' you know, 'Write about your mother'—very simple topics. I'm sure you were allowed to write very personal things, or critical things, but I don't think that's done. We very seldom wrote about ourselves. I don't think I ever did. In 105, I enjoyed writing, and I wrote a lot in my journal. Frankness, that's a nice thing that I think is the American way: to recognize the truth, and say it, don't make excuses. Shall I tell you something? Sometimes I used to think that when I wrote so much about my feelings, it was too strong. I thought it was really very cruel to the teacher, too disturbing for the reader. When I was writing, I felt a load lifting from my shoulders. In my essays, as you can see, I learned a powerful lot about me; you don't know it until you're writing it down. And then you say 'Wow,' you know.

"Why did I improve so quickly? There were a number of reasons, but most particularly is that—I don't know who said this—we're all unpolished, we need to be shaped, to be shined, whatever. And I believe everyone has it: you know, knock on the right door, have the right key to open it, and to allow something to come out.

"I read a lot; my husband taught me a lot, to go beneath the surfaces of things. And I travel a lot. As a result of my experience in the class, I definitely read more closely now. I keep in the back of my mind the theme, and how they end the story, how they begin, they trace back: you know, I notice these things, from what I have learned. And that itself is a story, there: how a person tell you a few paragraphs about what is happening now, and then all of a sudden you find that he's talking about 20 years ago. Most of the time I flip back, and I start again because I don't want to lose anything: so that I can understand when the character is talking about now or, when he sees something, he remembers 20 years ago when he saw the same thing, which meant something else to him, you know, and I like that. I definitely reread more than I did years ago.

"I didn't have any friends at school really. Mostly I kept to myself in the class, because most of the other students were younger than me. When I looked at them, I felt for them: they are all struggling so hard, and I felt the pain and frustration they go through, and the embarrassment when they cannot understand what the teacher wants, or how to put down in words. They probably have all the knowledge in their heads, they cannot put down in paper, so when it comes out it's so elementary. And that's so frustrating.

" . . . But the timing was right for me. I was ready. And that answer corresponds to why I quit. You discover yourself; you know what's important to you. At that time entering Queens College, getting a diploma was very important to me. I'm not saying I finished 105 and then discover that getting a diploma is not important! No, that doesn't jump one to the other. But I found that as a person, sometimes you go around in circles, you think that you're getting to the point that you wanted to be. That's how I was: I felt that I was running in circles. I reached my destination; but I didn't think I did. So I needed all these things to support me, like a person would need a house, need a car, need a Mercedes, to support that you are a successful person. I didn't need the diploma to say, 'Hey, Mimi, you're OK.' I began to see myself through the English course. English 105 was like a therapy, like you went to an analyst. I was my own analyst, and went through a lot of obstacles that I tripped over most of my life, that I discovered this didn't have to be there. All my life I wanted recognition, but I realized the recognition is not from somebody else but from myself. So once you know that, you don't need all this approval or these visa stamps—you're there already, you've passed the . . . threshold?

"I liked the history, I learned about Renaissance times, I know about a lot of paintings, through the music class I recognize a lot of pieces by Mozart or Beethoven. Before, it was like, 'it's not enough—there's so much more I don't know,' and forever you're hungry, you're like a dry sponge, you don't have enough water. But later on I discovered that I was happy that I know a piece, I was happy that I recognize something. It's not the things that I don't know, it's the things I know that I'm happy for. So that was a big change for me, as a person, to be more content. Of course I'm sure that I didn't feel that way when I just left school, though after I left school I did feel strong enough to enter another business, a printing shop my husband had shares in, and hang on until I got my shares out. So school gave me a sense of power. Later, I went back into the import-export business with my husband. But from the time I left school until today, I've discovered more. And I think other things in my life, like Buddhism, which I started just two years ago—I was reared as a Catholic—have given me a great sense of peace.

"Now this makes sense at this point in my life. Next year I might find I really would like to find out more about the history, so I might continue school again: you have a different kind of need. But the need is different from when I first went to college. I was so unsatisfied about myself. I was, like, drowning; now, if I would have anything more, it would just add to Mimi. When I wrote this paper ["I used to think going to school was a waste of time"], that was another change in my life. There are many stages. Before it was so dramatic, that I told my kids, 'Don't, don't neglect something or you'll have to go back and finish.' Now I feel, if you do have to go back, that's not so bad! When you know more, you say, 'So you go back—what's the big deal?'

"I've just turned 40, and I told my husband that he should start looking for someone to replace me in the business, that I'm coming out. I want to start something, a business, on my own. I still have this feeling, from time to time, of victim; like I said, I don't think a person really changes that much—I mean, to forget. I know that feeling is there, but I don't want to touch it. I know it, I know when it's coming, and I say goodbye to it. You grow. I think when you publish a book about how one becomes a woman, what makes a woman—something about a woman—these essays will probably be more useful than how a person progresses in English. Do you think so?"

6

Some "Japanese" and "American" Rhetorical Preferences

Prologue: A "Dialogue on Language"

Here is the first draft of a description written by Hiroyuki Araseki for an introductory composition course:

A Good Neighbor Is Better Than a Relative Afar Off

Two days ago, he came over to our house with a basketful 1
of apples. He said that his daughter had gone to pick up apples.
His name is Joe; he lives right in front of our house.

He is about 5 feet 7 inches in height, his shoulders some- 2
what narrow and a little stooped, his weight about 140 pounds.
He is fifty years old and the color of his hair is changing into
gray. But perhaps because he is short and skinny, he looks
younger than he actually is.

It is a habit with him to say, "you know," when he talks, as 3
many people in this country do. But unlike most Americans, he
doesn't use gestures very much. He speaks rather fast; however,
his voice sounds very soft despite his rapid speaking. He gazes at
me when I talk to him. He never opens his mouth until I finish
what I am saying, even though I often have to take time to think
about what I want to say. He knows how to be patient with a
poor speaker in English.

I have never seen him wearing a suit except on his daugh- 4
ter's wedding day. He usually wears a polo shirt or T shirt and
jeans even when he goes to work. He is a welder, and he teaches
welding twice an week at an institute in Brooklyn. I wonder if the
students in his class understand him, for as I have told you, he
speaks very gently.

He has two sons and three daughters. One of his daughter 5
has gotten married recently. He had wanted to buy a new car before her wedding. We went to a car dealer to take a look at some
of the cars he had on his mind. But after his daughter's marriage,

149

he has never talked about getting a new car. He must have spent the money he had saved for a car on the wedding.

His other daughter lives separately. She has delivered a 6 baby. Whenever she visits Joe with her baby, he comes over to our home with his granddaughter in his arms. We say, "She resembles you very much and cute!" Imagine what kind of face he makes; he has fallen in love with his granddaughter.

Sometimes he comes to our home with his wife to spend 7 spare time, they chat for a while and leave. I could say he is nothing but an avarage man; you will see a person like him no matter where you may be. Still, he is something special to us. We enjoy having him as our neighbor.

This chapter and the next will examine the written performances of Japanese students of English like Hiro Araseki in light of the controversial question of comparative rhetoric. The present chapter provides sociolinguistic background that will, I hope, illuminate the longer student texts discussed in the chapter that follows. Here I will be highlighting certain features of Japanese language, mores, art, and education, but ideally the reader should project this material against the backdrop of certain American social conventions and rhetorical expectations, particularly as they are reflected in the syllabi of composition classes around the United States. Allowing for the different emphases and methods of such classes, the range of assignments might include some or all of the following: journals, personal narratives, descriptions, procedural papers, explanations, analyses, and persuasive or argumentative essays. This last rhetorical category, brought to the fore (often with a certain reluctance on the teacher's part) in a number of introductory writing classes in my own department because of our need to prepare students for the agree/disagree format of the CUNY Writing Assessment Test, will be the focus of the chapter to come.

Toward the end of this chapter we will be looking at some of the guidelines of Japanese exposition as described in several representative Japanese textbooks. Perhaps, then, I should begin by stating some general guidelines of English exposition, at least as it is typically depicted in textbooks and frequently taught in American high schools and colleges. Much of the following formula is parody, of course, a matter of prescription rather than description of exposition as it is actually practiced, and one need only glance at any chapter of this or any other book in English to see the rules violated. Still, the emphasis that English speakers, particularly Americans, place on clearly marked and linear structure in our characterizations of exposition is a fair indication of principles enshrined in our discourse. Thus: in English exposition the topic of the essay, typically announced near the beginning of the text, is broken down into a series of subtopics or perspectives, each supported by examples and illustrations. The main point of each paragraph is generally related to the thesis of the essay. A paragraph is usually defined through a uniform orientation, its subject established early on in the paragraph. Expository paragraphs often have a hierarchical structure, either progressing deductively from important topic information to smaller and more specific details, or inductively from a series of details to a general statement that draws them together.

I certainly do not wish to hold Hiro Araseki's lovely essay, nor indeed any essay, to these martinet standards of organization. But since the perspectives of the paragraphs in Hiro's paper seem rather more loosely connected than American readers are led to expect, I would like to examine the ways in which these perspectives might be related. The paragraphs deal with Joe's appearance (paragraph 2), his speech patterns (3), his dress and his job (4), the car-hunting incident and his daughter's recent marriage (5), his love affair with his granddaughter (6), his visits to the author's home, and the author's feeling toward him (7). Although the thesis of the essay (as in many descriptive pieces) is unstated, upon finishing the essay we recognize how the theme is obliquely suggested in the first and last paragraphs, and in the title of the piece. Our realization of Hiro's point—Joe, an average man, once a stranger, has because of his gentleness and generosity become a special neighbor—allows us to return to the essay with a better sense of how its parts fit together.

Apart from repeated pronoun reference to Joe, whose name appears only in paragraph 1, the transitions that provide the essay with some surface cohesion are not difficult to sort out. After Joe is introduced and described in the first two paragraphs, the remaining paragraphs dovetail through Hiro's repetition of key phrases. Joe's soft voice, mentioned in paragraph 3, is heard again in the following paragraph; the occasion of his daughter's wedding comes up in paragraph 4 and again introduces paragraph 5; Joe's other daughter, mentioned at the opening of paragraph 5, introduces paragraph 6; Joe's visits to the author's home, alluded to in paragraph 6, provide the link with the essay's conclusion in paragraph 7.

Interestingly enough, though, these linking phrases may not be the elements of the portrait that the author wishes to emphasize, nor do they necessarily announce, even when they appear in the initial sentence of the paragraph, what the paragraph is about. We might say that the focal point of paragraph 3 is not Joe's soft voice but rather the way he listens attentively, patiently, to the author's halting English. Paragraph 4 brings up the daughter's wedding to underscore by contrast Joe's working man's attire, and mentioning Joe's job allows the author at the conclusion of the paragraph to imagine how difficult it might be for Joe's students to understand his gentle speech. The wedding is mentioned again in the following paragraph as a way of getting into the car search, the point of which is the author's inference that Joe, although he never talked about the car again, must have spent the car money on the wedding. Referring to Joe's other daughter allows Hiro to talk about Joe's love for his granddaughter, and, just as important, to let us know that Joe brings the child to the author's home. In the concluding paragraph, Joe is again shown visiting Hiro's home. It is here that the author articulates for the first time his feelings toward his subject: I could say Joe is an average man, but he is special to us; we enjoy having him as our neighbor. We can now see that the conclusion simply spells out the themes that have been intimated in the essay's introduction, where we are told that Joe visited the other day, bearing a modest gift, and that he lives nearby.

If not the repeated linking phrases, is there something else that holds this essay together, some underlying concept other than the repeated demonstrations of Joe's unassuming generosity and love for family and friends? I believe there is, though the connections are implicit rather than stated. Joe, however unremarkable he might seem to other observers, is in the author's estimation somehow set apart from his countrymen. He is rather small and slight, and "unlike most Americans" keeps his gestures to a minimum. He never interrupts or hurries a poor speaker of English, and speaks so softly that the author wonders if Joe's American students can understand him. In his occasional visits or "chats" with the author, Joe remains silent on the subject of his own feelings—his disappointment about the car, his family pride, his love for his grandchild (though that love is apparent in his expression). It remains for the author to read and interpret what Joe is silently communicating, and so Hiro's essay proceeds by observation, suggestion, inference, speculation. It appears that Joe is different from other Americans, but very like his Japanese friend, so much so that Hiro in the title of the essay pays him the ultimate compliment: Joe is a close neighbor, something better than a distant relative. If you have read any literature about the Japanese, you are aware of the distance they maintain from those outside their own culture, and you know what a tribute Hiro's essay is meant to be.

Readers of Hiro's essay might point out with justification that many native students' essays similarly lack thesis statements and exhibit the same loosely structured paragraph units, especially in an assignment such as the descriptive essay, in which there is no obvious chronology on which to rely. What I wish to investigate in this chapter and the next is the proposition that the values implied in Hiro's esteem for his subject, as well as his nondirective, elliptical descriptive method, are indicative of certain social and linguistic preferences in his native culture, which often differ from our own in this country.

The question of cultural contrasts in rhetorical styles—and, by extension, patterns in thinking and valuation—has received some critical attention over the years. The matter merits closer examination, since it calls up fundamental questions about our aims and methods in teaching writing to nonnative speakers. Are there, in fact, recognizable national styles of oral and written discourse? There is plentiful evidence that certain national preferences in rhetoric do in fact exist, and much of the discussion in the following pages is devoted to description of these tendencies as they are manifested in Japan. It is a far more difficult matter, however, to document how or indeed whether ESL learners carry over first-language rhetorical structures into English, and I shall only move timidly, anecdotally into this terrain at the end of Chapter 7. As I have indicated earlier, I believe only a weak form of the contrastive rhetoric hypothesis can be supported. The fact that different cultures often do favor different rhetorical structures and strategies does not predict the form a given ESL student's expository paper will take, any more than it enables us to read an essay "blind" and determine with any certainty the writer's country of origin. But knowledge of various cultural systems should deepen our own reading and teaching, and help us to make sense, after the fact, of certain departures a student makes from the forms of exposition most frequently taught in English classes in American colleges.

Please note that I have ventured to advance this "soft" form of the hypothesis on the safest possible ground: I have chosen examples from the writing of Japanese students, for as we know from the considerable and growing body of work written on the Japanese, particularly on the contrast between Japanese and American educational systems, theirs is an extraordinarily homogeneous culture. This cultural uniformity has been fostered by several interlocking conditions: by geographical isolation, strengthened through centuries of self-imposed isolation from Asia and the rest of the world during the Edo period; by Japanese nationals' much-discussed sense of their own uniqueness; and by their extremely strong patterns of group organization. I shall consider the effects of these conditions on discourse further on in this chapter. Ultimately I want to focus on a rhetorical activity that seems to me to highlight most emphatically the difference between Japanese and American cultures, the matter of that time-honored tradition in Western discourse, argumentation.

I am mindful of the misleading reductivism of such cultural contrasts. This binary view is fostered as much by the Japanese concept of *Nihonjin-ron*—the *uniqueness* of Japanese culture—as by Western contrastive linguistic studies. One sees this dialectic rehearsed in Heidegger's "Dialogue on Language [between a Japanese and an Inquirer]," the text of which, Heidegger notes, originated in conversations during 1953–1954 with a colleague from Tokyo's Imperial University. The dialogue presents European discourse as hermeneutical and insistently rationalist, as opposed to the Japanese privileging of stillness and the radiance of the unsayable. The Japanese speaker remarks that in his culture's "encounter with European thinking, there has come to light a certain incapacity in our language. . . . It lacks the delimiting power to represent objects related in an unequivocal order above and below each other" (2). The two speakers proceed to expatiate on the link between lexical and grammatical forms and rhetorical constructs. According to the Japanese observer, "We Japanese do not think it strange if a dialogue leaves undefined what is really intended, or even restores it back to the keeping of the undefinable" (13). This comfort with indeterminacy is contrasted with Western need for closure and what Heidegger characterizes as "greed for explanations."

Each speaker's essentialist critique of his own culture may strike the reader as a bit disingenuous, even self-serving. In the same way, the principles and preferences of "national" styles of exposition may become reified in our thinking and teaching. Ironically, through his evasiveness and irresolution, his denigration of reason in favor of wise passivity, Heidegger reveals in this dialogue on difference many affinities with his Japanese interlocutor, a kinship noted by the Japanese gentleman himself. Thus we are indirectly reminded that any characterization of Western models of exposition must also make room for the "otherness" of Heidegger, as well as for the disorderly baroque digressions of Montaigne and the aphoristic style of Emerson's later essays, which habitually omit the connectives of "logical" discourse. I merely cite these examples to complicate the model guidelines of Western linear discourse described at the opening of this chapter.

Moreover, as we have seen in earlier chapters, dialogues have a way of breaking down essentialist positions and bringing speakers closer together. Heidegger's Japanese visitor predicts that "modern technicalization and industrialization" will force the Japanese to adopt more "European" conceptual systems; and indeed a few examples of this phenomenon will be presented further on in this chapter. Reciprocally, Westerners' increasing contact with Japan has lately given rise in countless books and articles to reevaluation of the assumptions on which our own commercial and educational institutions are founded. I would like to examine the question of cultural difference, then, with these observations of cultural fluidity in mind.

Linguistic Patterns

Before looking at longer pieces of discourse written by Japanese-born students of English, I want to back up for a moment to examine a few English sentences produced by a Japanese student. It is comparatively easy to see how a student's native culture, combined with the exigencies of writing in a second language not yet mastered, may influence aspects of his written performance such as grammar, spelling, and diction. The following illustrations come from impromptu work produced by Seiichi Masuda[1] in an English 105 class. Again, and by way of reinforcing my comments with respect to rhetoric, I should reiterate the "weak" form of the contrastive analysis of grammar error: the errors illustrated below are by no means the exclusive province of Japanese speakers of English, nor are all Japanese speakers bound to make them. A brief survey of certain properties of languages other than English simply helps us as teachers to read ESL papers more attentively and to clarify our explanations of English grammar for speakers of a given linguistic group.

In Japanese, nouns are not marked for number, and accordingly, the language, like Chinese and Russian, lacks exact equivalents for the English articles *a(n)* and *the*. Nor do Japanese verbs inflect for person or number. You will find several noun and verb inflection errors in the examples below. Another significant feature of the Japanese verb system is that the verbs in

---

[1]Because errors alone are being singled out here, the student's name has been changed.

the main and subordinate clauses of a sentence need not agree in tense, even if the actions or states described occur simultaneously. This is perhaps why Seiichi writes,

> Although I *tried* to convince her it *is* stupid for me to spend
> so much money, I could not help postphoning the wedding. . . .

Notice that in this sentence Seiichi has eliminated the relative word *that* (as in "to convince her that it was stupid . . . "). Of course in English the word is optional in this case; but much of Seiichi's work shows recurring difficulty with relative pronouns and conjunctions such as *who, whom, whose, which, that,* and *where,* presumably because his own language lacks functional equivalents for these words. In Japanese, relative clauses directly precede the head noun, unaccompanied by relative pronouns or conjunctions. Here are a few examples from Seiichi's work of errors resulting from misunderstanding of the usage of relative words and clauses:

> When I was sixteen, I went to north part of Japan, where is
> about one thousand miles away from home, by myself.

> In early spring, I heard the sounds which the mountain was
> awaking from the long sleep of winter.

(In this next example, Seiichi replaces the relative pronoun + verb with an infinitive modifier of the subject—)

> There are hundreds of proverbs in Japan. Although most of
> them fit to modern life, some of them doesn't fit anymore. There-
> fore there are some common sayings *to be* new proverbs.

In English, as in French and German, sentence structure usually requires an overt subject for finite verbs as well as an object for transitive verbs. In Japanese, however, sentences may have missing subjects, and transitive verbs need not always have objects. In a paragraph I'll quote from more fully later on, Seiichi writes:

> But also it is important how fathers treat sons correctly, not
> how much time they spent with.

According to some linguists, the kind of ellipsis indicated by Seiichi's omission of the pronoun *them* in the above sentence may be traced to the rather free word order of Japanese sentences. Whereas languages such as English, French, and Chinese are so-called SVO (subject-verb-object) languages, Japanese, like Korean, is an SOV language, and the only immutable restriction on the word order of Japanese sentences is that each clause must end in a verb. Most SOV languages are postpositional; that is, all functional relations that English expresses with prepositions and subordinating and coordinating

conjunctions are expressed in Japanese by particles that are postpositional in
the sentence (Kuno 17). Japanese thus has what seems in comparison with
English a less rigid and explicit way of expressing the relationship between
sentence parts. The phenomenon of ellipsis is widespread in Japanese. Omission of subjects and direct objects is common, as is the tendency to leave out
main clause verbals, postpositional particles that identify grammatical relationships, and clear markers that distinguish between direct and indirect
speech. This tendency may tell us something of the way social forms can be
manifested in grammatical conventions, a point I will return to later on.

Apart from these grammatical considerations, a student's lexical choices
are occasionally colored by his or her native language. Before looking at a
revealing example of this phenomenon, we should review a few lexical errors
that might crop up *regardless of* an ESL student's country of origin, or,
alternatively, that have to do with phonetic rather than conceptual differences in languages. We know, to begin with, that Japanese, like Chinese, has
no exact equivalent phoneme for the English /l/, so we can determine the
cause of the following error, which is clearly not a matter of incorrect (though
provocative) word choice but of phonology:

> In fact, I wanted to marry this summer, but I did not want
> to spend a lot of money for it. At the beginning, my parents
> *cerebrate* my luck, however my mother did not allow me to marry
> if I would not spend more than U.S. $50,000 for the wedding.

Obviously, not all lexical errors are attributable to interference from the
native language. The next paragraph, part of which was quoted earlier,
shows the student creating a portmanteau based on what he hears and
understands as the meaning of the word:

> Although I tried to convince her it is stupid for me to spend
> so much money, I could not help *postphoning* the wedding because
> I love my mother. I recognized that some Japanese are still very
> traditional. Right now I don't know if I made right decision that I
> *postphoned* my marriage.

"Postphoned" makes sense—it means "to call off temporarily," after
all. A similar sort of error arises from mishearing the word boundaries of the
term "prime minister" in the following sentence. Note, too, Seiichi's logical
though incorrect application of affixes to create the words "unrespectable"
and "dreamable":

> From my point of view, a driver of the train is *unrespectable*
> job these days; the children could not dream anymore these days.
> There were a lot of them who wanted to be *dreamable* jobs, such as
> a pilot, a *priministor* or an astronot.

On the other hand, certain lexical errors in Seiichi's work have less to do
with phonology or morphology than with the fact that some concepts are not

readily translatable from one culture to another. Years ago, a Japanese student in my native-speaker composition class noted in one of her papers that Japanese sons, although not encouraged to show affection, nevertheless needed a little "skinship." This delightful neologism I took to be my student's private creation. In fact, I recall that when the student read this sentence aloud during her conference with me, my officemate shouted over the thin partition between our desks, "Who's writing poetry in there?"

I have since learned that other Japanese speakers of English employ the same lexical invention. In their use of the word "skinship" these speakers may have in mind several important Japanese concepts for which there are no direct English equivalents. I refer, first of all, to the phrase *hada to hada*, literally "skin to skin," which has been defined as a mutual willingness to expose one's sincerity; and second, to *amae*, a concept that psychologist Takeo Doi considers of primary significance in the personality structure of the Japanese. *Amae* is the noun form of *amaeru*, an intransitive verb that means something like "to be passively dependent on and presume upon another's affection and benevolence." Doi has developed various modifications of Freudian theory based on the concept of *amae*, which he maintains is a universal phenomenon but more visible in Japan, since that country lacks certain cultural proscriptions that conceal the presence of *amae* in the West. In Japan the term is most often used to describe a child's attitude toward his or her parents, particularly toward the mother, but the term is extended by analogy to characterize the protégé/mentor relationships pervasive in most Japanese institutions.

More important to our understanding of "skinship," though related in feeling to the foregoing concepts, is the phenomenon of the constant body contact a Japanese mother maintains with her young child. As one well-known study contrasting maternal care in Japan and America has demonstrated, American mothers spend less time with their infants, emphasize verbal interaction over physical closeness, and have as their goal active and self-assertive babies. Japanese mothers, in contrast, have greater bodily contact with their infants and soothe them toward physical quiescence, passivity, and silence (Caudill and Weinstein 226, 264). These patterns of infant behavior, of course, fall in line with the differing expectations for adult behavior in the two cultures. Later in this chapter I hope to show how such behavioral differences may also be reflected to some degree in our Japanese students' performance in class and on certain written assignments.

It is this last-mentioned concept of continual physical proximity of mother and infant for which, according to one source (Lebra 138), many Japanese speakers of English use the coinage "skinship." It would seem that the Japanese have taken the English word *kinship* and supplied the missing element of necessary and frequent "contact comfort." The coinage appears to have gained currency: I came across the same morphological invention in Seiichi's journal, presumably arising from the writer's need to fill a conceptual and lexical gap between cultures. Here is the paragraph in question, from Seiichi's impressions of the father in Sherwood Anderson's story "I Discover My Father":

> Sometimes father should treat his son differently, I guess.
> From my point of view, skinships between a father and the son is
> very important. But also it is important how fathers treat sons cor-
> rectly, not how much time they spent with. Anyway. I felt very
> sorry about the father. Really he was a nice guy, but the son was
> not the one who loves his father the way he is.

A further word on diction. Writing about the same story in his journal
the next day, Seiichi compares the father in Anderson's narrative to his own
father. His observations suggest how not only his familial relationships but
also his cultural orientation have influenced his interpretation of what he has
read, and the terms in which he casts his opinion:

> As the author wanted something from his father, I wanted
> my father to be like another father. My father is too respectable
> for me to feel like my own father. I used to talk him very politely.
> (I think I still do sometimes.) People, who do not know us, may
> think we (I and my father) are a professor and the student. By the
> way, a professor is a very respectable job in my country.

In Seiichi's paragraph, "respectable" and "politely" have meanings not
precisely translatable in English; or rather, the words are used in roughly the
same contexts in both languages, but are assigned different values. In Japanese these terms have much wider applications. Japanese is well known for
its wealth of grammatical and lexical means for expressing various levels of
respectfulness, although honorific usage in recent years has tended to be
leveled out by the younger generation. There are, to begin with, four levels of
sentence styles to express politeness: informal, polite, superpolite, and formal writing. These patterns apply to all copulative, adjectival, and verb
expressions in Japanese. Actually the four levels of style have less to do with
degrees of respect than with how close the speaker is justified to feel toward
the listener. The informal style, to take an obvious instance, can never be
used when a student addresses a teacher, nor, for that matter, when a young
child addresses his or her father. Furthermore, for each stylistic level there
are two different honorific forms: in the first the speaker expresses respect to
the *subject* of the sentence, whereas in the second the speaker expresses
respect to the *object* of the sentence (Kuno 18–20). So when Seiichi adds
parenthetically that being a professor is a very respectable position in his
country, he is expressing not only what he perceives as the difference in the
relative status of Japanese and American professors, but also the accompa-
nying disparity in forms of address. For these grammatical and lexical ways
of showing respect English has no direct equivalents.

Seiichi's cultural and personal background similarly affect his reading of
another selection, D. H. Lawrence's "The Rocking-Horse Winner." Here
Seiichi responds to the character of the mother in the story, a woman emphatically depicted by Lawrence as cold and obsessively materialistic:

> In a way, Paul's mother was not so unusual woman. There
> are many women like her in middle class. I would not complain
> her.

We may interpret Seiichi's summation of character and his reluctance to
criticize the mother in the story in light of what he has said about his own
family in his journal entries, as well as in view of the kind of respect
accorded (at least publicly) to parents more automatically in Japan than
in the United States. I need hardly point out that this kind of fealty is not
limited to the Japanese. The last time I taught Anderson's "I Discover My
Father" in English 105, several Iranian students became quite upset during
our discussion of the protagonist's ne'er-do-well father. "Why are all American children so critical of their parents?" demanded one young woman.
"In my country, we never say such terrible things about our fathers."

The question of how ESL students may approach literature in English
will be discussed in some detail in the last two chapters of this book. For now
I simply want this brief contrast of grammatical systems and lexicons to pave
the way for a consideration of the more subtle means by which culture
influences the composing process. We have noted several properties of the
Japanese language, but what do these features signify? In contrast to English,
most Japanese nouns, verbs, and even adjectives and adverbs, are nonrecip-
rocal: they are subject to change, depending on the relative status and group
affiliation of speaker and audience. From this observation we may infer that
Japanese speakers develop a strong linguistic bond with the group to which
they belong. And indeed, as virtually every recent article on the Japanese will
attest, the submergence of individual will in order to preserve group harmony is the central fact of their culture.

Further, much—perhaps too much—has been made of the fact that in
an SOV language, especially given the Japanese speaker's reluctance to create
discord, the speaker can always change the verb according to the auditor's
reactions. The topic is thus left open-ended, and the speaker can avoid
imposing his or her own ideas before knowing the listener's feelings (Doi
1974, 24ff.). The fact that negatives come at the end of a Japanese sentence
makes it even easier for the speaker to avoid commitment to a position (Lebra
38). That the Japanese are prone to speak in the transitive mode and to leave
verbs out of sentences altogether suggests to some observers that the Japanese are more process-oriented, more comfortable with ambiguities and
alternatives, than Americans, who tend to focus on "the bottom line" (Pascale and Athos 152).

It is a matter of debate as to whether ambiguity is virtually built into the
Japanese language. Certainly Japanese in its written form is astonishingly
complex. Modern Japanese is an amalgam of two utterly dissimilar elements—the original unwritten Japanese language of 15 centuries ago and
archaic Chinese. Since the sixth century, the Japanese have borrowed thousands—all told, nearly 50,000—of Chinese pictographs, or *kanji*; youngsters
in school today, however, are required to learn "only" around 2,000 charac-

ters. In addition, the Japanese make simultaneous use of two different sets of syllabic phonetic symbols, each set consisting of almost 50 symbols. These symbols are used phonetically for certain words or parts of words, but always in conjunction with Chinese characters. Understandably, the task of learning and remembering this writing system requires great effort and constant reinforcement, as illustrated in the following journal entry from Tatsuya Suzuki, a student who has lived in the United States for four years:

> Today I found out that I am in trouble with my native language, when I went to the Japanese consulate to extend my passport.
>
> Unlike English, we have thousands of letters and characters in our language, which we forget very easily if we do not constantly read and write in Japanese.
>
> When I was asked to fill out the form in the consulate, I was almost panicked, since I could not figure out what was written on the form. Maybe it is because I had not used my language for a long time.
>
> I guess that it is time for me to start reviewing the Japanese language, in order to avoid further trouble when I return to my country.

In conversation, one effect of this extraordinary linguistic complexity is that when a speaker uses one of the many homophones that occur in Japanese, the meaning may not be clear from the context of the utterance. The Japanese are the first to say that vagueness is inherent in their language, whether spoken or written. We have seen how Heidegger's Japanese interlocutor notes a certain "incapacity" of his own language in the dialogue with the West. Similarly, Hajime Nakamura, one of Japan's most distinguished philosophers, has delivered diatribes on his native language's deficiencies as a tool of logical exactness. He points to the difficulty in Japanese of making derivatives that represent abstract nouns, the lack of the relative pronoun *which* to link clause with antecedent, and other such "handicaps" (cited in Miller 116–17).

On the other hand, linguist Roy Andrew Miller dismisses Nakamura's argument as part of the myth of mystery and uniqueness surrounding the Japanese language that is promulgated by the natives themselves. (An extreme example of the ongoing Japanese obsession with *Nihonjin-ron,* or "what it means to be Japanese," is the Japanese best-seller of a few years back written by a physician who argued that the Japanese brain processes certain sounds differently from all other brains.) Along with fellow Japan-watcher Edwin O. Reischauer, Roy Miller insists there is nothing about the Japanese language that prevents clear, logical presentation of ideas if that is what a speaker or writer really wishes. Reischauer notes that when the Japanese want to be clear, as in drafting laws or explaining technological processes, they are as precise as English speakers, while in literary writing they typically opt for a more suggestive, often ambiguous style (1981, 381).

In presenting the two sides of this debate, I should like to keep in mind, here and in the following pages, that key terms of the discourse such as "clear," "logical," and "ambiguous" are more subjective, culturally determined descriptors than American observers' use of them would suggest. They point to notions of objectivity and directness of thought and speech that are fundamental to what might be called our own "American-ron."

The Discourse of "Acceptable Forms"

The issue at hand is a matter of language not as something somehow objectively set apart from the societal values it is used to express, but as a system that is itself irreducibly social in nature. Japanese often find "straight talk" alien and disturbing, an attitude that can be inferred from two Japanese students' notebook entries on the subject of cultural contrasts:

> One thing I like about Americans is that they are very straightforward and they really know how to express themselves. I, brought up in a traditional Japanese family, am sometimes lack of the facial expression of my emotions, which creates misunderstandings between me and Americans. Not only I but also most Asians do not let their feelings show on their faces, so I guess that it must be very hard for Americans to tell how Orientals feel. Some Americans say that our smiles are even mysterious, but it is just because of the way we look. I mean that Oriental people's slanting eyes make their smiles look unfriendly ones.
>
> Once in a while, I am asked if I am angry, even when I am not. My friends say that I look too serious. My answer is always "This is the way I look. What can I do?"
>
> Apart from facial expression, we Japanese really do not talk straightforwardly. Maybe I talk much more frankly than most Japanese people, because I am Americanized. However, I still refuse to come out and say how I feel. I know that all I have to do is to say "yes" or "no" and make everything clear, but sometimes it is hard for me to do it.
>
> Since I live in the States, I should talk more straightforwardly as Americans do in order to avoid misunderstandings and resulting troubles. I should also show my feelings more on my face.
>
> —Tatsuya Suzuki

Some Difference between My Culture and American Culture

> When I first came to America, I was puzzled with the difference between Eastern culture and Western culture; it took time to get used to the difference.
>
> First of all, when people meet for the first time, in America they shake hands each other or just say "Hi! Nice to meet you";

but in my country, they bow all the times. It is necessary and
should be done. The deeper you bow, the better—that means
you express or pay respect to another person. If you don't do
that, people think you are rude and are stigmatized as a out-of-
society. For a little while, I couldn't get rid of that custom when I
see American people because that custome is so strong that it is
very, very difficult not to do it. So to speak, that is the deep, basic
custom in Japanese society.

Second, in Japan we have the faith that not to speak up,
demand and insist your opinion. It is believed to be a virtue to
keep silent and not easily express your feeling outside. We have a
saying: The able eagle hides his nails; which is a direct translation.
As you can imagine, Japanese custome is setting back custom, I
mean, you have to be generous to others. When you need to act,
you show your ability at that point. For example, if you give
present, you'll say "This is a humble present, and might be hard
to please you, but I'd like you to accept if you can." Everything is
like this way. On the other hand, American custom is very direct
and easily express your feeling such as yes or no—very frank and
clear. We try to be ambiguous in every respects not to hurt other's
feeling. I'm really interested in both American Culture and Japanese one and I'd like to pick up good customs from both and
create my own way.

                                                        —Masaaki Ito

Precise, straightforward discourse is deemed undesirable by the Japanese, who prefer instead to rely on "acceptable forms" in navigating the
straits of social intercourse. Observers of Japanese culture have remarked
on the pervasive concept of *hanashi-kata*, the conviction that there are specific words and phrases to express what is required in any given situation
if only the speaker is aware of the right forms—such as the formal response Masaaki Ito cites in his journal entry to show the proper form for
gift-giving in Japanese. Note that Japanese speakers do not attempt to mod-
ify these expressions, but instead must reproduce them verbatim once they
become aware of the nuances of a particular social situation. This information must be acquired passively; the speaker who asks what the appropriate forms are risks rebuke and loss of face, for himself and for the supe-
riors and contemporaries responsible for fostering his social awareness. Thus
Japanese are taught to remain silent until the suitable response comes to
them.

It should be clear by now that different speech communities prefer
different strategies for manipulating language. These dissimilarities in turn
may lead learners to produce inappropriate speech or writing when they
attempt to transfer native conventions to their second language. For example,
it has been shown that native Hebrew speakers are apt to use more direct
ways of making requests than English speakers. The conventional way of
asking street directions in Hebrew, for instance, is the structural equivalent of
the English phrase "Where is the . . . ?", whereas English speakers in most

cases will use a less direct form such as "Can you tell me where . . . ?" (Blum-Kulka). Similarly, researchers have found that in role-playing, native speakers of Hebrew are less likely than English speakers to express apologies in a variety of social situations (Cohen and Olshtain). According to the same principle of cultural variation, it will come as no surprise that Japanese speakers find many more occasions for formulaic apologies and thanks than English speakers. Moreover, as Loveday (1982) has noted, the Japanese tend to transfer to English these ceremonial formulae.

This emphasis on stock expressions and behavior patterns in Japanese culture contrasts with the verbal disposition of English speakers, particularly Americans. In this country we tend to view language primarily as a tool of personal communication—regardless of the respective social positions of the speaker and audience—and to prize sincerity, novelty, and creativity in a speaker's response to social occasions such as those mentioned above. It has been postulated that the influence of *hanashi-kata* can inhibit Japanese students of English as a foreign language. One instructor of English in Japan maintains that students grounded in the concept of *hanashi-kata* can be expected to place less emphasis on grammar than on amassing vocabulary, memorizing set expressions, and investigating social nuances. In keeping with their cultural training, he finds, Japanese students tend to be passive in their acquisition of these forms and to remain silent when in doubt. They are likely to forgo oral practice until they feel they have mastered a particular form (Bowers).

On the subject of cultural differences in classroom demeanor, it is worth adding here that the Japanese have quite different expectations from Americans for oral scholastic discourse. In academic lectures, native speakers in the U.S. typically try to establish eye contact with some of their auditors, thereby inviting a nod of acknowledgment or an occasional question. Japanese lecturers, in contrast, tend to look over the heads of the audience; listeners do not register reactions to what is said, nor interrupt, even for necessary clarification of a point (Hinds 1976, 48–49). Thomas Rohlen reports that during a year of field work in Japanese high schools in the mid-1970s, the classes he observed usually took the form of lectures, rarely interrupted by class discussion. Few teachers solicited students' opinions on matters of interpretation, and on only one occasion, clearly anomalous, did students (at Nada, one of Japan's top schools) engage in classroom debate on the relative merits of several viewpoints (34, 20).

Thus, according to a recently published report by the U.S. Department of Education, Japanese youngsters have great difficulty readjusting when they return home from the United States, for they no longer display traditional patterns of behavior expected in the Japanese classroom. Children returning from the States tend to express themselves too adamantly, since self-assertion, rather than group harmony, is the norm in the American classroom (Dorfman 3). As a result, to reinforce Japanese socialization patterns, as well as to maintain the somewhat higher scholastic standards set by the Japanese educational system, the great majority of Japanese students living overseas and enrolled in American schools also attend Japanese-language schools after hours and on weekends.

Having noted examples of the influence of the nonnative student's culture on sentence formation as well as on appropriateness of behavioral and speech acts, we might now see more clearly how the same forces might shape that student's approach to written discourse. The two writers whose journal entries are quoted on pages 161 and 162 are commenting on a mode of behavior, but surely they tell us as well about a characteristic way of perceiving and of imparting information. Both students point to what they see as essential elements of the Japanese way of communicating: passivity, ambiguity, reserve, indirection.

Such communicative and aesthetic choices have traditionally informed not only the literary but the visual arts in Japan. We have seen how Japanese grammar features ellipsis, and how Japanese culture valorizes the role of silence. Similarly, traditional Japanese painting, shaped by early contact with Chinese culture, is suggestive rather than explicit in method. One of the earliest formulations of a Japanese theory of painting (as independent from Chinese painting[2]) appears in the work of the seventeenth-century court painter, Tosa Mitsuoki, who writes,

> If you are handling a poetic theme, do not describe it in detail,
> but leave its meaning unsaid. A blank space is also part of the pic-
> ture; leave white space and fill it with unspoken meaning. Foreign
> painting is like prose; Japanese painting is like poetry (quoted in
> Makoto Ueda 139).

In other words, the Japanese painter should merely hint at, and so inspire the spectator to reach for meaning. This spareness of expression has often been noted in the other arts of Japan, whether the haiku's "breach of meaning," to use Roland Barthes' term, the shorthand of Noh drama, or the absence of clutter in traditional Japanese furnishings. That the Japanese favor the elliptical over the explicit is again evident in their criticism of Akira Kurosawa's films as too "Western," too direct, in narrative technique.

Consider, too, the premise on which Japanese gardens (as opposed to European formal gardens) are fashioned: each landscape is designed to be enjoyed from many points of view. The designer leads visitors to stop at

---

[2]As David Pollack points out in *The Fracture of Meaning: Japan's Synthesis of China from the Eighth Through the Eighteenth Centuries*, the Japanese have traditionally "constructed" their culture in terms of its similarities to and differences from *their perception of* Chinese culture. To this crucial dialectic the Japanese have given the name *wakan*.

To illustrate the concept of *wakan*, Pollack cites, among many other examples, the eighteenth-century Japanese scholar Motoori Norinaga's commentary on Japan's first extant text (written in Chinese script), The *Kojiki* (A.D. 712). Norinaga characterizes "Chinese mentality" as dependent on "Chinese logic," the tendency of Confucian or Buddhist thinkers to consider philosophical or religious and moral instruction the ultimate purpose of writing. Further, Norinaga contrasts the "Chinese ornateness" of synonym-laden lexicon and style with the "simplicity" of the classical Japanese lexicon, in which the same word is used frequently in different contexts to mean several different things (44–47).

intervals, perhaps at the edge of a pool or an embankment, so that each can catch a glimpse of some unexpected vista. The point is to guide individuals to a spot where they can discover something for themselves. Analogously, as Makoto Ueda observes, in writing *about* aesthetic theory, the Japanese tend to favor the metaphorical over the analytical, the impressionistic over the rationalistic (225). Compare the quality of suggestiveness in Japanese art with the emphatic representationalism that has been the overriding legacy of American art, from its early portraiture to indigenous nineteenth-century schools of landscape painting to present-day movements such as the "new" realism and the hyperliteral photorealism. Faithful rendering of the material world, the most obvious and consistent characteristic of American painting, seems to reflect the nature of a practical-minded people, rooted in what we call the empirical world of concrete perception.

I offer this cursory and superficial contrast of Japanese and American art to point up what seem to me significant differences in the way the roles of artist or writer and audience are generally conceived in Japanese and English exposition. English exposition places emphasis on the responsibility of the writer to clarify his or her points through marked transitional phrases and coherent sequence. According to Japanese aesthetic theory, conversely, the burden lies equally with the reader to supply missing transitions and determine the (often inexplicit) relationship of a given part of the essay to the whole. What enables the reader to do so, of course, is precisely that homogeneity of culture, of tacit values and assumptions shared by writer and reader, which is everywhere apparent in Japanese culture. Robert Kaplan has remarked that much of "Asian" writing in general is marked by an "approach by indirection," in which statement is implicit, never insistent. I believe that Kaplan's observation—that Asian writers as a group tend to circle around a subject to show it from a variety of tangential views—is an assumption more clearly substantiated in what we have observed of Japanese culture than in the case of other, geographically dispersed and more diverse Asian groups.

In *The Japanese Mind*, Robert Christopher describes this stylistic phenomenon, forcibly impressed upon him when he was asked to assemble a team of non-American columnists for the international edition of *Newsweek* magazine:

> . . . virtually all the Japanese journalists and academics whose
> work I considered approached the task of making a point some-
> what the way my dog approaches his bed: they would circle com-
> pulsively around and around their central—but unstated—idea
> and then, just as they seemed about to settle down and spit it
> out, would abruptly veer away and wander off again at a tangent
> (180).

Christopher's impressions are seconded by another journalist of my acquaintance. Andrew Tanzer has lived in Japan for several years and serves

as Tokyo bureau chief for *Forbes* magazine, after having worked for three
years at the *Far Eastern Economic Review* in Taipei. His comments during a
recent conversation are worth quoting at length, I think, for their informal
elaboration of some of the sociolinguistic studies cited in this chapter, as well
as for what they tell us about Japanese expository patterns:

> Several variables affect what I'd call the "Japanese" style of
> writing prose. To begin with, the way the Japanese use language
> *in speech* is the opposite of the way English speakers try to express
> themselves. You're not supposed to be direct, or clear; you're sup-
> posed to be evasive and subtle.
>
> As far as the way writing is taught in the schools: Japanese
> methods of education and writing instruction are very different
> from those in the West. You're not supposed to be critical or ana-
> lytical. Of course, the Japanese like to say this about themselves:
> that they're not rational.
>
> There are other, more specific variables affecting newspaper
> writing. To begin with, the papers are not independent from the
> government. The system is the ultimate in pack journalism, be-
> cause the competitors (those who work for different mass-circula-
> tion dailies, along with representatives from the TV networks and
> major magazines) actually set up and conduct interviews together,
> discuss stories together at the end of the day. Every Ministry and
> company is covered in what are called "reporters' clubs," most of
> which don't allow foreign reporters and exclude representatives of
> the more independent intellectual publications as well as the scan-
> dal sheets that are liable to write about more volatile material.
> Anyone who disobeys the rules by writing about something sensi-
> tive or provocative is kicked out of the club and has less access to
> the "news."
>
> Apart from the political constraints on the newspapers, the
> articles themselves are often incomprehensible to English readers
> in terms of order and structure. I remember when I wrote the
> cover story for *Forbes* last year [July, 1987] called "The Land of the
> Rising Billionaires," about how in Japan the rich are getting richer
> while the middle class is disappearing: every Japanese newspaper
> attacked my piece the next day. I read these articles carefully, and
> they all seemed incoherent to me. They were completely emo-
> tional diatribes, lashing out; I would ask Japanese acquaintances
> to explain the authors' arguments, but they couldn't. Each article
> was an expression of anger, but without any real "logic" to it, so
> you could punch holes in each one. The writers, to an American
> reader, anyway, seemed to make false and unsupportable as-
> sumptions.
>
> Of course Japanese reporters are more overworked than
> American reporters; they have to write more stories and probably
> receive less editorial help. But at times I've read newspaper arti-
> cles in which I didn't know what the story was about—even
> some of my Japanese friends have noted that occasionally you get

to the end of the story without really knowing what the point is. I suppose the same thing sometimes happens with *Forbes* articles! Still, American news stories usually have a "lead," whereas the subject of the item need not appear in the first paragraph of a Japanese story. And if you're looking for transitions: they're often just absent. You don't know how the writer got from one paragraph to the other; it's like a synapse (telephone interview conducted October 22, 1988).

A sidelight is in order here: Tanzer is currently studying the Japanese language intensively in a school in Yokohama, and so was able to comment on Japanese methods of language instruction. Since this chapter and the next consider how the training of Japanese students in their own country affects their experiences in American schools, I'd like to quote Tanzer's observations of how the notion of *hanashi-kata* comes into play in the Japanese classroom:

> I've taken a brief leave of absence to improve my Japanese by attending the Stanford (or Inter-University) Center in Yokohama full time. Naturally all the teachers are Japanese. I'm learning now in class how to write letters in Japanese. For me it's really frustrating, because the process is the antithesis of the Western notion of originality. It's all set, the format as well as the phrases. Say, in a postcard, you start out by writing about the change of the season. You take a few paragraphs to get into the point of writing, which is, let's say, a thank-you note. You always end by saying again "it's getting cold," or "I hear you're working really hard; make sure you take care of your health," that sort of thing. But it's all fixed. There's no scope for creativity or much variation.
>
> The way for me to think of it and not get frustrated is to say it's all idiomatic. If you translate these phrases into English and think about what they mean, they all seem so artificial. The whole society, the language, has this very elaborate etiquette, which Chinese probably had 2,000 years ago, but no longer has. The Chinese language, in the structure of its sentences, is much closer to English, and not as elliptical. The Chinese have the same Confucian basic education, and the Chinese can also be very evasive in interviews; but they are more liable to ask pointed questions, and they're not nearly as reserved as the Japanese.

The testimonies of journalists like Tanzer and Christopher are corroborated to a great extent by the research of John Hinds, a specialist in Japanese discourse typology. According to Hinds, there is some expressed concern in Japanese expository writing for coherence, clarity, and logic, but a lot of this concern has been imported from Western tradition and does not extend much beyond texts that discuss rhetoric—chiefly because, he maintains, composition is not taught after sixth grade in Japan (1983, 78).

The latter observation is borne out, with minor modification, by the native-speaking Japanese informants still living in Japan with whom I have corresponded. For example, Kazuko Ouchi, a lifelong inhabitant of Tokyo, reports (after a recent survey of the bookstores selling Ministry of Education-approved texts) that the high school-level Japanese language texts currently on the shelves do not take up the teaching of composition. Formal writing instruction seems to leave off at the junior high school level, when most American schools are just beginning to approach the subject (personal communication, February 19, 1989). Further, that composition plays a relatively minor role in Japanese junior high schools may be gauged by the brevity of the composition sections in two standard, currently used eighth-grade textbooks on Japanese language arts. Both books emphasize reading and understanding materials selected from well-known novels, short stories, and criticism; in each book writing lessons appear in one or two brief chapters only.

Let's examine the way these writing lessons are presented. Much of the material cited in the next few pages has been provided by Michiru Arai, a former student of mine in an American literature class, now a graduate student in linguistics. (In the following chapter I will have more to report on Michiru's own progress through the English composition program at Queens.) In interviews conducted in February of 1989, Michiru kindly summarized and translated portions of the composition materials in the two textbooks sent me by Ms. Ouchi: *Gendai no Kokugo* (*Modern Japanese*), 1987, and *Chugakko Kokugo 2* (*Junior High School Japanese, Second Term*), 1987.

The former text contains a composition section on "Expressing Opinions." Yet revealingly, the sample student essay reprinted in this section would strike most readers as an exercise in exposition more than an expression of opinion or attempt at persuasion. The topic is "Students Cleaning Up the Classroom." While the subject might be a controversial matter in American schools, it is inarguable in Japan, where most schools have no hired janitorial staff; instead, selected students pitch in, scrubbing floors and so on, each day after school, and all participate in the end-of-term *dai soji* or "big clean-up." The essay concludes, "There might be some people who think the classroom doesn't have to be cleaned, but those people will feel bad when they see a dirty classroom. . . . Cleaning isn't much fun, but neither is it a hardship. So one should fulfill one's responsibilities; if everyone does that, the classroom will be cleaned." The topic is thus an expression of the civic pride and spirit of cooperation with which, by all accounts, Japanese citizens invest most activities of work and play. In the same spirit, the textbook offers a section on "Writing about Experiences" that focuses, in contrast to the characteristically American autobiographical narrative, on the experiences of *others:* "This chapter," Michiru remarks, "is more about how to listen to other people." And in a similar vein, I think, in the second-term textbook's lone section on composition—on writing the research report—students are advised not only to consult the encyclopedia and other books but, when interviewing experts, to be polite.

As Heidegger's dialogue predicted, and as Michiru Arai and John Hinds observe, current Japanese writing instruction has grafted some Western educational precepts, particularly an avowed concern with clarity and structure, onto native rhetorical traditions. The unit in *Modern Japanese* on expressing opinions, for instance, offers this guide: Choose a subject; Consider to whom and for what purpose you are writing; What is the problem? What impressed you?; Be clear on what you are saying; Structure your essay clearly; Don't mix facts and opinions; Don't insult those with counter-opinions; Proofread.

In the most telling evidence of Western influence, the book offers a brief section on argumentation, although the marginalized status of the activity is indicated by its being relegated, literally an afterthought, to the last two pages of the book. Further, Michiru tells me, "My textbooks [in the late 1970s] never had anything like it! The strategies are the same as Americans'. Entrance examinations to Universities didn't even have an essay part until 8 or 10 years ago. I think this shows how the Japanese have been influenced recently by Western culture."

The terms in which the lesson on argument is presented are ample indication of its foreign derivation, the rubrics being what Michiru characterizes as "Japanese English" phrases. As we will see from Michiru's translation of the lesson, following, the textbook authors seem to regard acts of argumentation much as ethnographers might describe arcane tribal rites of passage. Suitable occasions for argument are enumerated. (As I write this, it strikes me that my neighbors in Manhattan, where contention is our grossest national product, might more readily construct a shorter list of *unsuitable* occasions for argument, baby showers and funerals being the only two instances that come immediately to mind.) Even so, the authors describe activities that do not really get to the heart of what most Westerners recognize as argument, neither of the spontaneous and heated nor of the more circumspect variety. Instead these rubrics highlight the polite and cooperative aspects of the enterprise, emphasizing planned group discussion rather than individual combat:

To argue with people is not only to tell your own opinion, but also to listen to other people.

Different styles of arguments:

1. "Free-Talking"
   Participants raise hands when they want to express their opinion.
2. "Buzz Session"
   Participants form several groups and discuss. Each group reports the result at the end.
3. "Panel Discussion"
   Several "panelers" who represent different opinions will discuss the theme and then the audience joins the discussion later.

Beyond these formal lessons in Japanese secondary schools, several specific formulae for composition seem to be preferred by writers in Japan. Again, such stylistic preferences may initially affect the Japanese student's rhetorical choices in English. According to John Hinds (1983), two of these styles are influenced by literary tradition. One style descends from Noh drama, in which, like Western exposition, the composition proceeds "in fairly direct line" from introduction to climax or conclusion. The second, apparently more commonly practiced style derives from classical Chinese organization of poetry. This expository structure is described by four Chinese characters, the meanings of which are as follows:

(*ki*)	First, begin one's argument.
(*shoo*)	Next, develop that.
(*ten*)	At the point where this development is finished, turn the idea to a subtheme where there is a connection, but not a directly connected association [to the major theme].
(*ketsu*)	Last, bring all of this together and reach a conclusion.

While reviewing the two Japanese textbooks described above, my student Michiru, quite unprompted, drew for me this very outline, remembered from her own schooling in Japan. She emphasized that in the *ten* stage the writer's viewpoint changes, possibly to introduce an opposing view. In the following chapter we will be looking at Michiru's first college English essay, in which, I believe, ghostly traces of the same structure can be glimpsed. Other observers have also pointed to two aspects of this style that are especially relevant to comparative rhetoric studies. In *ten*, an abrupt shift takes place in which information only indirectly related to the major point is brought up with minimal syntactic marking. *Ketsu* presents a difference between English and Japanese definitions of "conclusion," the latter evidently being somewhat less "decisive."

Two additional common organizing schemata occur in the popular literature of Japan: the Japanese news story, in which, as Christopher and Tanzer have noted, the lead may be buried well into the article; and a type of essay found in popular Japanese magazines, the descriptive profile, similar in nature to the descriptive essay by Hiro Araseki quoted at the beginning of this chapter. Again, this type of Japanese expository prose is characterized by an author's selection of a "baseline theme" and his repeated return to this theme before progressing to a different perspective. In this manner, the theme of the article is continually reinforced, although that theme may never be explicitly stated. Information in each perspective often maintains a loose semantic cohesiveness, but the comments may seem only indirectly related (Hinds 1980, 1983).

The diffuseness or "indecisiveness" that so troubles Western readers may thus be the result of both unconscious communicative patterns and conscious aesthetic choices on the part of Japanese writers. And these stylistic features in turn appear to be preferred by Japanese readers. Takao Suzuki of Keio University explains,

> [Japanese authors] dislike clarification and full explanation of their views; instead, they like giving dark hints and attempt to drop nuances. But what we must not lose sight of in this connection is that in Japan this is exactly the type of prose that gets the highest praise from readers. Indeed, because readers seek just this kind of writing, and because they enjoy coming in contact with it, one suspects that this type of prose is, as a result, written more or less intentionally. . . . I think one might very well conclude that, rather than turning away from such writing, [Japanese] readers instead have a tendency to anticipate with pleasure the opportunities that it will offer them to savor this particular variety of "mystification through language" (quoted in Miller 121).

A quick survey of other related sociolinguistic studies reveals cultural attitudes that surely have bearing on the difficulties Japanese ESL students may experience with a range of expository forms they are typically asked to produce in American colleges. Observers have cited the Japanese reluctance to give analytic assessment of private experience (Barnlund 66–90) as well as to offer opinion or critical evaluation (Nakamura; Loveday 1982, 4). Moreover, Japanese speakers are far less inclined than English speakers to give commands, as in procedural or hortatory discourse, much less to express open disagreement in conversation. Hinds (1976, 52) notes that the Japanese generally consider it more effective to use expressions like "that way is probably better" than to use the imperative verb form; since World War II, advertisements in Japan have rarely employed the command form (see Higa), and even the street signs in Japan are as likely to use the cohortative verb form *yamemasyoo* ("Let's stop . . . ") as they are to use the command form, *yamero* ("Stop . . . "). By the same token, Nakane (35) observes that Japanese avoidance of words such as "no" or "I disagree" is rooted in the fear that negative expressions, like aggressive assertions, might disrupt the harmony of the group.

Given the evidence outlined in this chapter, as I have suggested, it may initially prove problematic for Japanese students to reconcile native linguistic and behavioral patterns with some of the demands made on them by the syllabi in U.S. college composition courses, which typically include personal narratives, journals, procedural essays, and persuasive or argumentative papers. It is this last category of discouse that the following chapter will investigate in greater detail.

7

In Which the Emphasis of Chapter 6 Is Shifted

Some "American" and "Japanese" Rhetorical Preferences

In 1827 Fanny Trollope set sail from London for America. She returned home over three years later, her ears filled with such a buzzing and whirring of discordant American voices that her book on *The Domestic Manners of the Americans* fairly vibrates with the din. Political debates, blunt harangues, querulous inquiries into the habits of foreigners: Trollope gleefully records each Congressional melee and drawing room imbroglio. Their frequency and vehemence she ascribes to a "hot-headed democracy"[1] and a system of public education which, unlike that of her native land, pays less attention to scholastic discipline and cultivation of "a correct and polished style" than to "the peculiar powers of the individual" (283–84).

In this chapter I would like to inquire into the causes and manifestations of a rhetorical activity that seems most clearly to demonstrate some of the cultural differences noted in the preceding chapter. I do not maintain that arguing is the great American pastime, simply that it remains one of the more sanguine features of the domestic manners of the Americans, and a point of emphasis in our schools.

Feminists over the years have remarked on what they perceive as the gender-specific bias of Western academic rhetoric. Walter J. Ong has suggested that the very origins of academic style in the West are peculiarly masculine and essentially polemic, even militantly so:

> Rhetoric is also ceremonial. It developed in the past as a
> major expression on the rational level of the ceremonial combat
> which is found among males and typically only among males at
> the physical level throughout the entire animal kingdom. . . .
> Rhetoric became particularly attached to Learned Latin, which

[1]Trollope was by no means the first weary traveler to find Americans' tendentiousness heightened after the Revolution. When Rip Van Winkle returns to Sleepy Hollow to find his beloved King George unseated by General Washington, he scarcely recognizes the place: "The very character of the people seemed changed. There was a busy, bustling, disputatious tone about it, instead of the accustomed phlegm and drowsy tranquillity" (Williams 101).

172

the male psyche appropriated to itself as an extrafamilial language when Latin ceased to be a "mother" tongue (that is, was no longer spoken in the home by one's mother). Latin, spoken and written for 1500 years with totally negligible exceptions only by males, became a ceremonial language institutionalizing with particular force the ceremonial polemic which set the style for all education until romanticism. For until the romantic age, academic education was all but exclusively focused on defending a position (thesis) or attacking the position of another person—even medicine was taught this way. Preromantic education was rhetorical and dialectical, dialectic and logic having developed out of rhetoric (615).

In 1973, Adrienne Rich quoted Ong's observations in her notes "Toward a Woman-Centered University" to underscore the metaphoric connections between social aggression and the traditional adversarial style of Western academic discourse. More recently, Belenky et al., in a study of *Women's Ways of Knowing,* have adopted the terminology of two different kinds of epistemological orientation, "separate"and "connected" knowledge. The latter emphasizes subjective experience and reciprocal personal relationships; the former represents the more "objective" and critical stance of the academy. Belenky and her coauthors concede the dearth of hard data demonstrating that an orientation toward critical reasoning, argumentation, and impersonal rules of discourse is in fact gender-specific. Although a number of observers have maintained that men are more apt than women to lean toward this "separate" knowing, evidence for the contention is chiefly anecdotal,[2] if compelling nonetheless. The Belenky study, for instance, summarizes the results of extensive interviews with women in American colleges.

---

[2] In *Feminism and Linguistic Theory,* Deborah Cameron takes issue with the contentions of what she terms "feminist folklinguistics." She charges that there is little evidence to support the widespread assertions in feminist literature (see, for example, Kramarae, Ardener, Spender, Zimmerman and West) that women's speech is more apt to be characterized by unfinished sentences, nonconformity with the "norms" of logic, greater silence or disfluency in mixed groups, and the tendency toward cooperative strategies in conversation where men tend to use competitive strategies.

Another dissenting opinion on the subject of gender differences in speech acts is relevant here. In Goodwin and Goodwin's recent study of children's arguing, data are drawn from audiotaped conversations of working-class black preadolescent girls and boys (ages 4–14) at play on the streets of Philadelphia. The authors conclude the following:

"When this activity is examined in detail, it is found that, rather than being disorderly, arguing provides children with a rich arena for the development of proficiency in language, syntax, and social organization. Moreover, in contrast to the prevalent stereotype that female interaction is organized with reference to politeness and a dispreference for dispute (Gilligan 1982:9–10; Lever 1976:482; Piaget 1965:77), we find that girls are not only just as skilled in argumentation as boys but have types of arguments that are both more extended and more complex in their participation structure than those among boys" (200).

Let me gloss the above findings with a few observations. First, the data Cameron uses to disprove aspects of "feminist folklinguistics" are drawn from a very limited sampling (see p. 36 of her discussion). Second, the Goodwin conclusions should be read against the background of a study that is ethnographically based, concerns the behavior of children rather than adults, and takes for its arena informal street activities rather than classroom situations. For the purposes of our cross-cultural investigation, let me point out finally that in both the aforementioned studies, conducted by native English speakers, argumentation is presented as a positive rather than disruptive intellectual enterprise, with its own agreed-upon rules.

The findings show most informants to be uncomfortable with argumentative critical discourse in informal conversation. At the same time, however, these interviewees recognized that "playing the power game" in the classroom, and typically in the "real world" beyond, meant taking a stand on some issue, assailing the opposing position, and making few concessions to the opponent's point of view.

Thus existing side by side with postromantic notions of self-fulfillment and personal expression promulgated in American writing classrooms since the 1960s, the academic tradition of rhetorical jousting that Ong describes as preromantic seems very much alive. My discussions with high school and college teachers and my own observations at CUNY—not to mention the typically argumentative format of the CUNY-mandated Assessment Test— offer further informal corroboration. The majority of composition textbooks published in the United States in recent years show a similar concern with argumentative discourse. Although a few observers have written that the teaching in America of the "principle modes" of discourse—narrative, description, exposition, argumentation—has been superseded, evidence suggests that in many cases this is wishful thinking more than fact.

The following discussion briefly surveys the history of rhetoric instruction in this country, and examines representative composition textbooks published in the United States in the past few years. Taking care not to equate the history of textbook publication with what actually goes on in classrooms throughout this country (the latter is of course impossible to ascertain with any precision), I want to see what these artifacts can tell us about the conventions of our own academic discourse, particularly with regard to argumentation. In this context I will then go on to consider the implications of the Japanese rhetorical preferences noted in the preceding chapter by looking at several argumentative essays produced by two Japanese students of English.

In Chapter 6 we saw some of the ways in which Japanese society proscribes self-assertiveness and confrontation. Group identification, not individualism, is the primary fact of Japanese social relationships. In their own country, the Japanese characteristically operate by consensus: as an often-quoted Japanese proverb has it, "The nail that sticks up gets pounded down." A *New York Times Magazine* article (July 8, 1984) on the Japanese computer industry points out that "The whole Japanese educational system . . . is committed to the spirit of compromise, not debate—students are actually taught to avoid the kind of intellectual confrontations that are fundamental to scientific instruction in the West." Let's examine how debate is fostered in American schools, and why.

The "Language of Argument" in the U.S.

In numerous studies conducted over the past few years contrasting secondary education in Japan and the United States, one theme keeps resurfacing. Americans, say observers from this country (see, for example, White on *The Japanese Educational Challenge*), have everything to learn from the Japanese when it comes to fostering cultural literacy—with one exception, acknowledged by Japanese and Americans alike: the personal expression of invention, spontaneity, opinion, dissent. For good or ill, the development of individuality has been the central tenet of the American educational system since the nineteenth century, so much so that when an American team was sent to overhaul and "democratize" the Japanese school system at the end of World War II, it presented with noteworthy hubris this dictum: "Freedom of inquiry, rather than exclusive memorization of factual knowledge for examination purposes, should be emphasized" (quoted in Rohlen 66).

In the spirit of free inquiry, with its implied responsibility of dissent, expressions of opinion such as oral debate and written argument have become a matter of practice in many high school and college classrooms in the United States. For the purposes of the present discussion, let me summarize the important features of this mode as categorized in several descriptive studies of argumentative discourse (see, for example, Kummer; Aston; Tirkkonen-Condit). These studies characterize the production of written argument as a cognitive process of problem solving, in which it is *the writer's goal and responsibility* to *change* the audience's initial *opposing position* by *winning* the reader over to the position proposed by the writer. The process typically involves the *structural units* of *situation* (background material), *problem, solution,* and *evaluation*. The studies show that the illocutionary forces in argumentative texts are typically *assertive* in the statement of the problem (the undesirable condition of things) and *directive* in the outlining of a *solution*.

With a heavy hand I have underscored the key terms of this description to suggest obvious points of departure for a sociolinguistic approach to the rhetorical format, given what we have learned about Japanese discourse in the preceding chapter. As I say, there is naturally great variance in the United States as to how or even whether argument is broached in high school[3] and

---

[3]Even allowing for local divergence in curriculum, one can see certain trends in writing instruction in high schools in the United States. The following background information, although tangential to the present discussion of argumentation, is relevant to our brief consideration of composition methodology in high schools in the U.S. and in Japan, the latter described in Chapter 6.

For one thing, there is far more diversity in the U.S. than in Japan with respect to textbook selection and methodology, although book lists must be submitted for approval to each State Board of Education. For another, according to Kathleen Pierce and Miriam Kogan, both teachers in the New Jersey school system, while English grammar may or may not be taught on the junior high school level—they even mention one school district in which formal grammar instruction is strictly proscribed—composition is regarded (or at least paid lip service) as an important component of language arts instruction at each grade level in junior high and high school.

More germane to our concerns in this discussion, these teachers observe two conflicting methodological trends. Their observations are corroborated by recent articles in the field, as well as by information provided by a colleague at Queens College who has monitored numerous English classes in the local high schools in Queens and on Long Island. These sources agree, first, that the "process" method of instruction and "student-centered" workshop formats are gaining status in the classroom, although they are usually introduced marginally in the form of supplementary materials (see, for example, the teachers' handbooks by Atwell and by Moffett and Wagner, cited in the bibliography for this chapter). Indeed a 1988 survey from the Center for the Study of Writing at Berkeley shows increased favorable response among U.S. teachers to the process model (cited in *Educational Leadership,* February 1989). *At the same time,* however, my informants point out that American high school instructors are just as apt to stick to more traditional approaches, teaching writing according to prescriptive methods and rhetorical modes, and in their book selection tend to favor long-lived texts like Warriner's (personal communications February and March, 1989).

college classrooms. Surely there are teachers who do not assign any form, however disguised, of written persuasive or argumentative discourse (though it is difficult to conceive of an American classroom that discourages debate about reading material and the like). On the other hand, consider the findings Mike Rose reports from UCLA. In his 1983 proposal for remedial courses geared toward "academic" rather than "personal" writing, Rose describes the procedure used in developing UCLA's Freshman Preparatory Program. Having collected 445 essay and exam topics from 17 departments on campus, he and his colleagues found no "personal experience" assignments, but rather,

> Most called for exposition—transaction in James Britton's scheme. . . . The balance required argument (Britton's conative mode, Kinneavy's persuasive), but a special kind of argument I will label academic argument, that is, not a series of emotionally charged appeals and exhortations, as one often finds in oratorical persuasion, but a calculated marshalling of information, a sort of exposition aimed at persuading (111).

Judging from current research, certain premises about argumentation seem to be "understood" in the West. Let me cite just two studies of the way English-speaking teachers rate junior high and high school students' essays. The first study, conducted by Marion Crowhurst in 1980, examines the relationship between syntactic complexity and quality ratings of narrative and argumentative essays by British Columbian pupils in grades 6, 10, and 12, generally finding arguments, but not narratives, to be rated higher for syntactic complexity. And a more recent cross-cultural study by Ulla Connor of argumentative patterns in high school students' essays—the sampling was drawn from the work of English, Finnish, German, and U.S. students— reveals that the essays rated highest by graduate students at Purdue University were those conforming to the typical structure I have outlined a few paragraphs above. The findings show little difference in the average holistic scores of these language groups. Both studies suggest agreement on the part of Western writers and readers as to certain characteristics of effective argument, and further, I think, point up the shared underlying assumption that the task of arguing itself is a familiar and worthy exercise. Interestingly, the one cross-cultural variation discovered among the groups in the Purdue study was that the situation + problem + solution + evaluation structure was used less consistently in the Finnish and German compositions than in the English and American examples.

How has argument evolved in the United States as a mode traditionally privileged in many college composition courses, and what does it say about American culture? The American university that came into its own in the nineteenth century was strongly influenced by the Scottish educational system, which at the time was forming a commitment to broad-based liberal arts instruction not just for an elite group but for a great portion of its citizenry. In contrast to the English system of specialized classical studies designed for the well-born, the four major Scottish universities began to advocate a more "democratic" program in English, favoring discussion and theme writing over lecturing as the principal modes of instruction (Horner 85). While maintaining the traditional classical emphasis on persuasive rhetoric, the most influential Scottish rhetoricians rebelled against Aristotelian deductive logic, which demanded mastery of learned syllogisms and emotional and ethical appeals. In its stead, they substituted the scientific inductive logic posited by the philosophy of the Common Sense empiricists.

This epistemological and pedagogical shift perfectly suited American democratic and technocratic ideals. The evolution of the teaching of literature and composition in the United States during the nineteenth century reveals a comparable shift in emphasis from oratory to writing. As James Berlin has shown in his discussion of popular rhetoric texts in nineteenth-century America, by far the most frequently taught principles of writing in the United States well into the century were those set forth by several prominent eighteenth- and nineteenth-century Scottish rhetoricians (and reiterated in textbooks by American educators). Hugh Blair, whose *Lectures on Rhetoric and Belles-Lettres* (1783) was enormously influential, focused on the development of eloquence and style, but argued that the Aristotelian topoi for stimulating ideas might actually stifle inventiveness (Blair xxvi). George Campbell was among the earliest theoreticians to demonstrate how psychology and language acted on the faculties of the audience to achieve the goals of persuasion. Campbell's *Philosophy of Rhetoric* (1776) emphasized the use of the faculties for induction from direct observation. Nearly a century later, Alexander Bain, professor of logic and rhetoric at the University of Aberdeen, published his manual of *English Composition and Rhetoric* (1866), whence derives the classification of major modes of discourse: narration, description, exposition, argumentation. This taxonomy was to shape writing instruction in the United States for many years, and, from the looks of the textbooks we shall survey a bit farther on, continues in some measure to influence the pedagogy of composition. Bain also set forth another mainstay of the American composition course: the concept of the paragraph as a unit focused by a topic sentence and developed according to the principles of unity, coherence, and emphasis (Mulderig 95).

To this triumvirate of seminal British rhetoricians we might add the Oxford reformer Richard Whately, who announced in his *Elements of Rhetoric* (1828) the intention of confining his study *exclusively* to argumentative composition. Whately adapted Campbell's and Blair's distinction between argument as an appeal to reason and persuasion as an appeal both to reason and emotion. He analyzed argumentative fallacies, detailed the way rational argument should be structured, emphasized the narrowing of thesis, and encouraged the practice of outlining to ensure coherent and clear arrangement of the parts of the argument (Corbett 623–25).

The post-Civil War years in America saw the expansion of the university system and the introduction of more varied and scientific curricula. At the same time, Robert J. Connors points out, the aristocratic, belletristic concern for taste, eloquence, and style gave way to stricter emphasis in freshman English courses on the classification of the four rhetorical modes, which "seemed to be adaptable to anything which a rising young American might wish to say" (447). At the turn of the century, the progressive reform movement in the United States, finding its most eloquent spokesman in John Dewey, further challenged the idea that education should only empower an elite. Dewey's *Democracy and Education* (1916) signaled a movement in the secondary schools away from lectures and memorized lessons, toward greater concern for "socialization training" through students' increased participation in the classroom. Responding to record numbers of immigrants entering the system during this time, the progressives believed that education should be designed to integrate a diverse population into the "mainstream" of American society. This goal called for a greater emphasis on the communicative function of writing as a means of self-discovery and social interaction,[4] and on the fostering of individual response and inquiry as a process by which adolescents develop and become productive citizens (see Bizzell and Herzberg 3).[5]

It is this "democratization" of American higher education, of its diverse population and its methods, that appears to have dictated the U.S. post-War response to the Japanese educational system quoted earlier in this chapter. Certainly the "general education movement" that came to prominence in American secondary schools and colleges in the late 1930s, with its focus on language and communicative skills, was stepped up after World War II, and again during the Cold War years of the fifties and sixties in response to the perceived threats of fascism and communism. From the 1950s on we see the growth of college "communications skills" courses designed to develop exposition, argument, and critical analysis—the latter skill in particular encouraged by the literary theories of the New Critics (Berlin 1987, 97). During the space race of the sixties, federal funds poured into programs for the teaching of literature and composition—evidence of the burgeoning need for new specialists in technology, business, and government (see Applebee 198–202).

[4]James Berlin also traces what he sees as a second strain in American rhetoric, existing alongside (but related to) the more "practical" strain in the nineteenth century, namely the "romantic rhetoric" of Emerson and Thoreau. These authors, too, placed emphasis on the individual at the center of political action in democracy. Berlin sees this emphasis resurfacing in the 1960s and '70s in textbooks such as those by Macrorie and Stewart, which advocate the expression of the writer's unique voice.

The confluence of these two streams in American rhetoric will be considered a bit further on in the present discussion.

[5]Organizations like the National Council of Teachers of English (formed in 1911) further emphasized the importance of catering to special "adolescent needs" in secondary school education. At the same time, as Arthur Applebee has shown in his history of high school education in this country, despite the efforts of such organizations to guard against college domination of high school curricula, college entrance requirements exerted increasing pressure on secondary schools to concentrate on reading lists and writing instruction (51ff., 142).

It would seem, then, that the same ideology of free enterprise, personal autonomy, and advice and consent, has continued to spawn successive generations of American textbooks advocating, to varying degrees, the argumentative mode. Witness this explanation from Richard Larson's preface to Jeanne Fahnestock and Marie Secor's textbook, *A Rhetoric of Argument* (1982):

> Argument in this sense pervades our lives. We are asked to buy products, to give money, to participate in campaigns, to cast votes. . . . Furthermore, on many questions inviting judgment or action, the data permit reasonable people to reach different conclusions; therefore, a liberal education in a democratic society, some teachers assert, should equip people to recognize how an argument is built (viii).

A glance at a shelf of representative college composition texts published in the States in the past few years—books based on a variety of models from process orientation to writing across disciplines—shows 10 out of 39 books focusing *exclusively* on argument, and 21 more highlighting argumentation in one or more chapters. In an example of the former category, *Elements of Argument* (2nd ed. 1988), Annette T. Rottenberg writes, "Argumentation as the basis of a composition course should need no defense, especially at a time of renewed pedagogical interest in critical thinking" (v).

The approach of the authors of *The Writing Commitment* is fairly typical of the latter group. In the preface to the third edition of their book (1984), Adelstein and Pival explain that in their revision they have given more attention to the prewriting and composing *process* (concerns that have characterized the teaching of composition in this country since the 1960s), but that the units are still organized according to "a rhetorical approach that moves from writer-oriented narrative and personal essay writing to reader-oriented exposition and argument, and finally to research papers and laboratory reports for a specialized audience" (vii). The majority of these rhetoric texts similarly present the argumentative essay as the conceptual capstone of the writing course, as this task has traditionally been taken (in the work of Piaget and other cognitive psychologists) to presuppose greater sophistication on the part of the writer than the descriptive or narrative assignments with which the books typically commence.

The linchpin of argument as practiced in the West is the individual act of taking a stand. As Robert K. Miller observes in his introduction to *The Informed Argument: A Multidisciplinary Reader and Guide* (1986), "Argumentation is intellectual self-assertion designed to secure the consideration and respect of our peers" (1). Revealingly, for the sixth edition of his textbook *The Language of Argument* (1989), Daniel McDonald has chosen as frontispiece an advertisement for the constitutional liberties organization, People for the American Way. The ad shows a photograph of a blindfolded-and-earplugged sheep with the caption "The ideal American citizen?" and urges readers to combat government censorship of information lest we turn into a nation of sheep. In the context of the book, the ad effectively demonstrates the conflation of the language of argument with the professed American ideals of self-reliance, self-assertion, self-expression.

Perhaps in the impetus behind this rhetorical activity we can see where the two seemingly opposed directions composition classes often take—the personally expressive and the transactional or conative—might be said to converge. In his study of *English in America* (1976), Richard Ohmann, surveying the college composition manuals of the time, concluded that in them the student is almost invariably conceived of as an individual acting alone, discovering his or her "authentic self, " trying to persuade others, but rarely (save in exceptions like Peter Elbow's *Writing Without Teachers*) working with others to advance a common purpose. Twelve years later, one sees on the shelf evidence of the theories of collaborative classwork and peer editing, but still the same valorization of the individual, from whose unique personal experience much of American composition springs.

Ohmann noted in 1976 the way our writing textbooks envisioned argument as rational persuasion, the largely formalistic matter of shoring up logical support for a proposition, leaving aside the pathetic and emotional appeals that theorists since Aristotle have noted in argumentation. In the intervening decade or so, however, a number of textbooks have taken into account philosophical and linguistic treatises on argument such as those by Chaim Perelman and Stephen Toulmin, both of whom have demonstrated how persuasion often has more to do with cultural conventions and assumptions than with the universal rationality of a given proposition.

Still, linguistic and pedagogical habits die hard. In the 1970s influential composition theorists of the New Rhetoric such as Ann Berthoff and Kenneth Pike, and observers like James Moffett, whose work grew out of cognitive psychology and empirical linguistics, described rhetoric as epistemic, as a context-specific and dialectic means of generating truth. Their observations brought to the study of composition what linguistic and literary theorists from Saussure and Jacobson and Wittgenstein to the present have recognized, that meaning is not simply expressed in language but produced by it. Language in large measure creates the world by determining what is and is not perceived. Yet the majority of our more popular textbooks in the eighties, while advocating the "authentic" voice of personal expression in their opening chapters, contrarily seem to present argument according to the nineteenth-century positivist model. As in the work of the Scottish rhetoricians of two centuries ago, this approach asks audience and writer to shed personal and social concerns and cultural distortions—all "blocks to logical thinking and unsound reasoning," in the words of one current textbook—in the interests of "objectivity." In this view, induction from concrete facts has greater value and authority than deductive reasoning from syllogisms, since empirical data are taken to approximate more closely actual sensory experience, the basis of all knowledge in the positivist epistemology.

The keynote of most of these textbook discussions of argument is still logic over emotion, with the implication that the two are clearly separable: in Robert K. Miller's estimation, "Written arguments require that we think clearly, without letting our feelings dominate what we have to say" (1). The structural metaphor of "building" an argument prevails in our pedagogy; we "construct" an argument on the "support" or "concrete foundation" of "sound reasoning." With this conceptualization of the rhetorical mode, as Ohmann has observed, academic argument (as opposed to everyday "emotional" argument) is made to appear acontextual, seemingly "divorced from power, money, social conflict, class, and consciousness" (158).

But of course argument is neither disinterested nor separable from cultural context. In *The New Rhetoric: A Treatise on Argumentation*, Perelman and Olbrechts-Tyteca note many ways of arguing other than the "quasilogical" methods discussed in American textbooks. They observe that some arguments derive acceptability and the semblance of rationality by virtue of implicit culturally based assumptions about the nature of reality, about presumed relations between persons and their actions. Most subjects we argue about exist in the shadowy realm of contingency and are not subject to "scientific" demonstration based on self-evident premises. Certain claims to rationality are embedded in verbal structures we often suppose to be purely ornamental. We argue as effectively by metaphor as by what we assume to be logical induction.

Two linguists have demonstrated specifically how these processes of argumentation are tied to our language and conceptual systems, which are indeed metaphorical in nature. In *Metaphors We Live By*, George Lakoff and Mark Johnson focus on another prevailing metaphor for argument in English, juxtaposed to the structural conceit of "argument as building," namely "argument as war". Our official line on argument in the academy, in law and diplomacy, in journalism, may be coolly rational, but in less formal discourse, and even in the language of textbooks at times, the passion seeps through. Thus we attack an opponent's claim, use various strategies to wipe him out, shoot him down, demolish his defenses, and so on, in the battle to win. Accordingly, the authors conclude with Perelman, most so-called logical arguments contain "irrational" or "unfair" tactics like intimidation, flattery, bargaining, and the like, though these defenses are disguised by the conventions of formal diction and appeals to authority (64ff.).

The authors' point is that through such metaphors we conceptualize and structure a rhetorical form. Our metaphors systematically shape the way we talk and write, provide patterns for what we can and cannot do in argument. These structures are deeply ingrained, and, as we have seen in the preceding chapter, may vary from culture to culture. In the midst of verbal battle, we lose sight of, for example, the cooperative aspects of arguing: after all, one's "opponent" or auditor is in fact giving his or her time in an effort at mutual understanding. Lakoff and Johnson invite us to imagine a hypothetical culture "where argument is viewed as a dance, the participants are seen as performers, and the goal is to perform in a

balanced and aesthetically pleasing way" (5). I cannot say with what metaphors the Japanese conceptualize the act of arguing. Having looked at the
Japanese textbooks mentioned in the previous chapter, however, I would
maintain that their culture highlights the very element of cooperation our
metaphor hides, while hiding the combativeness our culture highlights, and
that this perspective affects how they conceive of and carry out the process
itself.

One last point is worth making concerning the interrelationship of
social institution, linguistic form, conceptual system, and rhetorical mode. As
I have explained elsewhere, I do not presume direct causal relations here,
merely connections. The link between the forcefulness and specificity Americans prize on the *sentence level* of diction, grammar, and syntax (we are
exhorted from high school on to "Be specific!" and "Use active verbs!") and
the assertiveness of the persuasive or argumentative *essay as a whole* is graph-
ically drawn, I think, by the Table of Contents of another representative
generalist text, *College Writing* by McCrea and Kemmerle (1985). As you read
the book's outline, which I consider instructive enough to reprint virtually in
its entirety, keep in mind the sharply contrasting features of Japanese grammar noted in the preceding chapter:

Chapter I: Sentences That Make an Assertion: Agent Prose
   Building Sentences Around a Specific Subject
   Disguising the Subject: Latinate Diction
   Guiding the Reader with Clear Pronoun Reference
   Empty Subjects: Expletives
   Agentless Subjects: Participles, Gerunds, and Gerund Phrases
   Words That Describe Actions: The Predicate
   Eliminating the Agent: The Passive Voice
   Weak Predicates: The Imprecise *To Be* and *To Do*
   Describing the Agent and the Action: The Complement . . .
   Sentence Variety and Sentence Structure
Chapter II: Developing Ideas: The Agent and the Paragraph
   Linking Features of Agency: The Topic Sentence
   Assertions and Supports: Deductive, Inductive, and
      Combination Paragraphs
   Making the Paragraph Complete: Paragraph Development
   Giving the Paragraph Focus: Paragraph Unity
   Making the Paragraph Readable: Sentence Variety
   Paragraph Content: Illustration, Comparison, Analysis,
      Definition
Chapter III: Combining Paragraphs: Essay Organization
   Finding Something to Say: Brainstorming as a Strategy
      of Invention
   Finding a Way to Say It: Organizing the Essay by Prewriting
   Five Models for Short Essays . . .
Chapter IV: Moving from Exposition to Argument: The
   Shaping Role of the Audience

How Expository Models Become Argumentative:
    Four Examples
Working Toward the Longer Essay: Three Models for
    Combining Arguments . . .
Anticipating Objections
First-Person Writing and Argumentative Writing:
    Establishing Personal Authority

Japanese Students and the "Dialogue" on Argument: Two "Test" Cases

What effect does the pervasive Japanese "spirit of compromise" have on the Japanese student's ability to produce argument, a rhetorical mode valued in the Western tradition since its inception and still promulgated vigorously in many present-day American classrooms? We should remember that the Japanese ascribe less importance to verbal skills like logic and coherence than they do to the emotive power of suggestion and obliquity. In fact, the Japanese have a pejorative term, *rikutsupoi*, which translates as "overly logical" (Pascale and Athos 153). More telling still, that the Japanese language has at least 16 circumlocutory ways of saying "no" (by the count of K. Ueda) should indicate to what extremes the Japanese will go to avoid conflict. The following Japanese student's journal response to an assignment in argumentation witnesses the confusion and discomfort of a writer asked to perform a rhetorical task that is prized in the target language but shunned in the native language:

> It is very tough to write an annoying argument as I don't have any such kind of argument, and I don't even remember if I had such argument before. Of course I have some problem that annoys me, but it is not an argument. The biggest one is about a girl. She is my friend, but I thought she was my girl friend. Actually we were like that. I had known that she had a boyfriend in her country, but we were so close that I thought she chose me rather than him. In fact she said to me like that.
>
> One day she suddenly changed. . . . [The student goes on to narrate the incident.]

In *Errors and Expectations*, her benchmark study of basic writers in the City University of New York, Mina Shaughnessey illustrated persuasively how the basic writers in her sampling, generally native speakers of English, are apt to falter when attempting arguments such as those demanded of them by the (then-newly instituted) CUNY Writing Assessment Test. Shaughnessey used sample responses to the Test to show how basic writers are liable to stray from the topic, fail to develop their ideas, even shift viewpoint midstream. These examples she contrasted with the more clearly elaborated and structured written responses of more experienced freshmen writers in English. The more experienced writers *knew the value*, so to speak, of topic sentences, uniformity of perspective, specificity, logical reasoning, and clear linear structure. On the other hand, as we have seen in Chapter 6, these very features are often regarded by Japanese writers and readers as discursive elements *to be avoided*.

That argument itself is considered a valuable skill in this country—or in the CUNY universe, at least—is evidenced by the agree/disagree format of the CUNY Test itself. And because the Test is used in many branches of the City University not only as an instrument of placement but as a criterion for exit from basic-level composition courses, the WAT subsequently reinforces these values. We have lately heard that changes are afoot in the Test format, chiefly as a result of the growing recognition that both the form and content of the Test questions are particularly problematic for the increasing numbers of international students entering the system. But it is a truth universally acknowledged that institutional reform moves at a glacial pace.

In the following discussion I want to consider the progress of two Japanese students of my acquaintance—both introduced in Chapter 6—in their successive attempts at the WAT examination. Let me emphasize that the following is an exercise in textual explication rather than a statistical study of the sort that the question of comparative rhetoric calls for but has seldom received. My purpose here is simply to draw further distinction between developmental-level native speakers (even when they are speakers of other dialects) and ESL students, who are often called upon to absorb an entirely different set of social values and "natural" assumptions along with the rules of a given rhetorical task. I do so in the supposition that it may be useful for our own pedagogy to examine the rhetorical "errors" in the work of nonnative students like the native Japanese speakers discussed in this and the preceding chapter not so much for their divergence from the norm (as in the case of Shaughnessey's important contrast between basic and experienced native writers in English) as for their consonance with what is desirable or normal in the writer's first language.

In offering these brief examples I am not advancing the proposition that all Japanese students' essays will be muddled as to what constitutes a proper argument in English, nor that Japanese writers will inevitably approach the task by transferring linguistic or rhetorical structures from their home culture. Rather, I have wanted to suggest reasons for these particular writers' discomfort with this specific task, as well as for the differences between the way they initially approach the assignment and subsequently conceive of responses more acceptable to native speakers of English.

And here is the chief connecting point between this and the preceding chapter. For such cultural contrasts, by revealing what is "foreign," tell us easily as much about the underlying assumptions and prejudices of our *own* teaching methods, rhetorical categories, and curricula. In the process they may even reveal how myths and methods, habits of conceptualizing, reading, and evaluating, can become a little stale—can benefit from fresh perspectives. It is worthwhile noting here that in the cross-cultural study cited earlier, Ulla Connor observes that the highest-rated U.S. composition used *narration* to develop the "problem" stage of argument—and was the only sample composition to do so. Connor concludes that the evidence bolsters the views of observers who have long suggested alternative ways of evaluating and teaching the structure and development of argument.

In view of the rhetorical preferences noted in this and the preceding chapter, then, we will begin with three successive impromptu essays written by Masaaki Ito, whose journal is quoted in Chapter 6. The essays were written as answers to the CUNY Writing Assessment Test, which as you will recall all CUNY graduates are required to pass, and which typically invites students to "agree or disagree" with a proposition. The first two papers are very definite failures on the sentence level alone. Yet just as significant, though at first glance less obvious, are problems that appear (at least to the reader gifted with hindsight) to be influenced by interference—if not always by native rhetorical strategies then by native proscriptions. By his third attempt at the WAT, however, the writer has not only acquired sufficient knowledge of grammar to write a comprehensible English sentence but has absorbed in the process just what it is that his American readers ask of an argument essay.

The first Test essay Masaaki wrote on entering Queens College; the second, four months later after taking an intensive language course. On both occasions he scored 4 out of 12 points:

Test #1

"Success means making a lot of money?" To this question I strongly disagree! Some might say "Yes, of course," but I personally feel that's wrong from lots of point of view.

At first I want to think about what success is. There might be many different answers as each people has different way of thinking and experience. At the same time it could be impossible to get this answer, in any case the value or deep meaning essencially of it must be the same. So I want to discuss it.

In our society usually people think that success is making fortune: money and material possession, that is to say, they only notice personal possession which can be seen, not invisable thing. To be sure in order to live we need money. Also money can do most of things in this world. Without it it is very difficult to carry out our desire—helping people who are poor and sick because of lack of so many stuff. Money talks!

On the other hand, historically speaking, there were so many people who contributed the peace, development of society, or people of the world. Everybody like them were not rich, but what they did are valuable and can't compare with making money, which people usually think success. The worth of our life shouldn't be measured by money or substancial matters.

In the near future I might get married and get my family. Then all I think as a measure of success and happiness will be having a good wife and children. I need money in order to live, but money is not everything. We can't buy love or happiness by money. If some people say, "Yes," that's not a true happiness. I know a lot of people who are very rich, but they don't have anyone whom they can depend upon. They worked very hard in order to make money spending most of their lives. But after that what is left for them? A lot of money? Nobody can take money to the next life. They are hungry for happiness even if they are rich. So money is money and it is not everything.

If I conclude what I have said, money is important. I can't deny that fact. But there are so many things which make our life happier and more valuable. In order to live we need least money, but most significant concept in my opinion is how to live not how much money I will make. I want to [?] quality of my life. I believe.

I don't want to persue momentally happiness—like dream which could vanish instantly!

Test #2

I'm agree somehow that men can raise children as well as women do, but not exactly because parents are indispensable for children absolutely. I have some ideas which supports the statement.

Divorce has been increasing in these days. Why? It depends on several reasons such as they get married instantly and get divorced because it is better to be seperate than to live together hating each other for their new life, there's something in it, but it sounds just excuse for me, if they have children, they aren't supposed to get divorced not matter what kind of reasons they have. Marriage is not a game, that's a serious, delicate matter. I strongly feel that children shouldn't get involved and be victims of their parents, since for children, they need love from both father and mother.

Men can give love as well as women can, but on the other hand, father's love is different from mother's in a way, that is, characteristically speaking, men's love is direct way and women's love is mentally deep, affectionate. Usual problem is for men cooking, cleaning the house, washing dishes, laundry, etc, in short housekeeping is one of the headaches to take care of his children, in that case, mother is very important. For example, I know one man who takes care of his child after getting divorced. He seems to get along well about cooking, cleaning and doing very well to his children, but I sometimes see that child looks lonely sitting the bench in the park. He needs mother's love, too.

If I summarize what I have written, I say that the courts took good decision to award custody to the father. It's a delicate dicision but I hope it will prove that men can do as well as women can to take care of their children.

In both essays, the author vacillates between alternatives—an appropriate response in his own culture, where the writer is not urged to commit either way to an opinion. The Test, on the other hand, asks for clear-cut agreement or disagreement on the part of the writer; the most Masaaki is willing to venture is "I'm agree somehow." In each essay, as in much of Japanese exposition, the question is examined tentatively, from as many perspectives as possible. And in both essays the author tends to return to the "baseline theme" at the initiation of each perspective.

In Chapter 6 we noted how Japanese writers often offer a number of approaches for examining a given proposition, a technique that may account for the antiphonal voices of Masaaki's first essay. However strongly he says he disagrees with the statement that "Success means a lot of money," he is at the same time compelled to articulate the opposite view by citing what "some people" might say, or what people "in our society" "usually" think. Since this opposing voice is given utterance many times in the course of the argument, it cannot be dismissed as simply a strawman device. More likely it is a reflection of the common Japanese expository technique (Hinds 1980, 147) of juxtaposing two antithetical statements to give a more even-handed view of the subject. Through such means Masaaki justifies his claim that there might be as many answers to the question as there are people to formulate them, so that "it could be impossible to get this answer."

In Test #2 the author's opinion is even more difficult to pin down, beginning with the equivocations of his introductory thesis statement. I *think* what Masaaki means in this opening sentence, despite the vagaries of its punctuation, is that men *in theory* can rear children as well as women can, but that the experiment in practice doesn't "exactly" work, because both parents are indispensable to children. Consequently, the discussion of divorce in paragraph 2, which seems at first only tangentially related to the topic, is in fact Masaaki's way of getting back to his thesis: children need both parents, regardless of the circumstances of the parents' separation. Paragraph 3 begins by returning to the "baseline theme" and proceeding to view the thesis from a slightly different perspective, namely the difference between a mother's and a father's love and the consequent inadequacy of one without the other.

Native English speakers are apt to be put off by the apparent lack of semantic cohesiveness of the perspectives in Test #2. Paragraphs begin in one place and end up in quite another; sentences seesaw between alternatives, double back on themselves, and are resolved in apparent contradiction. Yet this circling around the subject may simply be, as we have seen, the author's way of supporting his thesis. The debate on the pros and cons of divorce presents a situation in which the father's custody of the child might be necessary but is nonetheless detrimental to the real "victim," the child. Paragraph 3 of this exam, similarly, brings up the matter of the difference between a mother's and a father's love to demonstrate, through a specific example, how even a father who overcomes the gender stereotype by managing housework still cannot compensate for the loneliness created by the absence of the mother. The important thing here is that at no time does Masaaki contradict his thesis, summarized in the concluding paragraph, that men can care for children as ably as women can. Masaaki has supported his thesis by repeatedly suggesting that whatever failures result may have more to do with the needs of children than with the capabilities of fathers.

Masaaki was tested seven months later, having completed a semester in English 105. His third exam demonstrates that he has gained some fluency, although a number of errors remain. What is evidently far more important to the readers who determined his passing grade on the exam, Masaaki shows that he has changed his approach to argumentation:

Test #3

I agree that private ownership of handguns must be banned in this country no matter what the reasons would be claimed.

First of all, by possessing handguns, people feel that they can do anything they want. Some people can't control themselves and that increases the crime-rate in the United States. For example, if we hadn't being able to possess the handguns, there would not have happened the terrible murder of John Lennon or close call of President Reagan. As long as we allow people to carry handguns in the name of self-protection, the crime will never decrease.

On the other hand, in my country, Japan, the possession of the handguns is strictly prohibited in the law. People are not afraid of walking late at night even in Tokyo. Policemen feel secure comparing those who in New York. It shows that Japanese crime-rate is surprisingly low and the system of police for protecting citizens is well-organized. That's why I never felt being a victim of the crime over ther.

In conclusion, I really hope that in legisrature the plan of getting rid of the possession of the handguns would be made and fortunately passed. That is the only way to stop the crime of the bad circulation, which is to possess guns and kill people in order to secure the civic life. I do anticipate it.

In this third response to the WAT, Masaaki takes great pains to be assertive, to state the thesis up front and without equivocation ("no matter what the reasons would be claimed"), and to use clear transitions that point up the essay's three-part structure and surface cohesiveness as well as the hierarchical structure of its paragraphs—each of which proceeds from topic sentence to supporting examples. Part of the shift in Masaaki's argumentative stance may be attributable to the topic. He probably finds it easier to pass judgment on this matter than on the issues of success and parenthood he had written about earlier, especially since, as he points out, handguns are outlawed in his own country. The rest of the turnabout seems to have been schooled into him.

Perhaps the resulting essay sounds canned—safer and shorter, presumably because the author wanted to cut his losses. Nevertheless the paper gets a passing score because it fulfills its English-speaking readers' expectations for an argument essay, or at any rate for the peculiar sort of brief essay exam that with luck the student with a passing score will never have to produce again. Stripped of its ruminative tone and careful weighing of alternatives, much of the individual's voice has been lost. Still, the clear structure of his response seems to have mitigated in the readers' minds the effect of the essay's brevity and grammatical errors. Obviously I am somewhat ambivalent about the formulaic results we seem to be seeking and eliciting on such exams. But at the same time I am convinced that with his newfound sense of certain structures of English exposition, the same student, given more time, and assured by his instructors that digressions and alternative points of view are perfectly acceptable in English exposition *so long as* the author lets the reader know what bearing these digressions have on the topic at hand, can regain his original circumspection.

This conviction is borne out in the case of Michiru Arai, a young woman who entered Queens College in 1983 having spent two months in this country. I have chosen to conclude my discussion of Japanese rhetorical preferences with Michiru's two responses to the Assessment Test for a number of reasons. Mickie, for that is her American nickname, was a member of an experimental American literature class I taught in the spring of 1988. Thus I have been able to gauge her progress in English by comparing her performance as an entering student with her work in an upper-level class taken five years later (Mickie's career at Queens had been interrupted by a year-long return to Japan in 1985). Mickie's work for the literature class will be discussed at length in the final chapter of this book. In addition, in the semester following our class together, I interviewed Mickie (in September 1988) about her earliest forays into English, including her performances on the Assessment Test, and about some of the contrasts she herself has noted between her first and second cultures; our conversation is reprinted at the end of the present chapter. Finally, in February of 1989, five months after that interview, Mickie was able to help me with the discussion of the Japanese textbooks examined in Chapter 6, and, as you have seen, to offer her own observations as well.

Mickie wrote her first Assessment Test essay on enrolling in Queens College in August 1983. The examination question asked students to agree or disagree with the proposition that the death penalty acts as a deterrent to violent crime. As you read the exam, keep in mind the *ki-shoo-ten-ketsu* structure Mickie was able to recall years later, in the course of translating the Japanese textbooks I had given her. Recall, too, the Japanese speaker's technique of introducing contrasting views with phrases such as "some people say. . . . " To underscore the strength of these rhetorical patterns in the Far East, let me cite a similar pattern in Korean discourse, *ki-sung-chon-kyul*, noted by William G. Eggington, in which the theme is developed by concepts only indirectly connected with the argument. Eggington also points out the pervasive use of the "some people say" formula. This locution is certainly not unknown in English discourse (nor for that matter, I have noticed, in my own arguments in this chapter). But it is apparently "very common in Korean discourse when one is taking a somewhat controversial stand, either to protect one's own position by enlisting anonymous support, or to appear not too direct when criticizing another's position" (154). Mickie, like Masaaki Ito, makes use of this technique in her first essay:

> I disagree with this. Japanese law has the death-penalty. Some of us say that we shouldn't have it. But, the other people disagree because they are afraid that murder might increase. I don't know whether this is right or not.
>
> When I was in high school, I discussed this problem with my friends. We thought that a person who has been in prison all his life might be more painful. Of course, many people don't say so. Because they think everything will finish if people die. But I think both are almost the same. If people can't do what they want to, they will not be happy. The murders might think like this, too.
>
> If New York City bring back the death penalty to reduce the number of those violent climes, the murder rate will never reduce. The book which I read a few years ago said, "The laws which are too strict bring much worse crimes."

Only four months later, after she had taken a preparatory-level composition class, Mickie wrote this exam:

> I agree with the statement that coin-operated video games don't belong on a high school or college campus because these games distract students from their studies.
>
> First of all, video games hurt students' health, especially eyesight. For example, I have a friend who used to love video games. He had had good eyesight until he began to play these games. However, he is now wearing a pair of glasses. He recognized that it was because he had played video games, and he has stopped playing them. However, I don't think his eyesight will recover.
>
> Secondly, video games waste students' time. It is easy for most students to start playing these games. Nevertheless, it is hard for them to start studying. Therefore, they start playing these games easily, and then they regret playing these games instead of studying. If there's no coin-operated video games on a campus, they cannot spend their time playing such stupid games.
>
> Thirdly, coin-operated video games waste students money, also. Because these games are easy to start playing, and give students much more fun than study, students waste their money for these games without thinking. My younger brother, who is a high-school student, loved to play video games. In fact, he spent five dollars a day for them. He told me that video games were like a drug. He understood that money was important, but he

couldn't stop playing these games. Because of the reason about which my brother told me, people waste their money, I guess.

Some people might say that video games make them relax. However, on a campus there are many other things to make students relax. For example, doing exercises or sports is very good way to relax. Moreover, it will make students more healthy, and it's free. Students don't have to waste their money to relax.

In conclusion, I want to say that coin-operated video games interrupt students from their studies. Therefore there should not be coin-operated video games on a high school or college campus.

A comparison of these two responses, the latter a startling improvement, shows some of the same phenomena at work that characterize Masaaki Ito's Test answers. My interview with Mickie in September 1988, in which I asked Mickie to reread her Test essays and comment on them, confirms this assumption. The transcript of the interview is reprinted below, nearly in its entirety. As you will see, Mickie, at the time a senior linguistics major, is an especially knowledgeable informant, able to elaborate on many of the cultural contrasts noted in this chapter. As always, one must keep in mind the ways in which some of the subject's responses are influenced by the interviewer. Indeed, Mickie acknowledges as much at the end of our conversation, and no doubt she has also been influenced in some measure by the cultural studies she had read for her linguistics courses. All the same, the information she reveals falls in line with reports of the Japanese educational system as well as with what we have observed in American composition classes, and goes a long way toward explaining the striking differences between her two responses to the Assessment Test.

I begin our talk by asking Mickie to discuss some of the behavioral patterns she has noted during her stay in this country. Her remarks then lead us into a consideration of stylistic differences in discourse:

AT: . . . What about acceptance back into Japanese society? Would you be looked on as someone who is just irretrievably Americanized?

MA: (Laughs) I can act like other Japanese, but it's very tiring.

AT: Well, what would that entail? What are some of the things you'd have to do?

MA: O.K., say, if you have an opinion, you don't say it straightforwardly. You don't say, "I don't think so, you are wrong." That's American. It's just a different opinion, you know, "I could say this, but maybe you are right." You know, "nobody knows who is right," something like that.

AT: Of course, there are all sorts of circumlocutions that Americans use, too; for example, in class, I rarely say to a student, "You're wrong." I say, "Well, that's one way of looking at it." But in Japan, you're saying, it's more of the norm, whatever your opinion is, to give it, if you give it at all, in a delicate or circumlocutory way.

MA: In my case, if I'm talking to a friend, and we have a difference of opinion, I strongly disagree, I *might* express my opinion, but if I disagree and it's not very strongly, then I'll just say "maybe . . ." and then change the topic.

AT: You would change the topic; it is polite form simply to shift into another subject.

MA: Um-hm.

AT: Of course it's a stereotypical observation of Japan that consensus is so important, but you would say in everyday discourse that disagreement is avoided?

MA: Yes.

AT: This brings up the question of the Writing Assessment Test, which is always "Do you agree or disagree." And I saw an interesting change in your papers over those four months. First of all I saw a remarkable linguistic improvement, and an ability to expand on a topic; but I also saw certain things that seemed to be trained into you over those months, during the course of your taking CESL 21. And it was successful, obviously, in terms of your American readers, because you passed. Let's look at the first essay (reads first paragraph): Do you see a pattern of thinking there; can you characterize it for me?

MA: Well, I wasn't sure which way I really thought, my own opinion. . . .

AT: . . . and were you thinking about your reader, and whether he or she would rather you agreed or disagreed?

MA: No, I didn't have that much in my head (both laugh).

AT: O.K., reader-consciousness happens later, as you gain sophistication in writing . . . so you were thinking, "How do I feel?" How did you express that confusion in that first paragraph? Are there any methods that you're carrying over—this is a very leading question!—from your training in Japan?

MA: You see, over here, if you disagree, you just keep on saying you disagree, you don't think about if others agree with this opinion. But in Japan, if you disagree, you think about others who agree or disagree with you. So, let's say, you start seeing things from those peoples' points of view, and you see how those people have good opinions, and we have good opinions, and you start comparing those two good sides. And, in a sense, if we have more good opinions than those other people, we are right. You put them side by side. It's not you *must*, but you *should* give reader both sides.

AT: I agree with that method as an American; I think that unfortunately in our teaching, especially with an agree/disagree question like this . . . we do teach that you should come down on the side of one argument or the other, and I think that's unfair to the argument. But it is true that Americans are more comfortable with that kind of disagreement. You go on to say [reads next paragraph]. . . . Do you think you were conscious, as a writer trained in Japan, to say, "Well, on the other hand, a lot of people don't think that's true"?

MA: It's not something we learned precisely in the classroom; it's just something that *is* done, it's understood.

AT: I don't mean to make everybody in Japan the same, any more than you can generalize about all Americans. But perhaps because we're a young nation, and in a way "pioneers," we really don't obey in quite the same way certain acceptable forms. Do you feel when you're speaking Japanese that there are certain words or phrases that are demanded of a particular situation?

MA: Yes, you hear these phrases throughout the culture, in movies, in your house: you just know what to say. If you see a neighbor, in America you say "Hi!"; in Japan, I say, "Hello, what a nice day."

AT: Would you ask about her health? Here we usually say, "Hi, how are you today?"

MA: In Japan "How are you?" is not that common. If you haven't seen that person for a few months, you might say, "What have you been doing?" But usually we just talk about the weather; it's polite to talk about the weather because it doesn't touch anything personal. We avoid personal topics—even with very close friends, I can talk about my family, for instance; but boyfriends, sex—no.

AT: . . . What kinds of writing instruction did you have in Japan?

MA: First of all, we were given six years of grammar instruction, mainly verbal practice. Later, we were given a book and we were supposed to write in it every day, like a diary—I think this is common among all Japanese school children of 8 or 9. But there were certain things you just didn't write about in your diary—there were no regulations, but you didn't write about really personal things. Main assignments were to read a book and then write about it. In junior high school we studied Japanese literature, from the seventh century on—very old, so we couldn't understand it without dictionaries. And we formally learned Japanese grammar; and there were only one or two papers a year, basically book reports. We have to take examinations to get into senior high school, and some of those schools require essays. So to practice for those exams, we had some essays, on topics like air pollution—what you should do to avoid it, things like this. Not agree/disagree, no argument—just a discussion of a problem everyone agreed on. We never did research in my school—maybe because it was a new school and we didn't have a good library. American kids usually have some kind of research paper in high school. When I took English 110, I said "Research—what's research?" I knew I should go to the library, but I didn't know what to do.

AT: Well, when you got to CESL 21 over here, and to your second attempt at the WAT, can you tell me something about what your teacher taught you about how to approach an argument?

MA: First of all, this [points to first sentence of Test #2] is my opinion. And you just explain this opinion in two or three paragraphs, and those paragraphs should start, "first of all," "secondly," "thirdly" (laughs); and this is a conclusion. She told us you have to give examples, and you have to be *clear* about what you want to say.

AT: Now, let's get to this point of clarity; for Americans, it is a very important point. Would you say Japanese discourse avoids clarity to some extent, overemphasis on something, going directly to the point and "proving" it in each paragraph, first, second, third? . . .

MA: Yes, it's not taught, but it's something we feel, not to be too insistent.

AT: So some of these bicultural studies conducted in the sixties, where the Japanese woman says two different answers to the same question, depending on whether she's speaking Japanese or English to the same interviewer—Some of it has to do with rhetorical conventions associated with each language, and with what your listener expects of you. [I'm referring here to the study described by Ervin-Tripp and cited in Farb 210–211.]

MA: Yes, I read the same study; and it's funny, I think I'm doing the same thing. Say I'm talking to my [Japanese] roommate's father, who was here last week; and he asks me "Are you going to go back?" when I finish college, and so I said, "Ah, maybe, probably I will because my parents expect me to go back, and I don't have any money to go to school." That's not really true, I want to stay here, but that's more polite, that's what he expects me to say. . . .

AT: Whereas to me?

MA: To you or to American friends, then I'll say, "I don't want to go back, I want to go to graduate school; if I can get a job, I'll stay here and work, in the United States." That's what I'd say.

As of this writing, Mickie has in fact gone on to graduate school in this country to pursue her studies in linguistics. Her oral and written testimony—along with the research cited in this and the preceding chapter—reminds us that ESL students in college, unlike many of their native-born counterparts, often have to set aside habitual thought patterns and to absorb foreign organizational patterns along with the grammar system of their adopted language. Cognitive and communicative competence are interlocking but different skills, both of which the ESL student requires to succeed in native

English-speaking institutions of higher learning. The evidence of research in cross-cultural communicative interference (and corroborated by Mickie Arai's subsequent work in college, of which more later) shows us how second-language learners can come to associate a different behavior or linguistic pattern with a particular communicative situation if they learn that this new behavior is more comprehensible, more valuable, to the native inhabitants of the host country.

PART THREE

In the Literature Classroom

8

Breaking Literary Codes, or Reading Students' Notebooks

Each story is written in a foreign language, and the meaning of the story is in learning how to read it.

William S. Wilson, "Métier"

One of my colleagues was bemoaning his students' mystification in the face of poetry. "They think of each poem as having a secret message," he explained, "which the poet has planted somewhere in the Garden of Eloquence. The students sit quietly waiting for me to tell them where the answer lies buried. When I finally *do* dig up the meaning for them, they think I've done it by some magical process or sleight-of-hand: 'There, you see,' they say, utterly bemused; 'He's done it again!' "

This chapter considers ways to demystify the processes of reading by encouraging native and nonnative students to recognize the part they themselves play in making meanings. The experimental literature class described in these pages was conducted in 1984, its collaborative methods an extension of those used in the composition classes described in earlier chapters of this book. Doubtless the following notes, written up in 1985 and expanded as I looked into the students' texts a year later, will strike some readers as preliminary, for so they now seem to me. But in keeping with the project of this book to present the evolving processes by which some of my colleagues and I have come to "read" our students' performances and our own methods and curricula, I want to offer this discussion as a preface to the following chapter. The conclusions detailed here were in fact prerequisite to my experience a few years afterward in teaching and designing the American Studies course described in Chapter 9.

In the fall of 1984 members of the Queens College English department were asked to fill out a questionnaire regarding their adventures in English

120, our Composition II course, called Writing and Literature. Instructors had for some semesters raised questions about ways to address the increasing numbers of international students enrolled in their 120 classes. These students had passed the required writing courses, but clearly the tasks of reading and writing about literature in English demanded of them a huge linguistic and interpretive leap. The dropout rate for this population appeared higher than for native speakers. The silent minority who stuck it out tended to huddle in the back of the classroom.

Teachers of English 120 were surveyed as to what literary genres their students seemed to have most trouble with, what successes they could report or syllabi suggestions they could offer, and whether the presence of ESL students in the class had influenced their selection of reading or writing assignments. The consensus among the 19 respondents was that students of all persuasions seemed to find poetry the most inaccessible of genres. In their syllabi suggestions, several teachers determined to use more culturally diverse texts in future, one recommending works in translation such as *One Hundred Years of Solitude, Dream of the Red Chamber,* and *The Tale of Genji.* Others reported greatest success with discussions and assignments that invited students to bring background information or personal experience—including the experience of cultural difference—to bear on textual analysis:

> ESL students have particular difficulty reading colloquial English (Salinger, Updike); but often, after *long,* detailed "explications," they find this type of literature more rewarding than 19th-c. fare, which is usually more accessible initially. Often, cultural barriers prevent free discussion; again, working through this proves valuable.

> Social problems in American life are of interest to both natives and ESL students (who need to be encouraged to talk!), and can elicit interesting comparison-contrast, i.e., alternative viewpoints.

> The most lively discussions, I think, are those that concern "modern" literature, when we move from literary concerns to "life" concerns. I haven't found a difference between American and foreign-born students in terms of types of assignments on which they do well. Some of the best writing I've seen from my students in general has been "creative."

> Assignments: imaginative or personal experience essays relating to a piece of fiction. Discussions: most successful are discussions of literature in which students can be brought to see relationships between theme, incidents, or characters in the work and their own experience or observation.

As for whether the presence of ESL students in the class had influenced (or would influence in future) the instructor's choice of materials and assignments, the respondents, surprisingly enough in light of the problems that had been reported, were almost as likely to point out the students' strengths as their weaknesses. Here are the comments of the 10 instructors who answered this question:

> Perhaps ESL students should be introduced—even in English 110—to more American literature, both as a means for improving cross-cultural understanding and to bring them up to par with native students, who have often been reading Whitman, Dickinson, Poe, et al. since grammar school.

> I will certainly in the future avoid poems (especially) that take for granted American traditions in order to satirize them. ESL students are completely at sea with this kind of material. Most notable offender this semester: cummings' "next to of course god, I love you."

> I usually make separate "arrangements" with them—discreetly of course.

> I use the same standards, but have to work more with ESLers.

> This term I have only one [ESL student] and she's as good as most of the others. She certainly works harder.

> ESL students may rewrite or get outside assistance. Of course, special problems remain, but only time will help.

> If anything, the two or three ESL students I had were more sensitive to literature and better able to handle difficult literature than many of the native speakers. We did some Greek mythology and *Oedipus Rex*, and one of my Greek students knew that material well.

> In my experience, ESL students have been competitive and in many cases a welcomed addition to the class (bringing special knowledge that native speakers do not normally have).

> No. I don't think we should cater to that segment of the class to the detriment of the regular students. Furthermore, when it comes to the *content* of the literature, I find that frequently the foreign students are able to comprehend complex material better than the American-born ones—maybe because many of them have thought and suffered more.

> I started the semester with six ESL students. Five dropped the course.

The following semester we decided to run several special sections, each composed of roughly 10 native-born and 10 nonnative students. We would teach a variety of genres, including standard canonical material and a few cross-cultural selections—preferably not literature in translation—and see what came out of an artificial balancing of the class constituency. This chapter describes the mixed results of the experiment, according to my own experiences in one of these sections.

My observations in this chapter regarding my students' encounters with literature are offered as both informal elaboration and modification of the body of research on reading that has grown considerably in the past few decades, most of it based on the assumptions of schema theory. These assumptions have become a matter for scrutiny of late, since the standard bearers for cultural literacy, campaigning for more uniform curricula and measurements of literacy, have built their case to a great extent on schema hypotheses. Schema theory, borrowing from cognitive psychology the concept of patterns or schemata by which the mind takes in and analyzes experience, shows how reading comprehension of a text requires the reader's access to prior background knowledge. The theory predicts that expanding the reader's acquaintance with the presuppositions implicit in the material will enhance her comprehension of the text. Since schema theory informs most studies of how nonnatives read literature in English, I will begin the present discussion with a survey of this research.

By way of introduction, however, I would like to offer a few considerations that do not appear to have entered into the methods and conclusions of most of the schema studies summarized below. There is little doubt that cultural background is central to a reader's understanding of a text, and much of this chapter is devoted to demonstrations of this premise. Indeed, several reading studies dovetail with the evidence for culturally determined *writing* preferences discussed in the preceding two chapters. To cite just one example that illuminates data mentioned further on in these pages: in a study by Eggington (1987), Korean students of English, asked to rank the relative difficulty of English reading samples, clearly preferred and found easiest to decipher those samples that followed traditional, "nonlinear" Korean discourse patterns. Naturally I agree that the conventions of literary genres in English have to be clarified and contextualized for ESL students. But I believe the hypotheses of schema research need to be modified further by what we have learned about transactions between reader and text from reader-response criticism and from other poststructuralist approaches to literature.

Most reading studies, and by extension the arguments for a program of cultural literacy, presuppose an ideal reading, one in which the "experienced native reader," as described in one of the articles quoted below, possesses sufficient background knowledge to "allow him to gain access to the total informational content of that discourse." Researchers usually gauge their subjects' comprehension of a text—typically an expository passage but some-times a piece of fiction—by the number of propositions from the text the subjects are later able to recall and elaborate on in an "appropriate" fashion. This methodology does more than simply make of any reading passage a rather dry commodity. It implies not only that there is an agreed-upon and finite interpretation of a given text, but, more profoundly, a common set of values and assumptions about the texts we read and how we read them. As George Dillon has objected in *Constructing Texts,* "we need to test for what sort of altered understanding a text has brought about, not just what facts have been recovered." Further, Dillon argues, not all information is mean-ingful for all readers, whose convictions and knowledge guide their interest in and recall of a text (163). In several articles cited a few pages hence, we will see how readers' beliefs can, or should, mediate quantitative data collected in research on reading.

Hermeneutics, reception theory, poststructuralist criticism, all point up the limitations of positivist methodology. A literary text, and even, to some degree, the "objective" discourse of science, embraces indeterminacies which may be interpreted variously. Each reader brings a private as well as histor-ically and culturally determined repertoire to his or her interaction with the text, so that there is phenomenologically manifold and unpredictable "infor-mational content" in any literary passage, rather than one fixed and univer-sally correct reading.

The observations of reader-based literary criticism, brought to bear in the laboratory, thus compromise the results of intake-of-content research models. More happily, the effect of this kind of literary criticism is liberating in the classroom. After all, many of our students have been taught (all the more persuasively, I should think, in countries less encouraging of student participation than the United States) that if they wait quietly at the Garden gate their teacher, like the colleague quoted at the beginning of this chapter, will indeed excavate "the" meaning of the text for them. But to recognize that texts are polysemous is not to license all interpretations, however far-fetched. True, some formulations of reader-response theory—say, by Bleich and Holland—tend to consider the reader in isolation, thus presenting readings as the (theoretically unbridled) projections of the reader's psyche onto the text. Similarly, poststructuralism taken to the nether regions of indetermi-nacy has fanned the fears of humanists that a text deconstructed is one reduced to rubble. Left out of such descriptions of the reading process, however, is the consideration of what it is like to read within the social context of the classroom, supported and reined in by what Stanley Fish has called "the authority of interpretive communities"—communities, that is, bred by academic institutions. In the collaborative classroom, a variety of readings are heard and elaborated, so that the community of readers at once revises assumptions, complicates inferences, and places certain constraints on the range of readings of a particular text.

The literature class described in the following pages takes the implica-tions of this method one step further. The experience of reading literature in

English with international students demonstrates how native readers' interpretations might have become impoverished by too narrow a perspective on
the text, and how the views of international students—those perhaps un-
aware of certain cultural conventions—can enlarge native speakers' understanding. By interrogating what a native reader might accept as given, nonnative readers expose certain implicit cultural habits of perception,
interpretation, and valuation, and so help estrange and renew the texts and
reading strategies of native speakers.

Schema Theory: A Little Background Information

With these caveats in mind let's survey the relevant research on reading, chiefly as it pertains to nonnative speakers. Studies of the past few
decades on ESL students' reading performance in English have shown that
the cultural background of a text has a greater effect on readers' comprehension than the text's degree of linguistic complexity. In fact, research by
Honeyfield (1977) and Blau (1982) demonstrates that simplifying the syntax
and content of reading material does not facilitate ESL students' comprehension, but may actually impede their understanding because the simplified
version differs significantly from normal English in information distribution
and organization. A study by Steffensen, Jogdeo, and Anderson (1978),
comparing American and Indian subjects' reading of two passages describing
typical American and Indian weddings, shows that the subjects read their
native passage more rapidly, recalled more information from the native
passage, and were more likely to recall elements from both texts that were
rated as "important" by other subjects from the same cultural heritage.
Further, the subjects produced more culturally appropriate elaborations of
the native passage as well as more culturally based distortions of the foreign
passage. Johnson (1981) comes to similar conclusions in her comparison of
college-level American and Iranian ESL students' readings of stories from
American and Iranian folklore.

From related studies we see that in all forms of discourse, scientific as
well as literary, cultural background is a critical factor in the reader's comprehension of the text. Selinker, Lackstrom, and Trimble (1973) consider how
presuppositional elements in the English of Science and Technology (EST)
interact with explicit rhetorical elements, and how these in turn affect surface
grammatical forms, specifically the use of articles and verb tenses. Selinker,
Trimble, and Trimble (1976) suggest that the nonnative reader "often lacks
those abilities which will allow him to recognize the existence of certain types
of *implicit presuppositional rhetorical information*, abilities which the experienced
native reader of EST discourse does possess and which allow him to gain
access to the total informational content of that discourse" (282). Similar
difficulties arising from a lack of presuppositional *cultural* information are
reported in Gatbonton and Tucker's study of Filipino high school students'
reading of American short stories (1971), in Trivedi's analysis of native Eng-

lish speakers' interpretations of an Indian story translated from Gujarati (1978), and in Kujoory's examination of English majors in Iranian universities studying British and American literature (1978).

The schema theory of reading asserts that building readers' culturally determined background knowledge prior to reading will improve their comprehension and recall of the text. For instance, in their previously cited study, Gatbonton and Tucker gave one group of Filipino students special instruction in cultural differences in values and attitudes, and found that this group subsequently performed more like the American control group than the Filipino students who had not received this training. Kujoory reports similar success offering Iranian students an introductory course in the background of Western thought. Johnson (1982), testing this hypothesis with ESL students in an American university, found that the students' recent experience with the celebration of an American holiday gave them sufficient background information for better comprehension of a reading passage in English concerning that event. Subjects were able to recall more explicit and implicit information, and the sentences in their written recollections more accurately reflected the cohesive ties and relations between ideas and propositions in the familiar section of the passage.

Yet the conclusions we can draw from the studies outlined above are surely mitigated by the considerable body of research on affective variables in language learning, discussed at length in Chapter 5 of this book. Determining the necessary or meaningful cultural background of a text, the means by which that information is to be imparted to our students, and the standards by which their absorption of "content" is to be measured or quantified: these are far more complicated and ideologically freighted undertakings than the foregoing studies would indicate.

Several departures from the findings just surveyed are therefore pointedly relevant here. Yousef (1968) observes that even after intensive cultural orientation, advanced Middle Eastern students living in the United States had trouble interpreting texts from American culture because of their negative attitudes toward the culture. He concludes that the students' vehement though unconscious resistance to American beliefs reduced their motivation and efforts to learn about the target culture, and caused them to answer questions according to their own native behavioral patterns. Williams (1981), in a study of pupils in Nigerian primary schools reading English as a second language, reports that the learners' attitudes toward reading English, when considered along with the variables of learning environment and materials, contributed significantly to the prediction of the students' scores.

More recently, Markham and Latham (1987), assessing the influence of religion-specific background knowledge on the listening comprehension of adult subjects (self-described Muslims, Christians, and "religion-neutral" university students), report that the content of passages describing Christian and Muslim rituals exerted a powerful influence on the performance scores of listeners professing close ties to a particular religion. The authors quote, for example, from a particularly revealing interview with a Muslim student. The student had earlier been asked to write down what he recalled from a passage he had listened to explaining Muslim religious practices. In the subsequent interview he criticizes the passage, which contradicts his own cultural strictures against justifying the assumptions of one's religious beliefs. The authors of the article conclude that "Ahmed's views may have influenced his quantitative performance" (164–65).

In light of the last three studies, then, the question of motivating and empowering international students in their reading of literature in English becomes all the more encumbered. As I have indicated, the purpose of the discussion that follows is, first of all, to flesh out some of the findings of the relevant research by illustrating the range of problems that may crop up when students of heterogeneous backgrounds, and ESL students in particular, study a variety of literary texts in an introductory course in an American college. More than this, however, I would like to illustrate a feature of nonnatives' readings of English texts largely absent from the research on reading. As we have seen, these studies generally focus on students' comprehension as shown by correct or erroneous short answers in retrieving specified content from a text. I wish to consider how the foregrounding of cultural differences in the setting of the collaborative classroom can open up texts for native and nonnative readers alike.

Let me not wax too elegiac. As you will gather from the notes that follow, opportunities to test this hypothesis were occasional, owing to the self-consciousness of the experimental makeup of the class and the lingering silence of the nonnative students in particular, especially those less linguistically prepared. (Once more, as when I had taught literature classes in the past, I found myself muttering, "How did the grammatically malnourished make it past English 105? What are my colleagues *doing* in their composition courses?" Naturally I seldom ask myself such questions when teaching composition.) But when students were convinced their responses were privileged, when their journal entries were read and questions of interpretation and even miscues were made matters of discussion, something clicked. Classroom discussion led to more critical examination of our preconceptions as readers, and some of the students' formal essays in turn derived from this discovery of how meanings are created.[1] Collectively we began to sense how our culturally determined reading schemata and interpretive conventions might, in effect, be blocking off alternative avenues of inquiry and understanding.

Bridging Cultural Gaffes: Reading Students' Notebooks

Like many teachers, I ask the students in my composition and literature classes to keep journals in which they record ideas for papers and reactions to

---

[1]Chapter 9 will consider ways to develop longer and more formal writing assignments in literature courses. The present chapter is confined to discussion of students' responses to reading assignments in class discussion and in their journals.

reading assignments. In the experimental Writing and Literature (English 120) course I taught in the spring of 1984, a section composed of 10 native speakers and 10 ESL students, I was particularly interested in monitoring the students' written responses to what was going on in class. Leafing through the notebooks, sometimes weeks after a classroom discussion that appeared to have gone rather well despite the reluctance of some of the nonnatives to speak out, I would discover some misunderstanding on the student's part, and, just as often, on the part of the instructor, regarding a passage in the reading assignment whose meaning had seemed obvious at the time.

I'd like to use some of these excerpts from my students' journals[2] to point up the impediments and insights that can arise in the path of students approaching literature primarily written by and for members of other cultures. Ideally, readers should share some of the author's presuppositions and expectations about literature, so that they can recognize a textual clue when they see one. In illustration of this point, let me give you a few examples of the range of readings—all "competent" enough—elicited by a text I studied with my English 120 class: *The Woman Warrior,* Maxine Hong Kingston's memoirs as a Chinese-American growing up in California among the "ghosts" of two cultures.

In "No Name Woman," the first chapter of her book, Kingston tells a "secret story" about an aunt in China who killed herself and her illegitimate child. The text suggests several interpretations of the title of the piece. The disgraced woman has no name because, to the family members in America who never speak of her, it is as though she never existed. To her family in China she had begun to disappear once her pregnancy became apparent; she was suffered to remain among them, rather than to live with her husband's parents as a respectable married woman in China was expected to do. She disturbed the order of the village and was renounced by her neighbors. Her infant, without family, would be nameless too.

Before we discussed the first chapter in class, I asked the students to write down their initial responses to the story, paying particular attention to the way Kingston stitches together a narrative from the few scraps her mother has given her. The students seemed to enjoy this chapter, and most were able to make sound if rather general observations. Interestingly, in the notebooks of the native English speakers I picked up a common thread: most appeared self-conscious about their status as outsiders looking in on the text, often responding to elements in the narrative as though to sociological more than literary events. These excerpts from the notebooks of three native-born students are fairly typical:

[2]Two reminders. Because the illustrations in this chapter are drawn exclusively from my students' notebooks, they are offered as starting points for discussion rather than as a comprehensive catalogue of the questions raised by the reading of multicultural literature. I also ask the reader to keep in mind that as the ongoing journal assignment was more immediate and personal in nature than the more formal essays assigned in the course, my students understood that in jotting down their impressions they did not have to concern themselves with grammar, mechanics, and so on.

I found the small portions of info that we receive about Chinese culture also quite amusing. In China at the time, we are told, "Adultery is extravagance" (p.7). Isn't is ironic that adultery is considered an extravagance, not explicitly something forbidden, and that it is compared to a delicacy, like rich food? Another very interesting point is the "outcast table" mentioned on p.8. In Chinese tradition the powerful older people "made the wrongdoers eat alone. . . . " (Nancy Cohen)

Maxine Hong Kingston tells the story about her aunt because it tells a lot about Chinese culture, and even though Maxine is basically Americanized, she does write about her family in China, and I think she wanted to stress some points in the Chinese tradition. This particular story stood out in her mind. I think that this story about her aunt is not only interesting and mystifying, but it says a lot about Chinese people and their ways. (Sheri Grunin)

. . . Maxine begins to draw one elaborate theory of her aunt's life, using her knowledge of Chinese behavior, theory, and imagination. She uses some very strong images in this fascinating story, among them the interesting descriptions of Chinese life and behavior. For example, even with the obvious physical condition of the aunt's pregnancy, no one would speak of it, as if the words would betray some secret. (Kevin Brown)

In class we began by considering various meanings of the story's title. Kathy Borstock, an American-born student, speculating on these possibilities in her notebook, was more specific than her compatriots:

Kingston compares herself with the aunt with no name, as she is in America and doesn't really know what her background is, whether it is Chinese or American. The aunt had her name taken away because of her affair, and Maxine has no true name. Maxine may feel that in order to have a beginning one must have a name. She is unsure of her name, whether it is American or Chinese, and she realizes that her aunt had all her possessions, including her name, taken away.

Fine so far. But compare the foregoing commentaries with that of Mei-Ying Tsai, a student from Taiwan:

Chinese believes that "name" can influence a person's fate and personality. Sometimes we have two names, one for written purpose, the other for "calling" purpose, that is the one which is supposed to bring you good luck. Therefore, the more people call your name, the more good luck you are going to get. (It is not easy to decide a "calling" name. Most of the time, we have to go to a fortune teller, and he would match your birthday with the strokes of characters, then can come out with a name that is only good for you.)

Female can't carry any descent line; therefore, if a girl dies before she gets married, she will become a wild ghost without any family temple where she can stay and get her food as well as paper money from. Unless, her family wants to pay dowery to a man who is willing to accept her as his "ghost" wife and lists her name in his own family temple. Then, she is always entitled to share any gifts that is given by the man's living descents.

As it happens, Ku Chien-Chung, the Taiwanese student whose progress we've followed in earlier chapters of this book, was also enrolled in one of these 120 sections. When he came to my office for a conference, I read him Mei-Ying's commentary. He smiled and nodded: he was fairly certain Kingston had had all this background in mind when writing "No Name Woman." Did Ku have any other information, say, about the next chapter, entitled "White Tigers" — information to which an American audience might not be privy? In this second chapter, Kingston casts herself in the role of the young Fa Mu Lan, the legendary Chinese woman warrior who saved her people from conquerors. For our next class meeting Ku made the following observations in his notebook:

White tiger is a series of star in the sky. The ancient Chinese astrologer believed that when white tiger appears on the sky, the war always occurs. The white tiger or jinx in China is a symbol of bad, something to do with blood, death, etc.

In the second chapter, I think the author has put a few different Chinese stories into one: stories about Fa Mu Lan, the woman warrior, but also stories about a hero named Fei. The chapter is about a child who is directed by a bird to a mountain where she learns some war skills and becomes a famous warrior. When she starts out, her parents write Chinese characters on her back. [Kingston writes, " 'We are going to carve revenge on your back,' my father said. 'We'll write out oaths and names.' "]

This story refers to a very popular Chinese legendary hero, whose name, Fei, is the Chinese ideograph for "fly." Fei's mother told him, "don't stay home to protect me—you have to protect your country against the enemy. If you don't fight, your family will die anyway." This is what she wrote on Fei's back; she didn't write about revenge—that's not what the Chinese story is about.

I think this shows a difference between American and Chinese people. We're more conservative, we don't speak out; American people are more straight-out. Maxine lived all her life and had her education among American people. On her back is written revenge.

The heroine Maxine mentions is Fa Mu Lan, but really the chapter is made up of several Chinese stories that mean something different to Chinese people. But in my point of view, she

has done good research in Chinese, and heard stories from her
mother, and put them all into a Chinese-American heroine.

It became clear that while the rest of the class and I were reading *The
Woman Warrior*, my Chinese students were reading a different book, a far
richer one. I assume this would be the case for Argentinian students reading
Allende, Japanese students reading Tanizaki, and so on. Of course, what we
usually read in English 120 are works by native English speakers, however
increasingly these voices are likely to come from outside so-called mainstream American culture. So the first line of inquiry in this chapter on reading
parallels that of earlier chapters on writing: we will examine the special
problems nonnative readers are more likely to encounter, the more readily to
anticipate them in subsequent classroom discussions of literature. We will
then look at some of the ways collaboration in the literature classroom helps
not just foreign-born students, but their U.S.-born classmates, with material
that is inevitably culture-bound.

Consider my students' reactions to Browning's "My Last Duchess." As
you might imagine, native and nonnative students alike had a rocky passage
through this text. But while some of the native speakers got the details wrong
in their initial notebook responses, they still clung to the conviction that they
could make out the sense of the poem if they reread it a few times, and that
if they had trouble understanding the monologue it wasn't their fault so
much as a function of the poem. Doubtless our students too frequently cave
in to this kind of rationalization. But in this case their sense of the poem's
purposeful obscurity was both justifiable and useful. Michael Callahan's terse
commentary nears the mark:

> The duke is a very snakey guy.
> He wants to obscure his own meanings, he hints at everything.
> He comes out and says nothing.
> She is just a work of art to him.
> All of this is called up out of someone who isn't a humanist.
> She is quite alone.
> Her friends are the servants.
> The Duke lets you look at her when he is around but not when he is not.

The ESL students in the class, on the other hand, were often flum-
moxed not only by their linguistic deficiencies but by their *apprehension* of
these shortcomings. Echoing a number of her peers, Chung-Ae Park, a
Korean student, had this to say:

> For the first time I saw this poem, I had no idea what was
> going on. Even though I understand almost all meaning of words,
> it was hard to follow what the speaker was trying to say.

Perhaps we can locate a few areas of special difficulty for ESL students reading the poem. The following examples are drawn from the notebooks of several Korean students in the class, but analogically map out the terra incognita all readers face when reading literature from other cultures.

To begin at the most basic level, as we have seen in previous chapters, nonnative speakers will naturally have problems with phonology and intonation, and nowhere is this more apparent than in the reading of poems. In Browning's dramatic monologue, obviously, the reader's grasp of rhythm and rhyme is central to understanding the work: the convoluted syntax of the duke's speech is pointedly at odds with the silky virtuosity of the perfectly matched rhyming couplets of iambic pentameter in which his speech is cast. That most students are initially stymied by Browning's sentence inversions is clear to anyone who has taught the poem. Our concern here, though, is with rhyme and cadence, which logically present greater difficulty for ESL students than for their native-speaker counterparts. Ku Chien-Chung, for example, who while enrolled in this 120 class was also taking my colleague Marie Ponsot's poetry workshop, professed to have far more trouble writing rhyming couplets than writing sestinas. Ku added that he can usually "hear" the rhyme when it occurs in the predictable final position of a poetic line but rarely when it occurs medially or at the end of an enjambed line. (Ku may also have heard end-rhyme more clearly because it conforms to expectations set up in his native culture. Even more so than in English poetry, one of the most powerful determinants of meaning in classical Chinese poetry is end-rhyme.)

We can't know for certain what our ESL students hear or think they hear, but characteristic misspellings provide us with clues. Take for instance the Greek student in our 120 class who told of a pleasant "happizode," or the Israeli woman who wrote about leaving home and becoming "hearthsick"—a wonderfully evocative portmanteau appearing to result in part from an overcorrection for the -th sound found in English but missing from Hebrew as from many other languages.

Or consider the case of another Korean speaker, since Chung-Ae Park's commentary is the point on which this discussion turns. As in many other languages, the contrast between the /I/ sound as in *bit* and the /i/ as in *beat* is fast disappearing in most dialects of Korean (Chu and Park 9). Many Korean learners will find it difficult to hear and produce the two varieties of *i* correctly; for instance, Mi-Young Cho, a compatriot of Chung-Ae's, wrote this journal entry about a passage from *The Woman Warrior:*

> The little girl never talked in her class which made Maxine
> angry for they had same nationality. Maxine felt shame of her and
> her country, so she bit her up.

If we add to this pronunciation problem the fact that Korean, like Chinese, does not have two distinct phonemes for /æ/ as in *bad* and /ɛ/ as in *bed*, we may imagine the difficulty a Korean speaker will have, for example, with the couplet from "My Last Duchess" that rhymes the deceptively spelled "said" and "read," and which is embedded in an extraordinarily complex periodic sentence that depends in part on this past-tense reading.

For this same student, the question of word stress becomes more complicated still. For one thing, Korean speakers have trouble with English consonant clusters, especially when they occur at the beginning or end of a word—as, for instance, in the two words that begin the above-mentioned couplet, "Will't please you sit and look at her? I said. . . . " The Korean student is likely to insert a barred ɨ sound between the consonants in the cluster, to "decluster" the sounds, thus producing something like "will it pɨlease you," which leaves the meaning intact but sabotages the rhythm of the line.

English is a stress-timed language: the time an English utterance takes depends upon the number of *stressed* syllables it contains. On the other hand, Korean—like, for example, Japanese and Spanish—is a syllable-timed language in the sense that the time a Korean utterance requires is determined by the number of syllables it contains (Chu and Park 12, 17). Syllables in a syllable-timed language are almost evenly stressed, in contrast to the weak and strong syllables of a stress-timed language. Predictably, Korean learners often transfer their own intonation patterns to English, frequently assigning even stress to each syllable, and thus making English poetic meter an improbability. Examples like these should give us some insight into how ESL students' phonological patterns may interfere with their perceptions of intonation, stress, rhyme, alliteration, and assonance, and, in addition, may hinder their ability to make sense of any regional dialects found in literature in English.

Problems at the lexical level are perhaps more easily detected. An ESL student may stumble unexpectedly over a word which to an American reader seems rudimentary. Glancing through Mi-Young Cho's notebook glossary for "My Last Duchess," I was scarcely surprised to see definitions for "mantle" and "trifle," but was brought up short by her need to look up "bronze." Then too, the bilingual dictionaries to which ESL students often resort are apt to supply comically inappropriate synonyms, although now and again the result is a felicitous archaism, as when Chung-Ae remarked that "A Rose for Emily" was the tragic story of a woman who ended her life in misery though she had grown up "in noblesse."

Unanticipated as well were the kind of miscues in diction and register that showed up in the notebook of Sunhi Lee, a Korean student whose grasp of English was much shakier than that of the other ESL students in the class. When we read Roethke's "Elegy for Jane," for example, I asked my students to begin investigating the nature imagery of the poem by looking up words such as tendril, pickerel, wren, sparrow—not just unfamiliar words, but words they might have thought they knew. Following are the first two stanzas of the poem, along with Sunhi's gloss of them:

> I remember the neckcurls, limp and damp as tendrils;
> And her quick look, a sidelong pickerel smile;

And how, once startled into talk, the light syllables leaped for her,
And she balanced in the delight of her thought,

A wren, happy, tail into the wind,
Her song trembling the twigs and small branches.
The shade sang with her;
The leaves, their whispers turned to kissing;
And the mold sang in the bleached valleys under the rose.

Sunhi had trouble playing out the semantic properties of the pickerel, with its
narrow glinty smile, but then so did the other students in the class: their
dictionaries just didn't go far enough. The surprise comes in her definitions
for "shade"—in her confusion about gauging register to occasion, topic, and
audience. It is equally important to note, however, that the same confusion
that led Sunhi to overlook the noun "shadow" and include "sunglass[es]"
also led her to "ghost," a crucial meaning that only appeared in the notes of
two other ESL students, Maribel Lopez and Alka Patel (for the native speakers had evidently seen no need to look up "shade"). Had it been volunteered
in class, this definition would have greatly enriched the other students'
reading of the poem.

   An even more elusive level of lexical interpretation for the nonnative
reader concerns the signification of words not just through the weave of

connotation but through look and sound. Even those foreign-born students with the most extensive English vocabularies cannot be expected to possess the network of associations that give words texture and heft for their native-born counterparts. Definitions are far more supple than native speakers realize, else how should we know that *heart* can refer to a conventionalized design on a playing card or a hollow muscular organ in the body, the essence of darkness or the core of the country, the bulbous part of a celery plant, courage (if you have a lot of it), or a lack of desire (if you only have half of one)? These levels of meaning are part of the fabric of thought for a native speaker but not for the second-language learner. And if word meanings are more elastic for native speakers, sounds are surely more evocative. Glossing "skittery pigeon" in Roethke's "Elegy," Sunhi comes up with "skitter: to move lightly along the surface," whereas Mona Costanza, a native speaker, less literal but more attuned to nuance and implied rhyme, notes, "Skittery, from the verb—hops, alive, jittery."

Even proper names—I mean those of naturalistic rather than obviously allegorical cast—can take on the sheen of chivalric epithets, as we have seen in the comments of Mei-Ying and Ku regarding *The Woman Warrior*. Let me illustrate this point further with an analogy from a work Americans would likely encounter in a similar introductory course in Chinese literature, the eighteenth-century classic *Dream of the Red Chamber*. During one conversation in the novel a court member, Yu-tsun, comments that "trite" girls' names such as Welcome Spring or Compassion Spring are only affected by common folk. A second character explains,

> "It [The word 'Spring'] was chosen because their first daugh-
> ter happened, as I told you, to be born on the first day of the
> year, when spring begins. In the preceding generation, the girls
> all have names analogous to those of the boys. For instance, the
> name of your pupil's mother is 'Min,' which has the same radical
> as Sheh and Cheng. . . . "
>
> "It must be so," Yu-tsun said. "Now I understand why my
> pupil always reads the character 'min' as 'mi' and writes it with a
> stroke missing."

English speakers need a good deal of presuppositional material to make sense of this interchange. Some cues are supplied in the passage. But just as much information—concerning naming practices, social distinctions, calculations of the seasons of the year, differences between boys' and girls' names and between given and family names, and the look and sound of written Chinese characters—must be assumed on the part of the reader. As for Yu-tsun's understanding of the pupil's "misreading" of names, this must be explained for us by the English translator of the work, who notes that "The names of the sovereign and parents were taboo and could not be used except in a 'mutilated' form" (Wang 24).

I do not argue that the etiquette of proper names in the West in the late twentieth century is anywhere near so complicated. But I do want to attend to the kinds of unconscious connections native speakers are more apt to make among sound, social context, and significance. Take an example from another story we read in our 120 class, John Cheever's "The Swimmer." Many American-born readers have the potential, at least, to "hear" that when Neddy Merrill leaves the swimming pools of the Hammers, Lears, and Howlands, and moves on to the pools of the Bunkers and the Levys and finally to those of the Sachses and Biswangers, his descent is social as well as psychological. Hence Mona Costanza's note that Cheever's protagonist eventually "loses his social status in the community along with his sense of the socioeconomic realities in the United States." Of course some native speakers will miss the point, but then nonnatives surely cannot be expected to make this distinction.

What I have been trying to suggest is the encoded, nonsemantic symbolism of the most seemingly innocuous of lexemes. Such considerations complicate the tangle of relationships between signifier and signified, a thicket of representation less universally meaningful than most classroom discussions of symbolism would suggest. I recall an instance of cultural difference in interpretation from one of my earliest ESL writing classes. I used to give my students a standard combination assignment in narration, description, and analysis: Narrate a dream you've had recently and discuss what you think it means. A Japanese student whose name escapes me but whose dream I vividly recollect wrote that she dreamed she was walking through the Queens College quad when she noticed snakes writhing all about her. Pink ones, thousands of them, lolling on the greensward, and very friendly they were, too: "They was smiling at me and looks cute!" she exclaimed. The dream ended with a rocket exploding into the air from the center of the quad. As we two sat in my office going over her paper, I considered telling this student about her libido. But I kept my exegesis to myself. *Her* interpretation was that this was a dream about good luck for the coming year, since snakes and dragons and like Western bugaboos are taken as good luck symbols by the Japanese and Chinese.[3] My "reading" did not

---

[3]I realize here I am reducing the complex and powerful image of the dragon in Chinese culture to greeting-card proportions. For the Chinese the dragon has also traditionally symbolized nature's elemental laws. But I want to show popular conceptions of the figure, as interpreted by some of the students in my classes. For instance, on the same subject, Mei-Ying's sister Su-Chuan Tsai, wrote in her journal for an introductory composition class:

"In Chinese culture, dragon represents goodness and luck. The native Chinese dragon is quite different from a Western dragon, which usually stand in the evil side. I like dragon not only because it's a symbol of luck, but for its elegant and free form. In Imperial China, dragon pattern is exclusively a royal symbol. It reminds me of the mysterious and luxurious life that the emperors used to live. We can find dragon design is widely used in Chinese art, and even in some Japanese paintings."

On the other hand, I suppose one ought not be too doctrinaire about this or any other culture-specific difference in interpretation. A Mainland Chinese student in my American literature course, comparing notes with his compatriot in the class, said he had never heard of this "Chinese" interpretation of the dragon symbol.

preclude hers: for all I know she was in for a run of extraordinary fortune. But the incident made me wonder what non-Western readers make of the dragons and serpents of Western literature, from Grendel and his mother to the narrow fellow in the grass who made Emily Dickinson zero at the bone. Of course, the symbolism of my student's snakes is particularly slippery, arising as it does from the context of a personal storehouse of dream images. But I use this example to show the confluence of the private repertoire of oneiric activity with the symbolic image recognized by and perhaps specific to a given culture.

My 120 class afforded a number of demonstrations of culturally deter-mined interpretation in the study of literature. For instance, midway through the semester our class read Stevens's poem, "Thirteen Ways of Looking at a Blackbird." While this piece initially appears more accessible than "My Last Duchess," it is of course recondite and problematic for all readers. But if I had banked, in any case, on everyone sharing certain dark and brooding conno-tations for "blackbird"—a flock of images that for American readers of my generation might include, say, Poe's raven, the blackbird singing in the dead of night in the Beatles' song, and the bird Al Jolson said bye bye to—I was mistaken. This is from the notebook of Blanca Palacios:

> In Ecuador, South America, the indians who live on the ori-ental part of the country have the believe that black birds bring them good luck and health. All this I learned when I went to the jungle (oriental part), there the tribes are full of traditions and customs that are totally diferent from the ones that we have in the city. I used to believe that any black thing could bring me bad luck. One day before I was going back to my home a little girl brought me a black bird. . . . She said to me, "Don't be scare, this little bird for us is a meaning of health, love and prosperity; we believe that all of us should keep a black bird in our homes but it has to be dead. Now take it home and always keep it with you, you will see that all these good things will come to you." Since then I have my little black bird with me wherever I go.

In a larger context, beyond the associations connected with this or that image, the collaborative experiment urged upon us a recognition of how perception itself is constructed by culture. Just before we began Bernard Malamud's short story, "The Magic Barrel," I asked the students to bring in photographs or objects that carried symbolic significance in their native cultures. Carmen Cheng, born in Peru of Chinese parents, brought in a red card decorated with figures. Red in Chinese culture signifies a happy occasion; the card, which stands for a good luck wish, is ritually exchanged on New Years and birthdays; the three figures are gods symbol-izing long life, good fortune, and money. The Chinese students in the class "automatically" recognized and understood the significance of the card. An American student, Lenny Atlas, brought in a photo of himself and several other men, each wearing a tallis and yarmulka, looking up from the scrolls they were reading. Some of the class members were able to infer that the locale was a synagogue, some that the scrolls were the Torah. What no one noticed was that Lenny was clean-shaven in our classroom though bearded in the picture. Or if we saw this, we didn't charge the fact with meaning, though the beard would signify to more observant (in both senses) Jews like himself that at the time the photograph was taken Lenny had been in mourning.

For my own part, I had brought along a small reproduction of that mainstay of the art history class, Jan Van Eyck's *The Marriage of Giovanni Arnolfini*, a work whose iconography would have been readily grasped by viewers in fifteenth-century Bruges but now seems writ in a dead language. You will recall that behind the wedding couple in the painting is a convex mirror, and encircling that mirror are ten scenes, no bigger than silver dollars in the original and barely perceptible in my copy, depicting the Passion of Christ. I was just about to indicate these roundels, after some introductory comments on other Christian symbols in the painting, when Michael Callahan called from the third row, "Hey, aren't those scenes from the life of Christ?" He swore he had never seen the painting before; parochial school had apparently endowed him with x-ray vision. Visual schemata, like their verbal counterparts, guide our perceptions of form and content. What you see depends on what you're looking for.

One message to be gleaned from the foregoing exercise is hardly news but worth reiterating: no text is read independently of the reader's experience of other texts—other legends, rules, stories, customs, genres. Some textual riddles can only be unlocked by means of intertextual references to which the ESL student cannot always be expected to have access. At the same time, I have wanted to highlight an element of reading largely ignored in the research on schema theory: the way in which cross-cultural references expand the repertoire of nonnative and native-born readers by denaturalizing matters of perception and interpretation.

In light of these two "morals," then, I would like to examine the example of Malamud's modern fable, "The Magic Barrel," which our class read along with several other allegorical tales. I focus on this particular story for several reasons. First of all, the work itself presents in very apparent ways an allegory of reading: the protagonist is consciously engaged in interpreting the character of his beloved, as it is revealed in the photograph he has seen of her. Second, the story, although set within the confines of a specific subculture, seemed fairly accessible to the members of the class. Since parables and fables are found in most cultures, we met on common ground. Then too, the linguistic and narrative syntax of the Malamud story, especially in comparison with the Cheever and Faulkner stories we had read, is fairly straightforward—so much so that Chung-Ae, who had confessed to great difficulty with the Browning poem, was prompted to remark in her journal:

> First of all, I was glad to read this story without too much
> interruption. It was easier to follow what is going on to next sen-
> tence than any other stories we have read so far.

I turn your attention to the conclusion of the story. Leo Finkel is a rabbinical student whose lapsed faith has isolated him from God, from his fellow creatures, and from recognition of his own remorse and fear. Leo falls in love with the haunting photograph of Stella, a fallen soul who turns out to be the dishonored daughter of Salzman the matchmaker. To Leo, we are told, Stella seems somehow familiar, and frightening; she appears to have lived and suffered and known evil. Leo asks Salzman to arrange a meeting, and Salzman, protesting, at last agrees, leaving Leo with the suspicion that Salzman had planned it all to happen this way. The story concludes:

> Leo was informed by letter that she would meet him on a
> certain corner, and she was there one spring night, waiting under
> a street lamp. He appeared, carrying a small bouquet of violets
> and rosebuds. Stella stood by the lamp post, smoking. She wore
> white with red shoes, which fitted his expectations, although in a
> troubled moment he had imagined the dress red, and only the
> shoes white. She waited uneasily and shyly. From afar he saw
> that her eyes—clearly her father's—were filled with desperate
> innocence. He pictured, in her, his own redemption. Violins and
> lit candles revolved in the sky. Leo ran forward with flowers out-
> thrust.
>   Around the corner, Salzman, leaning against a wall, chanted
> prayers for the dead.

I want to consider a couple of "natural" assumptions on the part of native speakers concerning this passage. We'll leave aside linguistic concerns such as the use of the passive voice or the pronoun *she*, without antecedent, in the first sentence of the passage. These matters, however significant, readers are likely to skim over. Elsewhere in the passage, some readers may assume that Malamud the fabulist wishes to evoke the paintings of Marc Chagall, to quicken our feeling for the enchantment of the genre as well as our sense of the provincial shtetl that exists even here, in the upper reaches of Manhattan where the story is set. Alert (or schooled) native readers may see this and more.

I say these bits of knowledge enrich the story, but I cannot say they are crucial. My colleague Nancy Comley once reminded me that the Malamud story is especially opaque to WASPs, a neglected minority in New York, so perhaps at some later date we shall consider running special sections not only of ESL Composition but of WASP Comp, or of Semiotics for Goyim. Still, ethnic or religious differences notwithstanding, it is fairly certain that most native speakers will pick up the "troubling" meaning of the red dress Leo imagines, for in a sense we share Leo's expectations. Our reading of character, like Leo's, is largely a matter of expectations fulfilled and disappointed. We know a fallen woman by her red dress, whether she's Bette Davis in "Jezebel" or the gal who done in John Dillinger.

It is this last presupposition on which our understanding of the story's ending partly hinges. Judging from their notebook responses, most native speakers in the class seemed to get the point. Two examples should suffice.

Background information regarding Judaism certainly helped Nancy Cohen to interpret the story:

> The idea of a matchmaker is not at all farfetched to me. In the community I come from, there are many Hasidic Jews that always find a spouse through a matchmaker. . . .
> There is a law in Judaism that when someone marries a non-Jew he should be treated as dead. In the last line of the story Salzman is chanting prayers for the dead—I think he had the impression that Leo would be a Rabbi no more, because of his involvement with a girl that had "gone wrong." Even though Salzman tried to persuade him not to get involved with Stella, Leo would not listen and kept on thinking he could change Stella's way of life.

At the same time, Mona Costanza, while more tentative in her observations about the religious significance of the passage, still takes the meaning of the "red dress" fantasy into account in her notes on the story's conclusion:

> People usually appreciate something more if they have to fight for it than if it's handed to them on a platter. The girl in the story appears to be described possibly as a whore. Leo imagined her wearing a red dress yet when he saw her she was wearing white (white is a symbol of virginity).
> It seems strange to me that Salzman didn't want his daughter to go with Leo. I should think it would change her ways and better her, so he should want them together.

Needless to say by now, this reading of the image is not necessarily automatic with foreign-born students, still less so with non-Westerners. Carmen Cheng interpreted the white dress/red dress against the background of the two cultures, Spanish and Chinese, in which she had been reared:

> White is the color of purity and virginity; in Chinese, red means luck and happiness—people wear it on New Years and at weddings. But of course everyone has a different lucky color; you just have to look for the signs.

Similarly, I happened to speak in conference with Alka Patel, a student from India, some time after we had discussed the Malamud story in class. I asked her about the image in Malamud's final paragraph. Here is her interpretation:

> In India, a woman in white is someone whose husband has died. White is the color of mourning. Red shoes and dress are worn only on a woman's wedding day. So there's a contradiction in the story. This seems to be a woman who is married, but whose husband is dying. Leo expects her to wear a red dress because he doesn't want her to suffer, even though he's dead. He wants to seem alive for her.

Alka had been present for the classroom discussion of the story. In class we had gone over various aspects of the story's conclusion, although we did not dwell on the picture of a woman in a white dress and red shoes standing "by the lamp post, smoking," for I had operated under the delusion that in this case, at least, we were all seeing more or less the same thing. What Alka had heard (I cannot say how closely, or even whether, she had read the story) was superseded by what her own culture had taught. The upshot, in Alka's case as in Carmen's, was a rather painful and bizarre contradiction, the result of interpreting a work against the background of codes that differ drastically from those we can in this case assume were intended by the author.

I do not for a moment mean to suggest that these impediments to understanding are inevitable or insuperable, any more than I would insist that "sufficient" background information ensures understanding. On the contrary, I have maintained that cultural difference inspires interpretive felicities as well as miscues. Here is Michael Callahan's laconic commentary on the ending of "The Magic Barrel": "Why Leo finally picks Stella is news to me." Contrast Sunhi Lee's journal entry. For all her urgent problems with English, she seems to have hit upon the perfect word to characterize the relationship of Leo and Stella:

> But after reading this story, I was more sure the word "af-
> finity." In the beginning of story, it reflected me Leo may not
> marry with anybody because he never has any knowledge and
> even confidence about women. But when he saw a snapshot, he
> gazed at it a moment because he felt familiar and vivid impression
> that he had met her before. Also this photograph gave him the
> impression of youth. Also when Leo met Stella on a corner, she
> wore white with red shoes which fitted his expectations. All of
> these things relate "affinity."

Often, as I have said, such observations were relegated to the obscurity of my students' journals, owing to the lingering reluctance of the less linguistically proficient nonnatives to speak out in the company of their American-born peers. But I would like to demonstrate how the queries of the ESL students opened up the conclusion of the story for all of us. In class, Mi-Young Cho asked about the prayers for the dead, the nature of which many of us had taken for granted in our apprehension of Salzman's despair for Leo as well as for Stella. "But what exactly do these prayers say?" Mi-Young wanted to know. Lenny brought out that Kaddish, although chanted for the dead, never mentions death, but rather celebrates God's holiness and glory. It is exclusively a prayer of praise, and shows, in effect, that God's ways are not to be questioned, for He is the Truthful Judge. The ending is true to the other sense the story imparts, the sense of the potentially redemptive power of the coming together of strangers.

Blanca Palacio's successive notebook entries on the story, written before and after our classroom discussion, illustrate for me the uses, some quite unanticipated, of reading across cultures—and across stereotypes. I'll quote two excerpts from her lengthy discussions of the text. Before coming to class she wrote:

> It is amazing to find out how a writer usually narrates his story with a bias. What I want to say is that usually one writes something that bears relation to one's social class, or one's own culture or believes, either religious or political.
> In this case Bernard Malamud, a Jew, narrates a story of a young Jew also. I think that the author is giving us an image of how it is like to be a person who consecrates himself to study, forgetting that outside there is a life that keeps going on. I understand that Jews usually are people who love to work and study hard; this we can see from the Bible which narrates Jew's life from the beginning, where they become a strong nation in the world. All these things make me think that the author gives a message to them about love. . . . The matchmaker is a very important character because he is like a mirror to reflect how love can be distorted from its true value by means of material things such as money and social position. . . .
> The part I don't get its real meaning is the last sentence. It confuses me and does not let me get a conclusion about what he really planned. . . .

And this is from Blanca's second entry, dated two days later:

> According to what has been discussed in class, now I can add a little more of my personal opinion about the story and the ending.
> For me is really interesting to learn that in the Jew's culture, when a man has a suffering, he lets his beard grow as a sign of it. It would never have come to my mind to think about the real meaning of Leo's beard growing when he was facing his trouble about God's love in relation to him. Furthermore at the end when Salzman chanted the prayer for the dead I didn't even think it was because of his daughter's reputation; this is really interesting to know how the Jews tradition shows how they feel. As it was explained the Jews prayers for the dead are not totally about this, on the contrary they are related to love and life.
> As a catholic and believer I also infer that the prayers of Salzman were not only because of his daughter's reputation but to ask God for the death of her sins. As you may know when one dies to his sins, he will share eternal life and forgiveness for the sins of the past. Therefore I think that Salzman also prayed for the death of his daughter's sin, for a better and brand new life.

The meeting of strangers, it seems to me, creates more capable readers of texts, whether the readers are characters in a work of literature, ESL and native-speaking students reading poems and stories by professional writers, or teachers of writing and literature reading the notebooks of ESL students.

In thinking about these cross-cultural encounters, and in rereading my students' notebooks, I find myself returning to their comments on the final chapter of Maxine Hong Kingston's memoirs, entitled "A Song for a Barbarian Reed Pipe." Sheri Grunin wrote:

> Kingston writes about Ts'ai Yen, another woman warrior, who has been captured by barbarians in China. She has two kids who do not want to learn about their culture. She is in exile among barbarians who do not appreciate her culture. She creates a beautiful song that the barbarians and she can relate to. Kingston creates the same kind of beauty through her writing.

Here are Mei-Ying Tsai's speculations:

> 1. Chinese treasure their tradition and attach deeply to their land. Maybe the author wants to use the story of Ts'ai Yen to express her own feeling and longing for her home country. Although she was born and grew up in a foreign country, she still has Chinese blood in her body; maybe she cannot understand everything about Chinese, but she can also be moved, just like Ts'ai's two children are moved by their mother's song without knowing the literal meaning.
> 2. She wrote a book to tell the foreigners about the Chinese she knew, the Chinese ways of living or their thought. Maybe by writing the book she identified herself with Ts'ai Yen, who spread Han's culture to the barbarians thousands of years ago, and thought that she was also transfering Chinese ideas to the Americans.
> 3. Or she wants to say that being a Chinese, although she is far away from her home land now just as Ts'ai Yen was, she will always be concerned about her country and perhaps one day she will also go back to China.

Cultural dialogue thus gives shape not only to reading and discussion but to writing—personal or formal, expository or poetic. For one last instance of collaborative learning, then, I want to submit the evidence of a pair of poems Ku Chien-Chung submitted for his workshop with Marie Ponsot. Ku's first poem was composed in response to an assignment to "write a fable." Reprinted below is the nearly finished product, but as I write I also have before me three other versions that happened along the way. Version #1 was Ku's first draft, inspired under Marie's tutelage; #2 was written with Richard Bonomo, the tutor with whom Ku worked over the course of a year in the Writing Skills Workshop at our school; #3 was Ku's amalgamation of the previous two; #4 came about after he and I briefly discussed the work-in-progress in conference.

Dark and Bright

As the falling darkness gradually shades
The joy out of the colors in the spread

Of the pond, the black water ripples
Turn the web of floating birds to the center.

Somewhere a childish voice kindly calls to
The birds the way he thought a goose would,
As the crumbs from his vague fingers hit the water,
Radiating charming waves out of the blackness.

Some swans respond to his calling, and break
away the web to the dim edge where spreads
Incense of rye and tickling sensation
Against their breasts from those delightful waves.

I recall a sunny kindness on this dark blind:
An old lady shared her breakfast this morning
To the swan with her pure fingers and giggles.
She is revived in the boy's voice tonight.

A sudden seething outbursts from the center:
An abrupt back-up in the trend of joy,
With flopping wings, kicking legs, panting screams,
Disturbs the contented in the cold dark pool.

His fingerprints die on a swan's white neck.
The boy and lady once one in action,
Burst apart as he chokes and she fades
From mind to the elegy in the dark.

Powerful syntactic undertow notwithstanding, Ku swims, buoyant, in the element of this new language. It is evident that Ku's study of literature has colored and deepened his fable. Among influences he cited in our conversation were several elegies we had read in class, as well as the poems of Yeats and Coleridge he had read in his poetry workshop. Ku's next poem illustrates the movement of intertextuality, since the preceding poem provides a subtext for it. I want to conclude with this poem, for in it Ku articulates the nature (and the importance for him) of his collaboration with native speakers—especially, in this case, his tutor Richard. From Richard's own testimony as well as from internal evidence in the poem we can infer that the tutor, too, benefited from the collaboration. And all the while Ku negotiates so gracefully the rigorous form of the sestina.[4]

Friendship

Richard and I have little in common.
He seldom tells me anything 'bout his self
Only once I bumped into him half drunk,

---

[4]To recap what has been called one of the most difficult of English poetic forms, the sestina is composed of six stanzas of six ten-syllable lines and a three-line envoi; the stanzas are built on an intricate repetition of end-words: 1 2 3 4 5 6; 6 1 5 2 4 3; 3 6 4 1 2 5, and so on. These words must then appear in sequence in the envoi.

He treated me to a bar, a love poem
For his girlfriend was told between beers and smiles.
As we split, he said, "World is in trouble."

He majors in English, which I have trouble.
Once a week, he helps my problems, common
To most foreign students. He kindly smiles,
Listening to the English from my Chinese self.
He speaks slow and clear, rhythmic like a poem,
So charming that it almost makes me drunk.

He impresses me with an unique sense like—drunk.
Is it his sensitive looks that give me the trouble?
Or that moment in the bar his love poem
Affected me deeply? or his uncommon
Pure eyes, lined with sadness, speak for his self?
Or it is because of his self-conscious smiles.

Now needing his help with my poems, I smile
And come to him, confused like being drunk.
He's a full time student in school himself,
And has to take care of his own trouble,
But treats himself and students like me in common,
Delicately like dealing with a poem.

With his help, I finished my first English poem:
An old lady feeds geese by the pond with her smiles.
He told me that he went to that common
Pond, and fed the geese while his girlfriend was drunk.
He penetrates my pond without trouble,
As he was part of the pond like myself.

This is how we respond through mind to each self.
To him, I, raw and brave, try my best on poems.
To me, there is no word in him as "trouble."
He needs not to tell me more than his smiles.
We understand each other when sober or drunk,
Even if we do not have much in common.

A future is common to himself and myself.
Never drunk, we have to fight for the world beyond this poem,
And always smile no matter what is in trouble.

APPENDIX FOR CHAPTER 8

Spring 1984 Class Schedule for English 120*

1/30 Introduction: making inferences; keeping a Reader's Notebook.

2/1 Active reading: in-class writing on Hemingway's "Cat in the Rain." Short paper #1: Compose a coda to Hemingway's narrative.

2/6 Making inferences, continued. Narrative as detective story: Faulkner's "A Rose for Emily."

2/8 Fables, parables, and fairy tales. Bettelheim's analysis of "Snow White." Carter's "The Snow Child." Short paper #2: Narrate a well-known fairy tale from your culture and analyze the message you think it imparts.

2/13}

2/15} Fables, continued: student-selected tales from various cultures; Cheever's "The Swimmer"; Malamud's "The Magic Barrel."

2/22 Continue discussion of "The Magic Barrel." Short paper #3: an original parable.

2/27 Point of view: Stevens's "Thirteen Ways of Looking at a Blackbird."

2/29 Due: short paper #4 (exercise in description: X ways of looking at a _____).

3/5 Tall tales and legends: hand-outs and student samples.

3/7 *The Woman Warrior.*

3/12 *The Woman Warrior.*

3/14 *The Woman Warrior.*

3/19 Due: major paper #1 (a "family album" in the manner of Maxine Hong Kingston; see assignment sheet for essay structure).

3/21 Continue reading and discussing student essays.

3/26} "Realism" (?): O'Connor's "Everything That Rises Must

3/28} Converge"; Baldwin's "Sonny's Blues."

4/2 Introduction to poetry; poems in translation.

4/4 Dramatic monologue: "My Last Duchess"; "To His Coy Mistress." Short paper #5: dramatic monologue from Duchess's point of view.

4/9}

4/11} Drama/film: introduction to *Rashomon*. Point of view, revisited—notebook exercise: Select an event—say, an argument you had with a friend, or a brief news item that has caught your interest—and write two versions of the same story, as told from the perspectives of two people involved in the event.

*For expanded discussion of many of these topics and assignments, see Costello and Tucker, *Forms of Literature: A Writer's Collection,* Random House, 1989.

Spring break

4/25 *Rashomon*, (screenplay), continued. Student reports on research assignment: Investigate the historical background of twelfth-century Japan, the time in which *Rashomon* is set. What can you discover about the roles of the clergy and the samurai class, or about the status of women, or about the concept of "saving face" as compared with the Western notion of "guilt," and how does this research help you understand the screenplay?

4/30 *Rashomon*: film and discussion.

5/2 Selected poems.

5/7 Workshop on major paper #2—a comparison of two poems (see assignment sheet).

5/9 Selected poems, continued; discussion of major paper #2.

5/14 Final essay examination.

Major Paper #1 (Structure Based on *The Woman Warrior*)

You are invited to put together an autobiography that is really a kind of "family album," consisting of at least four sections (described below), each around two pages long, each modeled on a chapter from Kingston's book. There should, of course, be some common theme or thread that connects these sections, though the theme need not be stated explicitly. The point is to explore the ways your life has been influenced in some measure by your family and home culture.

1. (Optional) A "secret story" about a family member, such as the one Kingston tells about her aunt, the "no name woman." (If you write this section but don't want other students to read it, tell me so.)
2. A description of, or story about, a legendary hero or heroine whom you fantasized about or who influenced you when you were a child.
3. A story from the early life of one of your parents—the parent you feel closest to or most strongly identify with. Because the events you will narrate occurred before you were born, you will have to depend on your parents or other family members for "research." (And you may want to embellish on "the facts," as Kingston does.)
4. A story about another relative, such as an aunt or grandfather.
5. A story about you as a child—a key incident, such as Kingston recounts in the last chapter of her memoirs, that might help the reader to understand the adult you have become.

Remember to consider (especially in the case of 3 and 4, above) what significance these stories have for you. Why did you choose these particular events to narrate out of all the stories your family has told you? How did these stories shape your childhood?

Major Paper #2

I. Select two poems that have similar form (two sonnets, for example) or theme, and compare them to discover how two different authors handle the same structure or subject matter. You have dozens of options for this essay—here are just a few:

a. Two elegies—death laments—by, for instance, Jonson, Bradstreet, Harper, Levine, Wilbur, Merwin, or Roethke. Here you will want to focus on the ways each artist finds to deal with the death of a loved one. For example, we've looked at how Anne Bradstreet writes about the loss of her house and possessions; how, in her elegy, does she struggle with the far deeper loss of her young granddaughter? Does she reconcile herself to God's will, as in the poem on the burning of her house?

b. Two poems on love or death by Dickinson, or two poems by Roethke on either of these subjects.

c. Two poems on some other subject. Possibilities include: war (Reed and Levertov); fathers (Roethke and Hayden); freedom and slavery (Wheatley, Langston Hughes, Hayden); Brueghel's painting of Icarus (Williams and Auden); fish (Roethke, Bishop, Ted Hughes), or any other subject you'd like to suggest.

d. Two translations of the same poem, such as the poem by the Persian poet Sa'di we looked at in class.

In your essay of about four pages, it is your task to show how each poet has made the subject his or her own. The points of comparison are up to you. Among other elements we've discussed in class, appropriate matters for your consideration might include the attitude each poet takes toward the subject matter—the poem's mood and tone; the line lengths, sound patterns, rhythms, word order, and diction of the poem, the way imagery is used, the relationship between the poet and the speaker of the poem, and so on.

II. Here's an alternative: you may prefer to forgo comparison and instead analyze one poem in great detail, according to the elements mentioned in the above paragraph.

Please jot down preliminary notes for your paper before you sign up to see me, so that we can begin discussing your ideas for the project.

The Four Mountains. (From Gladys A. Reichard, *Navajo Medicine Man Sandpaintings,* 1939. New York: Dover, 1977.)

9

Notes for
an American Studies Course

I. Designing a Course by Committee

In the fall of 1987, several members of the Queens College English Department[1] received a grant from the Fund for the Improvement of Post-Secondary Education (FIPSE) to create an American Studies course for non-native students. Here is the abstract of the grant proposal:

> Our project addresses the special difficulties Queens College ESL students confront in typical humanities classrooms. We will design and teach a series of introductory humanities courses to provide students unfamiliar with the fundamental assumptions of American culture with more effective ways of understanding our national heritage and perspective. In conjunction with these courses, we will organize a faculty seminar to discuss and publish on the practical and theoretical issues involved in re-envisioning the American tradition from an international perspective.

In the present chapter I'd like to show how this kind of project, by building on an American tradition viewed from "an internationalist perspective," begins to dismantle certain "fundamental assumptions of American culture." For the sake of convenience and constituency, the special FIPSE course was listed under the catalogue title of English 152: Major Works of American Literature. But as you might expect, especially given the population of the new course, the questions raised in our faculty seminar were How major, What works, Which American, and Whose literature?

The ensuing debate, summarized below, was simply a local version of the larger controversy that has raged around the country for the past several years, as various media events regarding higher education in the United

---

[1]Frederick Buell and William Kelly wrote the grant, with minor addenda from Jackie Costello and me. Our original faculty seminar consisted of the four of us plus Barbara Bowen, Melvin Dixon, and Robert Lyons (English Department); Joan Dayan (Comparative Literature); and Frank Warren (History).

States have made apparent. By now these skirmishes are familiar to all and
needn't be reenacted here, save (once more) to review the troops as they
lined up in 1987, when our experiment in American Studies began. Milling
about the corridors of the academic Bastille, legions had been advocating the
overhaul of a largely Eurocentric curriculum, as in the notable to-do at
Stanford University in 1987. Researchers for the Carnegie Foundation for the
Advancement of Teaching reported that year that fully two-thirds of the
colleges in the United States were similarly reviewing their general educational programs to attend more closely to non-Western traditions and to such
issues as the politics of race and gender in cultural representation. Guarding
the tower we had then-Secretary of Education William Bennett, criticizing
such efforts at revamping as "faculty trashing of Plato and Shakespeare."[2]
Flanking Bennett were E. D. Hirsch on the onerous subject of What Every
American Needs to Know (followed up in 1989 with a dictionary listing
precisely that), and Allan Bloom with the book that was on everyone's night
table in the summer of '87, *The Closing of the American Mind*. Bloom's call to
arms, as you know, focused on a generation of intellectually impoverished
philistines weaned on cultural relativism, and thereby closed out of "the real
community of man" (the phrase is Bloom's) consisting of seekers of "the
truth." The fount of truth again seemed to be the Great Books of Western Civ
class, which Bloom's Chicago colleague Saul Bellow defended against
charges of racism by asking, "Who is the Tolstoy of the Zulus? The Proust of
the Papuans? I'd be glad to read them" (quoted in *The New York Times
Magazine*, January 3, 1988).

I agree with Bellow that if we go to the Zulus looking for Tolstoy, or,
analogously, to Native American texts expecting them to sound like Henry
James, we will indeed be disappointed—and, I would add, our classrooms
so much the poorer. As other observers have objected, the difficulty with
arguments such as those presented by Bennett and his fellows lies with their
presumption of a common national heritage to which our students should be
returning, along with a shared set of values and principles to be imbued. This
is patently not the case, neither for our diverse student population, nor even,
as I shall demonstrate in the next few pages, for a fairly homogeneous group
of faculty members with similar interests and educational backgrounds.

This chapter begins, then, with a summary of the discussions of the
faculty seminar sponsored by the FIPSE grant, and then proceeds to examine
the work of a group of students in the American literature class for nonnatives I taught in the spring of 1988. I believe the progress of these students
through the course holds important implications for our teaching in general,
whatever the class, whatever the population. After all, the FIPSE course was
designed eventually to be offered as an American Studies course for native

[2]I might add that our own curriculum committee in the English Department at Queens ran
up against similar arguments when we submitted new courses containing non-Western and
feminist material to the college's curriculum committee for approval. They said we were letting
politics determine our courses; we maintained politics had always been the basis of the en-
trenched curriculum and that we were merely trying to balance these ideological biases.

and nonnative students alike. Participants in the grant hoped the findings of our experiment would help native-born teachers and students discover competing traditions that have not been subsumed in the canon now known as The American Tradition. Those of us who return to literature courses having taught composition, and to native-speaker classes having taught nonnatives, find our perceptions of ourselves and others subtly changed. What nontraditional students have to tell us can help us to revise our curricula—if not to redefine, at least to divert what has been regarded for the past 40 years or so as the mainstream of American culture.

First some background on the FIPSE course and how it grew.

Before the Fall semester began, Fred, Bill, Jackie and I met to map out our initial seminar meeting. We decided on ways to recruit students for a pilot section of the course. We then agreed on two major concerns we thought should occupy seminar members for the next several meetings: creating model syllabi and reading lists, and devising evaluation procedures to measure the effectiveness of the course.

These plans more or less flew out the window at our first group meeting. The most pressing issue soon revealed itself to be our approach to "foreignness" and our confrontation with different cultures, both within and outside of American culture. According to my notes for the meeting, the interlocking questions raised by several seminar members were these: How might our syllabi be pluralistic and inclusive of material hitherto underrepresented—works by women and men, blacks and Hispanics, recent immigrants? How could we present American Studies material to other cultures without embedding those cultures in ours, co-opting dissenting voices, and promulgating an "up with America" view of our lives and letters? How to destabilize culture in the classroom to allow for alternative versions of, for example, typical American genres like frontier literature—perhaps balancing Fenimore Cooper's version with the wilderness as depicted in, say, slave narratives?

Obviously, not all nine members of our seminar were convinced of the urgency of these questions. But it seemed to some in the group that we were proceeding from a nativist view of Self versus Other rather than favoring a more enlightened if more troublesome concept of a nation constituted of Others—of groups whose writing had been shuffled to the margins of texts by dominant racial, ethnic, and gender groups.

The breach widened at our next meeting when some of our number presented suggestions for course syllabi. The process of constructing syllabi in fact seemed to solidify the allegiances of the two parties that had taken shape at the first meeting; please note, however, that in the interests of brevity I am simplifying and essentializing positions here. Earlier, we had considered the problem of adhering to the canon versus reconstructing the canon to allow for greater representation of nontraditional selection. Now we weighed syllabi based on the "tyranny of chronology"—that is, organized according to traditionally defined historical periods ("Puritan America," "The Revolution," "Jacksonian America")—against those based on the "arbitrariness of theme" ("Concepts of Nature," "Individualism and Community," and so on).

We occupied ourselves with these matters for weeks, sulking in the seminar room and lobbying in the halls, bombarding one another with a salvo of memos and counter-memos. The advocates of canon and chronology argued compellingly that there is of course a tradition in American literature, one that has been taught in our schools these many years, and that we owe it to our students, foreign- and native-born, to acquaint them with this mainstream version of American culture. Study of recognized authors, works, and themes—with the occasional dissenting voice of a marginalized selection—would better equip ESL students for the kind of work they would likely encounter in other humanities courses. Maintaining that we needed to situate works of literature in clear chronological context, several participants offered frightening evidence that many of our students lack all sense of the sequence of fundamental events in American history.

Naturally, the opposing team countered that the historical record itself was as overdetermined as the literary canon. We all spent a good deal of time talking about how the academy's definition of a national heritage had been taxidermied by the conditions under which texts have been selected for printing and reprinting over the decades. The thrust of every American literary anthology of recent years has been to rectify this unfortunate by-product of publishing history, and a kindred attempt at re-vision was one of the avowed purposes of our grant. Perhaps, then, positioning "minority" texts in opposition to the mainstream, or posing the antinomies of Us versus the Other, were impediments to unity and to the imagination.

The schism in our seminar group regarding reading selections was often indicative as well of fundamental differences in pedagogical approach. At times we spoke to the issue of student empowerment from two sides of the conference table. One side believed the more information imparted by the teacher and absorbed by the students, the more enabled this group of new-comers would be. The opposing side emphasized the ways students' increased participation in the classroom and on paper would strengthen their sense of the meaning-producing process of reading and writing. American literature would be more accessible to the students for its being contextualized through their experience of two cultures.

In the course of these planning sessions I revised my own suggested syllabus several times. My teaching methods chiefly derived from what I had learned in the writing and literature classes described in the preceding chapters of this book, but my reading list and class schedule were modified considerably according to our seminar discussions. I wanted to prepare my students to participate intelligently in this and subsequent humanities courses, and at the same time to draw on their advantage over native speakers as observers of American culture. In this sense, my course would play against the notion of naturalization. I refer both to the Immigration Department's definition of naturalize—to grant full citizenship to one of foreign birth; that is, to cause to conform, become acclimated, adapt—and to the concept as defined in social anthropology, which posits that those who live within a given social formation have little awareness of the *conventional* nature of the values, beliefs, rituals, and myths that constitute their "reality." Norman Bryson has illustrated how this concept works visually in his study of *Vision and Painting*. Articulation of cultural values comes more easily to the observer who, not having been naturalized by the society under study, shares few of the unconscious assumptions of its members (Bryson 69).

Perceived differences between the student's native and adoptive cultures was therefore one of the themes the course would pursue. Another, less prominent theme, one suggested in the work of observers like Hazel Carby and Gerald Graff, would be the problem of the way canons themselves are constructed and changed over the years: the way they are produced by, and perpetuate, a prevailing view of literary and social history. By what critical standards and social conditions do once-revered authors of the genteel tradition like Riley and Longfellow cede ground to formerly reviled authors like Poe, Melville, and Dickinson? Since this debate has so consumed our colleagues of late, why not let students themselves in on the discussion?

Hence the methodology of the course: the students' writing in class and at home would be as important a component of the course as the reading selections. In addition to writing four or five formal papers and several in-class essays, each student would be asked to keep an extensive reader's notebook of responses to assigned texts, and occasionally to compare the ways native and American cultures might approach a particular genre or subject. The emphasis on the reading and writing connection is especially empowering to ESL students, who, as we have seen, are often reluctant to extemporize in class discussions. More generally, this kind of written dialogue highlights the active role of all of our students, whether ESL or native speakers, as commentators on American culture.

The overriding goal in each successive version of my American Studies syllabus was to blur customary divisions between writing and literature courses, canonical and nontraditional reading selections, outsiders and insiders, and academic disciplines. In my first, overambitious syllabus, I assigned as many genres as possible: paintings, plays, films, poems, essays, realia from popular culture, historical documents, fiction, autobiography. Later, rethinking the course according to our seminar discussions, I gave greater attention to chronology in each thematic unit, reduced the number of selections, and included more traditional material. I also appropriated bits from everyone else's syllabus—particularly regarding the opening activities of the course, which I attenuated to give students more time to discuss the issues of acculturation we had engaged in the seminar.

When I came to teach the course the following term, my class schedule (see Appendix 1, which also includes sample assignment sheets and the final exam) proceeded from these notions, but expanded and contracted according to the interests and capabilities of the students. So much for planning ahead. Who among us has actually made a syllabus before the fact and stuck to it—and who would want to?

As I write this prologue at the opening of the Fall 1989 term, our seminar group enters its third year having achieved, if not accord, a kind of respectful entente. The continuing dialogue of the seminar seems to have been salutary for all concerned. One measure of the worthiness of the experiment is that participants were forced by debate to articulate reasons for the vague notions and prejudices each had carried into the conference room. Another is that everyone's position has shifted a few degrees as a result of our discussions. We have all come to agree on the importance of providing our students with a sense of the complexity of cultural experience, rooted in a specific historical period and subject to change over time. On these accounts I would judge the seminar a success. And on the basis of the evidence offered in the remaining sections of this chapter I would say my students' and my own experiences in the course itself were productive. Certainly the class will change the way I teach "regular" American literature courses in future.

In the sections that follow, I'd like to show as specifically as I can how some of the ideas ventured above were put into action. Although our present subject is American Studies, the themes and structures of this chapter parallel those of Chapter 2, on the reading and rereading of multicultural texts. In a sense, the chapters of this book have come full circle, the experience of regarding other cultures having led us back to another look at American culture. Section II describes a two-part classroom lesson on the history of American painting. By way of introduction, several paintings from different cultures are juxtaposed to illustrate varying methods of representation, and to suggest how divergent vantage points might help us form a clearer picture of the American visual and literary canons. The significance of differing perspectives in the multicultural classroom is then underscored by several examples drawn from one student's work. Section III follows the progress of another student in greater detail, showing how her ideas evolved over the course of the semester through a series of interwoven reading and writing assignments. Finally, section IV suggests how a Native American writer's text —a story by Leslie Marmon Silko, examined in the preceding section— might be *reexamined* according to the interpretations offered by ESL students in class discussion. Each of these sections thus considers some of the implications such a course holds for our understanding of a national heritage, and for our teaching of literature and writing.

II. The Literature (and Art) of Exploration: Re-viewing the Canon

The FIPSE seminar group posed a question for our students to answer in their notebooks at the beginning of the semester: "This course is being designed for nonnative students. What specific questions would you like to discuss this semester regarding American traditions, lives, arts, and customs? What do you hope to get out of this course?" Fatima Tunis, a student from Sierra Leone who was enrolled in the section of 152 I taught in the spring of 1988, answered with this question: "Since America is made up of so many groups of people with very different backgrounds, traditions and cultures, which traditions should we consider 'American'?"

Precisely the point we had been hashing out in our seminar the semester before. Students' responses to the question varied, but this emphasis on pluralism in America emerged as a recurrent theme, seeming to signify for these writers a way toward enfranchisement in their adopted culture:

> As English is my second language, I would like to take this advantage not to be embarrassed by taking English class with Americans, and I would like to have more discussion about different culture, traditions besides American's.

> Since America is made up of all kind of people from all over the world how can we explain the American culture and its origin?

> I would like to know about American music. Besides that, American life style, their culture, the history of America—like who are Americans? Where are they originally from?

> I am more interested in American lives and arts, because the people in the U.S. have immigrated from all over the world & different nation's people brought their own culture. Should I say that the American culture is mixed with other nation's?

As you can see from the class schedule (Appendix 1), the course began with a unit on "culture as construct," discussion of which I would like to defer until the following section of this chapter. Let me begin these notes, instead, by flashing forward a few class meetings, to several lessons devoted to early views of the American landscape. I have chosen to begin this way so that the notion of diversity of viewpoint, introduced in the students' journal comments quoted above, might serve hereafter as a motif for the chapter.

The Queens College *Bulletin* says English 152 surveys the development of American literature "from its beginnings." As defined by the professors and anthologies of my generation, American literature commenced with the settlement narratives of William Bradford and John Smith. But according to several syllabi that emerged from our seminar, it made more sense to open discussion of American history with an earlier paradigm for the mutual discovery of native inhabitants and foreign explorers of the New World. So before looking at Bradford, Smith, and Company, our class briefly considered two other accounts of American colonization: Columbus' catalogue of the flora and fauna of the Caribbean islands—all of which he described according to the delusion that he had reached Asia—and Pedro de Casteñeda's narrative of Coronado's search in the American Southwest for the mythic

Seven Cities of Cibola. Classroom discussion centered on the ways the New World had been interpreted from the perspective of its first European explorers.

We commenced with an analogy drawn from painting. The conquest of America took place around the time artists in Italy were pioneering single-point linear perspective. Tsvetan Todorov has pointed out the significant coincidence of these two moments (121). Linear perspective validates the individual point of view, an element essential to the colonizing impulse, for it positions man as the a priori measure of the relative size of all things. A scene is sketched or painted from a determined vantage point, includes only what can be seen from this point, and thus does not acknowledge that objects or persons might be viewed otherwise.

I called up this illustration of perspective in the Age of Discovery in the belief that it characterizes the study of American literature from its beginnings, and to some extent still informs the way we conceive of the subject. Svetlana Alpers notes that for those of us who have inherited the view of artistic representation posited by Italian art theorists during the Western Renaissance, "it is hard to see it as a particular modality and not just the way representational art is" (43). Yet of course there are alternative ways of perceiving and picturing the world. While the so-called scientific perspective satisfies a certain logic about time and space perception for Westerners, members of other cultures have just as logically asked, "Since we know what lies on the other side of that mountain, why limit ourselves to painting only what can be seen from a fixed viewpoint?" (see Sullivan 155).

The culture-bound modality of representation therefore provided a subtext for the two-part slide lecture on American painting I put together for the class, as a capstone to our discussion of colonial literature.[3] My intention was, first of all, to give the class an extensive sampling of the canon of American painting. The core of the presentation was the depiction of American landscape, this genre having emerged in the nineteenth century as our greatest and most emphatic means of articulating national identity. Projected simultaneously on three screens and shown in roughly chronological order, these slides acquainted students with a partial history of this country's settlement, as well as with some of the important underlying themes and values of American art.

At the same time, as I say, the lectures gave us an opportunity to consider how perception and representation are shaped by culture. We began by comparing several American landscape paintings with a few examples from Iran, China, and Japan. The point of this visual prologue was to demonstrate the inapplicability of Eurocentric notions of illusionism or single-point or atmospheric perspective to traditional non-Western works of art. For example, in classical Chinese art, a landscape is viewed from a variety of

---

[3]Appendix 2 shows the list and order of the slides. Many of the choices were dictated by the availability of color reproductions and by my wish to emphasize works found in museums in the New York area.

perspectives, or what Shen Kua, an art theorist of the Sung Dynasty, called "viewing the part from the angle of totality." Where Western artists are traditionally restricted by the walls of the frame, Chinese artists record a fragment, deliberately avoiding a complete rendering because, as Michael Sullivan trenchantly observes in *The Arts of China* (152–56), they realize we can never know or describe or complete anything. Landscape painting seen from this angle is not a final statement but a starting point.

Of course, one need not travel to the Orient for examples of cultural difference in perspective. Included in the introduction to our slide show was an example closer to home: a copy of a sandpainting of *The Four Mountains* by a Navajo artist of the southwestern United States. (A schematic rendering of the sandpainting is shown at the beginning of this chapter.) To "see" this American landscape we must understand that Navajo culture traditionally conceives of time and space as unbounded. As Gladys Reichard explains in her commentary on the sandpaintings, in the Navajo universe there is earth, sky, a land beyond the sky, and a world under the earth. Landscapes such as *The Four Mountains* accordingly suggest the convergence of map, pictogram, aerial view, and profile. What Paula Gunn Allen, a literary critic of Laguna Pueblo and Sioux ancestry, has to say about American Indian ceremonial literature is helpful in this context:

> . . . the four mountains in the Mountain Chant do not stand for something else. They are those exact mountains perceived psychically, as it were, or mystically. The color red, as used by the Lakota, doesn't stand for sacred or earth, but it is the quality of a being, the color of it, when perceived "in a sacred manner" or from the point of view of the earth itself (69).

Equally significant, particularly in light of a student's essay we shall look at in a moment, are two additional features of this Navajo work of art. Created for use in a healing ceremony, it is defined by its function. More anomalous still (by Western standards) is the ephemeral nature of the artifact, which is destroyed at the end of the ceremony.

Differing ways of thinking about art informed our class discussion of the slides flashing on the screens before us. Several members of the group were able to guide the rest of us in reading paintings produced in their cultures, glossing both the work's iconography and its implied indices for depicting and viewing. Where some Westerners in the class perceived the components of a vertical Chinese silk scroll as two unrelated scenes, Huai-li Luo, from Peking, was able to identify the mountain above and the trees of the same size below as forming two parts of the same landscape. Though separated in time and space, bold stretches of countryside are simultaneously available to us through the artist's shifting perspective. When one student commented that the rendering of a horse in a scene from an Iranian manuscript was "childish," Albert Youssefi hastened to point out that in Iran, "this is the way a horse is supposed to look in fiction." Michiru Arai noted that the true subject of Hiroshige's woodcut of *Night Rain at Karasaki* was not really landscape, but the four seasons, and further that the season represented was not winter, as we had guessed, but summer, because "that kind of cloud" appears during summer in Japan, and is used to signify summer in Japanese art.

Appropriate reading of multicultural works, then, depends quite literally on familiarity with the lay of the land, or with the correspondence of geographic mountain and iconic representation. Knowledge of the terrain must be coupled with an understanding of the audience response posited by the work of art. Recent art criticism has been telling us just this: the act of seeing is constituted historically in the dialectic between internal experience and the external forms of representation.

In the same way, I wanted to emphasize to my students, the rendering and reading of our best-known nineteenth-century American landscapes have been determined by historical context. For example, for all the precise topographical detail of Thomas Cole's paintings of the Hudson River Valley, generally assumed by his contemporaries to be faithfully portrayed, present-day viewers can now see how much of Cole's oeuvre is less realistic than one might gather at first glance. Cole's actual subject, whether in allegorical series like *The Course of the Empire* or in naturalistic views of the Catskills, is typically the sublime romantic drama of his age: the cycle of violence and calm, death and regeneration, despair followed by optimism.

We looked closely at one of Cole's most frequently anthologized paintings, *The Oxbow* (1836). This painting (reproduced on the facing page) has long been considered a fairly accurate view from Mount Holyoke, Massachusetts, of the Connecticut River oxbow. Recent scholarship suggests otherwise. A comparison of Cole's preliminary sketches with the finished canvas shows how the artist molded the landscape to embody the heroic ideals of America's mission in the wilderness. As Oswaldo Rodriguez Roque has observed, Cole's rendering is properly read from left to right as a narrative progressing from the Salvatorian thunderstorm in the wilderness to the sunny Claudean cultivated valley below. The story thereby enacts the mid-nineteenth-century version of America's history and future. Roque points to the Hebrew letters carved into the mountains in the background of the painting, approximating the word "Noah," or, if read upside down, "Shaddai"—the Almighty (*American Paradise* 127). Through written characters and pictorial formulae, the artist has literally inscribed on the landscape the message of God's covenant with the European settlers of America.

Cole has quite literally put his stamp on the American landscape in several other ways. At the center of this canvas, nearly hidden among the foliage, the artist depicts himself in the act of painting, his gaze momentarily turned toward the viewer, an acknowledgment of his position as the prime mover in this saga of progress. Cole's signature appears on the sketchbook he has painted beside his self-portrait. The individual artist's mediating point of view is once again valorized, as is the colonial mission to civilize the wilderness. Examination of other nineteenth-century examples in our slide

Thomas Cole, *View from Mount Holyoke, Northampton, Massachusetts (The Oxbow)*, Oil on canvas, 51 1/2 × 76 inches. The Metropolitan Museum of Art, Gift of Mrs. Russell Sage, 1908.

show revealed how much of the visual history of the American landscape, like the written history of the continent's settlement, has similarly been organized to communicate this optimistic lesson of manifest destiny.

From the foregoing illustrations I want to draw two conclusions. First, the international discourse community in the classroom continually presents us with differing concepts of art and of perception itself, and, further, shows us how such matters have evolved into what Michael Baxandall calls the "cognitive style" of an epoch within our *own* culture in ways we are just beginning to recognize. Second, these conceptual differences are by no means insuperable for us or our students, and, once recognized, are fruitful topics for critical discussion and writing.

Let me expand on my first observation. In earlier chapters I have contended that cognitive and communicative differences deserve to be factored to a greater extent into writing and literature classes for native and nonnative speakers alike. The 152 class offered several examples of how conceptual differences, if left unexplored, can undermine a student's written performance. I refer you now to an essay composed by Fatima Tunis, the African student quoted at the opening of this discussion. Fatima's paper, reprinted in Appendix 3 of this chapter, was written in response to the second formal essay assignment of the semester, directly following our slide lecture. Students were asked to visit one or two local museums and write an essay comparing a work of art from the United States with a work from their home culture.

Fatima's written analysis tells us a good deal about culturally determined responses to art. As you will see from reading Part I of her essay, the author provides a fascinating discussion of a mask carved by the Mende men in Sierra Leone under the direction of the Sande (a female society of the tribe) and specifically designed to be used in a dance ceremony. Fatima's detailed description of the mask emphasizes its use as well as its beauty, a description consonant with the definition of traditional African works of tribal art as having prescribed social functions: ornately carved warriors' shields are carried into battle, walking sticks denote power and position, statues house ancestors' spirits, and so on.[4] The Mende mask Fatima describes plays a role in a secret rite that can no more be elucidated to the outsider than to the males of the tribe, lest the bond of sacredness, and the usefulness of the object, be broken. According to this taboo, Fatima's commentary can by definition only be what Westerners would in any other instance deem incomplete. But as the writer's explanation is plausible, most Western readers will, I think, accept the terms of her analysis—perhaps even value them the more for their exoticism.

Yet the same definition of art precipitates certain problems in Part II of Fatima's essay. For it is the belief in social function as an inherent property of the artwork that shapes Fatima's discussion of the American work she has

---

[4]Evidently, contemporary art critics in Africa continue to advocate the necessary social role of the work of art. See the article by Sheila Rule listed in this chapter's bibliography.

chosen to analyze. Thus she remarks of Alison Saar's sculpture of a gambler (in the Metropolitan Museum of Art):

> I think that this piece of sculpture—like the mask in my culture—can be put to a positive use in this society and that is as an advertising object to promote a gambling business. It can be placed right outside of the casino or any other building used as a gambling spot to attract people. The potential gambler on seeing this ad will be impressed by the attire (having a taste in clothing and material wealth similar to what he sees) and he would want to win some money and buy himself something like that. . . .
>
> This sculpture is by Alison Saar, an American; she made it in 1985. In comparing it to the mask in Mende society, what I think they have in common is that they each represent a group of people in their respective cultures and they can both be used for certain purposes by their group either for benefit or entertainment.

Generalizing from her own culture's definition, Fatima missed the notion of the "useless" object, of art for art's sake, underlying most Western conceptions of fine art. On the other hand, as I thought about how to reroute this student's interpretation, her analysis forced upon me a recognition of the generally "concealed" fact of Western art for consumer's sake.[5] That is, plastic arts in the West do of course serve a totemic though normally unspoken social function, that of announcing—both in the privileging of selected subject material as well as in the act of possessing the artifact—the wealth and position of the possessor.

Fatima's misunderstanding of certain tacit principles in Western art sidetracked her into an inappropriate excursus on the subject, in the middle of an otherwise effective essay. The error can be cleared up easily enough, and so I hope it was in subsequent conversation with the student. In presenting my slide lecture, I had not thought to point out these central propositions of Western art, as I had taken them either on faith or for granted. I will not do so the next time I teach the course.

Which emendation leads me to my second, corollary conclusion in our cross-cultural consideration of art, namely that discussions of painting or literature need not get mired in the endless regression of cultural relativism. Rather, observers can be trained to see inside and outside the conventions of their culture, as demonstrated not only by my own experience, related above, but by the student texts quoted later on in this chapter. International students come by this double vision quite naturally. As Mary Antin remarked in *The Promised Land*, the ur-narrative of an immigrant transplanted to American soil at the turn of this century,

[5]Regarding the influence of consumer on artifact see, for instance, Baxandall, Benjamin, Berger, Crow, all listed in the bibliography for this chapter.

Thus everything impressed itself on my memory, and with
double associations; for I was constantly referring my new world
to the old for comparison, and the old to the new for elucidation.
I became a student and philosopher by force of circumstances
(xxii).

Please don't misunderstand. In saying that we might occasionally
foreground cultural diversity as a strength rather than a hindrance in our
classrooms, I do not suggest we harp on the subject of national differences
in the classroom. Cultural comparison was the starting point of two writing assignments for the course, but would surely have become a tiresome
and strident theme if insisted upon further. Neither do I wish to mislead
my readers by playing up my students' strong suit while ignoring their
underpreparedness for advanced work. The fact is that too many of our
students, native as well as nonnative, lack the rudiments to succeed in
upper-level humanities courses. We begin such curriculum planning enterprises by acknowledging that nonnatives in particular are going to be ham-
pered in American literature classes not only by linguistic difficulties (abun-
dantly illustrated in earlier chapters of this book) but by insufficient
grounding in American literary history and protocol. These difficulties are
evidenced all too frequently by the thinness of their written responses and
their customary silences in classes with American-born coevals.

That said, it seems to me the questions that drive an American Studies
class for *any* group of students are these: How can we provide sufficient
contextualization to engage our students in discussions of American literature and to correct cultural miscues? How to provide them with the standard
rhetorical strategies their teachers generally expect from them? At the same
time, how do we use the multicultural resources that permit students and
teachers alike to break out of their cultural provincialism?

As I've implied in the foregoing discussion, we might begin by recognizing how we have been conditioned to see, and by reviewing traditional
texts to make explicit certain implicit conceptual and literary structures. To
elicit as full a response as possible to the course material, the literature class
is envisioned as a course in writing as much as reading, part of the contin-
uum of composition courses we have developed for all our undergraduates.
Emphasis on journal writing about culture as well as literature, synthesis of
personal writing and textual analysis, and assignment of a range of essays
that appeal to the student's authority: these techniques encourage collaborative work and a method of reader response that is inevitably, in this context,
multicultural response.

I do not pretend that this kind of classroom is utterly decentralized. The
teacher structures the syllabus and some of the discussion. She owes it to
her students to equip them with knowledge of canonical works (which, as
you can see from the appended syllabus, constitute the greater portion of
the semester's work). She has to present the conventions of the mainstream
if these assumptions are to be deconstructed in the classroom. At times

she lectures. And she's the one who dishes out the grades. Still, the goal here is a discourse less determined and more fluid, multivoiced. Topics are seldom presented exclusively from the single-point perspective of the official Westerner but rather explored from the ambulatory "angle of totality."

Permit me to illustrate the advantages of this more participatory method of reading and writing with a few self-serving examples, all drawn from the spoken and written observations of Fatima Tunis. After class one day toward the end of the semester, Fatima told me she had never spoken up in an English course. This declaration was seconded by the teacher of the Introduction to Poetry (English 140) class she had taken the previous semester. Yet the Fatima I knew was always waving her hand—was probably the most talkative of a very lively and engaged group of students. When Fatima dropped by my office to chat the following semester, I asked her to elaborate on her remark, and requested her permission to record our conversation. Here is what she said about the course and its effect on her:

> I never volunteered an answer in my 140 class, but now I see it doesn't matter what someone thinks about my accent as long as my ideas make sense. Even in my accounting class, which is large, I can answer without being too nervous. This has always been my biggest problem in college, but I think now somehow I'm overcoming it. It has to do with the fact that I took the 152 class. I knew the other students wouldn't ridicule my accent, and my ideas were encouraged. It happens in English classes, even if you're talking about something sensible, everyone turns around and just listens to the sound of my words, not the words themselves. At least that's how I feel.
>
> I still have that fear when the class is big. But I don't hesitate to talk and ask questions when the class is small, like my statistics class. I feel more free now. I'm even more active in the International Students' Club—I'm much more talkative, whereas last semester in the African club I never said anything. (I wish Asian students would take the class; they're very quiet in the International Club meetings.) In fact, I'm hoping to take a communications class next semester. I've been hesitant until now, but now after 152 I can think of it—not before. Now I feel I can take it.
>
> To be frank, I started thinking this semester about taking creative writing. Now I think I should go beyond 152.

I do not offer Fatima's comments to argue for separate tracks of literature for native and nonnative students. On the contrary, I have wanted to show how nontraditional voices like those encouraged in this experimental course might open up texts for students collectively in a typical literature classroom. I'd like to conclude this section on diversity of viewpoint by reprinting Fatima's final in-class exam essay (see the examination questions in Appendix 1), in which she makes a solid case for new perspectives on

the American canon. Perhaps the reader of this essay will think the student
has merely parroted her teacher's harangue. But I must assure you that
although the problem of the canon occupies us in the present chapter, and
was touched on briefly in class during the semester, none of the points
Fatima makes below was expatiated in class. Nor, alas, did we develop the
connections Fatima draws between the canon and the official historical
record. The class was not alerted that such a question would appear on
the exam. I tossed in the topic for the hell of it, and three or four students
took up the challenge, Fatima with greatest cogency. So let this student's
arguments serve as well for a pedagogy that swims against the mainstream
of the "classic" literature classroom, which often marginalizes students'
diverse responses and privileges the lecturer's "correct" reading of
the text:

> Those observers who think that "marginal" texts by women
> and minority writers should be disregarded for American Studies
> courses are wrong. Concentrating on "classic" texts only will
> make the subject very narrow.
>
> I think what goes on mainly in American Studies courses
> are the views of the people that make up this country and how
> these views affect the history of this country. If the study concen-
> trates on "classics" only, the course will not be complete.
>
> A writer like Gilman on women's issues brought awareness
> of the sufferings of women in the 1800s, and whether something
> was done about it or not, at least those women who did not at
> first care about how they were treated were now conscious about
> the situation after reading her book. Examples such as hers point
> out how the women's movement has come about, and that is
> worth spending a few weeks on in a semester.
>
> Frederick Douglass's *Narrative* is a very good account of
> what slavery was like in this country. Slavery has a lot to do with
> the development of this country—slaves did the farming, child-
> rearing, and a lot more. Douglass is a representative of what the
> majority of slaves were going through, and reading his work gives
> us an insight into what the civil rights movement is/was about,
> since slavery and the civil rights movement are stages in the black
> American struggle.
>
> Leslie Silko's poems are a work of art of a people who are
> almost disappearing off the face of this country. The American
> Indians were defeated and pushed to the side by the white set-
> tlers and now you can hardly hear about them. Silko is the first
> Indian whose work I have read, and I think it is very much a part
> of this country's literature, just as much as any "classic" work.
>
> With all their participations, contributions, and struggles to
> make this country what it is today, if works by minorities are ig-
> nored because of "lack of time," I think the title of the course—
> "American Studies"—should maybe be changed to just "Classical
> America."

III. Storytellers: Reading Traditional and Noncanonical Texts

Now let's go back to the beginning of the course. With Fatima's arguments in mind, I would like to offer a more detailed demonstration of how a sequence of reading selections, class discussions, and writing assignments can be mutually enabling. In the previous section we compared two paintings situated within and outside of the American canon, the latter a work by a Native American artist. To continue the discussion of diversity of viewpoint, in this section we will be looking at a work of literature that grows out of Native American tradition: the excerpt from Leslie Marmon Silko's *Storyteller* mentioned in Fatima's exam essay. Silko's book is an autobiographical montage of reminiscences, short stories, photographs, and legends from the Laguna Pueblo outside Albuquerque, New Mexico. The selection is in many respects representative of marginalized literature: its author is female and of mixed Hispanic, Native American, and European descent, and the characteristic sounds and forms of the piece originate in the rhythms of oral tradition.

Although the emphasis here is on interpretation of the noncanonical text, the reading and writing procedures outlined below seemed to work equally well with what have by now become more standard selections in the syllabus—with the autobiographies of Franklin and Douglass, essays such as Emerson's "Self-Reliance," and fiction such as Gilman's short story "The Yellow Wallpaper" and Cather's novel *My Ántonia*. So I would like the following observations about Silko's story, the students' responses to it, and the essay assignments described here, to serve more generally as an inquiry into the hermeneutics of the multicultural discourse community.

Our inquiry will proceed by tracing the performance of one student, pausing at several points in the semester to see how personal themes, literary materials, and class discussion were reflected in her work. The sequence summarized below includes the student's first journal entry; her classmates' responses to the reading selection and her own response as well; her first formal essay (engendered by the reading material), calling for narration and analysis of a folktale from the student's home culture; her revision of that assignment; and her final paper for the course.

The student whose passage through the course we will follow is Michiru Arai, whose earliest work in English, and later observations on Japanese rhetorical preferences, have been quoted in Chapters 6 and 7. In those chapters I argued that the foreign-born student can regain her distinctive voice and introspection once she has attained a measure of linguistic proficiency in the target language, and has figured out some of the favored communicative strategies of her adopted home. I believe Mickie's performance in this literature class confirms the prediction.

We begin with Mickie's response to the first journal assignment, which asked students to discuss to what extent they felt "Americanized." Mickie's observations have bearing on the present discussion for several reasons. First, she remarks with wit and perspicuity on cultural differences in behavioral norms and communicative preferences, and so picks up the argument of several earlier chapters of this book. In the process, she shows how her evolving feminist viewpoint both elucidates and subverts inherited notions of gender. Most important, Mickie's stance is characteristic of our foreign-born students' status as insiders and outsiders, participants and observers, no matter which culture they're commenting on. Here is her journal entry:

> Feb. 2, '88
>
> I am not sure what I've really lost or what I've really gained. I had been here for 2 years from '83 to '85. I went back to Tokyo, lived there for two years, and came back to NY last May. While I was in Tokyo, I was very uncomfortable. I felt I didn't fit into the society. I still don't know why. It might've been because they didn't have any rock-oriented radio stations or the subways were so crowded that I couldn't breathe. I've been looking for the very reason for so long. Here are two possible reasons I've thought of so far.
>
> The first one is that I had become less "feminine." To make you understand this, I have to explain "feminine." That's a direct translation from the Japanese word. In Japan women are supposed to speak in certain ways. They are also supposed to act in certain ways. For example, their knees should be stuck together whenever they are sitting, which is very tiring if you try. Since I had been in New York, I was used to easier way of life. I had to be very careful to look the same as Japanese women. It didn't come out naturally. I certainly have lost some of the femininity of Japanese women.
>
> The other possible reason is less visible. It's more psychological than physical. Japan consists of islands, so the population is very homogeneous. There are exceptions, but usually people feel more comfortable when they are doing the same things or they look the same as people around them. I don't feel that way anymore. I felt it's no fun to be same as others when I was in high school, but back then I didn't do anything different. Now I talk in class, which rarely happened in Japanese classrooms. I still have some hesitation, but here I look different, so no matter what I do, I am different. Those two years back in Tokyo, even though I didn't realize it, I probably felt oppressed because I couldn't be myself, since if I did something different, people gave me the "where this strange creature come from" look. Over here, I can feel that there is a life besides getting married and having kids, which Japanese women should lead. I only have to find a way to stay in NY after I finish school.

How is it that Mickie no longer fits into Japanese society? The author points to her now-inappropriate (because Americanized) deportment as a woman and as a student. I would maintain that the changes in Mickie's behavior in the schoolroom have also led her to certain behavioral differences on the page. The same spirit that prompts her to voice her opinions in class has produced a more assertive and personally revelatory writer—and one who can comment authoritatively on two cultures.

The earliest reading selection of the semester encouraged students to expand on the themes and strengths of their journal entries. Classroom discussion of the reading in turn initiated the first formal essay assignment. Let me summarize Silko's story (reprinted in Appendix 5 of this chapter) and the discussion it occasioned. Silko begins her book with a description of a storyteller, her Aunt Susie. As a child Susie had been sent away to an Indian school in Pennsylvania, according to the policy of the Bureau of Indian Affairs and Christian missionaries to root out Indian customs through education. Aunt Susie returned to Laguna Pueblo determined to preserve tradition through oral and written narrative. One of the legends she passed on was the story of the little girl who ran away:

A little girl asks her mother for yashtoah, a dish made from corn meal. Her mother sends her down the steep Acoma mesa to look for firewood, but when the child returns to the pueblo the wood has turned into snakes, and so she is sent back down to fetch more wood. Hurt and angry, the girl says she will drown herself in the Kawaik lake. At the Enchanted Mesa, near Acoma, she meets an old man and tells him her resolve. The old man cannot stop the little girl, but ascends the cliff to warn her mother. Now the mother cooks the yashtoah, and gathers the child's garments, which she takes down to the lake. She reaches out just as her daughter plunges into the water, and watches as the feather the child has tied in her hair (signifying death) whirls around in the depths below. The mother returns to the mesa to scatter her daughter's clothing. Shawl, manta dress, and moccasins turn into butterflies, red, white, blue, yellow.

That this American tale is elliptical, or so at least it might seem to the average American-born reader, suggests the inappropriateness of approaching the story with certain Western narrative expectations of signification and closure. At the same time, its open-endedness implies the reader's responsibility for transforming cultural material into meaning. What interests me here are the ways in which meaning in Silko's elusive story appeared to be more accessible to many of my students than it might have been to a group of native English speakers. Certainly they led the way in helping their instructor to read the text. I had chosen the tale chiefly as an introduction to oral traditions, and as a way to begin talking about the creative processes of storytelling, myth, legend, and history. The students, it turned out, had their own agenda.

Consider their reactions to the child's suicide in the story. Why, I asked, does the child drown herself, and why do the old man and the mother repeatedly fail to save the child? A number of non-Western students seemed to view the girl's death as tragic but necessary for the continuity of the community, thereby emphasizing the preeminence of the social order over the individual. An Iranian Jewish student I have mentioned earlier, Albert Youssefi, read this response from his journal:

A factor which is indispensable is destiny. There was
enough wood in the house to make "yashtoah"! The old man also
plays an important role in the story. Why not a young man?
Maybe if a young man tried to catch her, he would be more successful. It is as though the girl was destined to die to make history. She was destined to die to make us aware of a possible reason for Acoma having so many beautiful butterflies.

Similarly, César Nanzi, a Colombian student whose maternal grandmother is a Guarani Indian, immediately formulated this equation in class:
"She has to die because the world needs butterflies."

Quite unprompted by their instructor, these nonnative students were
especially alive to the metaphorical implications of the suicide. Many interpreted the story on their own as being about a culture threatened with
extinction. Thus Albert Youssefi continued,

   . . . one of the points that Leslie Silko could be alluding to
   in this story is the importance of your own native culture. The
   mother sends her daughter to get some woods. But after she
   hears that the daughter is about to jump in the lake she finds
   enough woods to make her "yashtoah," whereas she had told
   her, "I can't make you any yashtoah because we haven't any
   wood." This is a substantial evidence for either mother's ignorance or mother's attempt to increase the gap between the daughter and her own native culture.

Fatima Tunis wrote,

   "The girl who ran away" in my view is a story of a people
   who were invaded by strangers. This invasion caused them to be
   in conflict with their old traditions and customs since the invad-
   ers' new cultures were being imposed on them.
   The girl's running away could be the people's adoption of
   the new cultures instead of unsuccessfully resisting them. I think
   that the mother's refusal to make the yashtoah indicates the reluctance of the older people to keep their cultures alive or continue
   them for the younger generations.
   The end of the story is a sign of acceptance by the people of
   the new situation. The mother's grief turns into happiness when
   her daughter's belongings turned into butterflies, which depicts
   that after all the struggles the people went through to preserve
   their old traditions, they found it more peaceful to accept and to
   look on the bright side of the situation.

Huai-li Luo went on,

   I cannot quite understand the meaning of this simple story.
   But overall, the story gives me a feeling that Indian culture will

gradually fade away. In the story the little girl wants to eat yash-toah, which is typical Indian food. The girl wants to kill herself because her mother does not make the food for her. Neither the old man nor her mother saved her life, although they all tried. The girl follows the Indian traditional way to die, puts the feather in her hair. These are examples that Indians are losing their tradition ever since foreigners came into the New World. They made Indians change to the Westerner's ways. Even the religion has to be changed.

I don't know if my interpretation is too subjective.

Huai-li's interpretation might have been subjective, but it traveled to the heart of Silko's story. The note of loss of cultural identity was sounded repeatedly in the comments of these ESL students, who often see themselves as caught, like some of the characters in Silko's book, between a native culture that is increasingly distant and an adoptive culture not yet at hand.

Mickie Arai's ruminations on the story revealed her characteristic interest in cultural comparison. She demonstrated how such variations can comment on and enrich each other in the process of literary interpretation:

> The last part of the story, where the girl's clothes turned into butterflies, could have two meanings. If I see it from Japanese people's point of view, the butterflies are the mother's soul, which grieved over her daughter's death. It is the worst sin you can commit to die before your parents. If I see it from more religious point of view, the fact that the girl's clothes turned into butterflies means that the soul never dies. The body might disappear, but the soul will stay in the world. From the description of how Aunt Susie told the story, I think it's the latter. The people probably believed that the death is inevitable, but, even though people die, their souls remain here and so we should not be sad.

I searched for an essay assignment that capitalized on the common experience of the ESL students' vantage point "between cultures." Borrowing an assignment suggested by my colleagues Rosemary Deen and Bette Weidman, I adapted the task to the structure of Silko's piece. After the students had commented on the Laguna legend in their journals, they were to write down an oral tale, legend, or myth recalled from childhood, to describe the storyteller and circumstances of the telling, and to analyze the tale for what it reveals about their culture. The task reflects the underlying assumption of the reading selection, namely that the process of remembering is historical and cultural as well as personal. The assignment further assumes that examination of other myths inevitably denaturalizes the literary and critical myths that have shaped our reading.

I've indicated that our foreign-born students' papers often reflect a kind of dual literary citizenship. It is especially important in this context to keep in mind that many native-born Americans who belong to minority groups also experience and write about this sense of straddling cultures. But it would seem ESL students are made even more aware of the contrast because of their geographical and linguistic distance from their home cultures. Their papers frequently articulate at once the irresistible pull of acculturation and the resistance to assimilation. Mickie's essay effectively demonstrates these concerns. Ultimately, her reading and rereading of a popular native legend parallels the kind of reconsideration of a national heritage attempted in this American Studies class. For these reasons I reprint Mickie's paper in its entirety:

Stories for Children

My folks hardly ever told stories to me. However, they read me a lot of books, bedtime stories, so to speak. Even though my parents chose to read those stories, they have also orally survived in the Japanese culture for a long time. Anyway, the fact that my parents were reading didn't matter to a child who couldn't read. There were Japanese traditional stories and foreign stories, but those I remember most are all Japanese. I think it is because the stories reflected the cultural values of the traditional Japanese society.

Stories told to children are usually very simple and predictable from the points of view of adults who grew up in that culture. The sentences are short. The names of the heroes and heroines are repeated many times. In Japanese, pronouns don't appear so many times as in English. We can omit the subject of the sentence and the sentence still makes sense to us. The omission rarely occurs in the stories for children. Those stories also have certain rhymes. It might be another reason why I remember Japanese stories better than foreign stories. When stories are translated into different languages, it is hard to preserve the rhythms. Consequently, they lose certain flavours they originally had.

There was this story which my mother read me one night, and even though I don't remember, I'm sure some other people also told me on different occasions. Once upon a time, there was an old man and an old woman in a village. They didn't have any children, but besides that, they were living happily and quietly. Every day the old man went into the mountain to get firewood. The old woman went to the river to do the laundry. One day she found a big peach floating in the river. She carried it back home. At night, when they tried to cut the peach into halves, a little boy popped out of it. The old couple named the boy "Peach Taro." (Taro was a common name for boys.) He grew up very fast and became very strong.

One day, Peach Taro asked, "I heard there are devils who give people troubles. Is that true?" The old man said, "Yes, it is true." Peach Taro asked, "Doesn't anybody go and punish them?" "Everybody is afraid," the old man answered. Peach Taro said, "I'm going to get them." So his trip to the island where the devils lived started. On the way to the island, he met a dog, bird, and monkey, and they decided to join Peach Taro's trip to the island.

When they got to the island, Peach Taro shouted to the devils, "Stop bothering the village people." The devils said, "Stupid boy. We'll give you a lesson." Of course Peach Taro won the fight. However, for a child it was like the miracle had happened. The devils ran away, leaving a lot of treasure. Peach Taro and the animals brought the treasure home, and the old man and woman and Peach Taro lived happily ever after.

Every single Japanese child knows this story. When I think about this story now, I feel that it's such a male chauvinist story. Only woman in this story is the old woman, who did the housework and nothing else. The woman doesn't have any value in this story. That was how the Japanese society saw women in the old days. Women couldn't be any more use than animals could.

The obvious purpose of this story is to teach children, especially boys, to be brave and help other people. However, the less obvious purpose seems to me stronger and more important. It is that wherever you go, you should go back to your parents and take care of them. Peach Taro could have kept the treasure for himself, gone to the city, and had some fun. Instead, he went back to the village and lived with his parents.

In those stories we hear or read as children, there are usually hidden messages which we never notice until we grow up. However, the messages get planted in our brains. Right now, I'm away from my parents. The idea that I should be with or close to my parents makes me feel guilty. I try to justify myself with things I've learned after childhood, but I can't. The stories are made to give children the cultural values of the society and specific moral lessons. I guess that the Japanese society has succeeded in imposing its own cultural value system on its children.

If I have to tell stories to my children or somebody young, I would probably choose these stories about boys who suddenly appear from somewhere else and help people. There are at least ten similar stories. However, it is not because I appreciate the stories very much. It is because I feel it is important to preserve that part of the Japanese heritage.

There is one thing I would do differently when I tell stories. I would make up stories in which girls are the main characters. Maybe I don't have to make them up. There might be stories about girls now. Whether or not the stories survive in the culture is a question, though. Long time ago, I made up stories about brave girls and told them to my younger cousins. I don't think they remember the stories. Well, they weren't such fabulous stories anyway. Stories like "Peach Taro" are at least 1500 years old.

It is hard for new stories to catch up and have the same impact on children, but we should at least try. Some things just have to change.

Before we consider a few suggestions for American Studies proposed by Mickie's essay, I want to describe our approach to "revision" in this particular assignment. In class we read and discussed a number of students' essays. After a student had read his or her native tale, we paused before the author read the commentary on the tale, wrote down our own interpretations as outside observers of the text, read some of these responses, and compared them with the commentary that the author then read to us. For the next meeting, the students were asked to review their narratives and analyses, and to write codas to their papers: one more page or so of elaboration or second thoughts on the topic. Notice how in her addendum Mickie not only expands her exegesis of the story but deconstructs her own first response as well:

Further Thoughts on "Peach Taro"

I criticized the way the story treated women in the main part of this essay. However, I could see this story from different prospect. It saw the old woman as a role model for all women. She was calm, didn't complain, and took care of everything. It seems easy, but, in reality, it is very difficult to hide whatever the feelings we have and serve the family. The Japanese society still values those women very highly. By the way, even though it's not mentioned anywhere in this story, we should notice that the old woman became a complete woman finally by being given Peach Taro. The idea still remains in the modern Japanese society. Women are not complete until they have children.

The way "Peach Taro" came to the couple floating in the river symbolizes the idea that children are gifts from "Kamisama." "Kamisama" is like "God" in Christianity, but it's more abstract and he doesn't have anybody who represents him in this world.

The story also wants to teach children the importance of sharing by making Peach Taro bring the treasure back home. Even though the Japanese society is much more urbanized and sharing isn't as important as it used to be in those days when people were dependent on agriculture, taking something and keeping it for yourself doesn't have good image.

There are so many different messages in children's stories. The speed children absorb things is amazing. We should make sure that children hear plenty of stories which see things from different points of view. When they grow up, they will make their own judgment on these stories.

Mickie urges that children be exposed to stories with "different points of view," which they can later make sense of as adults. This kind of interpretation is precisely the task Mickie and her fellow students were asked to attempt. In the process of having to articulate implicit assumptions and cultural values underlying traditional narratives from their native lands— and digging still deeper in the coda—many members of the class came up with analyses that proved as illuminating to them, I think, as to their audience.

The structure of these assignments, with their juxtaposition of reading and writing, narrative and analysis, draft and coda, gave students a way to crystallize impressions they had jotted down in their notebooks during the first week of class. Succeeding essay assignments moved the class away from writing about personal experiences, but the final essay asked them to reexamine their own backgrounds, this time in the context of American fiction. They were to write about how the process of emigrating informed their interpretations of Willa Cather's novel of immigrant life in the Midwest at the turn of the century, *My Ántonia*. The description of the assignment and Mickie's lengthy final paper, to which the reader is now referred, are in Appendices 1 and 4 of this chapter. But a portion of Mickie's paper is quoted below so that we may see how her reading and commentary allowed her to enlarge on her initial topics, and, at the same time, to expand on a mainstay of the American literary canon in ways perhaps not given to native speakers.

In this final paper, entitled "Being a Stranger in America," Mickie takes up the theme of her notebook entry by recalling here that in returning to Tokyo after two years in America, "I was already hanging right in the middle of American and Japanese cultures." In her conclusion, she gathers together what she has learned from her studies as a linguistics major to contrast her own adaptation to life in America with the unhappy fate of the fictional immigrant, Ántonia's father. (Interestingly, in doing so, Mickie also reiterates some of the research on motivation summarized in Chapter 5 of this book):

> . . . On the surface, Mr. Shimerda seems integratively motivated because he intends to stay in America with his family, and I would be instrumentally motivated because I'm here to study. However, psychologically it's the other way around. Mr. Shimerda doesn't want to be an American. He wants to keep everything that is Bohemian. That's partly because he has to throw it away. He is threatened by American culture. If he doesn't hang on to Bohemian culture, it will go away. It might be wrong to call his motive instrumental. He is just too naive to have an idea that by learning a little bit of English he could get some kind of favor from American people. He is certainly not integratively motivated, though.
>
> As for my case, I am not only instrumentally motivated to survive in school, but also integratively motivated into American life which, by the way, is not possible because I will always look different. The way I look and the impossibility of my staying in

America makes me somewhat less integratively motivated, but more so that Mr. Shimerda.

When a person who has to stay and assimilate into a new culture can't accept the new culture, it is a disaster. However, when a person who can't stay in the new culture, but was influenced by the new culture and became someone different from the original him/herself, it is also a disaster. Mr. Shimerda is a victim of American culture. He may be too sensitive, but America is so big that unless you are careful, you will be eaten by this monstrous country. Being in this country, keeping foreign customs is very difficult, but everybody should keep something that is from their roots. It helps you to survive in this country without losing yourself, and also I believe it helps build up this country just as people from Europe did in the early days of America.

I have earlier said that Mickie's analysis of "Peach Taro" provides further suggestions for our pedagogy, and the same must be remarked of her comments here on motivation. I will conclude this section by elaborating briefly on her observations. In her first essay, Mickie speculates that Japanese legends starring little girls might exist, but doubts such tales can survive since they do not reflect the priorities of the dominant culture. The surmise certainly holds true for changing definitions of the canon in the United States and doubtless most other countries as well. For example, as Hazel Carby has shown in *Reconstructing Womanhood,* African-American women writing at the turn of the century exerted tremendous influence on the American novel, particularly in their concern with social protest. As the canon has evolved in this century, however, much of the influence of these writers has been forgotten, so that recent scholarship has been devoted to reclaiming their texts and resuming their social mission.

The research of Barbara Shollar, a colleague at Queens, substantiates the point from an internationalist perspective. Shollar has recently put together an anthology of international women's literature. She points to certain plots and fabulae common to narratives written by nonnative women living in the United States at the turn of the century. These narratives were quite popular in the literary journals of the day but have been passed over in the intervening years. Some of the themes that contribute to our extensive literature by immigrant women dovetail with those articulated by native-born minority groups in the United States: the issue of "passing" as opposed to asserting one's home culture; the metaphor of the wife and mother who follows the already assimilated husband to the States (and is often rejected there); the entrapment of the refugee who has no Old World to return to, whose former existence is no longer possible. As we have seen, these themes are elaborated in the writing of many of our foreign-born students.

Viewed in this historical and cultural context, émigré writers like Mickie Arai and her peers are working out of an established American tradition. I have offered the foregoing examples to suggest that closer study of ethnic writers, men and women, professionals and students, natives and nonnatives, inevitably guides us in the reassessment and enrichment of our concepts of national identity and literary heritage.

IV. Coda: Further Thoughts on *Storyteller*

The objective of the curriculum planning and teaching methods outlined above is to resist the colonial assumption that what is studied, whether a foreign culture or one of our several native American traditions, is something reified and utterly comprehensible. By reversing our habitual terms of alterity, of thinking about the Other, we begin to recognize what is exotic, or other, in ourselves. As Mickie and other writers have remarked over the years, we need creative and critical myths that adjust for temporal change and cultural difference. Accordingly, in this brief final section the comments of my international students provide impetus for further exploration of Leslie Marmon Silko's story of "the little girl who ran away."

In *Storyteller*, Leslie Silko puts a spin on many of the myths of what has come to be called the American Tradition, from structural tropes to images of the artist and the community. Nina Baym has characterized much of the literature favored by American critical theorists following World War I as "melodramas of beset manhood," stories in which women appear as representatives of a society that drags the hero down, and from whose stifling influence the male protagonists flee into the wilderness. Silko's modern versions of pueblo-inspired tales reflect a different kind of society, one based on the more powerful role of women in the community. The social conformations of the Acoma and Laguna pueblos are traditionally matrilinear and matrilocal. In the myths, ceremonies, and stories of these pueblos, the relationship of mother and daughter is central to holding together and preserving the life of the tribe.

Little wonder, then, that several of Silko's heroines in *Storyteller*—sisters, perhaps, to the mother in "the little girl who ran away"—find themselves fraught with domesticity. One group of stories concerns Yellow Woman, the heroine of many Laguna legends. For our purposes we'll call them tales of the American Eve, or The Scarlet Woman. In these stories, the protagonist sets forth into what white explorers call wilderness, though of course the terrain is quite familiar to her. She wanders away to search for food or water for the community, or to hunt buffalo—Laguna women are known to be expert hunters—or to satisfy a certain hankering for the sultry stranger she meets along the way. After a few days, or perhaps months, our heroine may return, somewhat reluctantly, to the obligations of husband, children, and settlement. Now, if these are not quite female counterparts of classic American "melodramas of beset manhood," neither do they neatly fit any other prominent critical assumptions about the American literary canon.

For a closer reading of tales like Silko's stories of Yellow Woman or of "the little girl who ran away," we must look to the combination of cultures out of which the tale grows, and then consider how Silko's (and her informant's) rendition departs from its traditional sources. Aunt Susie's story seems to derive elements from several story types. Stith Thompson's early compilation of North American Indian tales provides a category to which Susie's tale vaguely corresponds: stories of Deserted Children, examples of which are widely distributed over the continent but especially throughout the western United States. Structuralist analyses of this tale type (see Thompson's *The Folktale* 360, and Hymes 142–44) describe stories in which children are abandoned by a starving tribe, subsequently prosper, and are ultimately reclaimed by the repentant camp. In his collection of Laguna stories (1928), Franz Boas mentions one such tale. But whereas Boas's variant fits the template, Silko's does not.[6]

I would like to pursue the trail of Aunt Susie's variant by recalling my international students' commentaries. In their reading of the tale, many students had pointed to the underlying theme of cultural rupture. Taking care not to equate historical and fictional incident, we might inquire into the history of the Acoma and Laguna pueblos—and at the same time, into the personal history of the teller—for events that perhaps contributed to the making of a story set partly in Acoma, partly in Laguna.

In fact the intertwined history of these pueblos reveals a long series of cultural confrontations and disruptions, from the attack on Acoma by emissaries of Coronado in the sixteenth century, to the Pueblo Revolt against Spanish control in 1680 and the establishment some two decades later of the settlement at Old Laguna [Kawaika], to the Laguna Break in the late 1800s. At this point the history of the pueblo and of Leslie Marmon Silko's family become deeply interwoven. According to the *Handbook of North American Indians* (Sturtevant 9:447), in the 1870s Walter G. Marmon, a white Protestant, was appointed government school teacher and moved into the pueblo; Marmon, his brother Robert, and his cousins all married Laguna women, and their families formed a small colony on the edge of the village. Although they respected Laguna traditions, the Marmons viewed the old Pueblo beliefs as stultifying to the village, and the changes they instituted led to factionalism. Moreover, according to common practice of the time, Indian children were literally captured and sent away from the pueblo to government-run Indian boarding schools, where they were encouraged to reject their heritage. Walter G. Marmon's own wife attended the Indian school at Carlisle, while Marmon's Ohio relatives cared for their children.

---

[6]Several related tales recorded by Boas, concerning the migration of the Laguna people, are also relevant to our discussion of sources for Susie's tale. Further, Boas relates another Laguna story from which Susie's story seems to borrow elements. In "Yellow Woman and the Turkeys," the heroine discovers her husband and sister together; angry, she puts the eagle down in her hair, and drowns herself in the lake. Her husband arrives and throws down her manta, which is transformed into butterflies (147, 156). De Huff (cited in Boas) offers a variant in which a girl drowns herself, and her mother throws her clothing into the water: the dress turns into deer, the moccasins into bears, the belt into a water snake. Boas cites these as two of very few Laguna tales explaining the origin of natural phenomena (179–80).

From evidence in *Storyteller*, we find that Robert Marmon's children were Leslie Silko's grandfather Hank, and Walter K. Marmon, the husband of Silko's Aunt Susie. Remember that Aunt Susie, too, had been sent away to Carlisle. Her life story is a version of the classic American captivity tale, in which white narrators typically describe being kidnapped by Indians. Susie's is a captivity tale from the Indian's point of view. Many years later, this same storyteller relates to her great-niece the tale of the little girl who ran away because her mother did not make for her yashtoah, the tribal food. Aunt Susie and her auditor have left their stamp on the story type of the Deserted Child just as surely as Boas's informants (among whom was Robert Marmon), along with the ethnographer himself, left their imprint on the tales they related.

We can now see more clearly how the teller in oral transmutation merges tribal and personal history, tradition and change. In her commentary on a Japanese folktale, Mickie Arai analyzes at length the way storytellers pass on the values of the dominant group to their young listeners. Aunt Susie's story is a negative exemplum of the behavior expected of mothers and daughters in her culture, reflecting the teller's enforced separation from her mother's teaching and from tribal knowledge. Eventually, however, in returning home, daughters like Susie were able to combine elements of their native culture with what they had learned from schooling outside the pueblo. It is this creative process Silko has chosen to emphasize. Silko begins her book by describing Susie's habit of writing down legends from the oral tradition, and the act becomes a model for Silko's composing methods throughout *Storyteller*. The new stories, combining tradition and revision, ensure the continuity and vigor of the culture.

The inheritor of a complex weave of ancestral traditions, Leslie Marmon Silko uses the forms and themes of Native American oral literature, with its repetitions and rituals, its concern for the land, its affirmation of cultural values and communal solidarity. To this indigenous form she adds the European-derived element of autobiography, of the individual point of view. For writers like Silko and the women whose stories she tells, the pueblo is both the destination and the starting point of literary exploration. The mesa becomes a symbolic scene of ascent and descent (and those two words are spelled any way you like).

The same exploratory spirit is perpetuated in the infusion of cultures in our international students' writing. These students may bring with them other ways of perceiving and reading, and alternative modes of shaping rhetoric, but they must also learn to adapt to the methods favored in the host country. My question in considering the composition and literature courses described in the chapters of this study has been not simply what we should teach, but what we might learn from nontraditional students. In her essay on *My Ántonia*, you may recall, Mickie concludes that holding on to your roots "helps you to survive in this country without losing yourself, and also I believe it helps build up this country just as people from Europe did in the early days of America."

APPENDIX 1 FOR CHAPTER 9

Syllabus for English 152/Tucker

Texts:

The Autobiography of Benjamin Franklin, ed. Silverman (Penguin)
Narrative of the Life of Frederick Douglass, ed. Baker (Penguin)
The Yellow Wallpaper, Charlotte Perkins Gilman (Feminist Press)
Herland, Charlotte Perkins Gilman (Pantheon)
My Ántonia, Willa Cather (Houghton Mifflin)
The remaining reading selections will be photocopied and provided by the instructor.

Course requirements: Your written work for the course will consist of a number of short essays, a final exam, and a "reader's journal" in which you will be asked to respond, for each class meeting, to the assignments and issues we'll be discussing throughout the term. A good deal of this syllabus depends on your participation, so I ask that you attend faithfully.

Spring 1988 Class Schedule:

I. The Figure in the Landscape

2/1 Introduction: bicultural perspective.

2/4 In-class writing (diagnostic).

2/9 Cultural constructions of the family.

2/11 President's holiday—no class.

2/16 Views of the family, continued: representations in American popular culture.

2/18 The creation of history: excerpts from Leslie Marmon Silko's *Storyteller* and N. Scott Momaday's *The Way to Rainy Mountain*. Essay #1 due: personal/cultural narrative and interpretation (modeled on Silko).

2/23 Early views of the landscape: readings from Mayan, Apache, Okanagon, and Yamana Indians; early literature of exploration (Columbus, Casteñeda); Powhatan's letter; John Smith; William Bradford; Anne Bradstreet.

2/25 Continue discussion of readings. Later depictions of terrain: photocopies of "nineteenth-century views" and excerpts from Amelia Knight's Oregon Trail diary.

3/1 Nineteenth- and twentieth-century representations of American landscape: slide presentation, part 1.

3/3 Slide presentation, part 2.

3/8 Essay #2 due: detailed description of an American painting or sculpture, contrasted with description and analysis of painting or artifact from your native culture.

II. Public Lives and Documents

3/10 The construction of autobiography: introduction to Franklin and Douglass.

3/15 *The Autobiography of Benjamin Franklin*, Part I.

3/17 Franklin, excerpt from Part II.

3/22 *Declaration of Independence* and excerpts from Jefferson's *Notes on the State of Virginia*.

3/24 *Narrative of the Life of Frederick Douglass.*

3/29 Douglass, continued. Extended notebook piece: favorite/most moving/effective chapter and reasons for your choice.

3/31 Douglass; Fugitive Slave Law; Gettysburg Address. Collect notebooks. Essay #3 due: analysis of comparable vignettes from Franklin and Douglass (see assignment sheet).

Spring Break

4/12 Documents, continued: Emerson, "Self-Reliance"; Sojourner Truth, "Ain't I A Woman?"

4/14 Excerpts from *Herland*. Extended notebook piece: your own utopian design; pick one aspect—social/familial organization, education, etc.—and discuss as specifically as you can.

III. The Fictional American

4/19 Irving, "Rip Van Winkle."

4/21 "Rip Van Winkle," continued.

4/26 Gilman, "The Yellow Wallpaper."

4/28 "The Yellow Wallpaper," continued; excerpts from late nineteeth-century documents and diaries.

5/3–

5/12 *My Ántonia*; term essay #4 on immigrant experience and analysis of a passage from the novel (see assignment sheet); oral reports.

5/17 In-class essay (diagnostic).

5/19 Final examination.

Sample Essay Assignments

In-Class Writing (diagnostic)

You will have one hour to plan and write the essay assigned below. Your goal is to analyze culture more than it is to give personal opinions, so the way you develop your ideas is as important as the ideas themselves. Whenever possible, support your assertions with examples drawn from your reading, your experience, and your observations of others. Try to illustrate your thoughts with as many cultural references as possible. For example, you may refer to the behavior patterns of a particular group, aspects of American history and culture, and specific literary texts to develop your response. You may also wish to compare or contrast elements of American culture with those of other cultures, which may help to describe American ideas, values, and ways of life more exactly than you otherwise could.

Here is an excerpt from a speech delivered in August of 1963 by Martin Luther King at a demonstration in Washington, D.C., for civil rights for black people in America:

> . . . I say to you today, my friends, that in spite of the difficulties and frustrations of the moment I still have a dream. It is a dream deeply rooted in the American dream.
>
> I have a dream that one day this nation will rise up and live out the true meaning of its creed: "We hold these truths to be self-evident; that all men are created equal."
>
> I have a dream that one day every valley shall be exalted, every hill and mountain shall be made low . . . and the glory of the Lord shall be revealed. . . .
>
> When we let freedom ring, when we let it ring from every village and every hamlet, from every state and every city, we will be able to speed up that day when all of God's children, black men and white men, Jews and Gentiles, Protestants and Catholics, will be able to join hands and sing in the words of the old Negro spiritual, "Free at last! free at last! thank God almighty, we are free at last!"

In this speech, Martin Luther King speaks of his dream of equal rights for blacks. What do you think the "American dream" is *today?* What do the Americans you have observed seem to want most in their lives?

An experiment: this doesn't count! See if you can answer the following questions (brief answers—a few words are sufficient):

1. Who was Martin Luther King and what happened to him?
2. Where does the quotation in paragraph 2 come from?
3. Where does the quotation in paragraph 3 come from?
4. What is a Negro spiritual?

Assignment: Essay #3

This essay is to be a comparison/contrast of excerpts from Benjamin Franklin's *Autobiography* and Frederick Douglass' *Narrative.* Select two comparable incidents, one from each book—to show how each author treats, for example, the opening of his memoirs, an episode in his self-education, an important moral lesson he learned, his escape from indenture/slavery, and so forth. (Since this is to be a brief essay, don't attempt to discuss large chunks of narrative. Pick one aspect of an issue—choose very short excerpts to analyze, perhaps of one or two pages each.)

There are several ways to organize a comparison/contrast essay, but probably the simplest way to structure the paper is to state your thesis and chief points of comparison in an opening paragraph or two (in this paragraph, too, you should state the titles and dates of each book); then analyze the excerpt you have chosen from the earlier Autobiography (Franklin's); then discuss the Douglass Narrative according to the points you have raised about the episode from Franklin, and treat each of these points in roughly the same order, so the reader can easily follow the logic of your comparison.

As always, be sure to give your paper a title, and to proofread carefully. And remember that summary of literary events is given in the *present tense.*

(One more reminder: as we discussed in class, the original paper topic on a hero or heroine from your culture [as it appears on our original syllabus] has been changed from a short essay to a notebook entry. So please make sure you have written an extended analysis in your notebook of a representative hero or heroine from your culture: Briefly describe this figure's life, discuss the qualities he or she embodies, and analyze the cultural or national values that are implicit in his or her life story.)

Assignment: Essay #4

Your final paper will allow you to use your own experience—as someone who has moved between two cultures—as a starting point (or ending point) for analysis of a passage from Willa Cather's *My Ántonia.*

The theme of the essay is sounded in this quotation from a recent biography of Cather by Sharon O'Brien:

> A concern with uprooting, transplanting, and resettlement infuses much of her mature work. Cather was drawn again and again to individuals and groups forced to move from one home to another, [such as] the immigrants who settled the Divide. . . . She was particularly drawn to the rituals and traditions that provided continuity during the process of transplanting, those customs that allowed immigrants to integrate the past with the present and the future. Like Emerson and Whitman, Cather liked to celebrate the heroic individual, but she never advocated a radical break with the past or a separation from community. Her heroic protagonists invariably draw strength from their connection with people, places, and customs that sustain rather than oppress individual achievement.

In an essay of about four pages, examine a brief passage from *My Ántonia* with the above quotation in mind. Your essay will have two parts:

1. Discuss a tradition or custom that you or your family or friends have brought over to the United States from your home culture. How, if at all, has this tradition "provided continuity during the process of transplanting" to this country?

2. Analyze a passage from the novel in which Cather shows how an old-world custom or belief or set of values keeps an immigrant community together—or keeps them apart from their native-born American neighbors. Summarize the passage and discuss its significance in terms of the section of the book in which it appears.

You may, of course, reverse the order of these two parts of the essay. The important thing is to integrate the two sections, to relate them in some way. The insights of the two parts, personal experience and literary analysis, should illuminate each other. (Remember to use the present tense when you are discussing the events in a work of fiction.)

We'll have a final conference next week to talk about the paper—please bring along the passage you'd like to discuss and a one-page sketch of what you want to say.

Final Examination

I. In two or three sentences, identify (give dates where possible) and explain the significance of *12* of the following terms (4 points each):

1. Fugitive Slave Law
2. deism
3. *picturesque* and *sublime*
4. "imitation is suicide"
5. Niagara Falls
6. parthenogenesis
7. "this nation, under God, shall have a new birth of freedom"
8. nachträglichkeit
9. "Where did your Christ come from? From God and a woman!"
10. Cuzak's Boys
11. binary opposition in Douglass' *Narrative*
12. "Governments are instituted among Men, deriving their just powers from the consent of the governed."
13. Franklin's project for "arriving at moral perfection"
14. Douglass' escape, as described in *Life and Times*

II. In his "Essay on American Scenery" (1835), Thomas Cole wrote, "Yet American scenes are not destitute of historical and legendary associations—the great struggle for freedom has sanctified many a spot, and many a mountain, stream, and rock, has its legend, worthy of poet's pen or the painter's pencil. But American associations are not so much of the past as of the present and the future. . . ."

How have artists and writers in America made use of the American landscape? How have they used the physical facts of the continent to create American myths, legends, and finally a national identity? In your response, try to refer to some of the early literature of exploration and settlement (Bradford, Smith, Bradstreet, Native American works), and to at least one nineteenth-century painter's work, as well as to "Self-Reliance" and *My Ántonia* (26 points).

III. Choose *one* of these essays (26 points):

1. Some observers argue that American Studies courses should concentrate on "classic" texts; that we simply don't have enough time in a semester to focus on "marginal" texts by women or minority writers. What do you think? Whichever way you argue, try to support your case with specific references to the work of writers such as Gilman, Douglass, Silko and other (anonymous) Native Americans whose texts we read this semester.
2. The English novelist D. H. Lawrence wrote in a much-quoted essay that Ben Franklin "set up this dummy of a perfect citizen as a pattern to America." How have Franklin, Douglass, and Gilman (through the fictional narrator of "The Yellow Wallpaper") combined artifice and autobiography to create versions of a typically "American self"? Discuss the literary techniques and themes through which these three writers *construct* or *represent* an American self on paper.

APPENDIX 2 FOR CHAPTER 9

American Painting: Presentations of the Landscape

I. Ways of Seeing Landscape

1. Miguelito (b. 1865): (Navajo Sandpainting) *The Four Mountains*

2. (China) Ni Tsan: *Woods and Valleys of Yu-Shan* (1372)*

3. (Iran) Shah Tamapo: *Rustama Cleaves Witch* (1527–1528)*

4. (China) Sung Dynasty (10th–11th c.), *The Tribute Horse**

5. (China) Ma Yuan (active 1190–1225): *Scholar by Waterfall**

6. Alex Wyant: *The Mohawk Valley* (1866)*

7. (Japan) Hiroshige: *Night Rain at Karasaki* (1850s)*

8. Hiroshige: *Kameido Tenjin Keidai* (1856)*

9. J. Barralet: *Bridge Over Schuylkill* (c. 1810)

II. Early American Painting: Portraits

10. the G. Limner: *Young Lady With Rose* (1732)*

11. J. Smibert: *Francis Brinley* (1731)*

12. J. Blackburn: *Mary Sylvester* (1754)*

13. Susan Sedgwick: *Elizabeth Freeman* (1811)

14. Joshua Johnson: *Mrs. Kennedy Long and Children* (1805–1806)

15. Gilbert Stuart: *George Washington* (1803)*

16. James Peale: *George Washington at Yorktown* (c. 1782)*

17. J. S. Copley: *Joseph Sherburne* (c. 1767)*

18. Copley: *Midshipman Augustus Brine* (1782)*

19. Copley: *Paul Revere* (c. 1768–1770)

*In the Metropolitan Museum of Art, New York City.

III. American Landscape Painting: Influences, Confluences

20. (France) Claude Lorrain: *Sunrise* (c. 1647–1648)*

21. (Italy) Salvator Rosa: *Landscape w/Tobias and Angel* (c. 1650s?)

22. Washington Allston: *Italian Landscape* (1814)

23. (England) J. M. W. Turner: *Interior, Tintern Abbey* (1794)

24. (England) John Constable: *Stonehenge* (1836)

25. Thomas Cole: *View Near Tivoli (Morning)* (1832)

The picturesque:

26. (England) Francis Towne: *Grasmere fr. Rydal Road* (c. 1787)

27. (England) Joseph Wright of Derby: *Rydal Waterfall* (1795)

28. (England) J. Constable: *The Glebe Farm* (1827)

29. T. Cole: *View on the Catskill, Early Autumn* (1837)*

30. Asher B. Durand: *The Beeches* (1845)*

31. A. Durand: *View of Troy, N.Y.* (c. 1840s)

The sublime:

32. (England) Turner: *The Passage of the St. Gothard* (1804)

33. (England) J. Martin: *The Bard* (1817)

34. Thomas Moran: *The Chasm of the Colorado* (1873–1874)

The "uses" of landscape painting:

35. John White: *Indians Fishing* (c. 1585)

36. John Smibert: *A View of Boston* (1738)

37. A. Robertson: *Hobuck* (1808)

38. T. Davies: *View of the Lines at Lake George, 1759* (c. 1774)

39. Thomas Birch: *Fairmount Waterworks* (1821)

40. Wm. Strickland: *Ballston Springs, N.Y.* (c. 1794)

41. Francis Guy: *Carter's Tavern, Lake George* (1817–1820)

42. Charles Fraser: *View of the Palisades* (1818)

IV. Native Schools

Hudson River School, first and second generations:

43. Photograph: View of Hudson

44. Thomas Chambers: *Villa on the Hudson* (late 1840s)

45. T. Cole: *Sunny Morning on the Hudson* (c. 1827)

46. Thomas Doughty: *Scene in the Catskills* (c. 1820s)

47. T. Cole: *The Oxbow (Connecticut River)* (1836)*

48. Asher Durand: *Kindred Spirits* (1849)†

49. T. Whittredge: *The Trout Pool* (c. 1868)*

50. S. Gifford: *Kauterskill Falls* (1862)*

51. Jasper Cropsey: *Wyoming Valley, Pa.* (1864)*

Genre painting:
52. William S. Mount: *Cider Making* (1841)*

Luminism and later marine painting:

53. Fitz Hugh Lane: *Brace's Rock, Gloucester* (1863)

54. Martin Johnson Heade: *Thunderstorm Over Narragansett Bay* (1868)

55. John F. Kensett: *Passing Off of the Storm* (1872)*

56. Winslow Homer: *Moonlight—Wood's Island Light* (1894)*

57. Albert P. Ryder: *Moonlight Marine* (1870s–1880s)*

Exploration and westward expansion:

58. J. Thompson: *Belated Party on Mansfield Mountain* (1858)*

59. George Caleb Bingham: *Fur Traders Descending the Missouri* (c. 1845)*

60. Albert Bierstadt: *Sunset in the Yosemite Valley* (1868).

61. Thomas Hill: *View of Yosemite* (1885)*

62. T. Moran: *The Teton Range* (1897)*

63. A. Bierstadt: *The Rocky Mountains* (1863)

64. Ralph Blakelock: *Indian Encampment* (c. 1880s)*

65. C. Schreyvogel: *My Bunkie* (1899)*

66. Frederic Remington: *Cavalry Charge on the Southern Plains* (1907)*

Niagara and industrialization:

67. A. Bierstadt: *Waterfall and Rainbow* (c. 1870s)

68. A. Bierstadt: *Niagara Falls* (c. 1880)

†In the New York Public Library.

69. Frederic Church: 70. George Inness:
Niagara Falls (1857)   *Niagara Falls* (1893)

City/country:

71. Thomas Eakins: 72. George Bellows:
Max Schmitt in a Single   *The Red Vine* (1916)*
Scull (1871)*

73. Edward Hopper: 74. E. Hopper: *Manhat-*   75. Charles Sheeler:
Gas (1940)‡   *tan Bridge Loop* (1928)   *American Landscape*
                                                            (1930)‡

Abstraction of landscape:

76. George Inness: 77. Mark Rothko: 78. Stuart Davis: *Com-*
Peace and Plenty (1865)*   *Number 22* (1949)‡   *bination Concrete* (1958)

79. Richard Estes:
Ansonia (1977)

80. Georgia O'Keeffe: 81. G. O'Keeffe: *Black*   82. G. O'Keeffe: *New*
Cow's Scull (1931)*   *Iris* (1926)*   *Mexico—Near Taos*
                                                            (1929)

                              83. G. O'Keeffe: *Pool*
                              in the Woods, Lake
                              George (1922)

‡In the Museum of Modern Art.

APPENDIX 3 FOR CHAPTER 9

Essay by Fatima Tunis

Essay #2, Part I: The Helmet Mask (Mende)

The mask is carved out of wood and is polished in jet-black; it has an object on the top of the head which is surrounded by four horns. The shape is hard to describe: I can only describe it as the letter "U" turned upside down; the whole thing represents the parts of the body from the neck up. It has a ringed neck, a small face—small nose, mouth and eyes.

Some of the features are typical of such a mask—the ringed neck, the color—some are not (instead of the horns on the head sometimes it has braids); there is no back or front difference on some of them, but some have the face and the back of the head to which the ringed-neck extends, and designs are made to make it as beautiful as the face. It makes no difference, though, how it looks, it is still the same mask serving the same purpose.

It is usually big enough to be worn over the human head—which is probably why it is called "the helmet mask" in the Metropolitan Museum of Art. This mask plays a significant role in the Mende woman's life—the Mendes are a tribe in Sierra Leone to which I partially belong. The Mendes have a female society called Sande—I will not go into what goes on in the Sande society because it is strictly confidential and off limits to men and non-members. This mask belongs to the Sande society and it is worn only by special people called Sowe; the Sowe is the leader of the Sande and she performs a lot of duties, one of which is to wear the mask—Sowe-wei, (Sowe's head) as the Mendes call it—and a rafia costume and dance during Sande ceremonies and special occasions.

Men are not allowed to see the Sowe dance during Sande ceremonies, except on other occasions such as feast days when the Sowe will just be there as a dancing masquerade. The Sowe-wei is carved by men, under the instructions of the Sande women as to how it should look. As soon as it is done, it is handed over to the women and then becomes *sacred* and kept away from men and non-members (it is seldom to find a Mende woman who is not a member of Sande).

The Sowe-wei is regarded as the most beautiful thing in Mende tribes; features such as the ringed-neck, dark complexion, etc, are some of the Mendes' definition of beauty in women. It is so highly respected that not just any Sande woman can wear it; even those qualified, I am told, have to adhere to certain rules, (which are part of the secrets in Sande) or else their heads will get stuck in it or it will get so heavy that they will not be able to keep their balance—if such things happen, the other Sande women will get together and release the person. The Sowe wearing the mask to dance is the main purpose of the Sowe-wei but it is also kept as an artifact or a legacy of a family of Sowes (daughters of Sowes usually succeed after their mothers). Miniatures or medium sizes are also made as decorative pieces, but since these have not been worn by the Sowe, they are mere copies and thus can be outside of the Sande society—like the one in the Metropolitan Museum of Arts, which measures about 17 1/4 inches, and is a 19/20th century piece. The authentic pieces kept in families or tribes, and *not* for display in museums, are much older.

Part II: *Tinto en Tando y Suta*

This is a sculpture made out of tins and wood and it is painted in a variety of colors—yellow, orange, brown, and black and white.

It is carved out as a man wearing a bright colored suit (yellow/orange) and a brown hat which comes down to his face (his spectacles). On his feet he has black and white shoes and his feet are crossed. His face and hands are dark brown, he is holding two gambling dices in his right hand, and on the middle finger of his left hand he has a brown ring.

Looking at this piece of sculpture what I saw was a gambler hanging around a street corner waiting for his friends to join him in playing dice. His suit does not look expensive—maybe at a price that a gambler can afford. The hat brought down to the spectacles suggests to me that this man is ashamed of what he does, yet either out of need or habit, he does it anyway.

I think that the artist is trying to project an image of a particular set of people in American culture—the gamblers. The impression that I get from this piece is that, on the average, the gambler is not an educated or literary person; he is aware of the fact that what he is doing is not widely accepted in the culture, which is why he is hiding his face. This tells me that the American culture does not give much encouragement to gambling but tells the gamblers that they can do it as long as they are discreet and ashamed of it.

I think that this piece of sculpture—like the mask in my culture—can be put to a positive use in this society and that is as an advertising object to promote a gambling business. It can be placed right outside of the casino or any other building used as a gambling spot to attract people. The potential gambler on seeing this ad will be impressed by the attire (having a taste in clothing and material wealth similar to what he sees) and he would want to win some money and buy himself something like that, given that he has no other means of getting extra money that would enable him to do so because of his lack of education. This piece used in this manner can bring a lot of profit to the business owners.

This sculpture is by Alison Saar, an American; she made it in 1985. In comparing it to the mask in Mende society, what I think they have in common is that they each represent a group of people in their respective cultures and they can both be used for certain purposes by their group either for benefit or entertainment.

APPENDIX 4 FOR CHAPTER 9

Essay by Michiru Arai

Essay #4: Being a Stranger in America

Mr. Shimerda in *My Ántonia* is away from his native country, just like I am. His country is as far away from America as mine is. The situations both of us are in seem to be identical. However, Mr. Shimerda eventually kills himself in this strange country and I am still alive. What makes our lives so different?

When Mr. Shimerda, the Bohemian immigrant, visits Jim Burden's grandfather on Christmas day, we see parts of what Mr. Shimerda misses so much in this country. He doesn't have a warm family atmosphere or relationships with other people in America. We know that his parents resented him for marrying Antonia's mother, but the life in Bohemia must have been more comfortable. Although he probably was not rich—if he was, the Shimerdas wouldn't have come to America—he had many friends who shared his interests, and who would come over and talk to him for hours.

At his grandfather's house Jim sees Mr. Shimerda's expression and describes it as if Mr. Shimerda was relieved from pain. Mr. Shimerda senses the warmth of the family who have enough money, food, and love for each other. The pain Mr. Shimerda is feeling is the uncomfortableness in his own house. Mr. Shimerda still loves his family, but Mrs. Shimerda now blames everything on him and other people. I'm not sure if Mrs. Shimerda was complaining as much about everything in Bohemia as she is now, but she has probably never been satisfied with her life. Since she was not satisfied with the life in Bohemia, she convinced her husband to come to America, the place where more money, opportunities and happiness were supposed to exist. When the Shimerdas came over here, none of those good things existed. They have to create a new life by working hard. The difficulties which Mrs. Shimerda didn't expect make her more frustrated and more harsh toward other people. She is just another victim of the American dream.

Mr. Shimerda understands his wife's frustration, but he is not doing anything to change the situation. He is not lazy. I think he just doesn't know how to change their lives. He had never encountered the toughness of nature until he came to America. His childhood must have been similar to that of Jim's. He read books and learned to play instruments, but he has never learned to cope with the hard life.

When Jim lights the Christmas tree, Mr. Shimerda kneels before the tree and prays. He doesn't care what religion Jim's grandfather follows. His religion is something that he carried over to America and nobody can change it. Jim feels something has changed about the tree when Mr. Shimerda kneels before it. Mr. Shimerda brings in something that is not theirs, a foreign custom. Grandfather doesn't say anything because he respects Mr. Shimerda. Grandfather probably guesses what kind of life Mr. Shimerda had in Bohemia from the way he prays. In addition to the respect, he feels sympathy to Mr. Shimerda who had to leave his country, throwing away everything he had, and adjust to a totally new environment.

When Mr. Shimerda looks at Jim he feels Mr. Shimerda is looking into Jim's future. I think Jim is exactly right. Mr. Shimerda envisions Jim's bright future and hopes his own children's future is as bright as Jim's. Since his life is not going anywhere, Mr. Shimerda wants his children to have good lives in America. Mr. Shimerda envies Jim on two accounts. One is for his own children. He wishes his own children had everything Jim has. The other is for himself. He wishes he was as young as Jim is so that he could enjoy the life again. Mr. Shimerda is also seeing himself in Jim, the boy who didn't have to do all the hard work, could read a lot of books, and dream about the future. Jim makes Mr. Shimerda more aware of what he doesn't have in America.

Mr. Shimerda didn't have wealth, but had everything else he needed in Bohemia. Leaving everything he loved in his own country is the main reason Mr. Shimerda can't assimilate into America culture. Unlike Mr. Shimerda, I didn't have much in Japan. Of course, I have my family there. That makes my situation much different from Mr. Shimerda's, but I will discuss it later.

When I went back to Tokyo after my two year stay in New York, I was already hanging right in the middle of American and Japanese cultures. I was eighteen when I came to New York for the first time. I was sensitive to everything. In short, I was Americanized. I started questioning Japanese values. Why do they wear the same clothes? Why don't they value anything but academic achievement? In Japanese society, if you start questioning those things, you are an outsider. I tried to hide those doubts and to become more Japanese. It was a pain. The two years in New York completely transformed me into Japanese-American. I call myself Japanese-American because I am not really American nor Japanese. For the pain I experienced in Japan, I was relieved to come back to New York. It seems funny that a Japanese girl feels better in this infamous city, New York. However, this is 1988. We, Japanese, are everywhere in New York. We can get Japanese food, doctors, and TV programs. Unlike Mr. Shimerda who has to take everything that is American because there is no other choice, I can choose between Japanese and American. That is a big difference between me and Mr. Shimerda.

My family is still in Japan. What that means is that I'm not really uprooted. If I fail here, I expect my parents to welcome me back there and I know they will more than gladly. On the other hand, Mr. Shimerda has his own family now. He can't give everything up and go back to his mother's hands. Having my parents in Japan makes it easier for me to take chances. However, there is another side to the advantage. I can't settle down anywhere. If I didn't have my family there, I would do anything to stay here forever because my way of thinking and behavioral patterns are closer to American culture than to Japanese Culture, but in reality, I know someday I have to go back to Japan.

In Linguistics, two different motives for which people learn a new language are discussed, integrative and instrumental motives. The integratively motivated person wants to be completely assimilated into the new society. On the other hand, the instrumentally motivated person wants only to use the knowledge of the second language to study or work in the new environment. This person doesn't intend to stay in the new country for a long time. Thus the integratively motivated person will learn the new language much better than the instrumentally motivated person.

On the surface, Mr. Shimerda seems integratively motivated because he intends to stay in America with his family, and I would be instrumentally motivated because I'm here to study. However, psychologically it's the other way around. Mr. Shimerda doesn't want to be an American. He wants to keep everything that is Bohemian. That's partly because he has to throw it away. He is threatened by American culture. If he doesn't hang on to Bohemian culture, it will go away. It might be wrong to call his motive instrumental. He is just too naive to have an idea that by learning a little bit of English he could get some kind of favor from American people. He is certainly not integratively motivated, though.

As for my case, I am not only instrumentally motivated to survive in school, but also integratively motivated to assimilate into American life which, by the way, is not possible because I will always look different. The way I look and the impossibility of my staying in America makes me somewhat less integratively motivated, but more so than Mr. Shimerda.

When a person who has to stay and assimilate into a new culture can't accept the new culture, it is a disaster. However, when a person who can't stay in the new culture, but was influenced by the new culture and became someone different from the original him/herself, it is also a disaster. Mr. Shimerda is a victim of American culture. He may be too sensitive, but America is so big that unless you are careful, you will be eaten by this monstrous country. Being in this country, keeping foreign customs is very difficult, but everybody should keep something that is from their roots. It helps you to survive in this country without losing yourself, and also I believe it helps build up this country just as those people from Europe did in the early days of America.

APPENDIX 5 FOR CHAPTER 9

Excerpt from *Storyteller* by Leslie Marmon Silko

I always called her Aunt Susie
because she was my father's aunt
and that's what he called her.

She was married to Walter K. Marmon,
my grandpa Hank's brother.
Her family was the Reyes family from Paguate
the village north of Old Laguna.
Around 1896
when she was a young woman
she had been sent away to Carlisle Indian School
in Pennsylvania.
After she finished at the Indian School
she attended Dickinson College in Carlisle.

When she returned to Laguna
she continued her studies
particularly of history
even as she raised her family
and helped Uncle Walter run their small cattle ranch.
In the 1920's she taught school
in a one-room building at Old Laguna
where my father remembers he misbehaved
while Aunt Susie had her back turned.

From the time that I can remember her
she worked on her kitchen table
with her books and papers spread over the oil cloth.
She wrote beautiful long hand script
but her eyesight was not good
and so she wrote very slowly.

She was already in her mid-sixties
when I discovered that she would listen to me
to all my questions and speculations.

I was only seven or eight years old then
but I remember she would put down her fountain pen
and lift her glasses to wipe her eyes with her handkerchief
before she spoke.

It seems extraordinary now
that she took time from her studies and writing
to answer my questions
and to tell me all that she knew on a subject,
but she did.

She had come to believe very much in books
and in schooling.
She was of a generation,
the last generation here at Laguna,
that passed down an entire culture
by word of mouth
an entire history
an entire vision of the world
which depended upon memory
and retelling by subsequent generations.

She must have realized
that the atmosphere and conditions
which had maintained this oral tradition in Laguna culture
had been irrevocably altered by the European intrusion—
principally by the practice of taking the children
away from Laguna to Indian schools,
taking the children away from the tellers who had
in all past generations
told the children
an entire culture, an entire identity of a people.

And yet her writing went painfully slow
because of her failing eyesight
and because of her considerable family duties.
What she is leaving with us—
the stories and remembered accounts—
is primarily what she was able to tell
and what we are able to remember.

As with any generation
the oral tradition depends upon each person
listening and remembering a portion
and it is together—
all of us remembering what we have heard together—
that creates the whole story
the long story of the people.

I remember only a small part.
But this is what I remember.

This is the way Aunt Susie told the story.
She had certain phrases, certain distinctive words
she used in her telling.
I write when I still hear
her voice as she tells the story.
People are sometimes surprised
at her vocabulary, but she was
a brilliant woman, a scholar
of her own making
who has cherished the Laguna stories
all her life.
This is the way I remember
she told this one story
about the little girl who ran away.

The scene is laid partly in old Acoma, and Laguna.
Waithea was a little girl living in Acoma and
one day she said
        "Mother, I would like to have
        some *yashtoah* to eat."
"Yashtoah" is the hardened crust on corn meal mush
that curls up.
The very name "yashtoah" means
it's sort of curled-up, you know, dried,
just as mush dries on top.
She said
      "I would like to have some *yashtoah*,"
and her mother said
        "My dear little girl,
        I can't make you any *yashtoah*
        because we haven't any wood,
        but if you will go down off the mesa
        down below
        and pick up some pieces of wood
        bring them home
        and I will make you some *yashtoah*."
So Waithea was glad and ran down the precipitous cliff
of Acoma mesa.
Down below
just as her mother had told her
there were pieces of wood,
some curled, some crooked in shape,
that she was to pick up and take home.
She found just such wood as these.
She went home
and she had them
in a little wicker basket-like bag.

First she called her mother
as she got home.
She said
       "Nayah, deeni!
       mother, upstairs!"
The pueblo people always called "upstairs"
because long ago their homes were two, three stories high
and that was their entrance
from the top.
She said
       "Deeni!
       UPSTAIRS!"
and her mother came.
The little girl said
            "I have brought the wood
               you wanted me to bring."
And she opened
her little wicker basket
and laid them out
and here they were snakes
instead of the crooked sticks of wood.
And her mother says
            "Oh my dear child,
              you have brought snakes instead!"
She says
       "Go take them back and put them back
       just where you got them."
And the little girl
ran down the mesa again
down below in the flats
and she put those sticks back
just where she got them.
They were snakes instead
and she was very much hurt about this
and so she said
           "I'm not going home.
           I'm going to *Kawaik*,
           the beautiful lake place, *Kawaik*
           and drown myself
           in that lake, *bun'yah'nah*.
That means the "west lake."
           I'll go there and drown myself."
So she started off,
and as she came by the Enchanted Mesa
near Acoma
she met an old man very aged
and he saw her running and he says
                  "My dear child,
                  where are you going?"

She says
       "I'm going to *Kawaik*
       and jump into the lake there."
"Why?"
"Well, because,"
          she says
"my mother didn't want to make any *yashtoah*
for me."
The old man said "Oh no!
          You must not go my child.
          Come with me
          and I will take you home."
He tried to catch her
but she was very light
and skipped along.
And everytime he would try
to grab her
she would skip faster
away from him.
So he was coming home with some wood
on his back,
strapped to his back
and tied with yucca thongs.
That's the way they did
in those days, with a strap
across their forehead.
And so he just took that strap
and let the wood drop.
He went as fast as he could
up the cliff
to the little girl's home.
When he got to the place
where she lived
he called to her mother
          "Deeni!"
"Come on up!"
And he says
       "I can't.
       I just came to bring you a message.
       Your little daughter is running away,
       she's going to *Kawaik* to drown herself
       in the lake there."
"Oh my dear little girl!"
          the mother said.
So she busied herself around
and made the *yashtoah* for her
which she liked so much.
Corn mush curled at the top.
She must have found enough wood

to boil the corn meal
to make the yashtoah"
And while the mush was cooling off
she got the little girl's clothing
she got her little *manta* dress,
you know,
and all her other garments,
her little buckskin moccasins that she had
and put them in a bundle too,
probably a yucca bag,
and started down as fast as she could on the east side of Acoma.
There used to be a trail there, you know, it is gone now, but
it was accessible in those days.
And she followed
and she saw her way at a distance,
saw the daughter way at a distance.
She kept calling
           "*Stsamaku!* My daughter! Come back!
           I've got your *yashtoah* for you."
But the girl would not turn
she kept on ahead and she cried
                    "My mother, my mother.
                    She didn't want me to have any *yashtoah*
                    so now I'm going to *Kawaik*
                    and drown myself."
Her mother heard her cry
and says
           "My little daughter
           come back here!"
No, she kept a distance away from her
and they came nearer and nearer
to the lake that was here.
And she could see her daughter now
very plain.
                    "Come back my daughter!
                    I have your *yashtoah!*"
And no
she kept on
and finally she reached the lake
and she stood on the edge.
She had carried a little feather
which is traditional.
In death they put this feather
on the dead in the hair.
She carried a feather
the little girl did
and she tied it in her hair
with a little piece of string
right on top of her head
she put the feather.

Just as her mother was about
to reach her
she jumped
into the lake.

The little feather was whirling
around and around in the depths below.
Of course the mother was very sad.
She went, grieved back to Acoma
and climbed her mesa home.
And the little clothing,
the little moccasins
that she's brought
and the *yashtoah,*
she stood on the edge
of the high mesa
and scattered them out.
She scattered them to the east
        to the west
to the north and to the south—
in all directions—
and here every one of the little clothing—
        the little *manta* dresses and shawls
        the moccasins and the *yashtoah*—
        they all turned into butterflies—
        all colors of butterflies.
And today they say that acoma has more beautiful butterflies—
red ones, white ones, blue ones, yellow ones.
They came
from this little girl's clothing.

Aunt Susie always spoke the words of the mother to her daughter
with great tenderness, with great feeling
as if Aunt Susie herself were the mother
addressing her little child. I remember there was something mournful
in her voice too as she repeated the words of the old man
something in her voice that implied the tragedy to come.
But when Aunt Susie came to the place
where the little girl's clothes turned into butterflies
then her voice would change and I could hear the excitement and wonder
and the story wasn't sad any longer.

Bibliography

INTRODUCTION

"Trying to Handle Two Languages at Once": ESL Students in the College Classroom

Andersen, Roger, ed. *New Dimensions in Second Language Acquisition Research*. Rowley, Mass.: Newbury House, 1981.

Ardener, E. W. "The Problem (of Women) Revisited." *Perceiving Women*. Ed. S. Ardener. London: Dent, 1975.

Ardener, S., ed. *Defining Females*. London: Croom Helm; New York: Halsted, 1978.

Bakhtin, Mikhail. "Discourse in the Novel." *The Dialogical Imagination*. Ed. Michael Holquist. Austin: U of Texas P, 1981. 259–442.

Basso, Keith H. *Portraits of "The Whiteman": Linguistic Play and Cultural Symbols Among the Western Apache*. Cambridge: Cambridge UP, 1979.

Chen, Xuya. "Studying in the United States: The Experience of Chinese Students in Queens College." Term paper submitted April 1988.

Cheong, George S. "A Cursory Comparison Between Chinese and English on Precision." *Elementary English* 49.3 (1972): 341–348.

James, Carl. *Contrastive Analysis*. Essex, England: Longman, 1980.

Kuhn, Thomas S. *The Structure of Scientific Revolutions*. 2nd ed. Chicago: U of Chicago P, 1970.

LoCoco, V. "An Analysis of Spanish and German Learner's Errors." *Working Papers on Bilingualism* 7 (1975): 96–124.

Martin, Anne V. "ESL Students' Perceptions of L1-L2 Differences in Organizing Ideas." Paper presented at TESOL '83. Toronto, Canada, 16 March 1983.

Otani, Yasuteru. "The Influence of the Mother Tongue on Achievement in Mathematics: A Contrastive Study of English and Japanese." *Workpapers in Teaching English as a Second Language* 9 (1975): 67–73.

Reynolds, David. *Naikon Psychotherapy*. Chicago: U of Chicago P, 1983.

Richards, Jack C., ed. *Error Analysis: Perspectives on Second Language Acquisition*. London: Longman, 1974.

Ritchie, William C. *Second Language Acquisition Research: Issues and Implications*. New York: Academic, 1978.

Roland, Alan. *In Search of Self in India and Japan: Toward a Cross-Cultural Psychology*. Princeton: Princeton UP, 1988.

Rorty, Richard. *Philosophy and the Mirror of Nature*. Princeton: Princeton UP, 1979.

Scarcella, Robin, and Stephen Krashen, eds. *Research in Second Language Acquisition: Selected Papers of the Los Angeles Second Language Acquisition Research Forum.* Rowley, Mass.: Newbury, 1980.

Schachter, Jacqueline, and Marianne Celce-Murcia. "Some Reservations Concerning Error Analysis." *TESOL Quarterly* 11.4 (1977): 441–451.

Schachter, Jacqueline, and William Rutherford. "Discourse Function and Language Transfer." *Working Papers on Bilingualism* 19 (1979).

Schumann, John. "The Relationship of Pidginization, Creolization and Decreolization to Second Language Acquisition." *Language Learning* 28.2 (1978): 367–379.

Schumann, John, and Nancy Stenson, eds. *New Frontiers in Second Language Learning.* Rowley, Mass.: Newbury, 1974.

Sleeter, Christine E. and Carl A. Grant. "An Analysis of Multicultural Education in the United States." *Harvard Educational Review* 57.4 (1987): 421–444.

Vygotsky, Lev. *Thought and Language.* Ed. and trans. Eugenia Hanfmann and Gertrude Vakar. Boston: M.I.T. P, 1962.

White, Merry I. and Susan Pollack, eds. *The Cultural Transition: Human Experience and Social Transformation in the Third World and Japan.* Boston: Routledge, 1986.

PART I

Cross-Cultural Literacy: What Do Readers Need to Know?

CHAPTER 1

On First Reading

Dasenbrock, Reed Way. "Intelligibility and Meaningfulness in Multicultural Literature in English." *PMLA* 102.1 (1987): 10–19.

Gilsenan, Michael. *Recognizing Islam: Religion and Society in the Modern Arab World.* New York: Pantheon, 1982.

Hirsch, E. D., Jr. *Cultural Literacy: What Every American Needs to Know.* Boston: Houghton, 1987.

Merriam, Allen H. "Comparative Chronemics and Diplomacy: American and Iranian Perspectives on Time." Paper presented at Annual Meeting of the Southern Speech Communication Association, Hot Springs, Arizona, Apr. 1982. ERIC ED 216 420.

Rushdie, Salman. "Good Advice Is Rarer Than Rubies." *The New Yorker,* 22 June 1987: 26–28.

Said, Edward W. *Covering Islam: How the Media and the Experts Determine How We See the Rest of the World.* New York: Pantheon, 1981.

Tyler, V. Lynn, and James S. Taylor. "Reading Between the Lines: Language Indicators Project." Interim Research Summary. Provo: Eyring Research Institute, 31 May 1978. ERIC ED 175 254.

CHAPTER 2

Rereading Chapter 1

"The Afghani." Fact Sheet Series #5. Center for Applied Linguistics, Washington, D.C., Sept. 1981. ERIC ED 216 519.

Ahmed, Leila. "Feminism and Feminist Movements in the Middle East, a Preliminary Exploration: Turkey, Egypt, Algeria, People's Democratic Republic of Yemen." *Women and Islam.* Ed. Azizah Al-Hibri. Oxford: Pergamon, 1982. 153–68.

Atil, Esin. *The Age of Sultan Suleyman the Magnificent.* Washington, D.C.: National Gallery of Art; New York: Abrams, 1987.

———. "The Age of Sultan Suleyman the Magnificent." *USA Today* July 1987: 78–86.

Belsey, Catherine. *Critical Practice.* London: Methuen, 1980.

Bhabha, Homi K. "Signs Taken for Wonders: Questions of Ambivalence and Authority under a Tree outside Delhi, May 1817." *"Race," Writing, and Difference.* Ed. Henry Louis Gates, Jr. Chicago: U of Chicago P, 1986. 163–84.

Bird, Jon. "On Newness, Art and History: Reviewing *Block* 1979–85." *The New Art History.* Ed. A. L. Rees and Frances Borzello. Atlantic Highlands, N.J.: Humanities, 1988. 32–40.

Bryson, Norman. *Tradition and Desire: From David to Delacroix.* Cambridge: Cambridge UP, 1984.

Burke, Kenneth. *Language as Symbolic Action.* Berkeley: U of California P, 1966.

Carr, Philippa, who is also Victoria Holt. *The Return of the Gypsy.* New York: Ballantine, 1985.

Cartland, Barbara. *Love Is Invincible.* New York: Berkley, 1988.

Chesney, Marion, writing as Jennie Tremaine. *Ginny.* New York: Dell, 1980.

Clark, T. J. *The Painting of Modern Life: Paris in the Art of Manet and His Followers.* Princeton: Princeton UP, 1984.

Clifford, James. *The Predicament of Culture: Twentieth-Century Ethnography, Literature, and Art.* Cambridge: Harvard UP, 1988.

Cowart, Jack, and Dominique Fourcade. *Henri Matisse: The Early Years in Nice 1916–1930.* Washington, D.C.: National Gallery of Art; New York: Abrams, 1986.

Culler, Jonathan. *On Deconstruction: Theory and Criticism After Structuralism.* Ithaca: Cornell UP, 1982.

Dawood, N. J., trans. *The Koran.* 1956. Harmondsworth, England: Penguin, 1986.

El Sa'adawi, Nawal. *Death of an Ex-Minister.* Trans. Shirley Eber. London: Methuen, 1987.

———. *The Hidden Face of Eve: Women in the Arab World.* Trans. and ed. Dr. Sherif Hetata. Boston: Beacon, 1982.

———. *Memoirs From the Women's Prison.* Trans. Marilyn Booth. London: Women's P, 1986.

———. *Two Women in One.* Trans. Osman Nusairi and Jana Gough. Seattle: Seal, 1986.

Ettinghausen, Richard. *Arab Painting.* New York: Rizzoli, 1977.

Ettinghausen, Richard, and Oleg Grabar. *The Art and Architecture of Islam, 650–1250.* Harmondsworth, England: Penguin, 1987.

Fernea, Elizabeth Warnock, ed. *Women and the Family in the Middle East: New Voices of Change.* Austin: U of Texas P, 1985.

Flam, Jack D. *Matisse on Art.* New York: Dutton, 1978.

———. *Matisse: The Man and his Art 1869–1918.* Ithaca: Cornell UP, 1986.

Fleenor, Juliann E., ed. *The Female Gothic.* Montreal: Eden 1983.

Foucault, Michel. *The Archaeology of Knowledge (and The Discourse on Language).* New York: Harper, 1976.

———. *The Order of Things: An Archaeology of the Human Sciences.* New York: Vintage, 1973.

Gilsenan, Michael (see Chapter 1).

Hamburger, Philip, "Lighted by Matisse." *The New Yorker* 10 Aug. 1987: 61–65.

Harari, Josué V., ed. *Textual Strategies: Perspectives in Post-Structuralist Criticism.* Ithaca: Cornell UP, 1979.

Hobhouse, Janet. "Odalisques: What Did They Mean to Matisse?" *Connoisseur* Jan. 1987: 60–67.

Horn, Miriam. "The Masters Behind the Masterpieces." *U.S. News & World Report* 2 Mar. 1987: 70–71.

Horn, Miriam, and Charles Fenyvesi. "Sultan Suleyman Courts America." *U.S. News & World Report* 9 Feb. 1987: 72.

Hughes, Robert. "Inventing a Sensory Utopia." *Time* 17 Nov. 1986: 98–99.

Kremer, Randall. "Henri Matisse: The Early Years in Nice." *USA Today* Mar. 1987: 84–87.

Larson, Kay. "Into the Light." *New York* 17 Nov. 1986: 93–94.

———. "Stella Performance and Other Exhibitions." *New York* 26 Oct. 1987: 123–25.

Lyman, Christopher M. *The Vanishing Race and Other Illusions: Photographs of Indians by Edward S. Curtis.* New York: Pantheon, 1982.

McGuigan, Cathleen. "A Golden Trove Fit for a Sultan." *Newsweek* 2 Feb. 1987: 66–67.

Marin, Louis. "On the Interpretation of Ordinary Language: A Parable of Pascal." Harari. 239–59.

Minces, Juliette. *The House of Obedience: Women in Arab Society.* Trans. Michael Pallis. London: Zed, 1982.

Mulvey, Laura. "Visual Pleasure and Narrative Cinema." *Screen* 16.3 (Autumn 1975): 6–18.

Nochlin, Linda. "The Imaginary Orient." *Art in America* May 1983: 118–31, 187–91.

Perl, Jed. "His Sultanic Majesty's Bequest." *Vogue* Apr. 1987: 74.

———. "Matisse in Love." *Vogue* Dec. 1986: 84, 88.

Plaidy, Jean, who is also Victoria Holt. *Myself My Enemy.* New York: Ballantine, 1983.

Radway, Janice A. *Reading the Romance: Women, Patriarchy, and Popular Literature.* Chapel Hill: U of North Carolina P, 1984.

Rice, David Talbot. *Islamic Art.* New York: Oxford UP, 1965.

Rushdie, Salman. *Midnight's Children.* New York: Avon, 1980.

———. *Shame.* London: Picador, 1984.

Said, Edward W. *Orientalism.* New York: Pantheon, 1978.

———. "The Text, the World, the Critic." Harari. 161–88.

Schneider, Pierre. *Matisse.* Trans. Michael Taylor and Bridget Stevens Romer. New York: Rizzoli, 1984.

Severy, Merle. "The World of Suleyman the Magnificent." *National Geographic* Nov. 1987: 552–601.

Silver, Kenneth E. "Matisse's Retour à l'ordre." *Art in America* June 1987: 111–23, 167–69.

Spivak, Gayatri Chakravorty. *In Other Worlds: Essays in Cultural Politics.* New York: Routledge, 1988.

Stevens, Mark. "Palette Nicoise." *New Republic* 16 Mar. 1987: 28–31.

Watkins, Nicholas. Rev. of "Matisse: The Early Years in Nice." *Burlington Magazine* Apr. 1987: 273–74.

White, Hayden. *Tropics of Discourse: Essays in Cultural Criticism.* Baltimore: Johns Hopkins UP, 1978.

PART II

In the Composition Classroom

CHAPTER 3

How to Do Things with Function Words: A Russian Student's Acquisition of English Articles

Akhmanova, Olga, et al. *Approaches to Contrastive Linguistics.* Moscow: Moscow State U, 1972.

Bialystock, Ellen. "Some Evidence for the Integrity and Interaction of Two Knowledge Sources." *New Dimensions in Second Language Acquisition Research.* Ed. Roger W. Andersen. Rowley, Mass.: Newbury, 1981. 62–74.

Croft, Lee B. "The Expression of Modality in English and Russian: A Contrastive Analysis." *Russian Language Journal* 29.104 (1975): 5–24.

Dulay, H., and M. Burt, "Errors and Strategies in Child Second Language Acquisition." *TESOL Quarterly* 8 (1974): 129–36.

Duškova, L. "On Sources of Error in Foreign Language Learning." *International Review of Applied Linguistics* 7 (1969): 11–36.

Hakuta, K. "Becoming Bilingual: A Case Study of a Japanese Child Learning English." *Language Learning* 26 (1976): 321–51.

Hartwell, Patrick. "Grammar, Grammars, and the Teaching of Grammar." *College English* 47.2 (1985): 105–27.

Kellerman, E. "Giving Learners a Break: Native Language Intuitions as a Source of Predictions About Transferability." *Working Papers on Bilingualism* 15 (1978): 59–92.

Krashen, Stephen. *Second Language Acquisition and Second Language Learning.* Oxford: Pergamon, 1981.

Lake, J. Joseph. "Predicate-Subject Order in Russian: What to Tell the Student." *Russian Language Journal* 28.100 (1974): 44–49.

Launer, Michael K. "Element Order in Russian: A Methodology for Elementary Courses." *Russian Language Journal* 29.103 (1975): 61–69.

Mentcher, E. "Teaching English to Russian Students." *English Language Teaching Journal* 34.1 (1979): 47–52.

Morris, William, ed. *American Heritage Dictionary.* 2nd college ed. Boston: Houghton, 1980.

Nabokov, Vladimir. *Nikolai Gogol.* Norfolk, Conn.: New Directions, 1944.

Rowse, A. L., ed. *Shapespeare's Sonnets.* New York: Harper, 1964.

Schaarschmidt, Gunter. "A Natural Learning Sequence: Passives and Participles in Russian." *Russian Language Journal* 33.115 (1979): 6–18.

Schachter, J. "An Error in Error Analysis." *Language Learning* 24 (1974): 205–14.

Seliger, Herbert W. "On the Nature and Function of Language Rules in Language Learning." *TESOL Quarterly* 13 (1979): 359–69.

Thompson, Irene. "Russian Word Order: A Comparative Study." *Slavic and East European Journal* 21.1 (1977): 88–104.

Wode, H. "Developmental Sequences in Naturalistic L2 Acquisition." *Second Language Acquisition.* Ed. E. Hatch. Rowley, Mass.: Newbury, 1978. 101–17.

Zobl, Helmut. "A Direction for Contrastive Analysis: The Comparative Study of Developmental Sequences." *TESOL Quarterly* 16.2 (1982): 169–83.

CHAPTER 4

A Greek Writer's Idiolect: What Is Not an ESL Error?

Allen, R. E., trans. *The Dialogues of Plato. Vol. I.* New Haven: Yale UP, 1984.

Bien, Peter. *Kazantzakis and the Linguistic Revolution in Greek Literature.* Princeton: Princeton UP, 1972.

Bruffee, Kenneth A. "Collaborative Learning and the 'Conversation of Mankind.' " *College English* 46.7 (1984): 635–52.

Bruner, Jerome. "Life as Narrative." *Social Research* 54.1 (1987): 11–36.

Efstathiadis, S., and P. King. "Some Lexical and Structural Errors Made by Greek Learners of English." *English Language Teaching* 26.2 (1972): 159–67.

Joseph, Brian D., and Irene Philippaki-Warburton. *Modern Greek.* London: Croom Helm, 1987.

Kazazis, Kostas, and Joseph Pentheroudakis. "Reduplication of Indefinite Direct Objects in Albanian and Modern Greek." *Language* 52.2 (1976): 398–403.

Kinneavy, James L. "Translating Theory into Practice in Teaching Composition: A Historical View and a Contemporary View. *Essays on Classical Rhetoric and Modern Discourse.* Ed. Robert J. Connors, Lisa S. Ede, and Andrea A. Lunsford. Carbondale: Southern Illinois UP, 1984.

Kleinmann, Howard H. "Avoidance Behavior in Adult Second Language Acquisition." *Language Learning* 27.1 (1977): 93–107.

Koutsoudas, Andreas, and Olympia Koutsoudas. "A Contrastive Analysis of the Segmental Phonemes of Greek and English." *Language Learning* 7.3 (1962): 211–30.

Markus, H. "Self-Schemata and Processing Information about the Self." *Journal of Personality and Social Psychology* 35 (1977): 63–78.

Neisser, Ulric, ed. *Memory Observed: Remembering in Natural Contexts.* San Francisco: Freeman, 1982.

Ohmann, Richard. "Use Definite, Specific, Concrete Language." *College English* 41.4 (1979): 390–97.

Ponsot, Marie, and Rosemary Deen, *Beat Not the Poor Desk.* Upper Montclair, N.J.: Boynton/Cook, 1982.

Rosenfield, Israel. *The Invention of Memory: A New View of the Brain.* New York: Basic, 1988.

Rubin, David C., ed. *Autobiographical Memory.* Cambridge, England: Cambridge UP, 1986.

Schor, Sandra. "An Alternative to Revising: The Proleptic Grasp." *Journal of Basic Writing* 6.1 (1987): 48–54.

Seiler, Hansjakob. "Abstract Structures for Moods in Greek." *Language* 47.1 (1971): 79–89.

Wenden, Anita. "Helping Language Learners Think About Learning." *English Language Teaching Journal* 40.1 (1986): 3–12.

CHAPTER 5

"What Changed Me":
Mimi Soo and the Question of Motivation

Austin, J. L. *How To Do Things With Words.* Cambridge, Mass.: Harvard UP, 1962.

Beebe, Leslie M. "Risk-Taking and the Language Learner." *Classroom Oriented Research in Second Language Acquisition.* Ed. Herbert W. Seliger and Michael Long. Rowley, Mass.: Newbury, 1983.

Birdsong, David, and Terence Odlin. "If Whorf Was on the Right Track: A Review of *The Linguistic Shaping of Thought: A Study of the Impact of Language and Thinking in China and the West.*" *Language Learning* 33.3 (1983): 401–10.

Bloom, Alfred H. *The Linguistic Shaping of Thought: A Study of the Impact of Language and Thinking in China and the West.* Hillsdale, N.J.: Lawrence Erlbaum, 1981.

Brown, H. D. "Cognitive and Affective Characteristics of Good Language Learners." Paper presented at Los Angeles Second Acquisition Research Forum. UCLA, February 1977. Cited in Krashen, *Second Language Acquisition* (see Chapter 3).

———. *Principles of Language Learning and Teaching.* Englewood Cliffs, N.J.: Prentice-Hall, 1987.

Busch, D. "Introversion-Extroversion and the EFL Proficiency of Japanese Students." *Language Learning* 32.1 (1982): 109–32.

Carroll, J. B. "Foreign Language Proficiency Levels Attained by Majors Near Graduation from College." *Foreign Language Annals* 1 (1967): 131–51.

————. *The Teaching of French as a Foreign Language in Eight Countries.* New York: Wiley, 1975.

Chen, Y. F. *Teaching Advanced English Composition to Chinese College Students.* M.A. thesis, California State University, Fresno, 1982.

Chiang, T. H. *Error Analysis: A Study of Errors Made in Written English by Chinese Learners.* Taipei: Crane, 1981.

Chihara, T., and J. Oller. "Attitudes and Attained Proficiency in EFL: a Sociolinguistic Study of Adult Japanese Speakers." *Language Learning* 28 (1978): 55–68.

Chu, Chauncey C. "A Semantico-Syntactic Approach to Contrastive Analysis—Some 'Be' and 'Have' Sentences in English and Chinese." *International Review of Applied Linguistics in Language Teaching* 16.4 (1978): 273–96.

Clément, R., R. C. Gardner, and P. C. Smythe. "Motivational Variables in Second Language Acquisition: A Study of Francophones Learning English." *Canadian Journal of Behavioural Science* 9 (1977): 123–33.

Clément, R., and Bastian G. Kruidenier. "Orientations in Second Language Acquisition: I. The Effects of Ethnicity, Milieu, and Target Language on Their Emergence." *Language Learning* 33.3 (1983): 273–90.

A Contrastive Study of English and Mandarin Chinese. Monterey, Calif.: Defense Language Institute, 1974.

Day, Richard R. "Student Participation in the ESL Classroom Or Some Imperfections in Practice." *Language Learning* 34.3 (1984): 69–98.

Ely, Christopher M. "An Analysis of Discomfort, Risktaking, Sociability, and Motivation in the L2 Classroom." *Language Learning* 36.1 (1986): 1–25.

Fenollosa, Ernest. *The Chinese Written Character as a Medium for Poetry.* Ed. Ezra Pound. San Francisco: City Lights, 1936.

Flege, James Emil. "A Critical Period for Learning to Pronounce Foreign Languages?" *Applied Linguistics* 8.2 (1987): 162–76.

Gardner, R. C. "On the Validity of Affective Variables in Second Language Acquisition: Conceptual, Contextual, and Statistical Considerations." *Language Learning* 30.2 (1980): 255–70.

Gardner, R. C., and W. E. Lambert. *Attitudes and Motivation in Second Language Learning.* Rowley, Mass.: Newbury, 1972.

————. "Motivational Variables in Second Language Acquisition." *Canadian Journal of Psychology* 13 (1959): 266–72.

Gardner, R. C., R. N. Lalonde, and J. MacPherson. "Social Factors in Seocnd Language Attrition." *Language Learning* 35.4 (1985): 519–40.

Gardner, R. C., R. N. Lalonde, and R. Moorcroft. "The Role of Attitudes and Motivation in Second Language Learning: Correlational and Experimental Considerations. *Language Learning* 35.2 (1985): 207–27..

Genesee, Fred, Pierre Rogers, and Naomi Holobow. "The Social Psychology of Second Language Learning: Another Point of View." *Language Learning* 33.2 (1983): 209–24.

Halliday, M. A. K., and R. Hasan. *Cohesion in English.* London: Longman, 1976.

Harvey, Paul. "A Lesson to be Learned: Chinese Approaches to Language Learning." *English Language Teaching Journal* 39.3 (1985): 183–86.

Hermann, G. "Attitudes and Success in Children's Learning of English as a Second Language: The Motivational Versus the Resultative Hypothesis." *English Language Teaching Journal* 34 (1980):247–54.

Heyde, A. "The Relationship Between Self-Esteem and the Oral Production of a Second Language." *On TESOL '77: Teaching and Learning English as a Second*

Language: Trends in Research and Practice. Ed. H. D. Brown, C. Yorio, and R. Crymes. Washington, D.C.: TESOL, 1977. 226–40.

Jones, Irene. "Some Cultural and Linguistic Considerations Affecting the Learning of English by Chinese Children in Britain." *English Language Teaching Journal* 34.1 (1979): 55–60.

Kaplan, Robert B. *The Anatomy of Rhetoric: Prolegomena to a Functional Theory of Rhetoric.* Philadelphia: The Center for Curriculum Development, 1972.

———. "Cultural Thought Patterns in Inter-Cultural Education." *Language Learning* 16.1–2 (1966): 1–20.

Kingston, Maxine Hong. *The Woman Warrior: Memoirs of a Girlhood Among Ghosts.* New York: Knopf, 1976.

Li, C. N., and S. A. Thompson. *Mandarin Chinese: A Functional Reference Grammar.* Berkeley: U of California P, 1981.

Lukmani, Y. M. "Motivation to Learn and Language Proficiency." *Language Learning* 22 (1972): 261–73.

Ma, Helen. "The Problems Faced by Chinese Students Learning Spoken English in Secondary Schools in Hong Kong." Unpublished M.A. thesis. Hong Kong: Ealing College of Higher Education, 1982.

Madden, Edith H. "The Effect of Training on Pronunciation." *ORTESOL Journal* 4 (1983): 69–80.

Matalene, Carolyn. "Contrastive Rhetoric: An American Writing Teacher in China." *College English* 47.8 (1985): 789–808.

McLaughlin, Barry. "The Monitor Model: Some Methodological Considerations." *Language Learning* 28.2 (1978): 309–31.

Mo, J. C. "A Study of English Reading Comprehension from the Point of View of Discourse Function." *English Teaching and Learning* 6.3 (1982): 39–48. Translated and cited by Tsao (see below).

Oller, J. W., Jr. "Research on the Measurement of Affective Variables: Some Remaining Questions." *New Dimensions in Second Language Acquisition Research.* Ed. R. Andersen. Rowley, Mass.: Newbury, 1981. 14–28.

Oller, J., L. Baca, and A. Vigil. "Attitudes and Attained Proficiency in ESL: A Sociolinguistic Study of Mexican-Americans in the Southwest." *TESOL Quarterly* 11 (1977): 173–83.

Oller, J., A. Hudson, and P. Liu. "Attitudes and Attained Proficiency in ESL: A Sociolinguistic Study of Native Speakers of Chinese in the United States." *Language Learning* 27 (1977): 1–27.

Oller, J., and K. Perkins. "Intelligence and Language Proficiency as Sources of Variance in Self-Reported Affective Variables." *Language Learning* 28.1 (1978): 85–97.

Pierson, Herbert D., Gail S. Fu, and Sik-yum Lee. "An Analysis of the Relationships Between Language Attitudes and English Attainment of Secondary Students in Hong Kong." *Language Learning* 30.2 (1980): 289–305.

Ponsot, Marie, and Rosemary Deen (see Chapter 4).

Qu, Xinpei. *A Preliminary Study of Organizational Structures of Argumentative Essays Written By Chinese Students at Two Levels of English.* Unpublished M.A. thesis, City College, CUNY, 1988.

Savignon, Sandra J. *Communicative Competence: An Experiment in Foreign Language Teaching.* Philadelphia: The Center for Curriculum Development, 1972.

Schumann, John H. "Social Distance as a Factor in Second Language Acquisition." *Language Learning* 26 (1976): 135–43.

Scovel, Thomas. "The Effect of Affect on Foreign Language Learning: A Review of the Anxiety Research." *Language Learning* 28.1 (1978): 129–42.

Seliger, H. "Does Practice Make Perfect? A Study of Interaction Patterns and L2 Competence." *Language Learning* 27 (1977): 263–78.

Stevick, E. *Memory, Meaning, and Method.* Rowley, Mass.: Newbury, 1976.

Strong, Michael. "Integrative Motivation: Cause or Result of Successful Second Language Acquisition?" *Language Learning* 34.3 (1984): 1–14.

Svanes, Bjorg. "Motivation and Cultural Distance in Second-Language Acquisition." *Language Learning* 37.3 (1987): 341–59.

Thompson, J. Charles. "Aspects of the Chinese Verb." *Linguistics* 38 (1968): 70–76.

Tsao, Feng-Fu. "Linguistics and Written Discourse in Particular Languages: Contrastive Studies: English and Chinese (Mandarin)." *Annual Review of Applied Linguistics: 1982.* Ed. Robert B. Kaplan et al. Rowley, Mass.: Newbury, 1983.

Upshur, J., W. Acton, B. Arthur, and A. Guiora. "Causation or Correlation: A Reply to Oller and Perkins." *Language Learning* 28.1 (1978): 99–104.

Wang. L. *Jungguo Yufa Lilun* (*Theory of Chinese Grammar*). Shanghai: Commercial, 1955.

Witte, S. P., and L. Faigley. "Coherence, Cohesion and Writing Quality." *College Composition and Communication,* 32 (1981): 189–204.

CHAPTER 6

Some "Japanese" and "American" Rhetorical Preferences

Barnlund, D. C. *Public and Private Self in Japan and the US.* Tokyo: Simul, 1975.

Barthes, Roland. *Empire of Signs.* Trans. Richard Howard. New York: Hill and Wang, 1982.

Berlin, James A. "Contemporary Composition: The Major Pedagogical Issues." *College English* 44.8 (1982): 765–77.

Blum-Kulka, S. "Learning to Say What You Mean in a Second Language: A Study of the Speech Act Performance of Learners of Hebrew as a Second Language." *Applied Linguistics* 3 (1982): 29–59.

Bowers, James R. "The Japanese Concept of *Hanashi-Kata* and Its Potential Influence on Foreign Language Acquisition." *Cross Currents: Communication/Language/Cross-Cultural Skills* 5.2 (1978): 1–8.

Brownscombe, E. Carol. "Towards Characterizing Perceptual Strategies of Second Language Learners." *Occasional Papers on Linguistics* 1 (1977). Carbondale: Southern Illinois U., Department of Linguistics.

Caudill, William, and Helen Weinstein. "Maternal Care and Infant Behavior in Japan and America." Lebra and Lebra. 225–76.

Christopher, Robert C. *The Japanese Mind.* New York: Ballantine, 1983.

Chugakkou Kokugo 2 (*Junior High School Japanese, Second Term*). Tokyo: Gakkou Tosyo, 1987.

Cohen, A. D., and E. Olshtain. "Developing a Measure of Sociocultural Competence: The Case of Apology." *Language Learning* 31.1 (1981): 113–34.

Doi, L. Takeo. "*Amae:* A Key Concept for Understanding Japanese Personality Structure." Lebra and Lebra. 145–54.

————. "Some Psychological Themes in Japanese Human Relationships." *Intercultural Encounters with Japan.* Ed. J. C. Condon and M. Saito. Tokyo: Simul, 1974.

Dorfman, Cynthia Hearn, ed. *Japanese Education Today: A Report from the U.S. Study of Education in Japan.* Washington, D.C.: U.S. Department of Education, 1987.

Duke, Benjamin. *The Japanese School: Lessons for Industrial America.* New York: Praeger, 1986.

Farkas, Jennifer Burkard, and Morio Kohno. *America no Nihonjin Seitotachi. (Japanese Students in America).* Trans. Takako Futatsugi. Tokyo: Tokyo Shoseki, 1987.

Gendai no Kokugo (Modern Japanese). Tokyo: Sanseido, 1987.

Goldstein, Bernice Z., and Kyoka Tamura. *Japan & America: A Comparative Study in Language and Culture.* Rutland, Vermont: Tuttle, 1975.

Heidegger, Martin. "A Dialogue on Language." *On the Way to Language.* Trans. Peter D. Hertz. San Francisco: Harper, 1971. 1–54.

Higa, Masanori. "The Use of the Imperative Mood in Postwar Japan." *Transcultural Research in Mental Health: Vol. II of Mental Health Research in Asia and the Pacific.* Ed. W. P. Lebra. Honolulu: UP of Hawaii, 1972.

Hinds, John. "English and Japanese." *Annual Review of Applied Linguistics 1982.* Ed. Robert Kaplan et al. Rowley, Mass.: Newbury, 1983. 78–84.

————. *Japanese.* London: Croom Helm, 1986.

————. "Japanese Expository Prose." *Papers in Linguistics: International Journal of Human Communications* 13.1 (1980): 117–57.

————. "A Taxonomy of Japanese Discourse Types." *Linguistics* 184 (1976): 45–53.

Kaplan, Robert (see Chapter 5).

Kinneavy, J. L. *A Theory of Discourse.* Englewood Cliffs, N.J.: Prentice-Hall, 1971.

Kobayashi, M. K., and W. Warner Burke. "Organization Development in Japan." *Columbia Journal of World Business* 11.2 (Summer 1976): 113–23.

Kuno, Susumu. *The Structure of the Japanese Language.* Cambridge: MIT P, 1973.

Lebra, Takie, and William P. Lebra, eds. *Japanese Culture and Behavior.* Honolulu: UP of Hawaii, 1974.

Lebra, Takie Sugiyama. *Japanese Patterns of Behavior.* Honolulu: UP of Hawaii, 1976.

Littlewood, William T. "Contrastive Pragmatics and the Foreign Language Learner's Personality." *Applied Linguistics* 4.3 (1983): 200–6.

Loveday, Leo J. "Communicative Interference: A Framework for Contrastively Analysing L2 Behavior of Japanese Performing in English." *International Review of Applied Linguistics in Language Teaching* 20.1 (1982): 1–16.

————. "Japanese Donatory Verbs: Their Implications for Linguistic Theory." *Language Sciences* 3.1 (1981): 58–90.

Miller, Roy Andrew. *Japan's Modern Myth: The Language and Beyond.* New York: Weatherhill, 1982.

Nakai, Satoru. "A Method of the Contrastive Analysis of English and Japanese." *Doshisha Literature* 27 (1973): 86–105.

Nakamura, Hajime. *Ways of Thinking of Eastern Peoples: India-China-Tibet-Japan.* Rev. Eng. trans. Ed. Philip P. Wiener. Honolulu: East-West Center, 1964.

Nakane, C. *Japanese Society.* London: Weidenfeld & Nicolson, 1970.

Pascale, Richard Tanner, and Anthony G. Athos. *The Art of Japanese Business Management.* New York: Warner, 1981.

Pollack, David. *The Fracture of Meaning: Japan's Synthesis of China from the Eighth Through the Eighteenth Centuries.* Princeton: Princeton UP, 1986.

Ree, Joe J. "Contrastive Analysis and Language Tendencies." 1975. ERIC ED 116 466.

Reischauer, Edwin O. *Japan: Story of a Nation.* 3rd ed. New York: Knopf, 1981.

————. *The Japanese Today*. Cambridge: Harvard UP, 1988.

Rohlen, Thomas P. *Japan's High Schools*. Berkeley: U of California P, 1983.

Silberman, Bernard S., ed. *Japanese Character and Culture: A Book of Selected Readings*. Tucson: U of Arizona P, 1962.

Smith, Donald L. "Mirror Images in Japanese and English." *Language* 54.1 (1978): 78–122.

Smith, Robert J., and Richard K. Beardsley, eds. *Japanese Culture: Its Development and Characteristics*. Chicago: Aldine, 1962.

Suzuki, Takao. *Tozasareta Gengo—Nihongo no Sekai*. Tokyo: Sincho-sha, 1975. Cited in Miller.

Tarallo, Fernando, and John Myhill. "Interference and Natural Language Processing in Second Language Acquisition." *Language Learning* 33.1 (1983): 55–76.

Ueda, Makoto. *Literary and Art Theories in Japan*. Cleveland: P of Western Reserve U, 1967.

White, Merry. *The Japanese Overseas: Can They Go Home Again?* New York: Free, 1988.

Wolfson, Nessa. "Compliments in Cross-Cultural Perspective." *TESOL Quarterly* 15.2 (1981): 117–24.

CHAPTER 7

In Which the Emphasis of Chapter 6 Is Shifted: Some "American" and "Japanese" Rhetorical Preferences

Adelstein, Michael E., and Jean G. Pival. *The Writing Commitment*. 3rd ed. San Diego: Harcourt, 1984.

Applebee, Arthur N. *Tradition and Reform in the Teaching of English: A History*. Urbana: NCTE, 1974.

Ardener, E. W. (see Introduction).

Ardener, S. (see Introduction).

Aston, G. "Comprehending Value: Aspects of the Structure of Argumentative Discourse." *Studi Italiani di Linguistica Teorica ed Applicata* 6 (1977): 465–509.

Atwell, Nancie. *In the Middle: Writing, Reading and Learning with Adolescents*. Portsmouth, N.H.: Boynton/Cook, 1987.

Barnet, Sylvan, and Hugo Bedau. *Current Issues and Enduring Questions: Methods and Models of Argument from Plato to the Present*. New York: St. Martin's, 1987.

Belenky, Mary Field, et al. *Women's Ways of Knowing: The Development of Self, Voice, and Mind*. New York: Basic, 1986.

Berlin, James A. *Rhetoric and Reality: Writing Instruction in American Colleges, 1900–1985*. Carbondale: Southern Illinois UP, 1987.

————. *Writing Instruction in Nineteenth-Century American Colleges*. Carbondale: Southern Illinois UP, 1984.

Berthoff, Ann E. *Forming/Thinking/Writing: The Composing Imagination*. Rochelle Park, N.J.: Hayden, 1978.

Bizzell, Patricia, and Bruce Herzberg, *The Bedford Bibliography for Teachers of Writing*. New York: St. Martin's, 1987.

Blair, Hugh. *Lectures on Rhetoric and Belles Lettres.* 1783. Ed. Harold F. Harding. Carbondale: Southern Illinois UP, 1965.

Cameron, Deborah. *Feminism and Linguistic Theory.* New York: St. Martin's, 1985.

Connor, Ulla. "Argumentative Patterns in Student Essays: Cross-Cultural Differences." *Writing Across Languages: Analysis of L2 Text.* Ed. Ulla Connor and Robert B. Kaplan. Reading, Mass.: Addison-Wesley, 1987.

Connors, Robert J. "The Rise and Fall of the Modes of Discourse." *College Composition and Communication* 32 (Dec. 1981): 444–63.

Corbett, Edward P. J. *Classical Rhetoric for the Modern Student.* 2nd ed. New York: Oxford UP, 1971.

Crowhurst, Marion. "Syntactic Complexity and Teachers' Quality Ratings of Narrations and Arguments." *Research in the Teaching of English* 14.3 (1980): 223–31.

Eggington, William G. "Written Academic Discourse in Korean: Implications for Effective Communication." *Writing Across Languages: Analysis of L2 Text.* Ed. Ulla Connor and Robert B. Kaplan. Reading, Mass.: Addison-Wesley, 1987.

Elbow, Peter. *Writing Without Teachers.* New York: Oxford UP, 1973.

Ervin-Tripp, Susan. "Interaction of Language, Topic, and Listener." *American Anthropologist* 66 (1964): 86–102. Cited in Peter Farb. *Word Play.* New York: Bantam, 1976.

Fahnestock, Jeanne, and Marie Secor. *A Rhetoric of Argument.* New York: Random, 1982.

Gage, John T. *The Shape of Reason: Argumentative Writing in College.* New York: Macmillan, 1987.

Gilligan, C. *In a Different Voice: Psychological Theory and Women's Development.* Cambridge, Mass.: Harvard UP, 1982.

Goodwin, Marjorie Harness, and Charles Goodwin. "Children's Arguing." *Language, Gender, and Sex in Comparative Perspective.* Ed. Susan U. Philips et al. Cambridge: Cambridge UP, 1987.

Hinds, John (see Chapter 6).

Horner, Winifred Bryan. "Rhetoric in the Liberal Arts: Nineteenth-Century Scottish Universities." *The Rhetorical Tradition and Modern Writing.* Ed. James J. Murphy. New York: MLA, 1982.

Kramarae, Cheris. *Women and Men Speaking.* Rowley, Mass.: Newbury, 1981.

Kummer, W. "Aspects of a Theory of Argumentation." *Text Sorten.* Ed. E. Gulich and W. Raible. Frankfurt: Athenaum, 1972. 25–49.

Kytle, Ray. *Clear Thinking for Composition.* 5th ed. New York: Random, 1987.

Lakoff, George, and Mark Johnson. *Metaphors We Live By.* Chicago: U of Chicago P, 1980.

Lever, J. "Sex Differences in the Games Children Play." *Social Problems* 23 (1976): 478–87.

Levin, Gerald. *Writing and Logic.* New York: Harcourt, 1982.

McCrea, Brian, and Toni Lopez Kemmerle. *College Writing.* Indianapolis: Bobbs, 1985.

McDonald, Daniel. *The Language of Argument.* 6th ed. New York: Harper, 1989.

Macrorie, Ken. *Telling Writing.* 3rd ed. Hasbrouck Heights: Hayden, 1980.

Miller, Robert K. *The Informed Argument: A Multidisciplinary Reader and Guide.* San Diego: Harcourt, 1986.

Moffett, James. *Teaching the Universe of Discourse.* Boston: Houghton, 1968.

Moffett, James, and Betty Jane Wagner. *Student-Centered Language Arts and Reading, K-13: A Handbook for Teachers.* 3rd ed. Boston: Houghton, 1983.

Mulderig, Gerald P. "Nineteenth-Century Psychology and the Shaping of Alexander Bain's *English Composition and Rhetoric.*" *The Rhetorical Tradition and Modern Writing.* Ed. James J. Murphy. New York: MLA, 1982.

North, Stephen M. *The Making of Knowledge in Composition.* Upper Montclair, N.J.: Boynton/Cook, 1987.

Ohmann, Richard. *English in America: A Radical View of the Profession.* New York: Oxford UP, 1976.

Ong, Walter J., S. J. "Review of Brian Vickers' *Classical Rhetoric in English Poetry.*" *College English* 33 (1972): 612–16.

Pascale and Athos (see Chapter 6).

Perelman, Chaim, and L. Olbrechts-Tyteca. *The New Rhetoric: A Treatise on Argumentation.* 1958. Trans. John Wilkinson and Purcell Weaver. Notre Dame, IN: Notre Dame UP, 1969.

Piaget, J. *The Moral Judgment of the Child.* 1932. New York: Free, 1965.

Pike, K. L. *Language in Relation to a Unified Theory of the Structure of Human Behavior.* The Hague: Mouton, 1967.

Rich, Adrienne. *On Lies, Secrets, and Silence: Selected Prose 1966–1978.* New York: Norton, 1979.

Rohlen, Thomas P. (see Chapter 6).

Rose, Mike. "Remedial Writing Courses: A Critique and a Proposal." *College English* 45.2 (1983): 109–28.

Rottenberg, Annette T. *Elements of Argument: A Text and Reader.* 2nd ed. New York: St. Martin's, 1988.

Shaughnessy, Mina. *Errors and Expectations: A Guide for the Teacher of Basic Writing.* New York: Oxford UP, 1977.

Spender, Dale. *Man Made Language.* London: Routledge, 1980.

Sternglass, Marilyn S. *Reading, Writing, and Reasoning.* New York: Macmillan, 1983.

Stewart, Donald C. *The Authentic Voice: A Pre-Writing Approach to Student Writing.* Dubuque: Brown, 1972.

Suhor, Charles. "Trends." *Educational Leadership.* Feb. 1989: 84.

Tirkkonen-Condit, S. "Towards a Description of Argumentative Text Structure." *Proceedings from the Second Nordic Conference for English Studies.* Ed. H. Ringbom and M. Rissanen. Abo: Meddelanden fran Stiftelsens for Abo Akademi Forskningsinstitut 92 (1984).

Toulmin, Stephen. *The Uses of Argument.* Cambridge: Cambridge UP, 1958.

Trollope, Frances. *Domestic Manners of the Americans.* 1832. Ed. Richard Mullen. Oxford: Oxford UP, 1985.

Ueda, K. "Sixteen Ways to Avoid Saying 'No' in Japan." *Intercultural Encounters With Japan.* Ed. J. C. Condon and M. Saito. Tokyo: Simul, 1974. 185–92.

White, Merry. *The Japanese Educational Challenge: A Commitment to Children.* New York: Free, 1987.

Williams, Stanley T., ed. *Washington Irving: Selected Prose.* New York: Holt, 1950.

Zimmerman, D., and C. West, "Sex Roles, Interruptions and Silences in Conversation." *Language and Sex: Difference and Dominance.* Ed. B. Thorne and N. Henley. Rowley, Mass.: Newbury, 1975.

PART III

In the Literature Classroom

CHAPTER 8

Breaking Literary Codes, or Reading Students' Notebooks

Blau, Eileen K. "The Effect of Syntax on Readability for ESL Students in Puerto Rico." *TESOL Quarterly* 16.4 (1982): 517–27.

Bleich, David. *Subjective Criticism*. Baltimore: Johns Hopkins UP, 1978.

Chu, Harold S., and Young-Hee Park. *A Contrastive Analysis Between Korean and English for ESL Teachers*. Washington, D.C.: Office of Bilingual Education and Minority Languages Affairs, 1979.

Dillon, George L. *Constructing Texts*. Bloomington: Indiana UP, 1981.

Eagleton, Terry. *Literary Theory: An Introduction*. Minneapolis: U of Minnesota P, 1983.

Eggington, William G. (see Chapter 7).

Fish, Stanley E. *Is There a Text in This Class? The Authority of Interpretive Communities*. Cambridge, Mass.: Harvard UP, 1980.

Gatbonton, E., and G. R. Tucker. "Cultural Orientation and the Study of Foreign Literature." *TESOL Quarterly* 5.2 (1971): 137–43.

Holland, Norman N. *5 Readers Reading*. New Haven: Yale UP, 1975.

Honeyfield, John. "Simplification." *TESOL Quarterly* 11.4 (1977): 431–40.

Johnson, Patricia. "Effects on Reading Comprehension of Building Background Knowledge." *TESOL Quarterly* 16.4 (1982): 503–15.

———. "Effects on Reading Comprehension of Language Complexity and Cultural Background of a Text." *TESOL Quarterly* 15.2 (1981): 169–81.

Kingston, Maxine Hong. (see Chapter 5).

Kintsch, W., and T. A. van Dijk. "Toward a Model of Text Comprehension and Production." *Psychological Review* 85.5 (1978): 363–94.

Kujoory, Parvin. "Iranian Students and Western Cultural Concepts in Literature." *English Teaching Journal* 32 (1978): 221–25.

Markham, Paul, and Michael Latham. "The Influence of Religion-Specific Background Knowledge on the Listening Comprehension of Adult Second-Language Students." *Language Learning* 37.2 (1987): 157–70.

Selinker, L., J. E. Lackstrom, and L. Trimble. "Technical Rhetorical Information in EST Discourse." *TESOL Quarterly* 7.2 (1973): 127–36.

Selinker, L., R. M. Todd Trimble, and Louis Trimble. "Presuppositional Rhetorical Information in EST Discourse." *TESOL Quarterly* 10.3 (1976): 281–90.

Steffenson, M., C. Jogdeo, and R. C. Anderson. *A Cross-Cultural Perspective on Reading Comprehension* (Technical Report #97). Champaign, Ill.: Center for the Study of Reading, University of Illinois, 1978.

Swinney, David A., and David T. Hakes. "Effects of Prior Context Upon Lexical Access During Sentence Comprehension." *Journal of Verbal Learning and Verbal Behavior* 15 (1976): 661–89.

Trivedi, H. C. "Culture in Language Learning." *English Language Teaching Journal* 32 (1978): 92–97.

Wang, Chi-Chen, trans. *Dream of the Red Chamber* by Tsao Hsueh-chin. Garden City, N.Y.: Doubleday, 1958.

Williams, David. "Factors Related to Performance in Reading English as a Second Language." *Language Learning* 31.1 (1981): 31–50.

Wilson, William S. "Métier: Why I Don't Write Like Franz Kafka." *Why I Don't Write Like Franz Kafka.* New York: Ecco, 1977.

Yousef, Fathi S. "Cross-Cultural Testing: An Aspect of the Resistance Reaction." *Language Learning* 18.3–4 (1968): 227–34.

CHAPTER 9

Notes for an American Studies Course

Allen, Paula Gunn. *The Sacred Hoop: Recovering the Feminine in American Indian Traditions.* Boston: Beacon, 1986.

Alpers, Svetlana. *The Art of Describing: Dutch Art in the Seventeenth Century.* Chicago: U of Chicago P, 1983.

Andrade, Manuel J. *Quileute Texts.* New York: Columbia UP, 1931.

Babcock, Barbara A., and Guy and Doris Monthan. *The Pueblo Storyteller: Development of a Figurative Ceramic Tradition.* Tucson: U of Arizona P, 1986.

Bataille, Gretchen M., and Kathleen Mullen Sands. *American Indian Women: Telling Their Lives.* Lincoln: U of Nebraska P, 1984.

Baxandall, Michael. *Painting and Experience in Fifteenth-Century Italy: A Primer in the Social History of Pictorial Style.* 2nd ed. Oxford: Oxford UP, 1988.

Baym, Nina. "Melodramas of Beset Manhood: How Theories of American Fiction Exclude Women Authors." *The New Feminist Criticism: Essays on Women, Literature, and Theory.* Ed. Elaine Showalter. New York: Pantheon, 1985. 63–80.

Benedict, Ruth. "Eight Stories from Acoma." *Journal of American Folk-Lore.* 43:167(1930): 59–87.

Benjamin, Walter. *Illuminations: Essays and Reflections.* Ed. Hannah Arendt. Trans. Harry Zohn. New York: Schocken, 1969.

Berger, John. *Ways of Seeing.* Harmondsworth, England: Penguin, 1972.

Bloom, Allan. *The Closing of the American Mind: How Higher Education has Failed Democracy and Impoverished the Souls of Today's Students.* New York: Simon, 1987.

Boas, Franz, ed. *Keresan Texts.* Vol. 8, I. New York: Publications of the American Ethnological Society, 1928.

———. *Tsimshian Texts.* Washington, D.C.: Government Printing Office, 1902.

Bryson, Norman. *Vision and Painting: The Logic of the Gaze.* New Haven: Yale UP, 1983.

Carby, Hazel. *Reconstructing Womanhood: The Emergence of the Afro-American Woman Novelist.* New York: Oxford UP, 1987.

Crow, Thomas E. *Painters and Public Life in Eighteenth-Century Paris.* New Haven: Yale UP, 1983.

Graff, Gerald. *Professing Literature: An Institutional History.* Chicago: U of Chicago P, 1987.

Howat, John K., et al. *American Paradise: The World of the Hudson River School.* New York: Metropolitan Museum of Art, 1987.

Hymes, Dell. *"In Vain I Tried to Tell You": Essays in Native American Ethnopoetics.* Philadelphia: U of Pennsylvania P, 1981.

Nygren, Edward J., et al. *Views and Visions: American Landscape Before 1830.* Washington, D.C.: The Corcoran Gallery of Art, 1986.

Parsons, Elsie Clews. "The Laguna Migration to Isleta." *American Anthropologist* 30 (1928): 602–13.

———. *Notes on Ceremonialism at Laguna.* New York: Anthropological Papers of the American Museum of Natural History 19:4(1920): 83–131.

Reichard, Gladys A. *An Analysis of Coeur D'Alene Indian Myths.* Philadelphia: American Folklore Society, 1947.

———. *Navajo Medicine Man Sandpaintings.* 1939. New York: Dover, 1977.

Rule, Sheila. "Kenyan Artists Struggle to Maintain Artistic Integrity Against the Lure of Tourist Money." *New York Times* 31 July, 1988: Sec. 2: 35.

Silko, Leslie Marmon. *Storyteller.* New York: Seaver, 1981.

Sturtevant, William C., ed. *Handbook of North American Indians.* Vol. 9 (Southwest). Ed. Alfonso Ortiz. Washington, D.C.: Smithsonian Institution, 1979.

Sullivan, Michael. *The Arts of China.* 3rd ed. Berkeley: U of California P, 1984.

Swann, Brian, and Arnold Krupat, eds. *I Tell You Now: Autobiographical Essays by Native American Writers.* Lincoln: U of Nebraska P, 1987.

———. *Recovering the Word: Essays on Native American Literature.* Berkeley: U of California P, 1987.

Thompson, Stith. *The Folktale.* New York: Dryden, 1946.

———, ed. *Tales of the North American Indians.* 3rd ed. Bloomington: Indiana UP, 1968.

Todorov, Tzvetan. *The Conquest of America: The Question of the Other.* Trans. Richard Howard. New York: Harper, 1984.

Index

Note: references to footnotes are shown by a page number followed by an italic *n*.

Affective variables in learning, 99
  measurement of, 132–133
  in reading literature, 205
  (*See also* Motivations of ESL
    students)
Ahmed, Leila, 47
Allen, Paula Gunn, 237
Ambiguity, in Japanese, 159–160
American culture:
  educational system in, and
    argumentation, 174–183
  versus Japanese culture, Japanese
    students on, 161–162
  (*See also* American Studies course for
    ESL students)
American Studies course for ESL
  students, 229–279
  and American culture, definition of,
    234–235
  designing of, 229–234
  re-viewing the literary and artistic
    canon in, 234–244
  syllabus for, 258–263
Antin, Mary, 240–241
Applebee, Arthur, 178*n*
Approximative system, 5
Argumentation:
  in American classrooms, 174–183
    by Japanese students, 183–195
  and culture, 181–182
    Chinese culture, 11–12

Argumentation, and culture (*Cont.*):
    Japanese culture, 169
  metaphors of, 181–182
  (*See also* Rhetoric)
Aristotle, on rhetoric, 112
Art:
  in American Studies course, 236–
    241
  in Japanese culture, 164–165
Articles (function words) in writing of
  Oleg Gokhman (Russian), 73–84
Audience, for native versus nonnative
  writers, 52–53
Autobiography in student writing:
  importance of, 94–95
  by Koula Markantonatous (Greek),
    100–104

Bain, Alexander, 177
Barclay, Craig R., 101*n*
Basso, Keith, 7
"be" (verb), in English versus
  Chinese, 120
Belenky, Mary Field, 173–174
Bellow, Saul, 230
Belsey, Catherine, 61
Bennett, William, 230
Berlin, James, 178*n*
Bird, Jon, 40
Blair, Hugh, 177

Bloom, Alfred H., 120*n*
Bloom, Allan, 230
Boas, Franz, 256, 256*n*
Bowman, Barbara, 54*n*
Browning, Robert, 210–212
Bruner, Jerome, 100
Bryson, Norman, 40, 233
Busch, D., 135*n*

Cameron, Deborah, 173*n*
Campbell, George, 177
Cartland, Barbara, 55
Cather, Willa, 252
Chinese culture:
  and argumentation, 11–12
  dragon in, 215*n*
  in *Dream of the Red Chamber*,
    214
  educational system in, 137–138
  good luck symbols in, 216
  indirectness in, 126–128
  and Japanese culture, 164*n*
Chinese language:
  cognitive effects of, 120*n*
  dialects of, 117*n*
  versus English, 116–129
    gerunds in, 121
    "have" in, 120
    nouns in, 121–122
    phonemes in, 123–125
    plurals in, 121–122
    in precision, 8–9
    prepositions in, 121
    pronouns in, 117
    spelling in, 123–125
    subjects in, 117
    time in, 118
    verbs in, 117–121
Chinese students:
  majors of, reasons for, 12, 12*n*
  organization of writing by, 125–129
  and reading of Maxine Hong
    Kingston's *The Woman Warrior*,
    141, 208–210
  sociocultural variables' effects on,
    137–139
  (*See also* Students, individuals,
    Chinese)
Christopher, Robert, 165
Chu, Chauncey C., 120*n*

City University of New York:
  cultural literacy of students at, 20
  Writing Assessment Test of, 11,
    183–184
  (*See also* Queens College)
Cole, Thomas, 238, 239
Connor, Ulla, 185
Contrastive analysis, 4
Cross-cultural literacy, 20–63
Culture:
  and aesthetics, 22–24
  and argumentation, 181–182
  and cross-cultural literacy, 20–63
  and discourse, 25–26
    (*See also* Rhetoric, and culture)
  and gender roles, 24–25
  as individual's creation, 57
  and provincialism, 13–14
  and readings in classes, 25, 29–31
  literary, 202–227, 230–231
    Bernard Malamud's "The Magic
      Barrel," 216–221
    John Cheever's "The
      Swimmer," 215
    Leslie Marmon Silko's
      Storyteller, 245–257, 273–279
    Maxine Hong Kingston's *The
      Woman Warrior*, 207–210, 222
    and religion, 205–206
    Robert Browning's "My Last
      Duchess," 210–212
    Salman Rushdie's "Good Advice
      Is Rarer Than Rubies," 30–35,
      59–64
    and schema theory, 204–206
    Theodore Roethke's "Elegy for
      Jane," 212–214
    Wallace Stevens's "Thirteen
      Ways of Looking at a
      Blackbird," 216
  and respect, 24
  stereotyping of cultural groups, 8*n*
    and interpretation of students'
      writing, 48
  vague definition of, 56–57
  (*See also* American culture; Chinese
    culture; Interpretation and culture;
    Islamic culture; Japanese culture;
    Jewish culture; Mende culture;
    Navajo culture; Perception and
    culture; Rhetoric, and culture)

Day, Richard R., 135*n*
Debate (*see* Argumentation)
Dewey, John, 178
Dillon, George, 203
Directness versus indirectness:
  in Chinese culture, 126–128
  in Japanese culture, 160–171
Discourse:
  cultural variations in, 25–26
  (*See also* Rhetoric)
Doi, Takeo, 157

Education:
  American systems of:
    and argumentation, 174–183
    rhetoric in, in higher education,
      177–183
    writing instruction in, in
      secondary school, 71–73
  Chinese system of, 137–138
  Japanese system of, 167–168
    versus American system, 163
Eggington, William G., 189–190
Ellipsis, in Japanese versus English,
  155–156
Ely, Christopher, 135*n*
English as a second language (ESL),
  history of research in, 4–6
English language:
  articles in, in writing of Oleg
    Gokhman (Russian), 73–84
  versus Chinese, 116–129
    gerunds in, 121
    "have" in, 120
    nouns in, 121–122
    phonemes in, 123–125
    plurals in, 121–122
    in precision, 8–9
    prepositions in, 121
    pronouns in, 117
    spelling in, 123–125
    subjects in, 117
    time in, 118
    verbs in, 117–121
  versus Greek, 98*n*, 103
  versus Hebrew, 162–163
  versus Japanese, 154–159
    and ellipsis, 155–156
    and mathematics, 9
    nouns in, 154

English language, versus Japanese
  (*Cont.*):
    relative pronouns and
      conjunctions in, 155
    word order in, 155
  versus Korean, 211–212
  present tense in, 118
  versus Russian
    pronunciation of, 71
    verbs in, 71–73
Error analysis, 5
Errors in students' writing:
  analysis of, 4–5
  of Chinese students, 116–129
    of Mimi Soo, 142
  errors that are not ESL errors,
    93–113
  of Oleg Gokhman (Russian), 71–74,
    75–84
  of Seiichi Masuda (Japanese),
    154–159
  (*See also* Writing by ESL students)
ESL (English as a second language),
  history of research in, 4–6
Essays:
  forms of, cultural variations in, 6–8
  (*See also* Rhetoric)
Exposition by Chinese students, 125–129

Fables, writing of, by Koula
  Markantonatous (Greek), 104–107
"Face" and second-language
  acquisition, 137
Fenollosa, Ernest, 117
Fossilized structures, 84, 134
Four Mountains, The (Navajo
  sandpainting), 228, 237
Function words:
  articles, in writing by Oleg
    Gokhman (Russian), 73–84
  in English versus Chinese:
    prepositions, 121
    "to be" and "to have," 120
    modals and modal auxiliaries,
      119–120

Gender bias of rhetoric, 172–174, 173*n*
Gender roles, cultural variations in,
  24–25
Gerunds, in English versus Chinese, 121
Goodwin, Charles, 173*n*

Goodwin, Marjorie Harness, 173*n*
Grammar:
 correction of, in student writing,
  95–96
 instruction in, usefulness of, 68*n*
 of interlanguage, 67–68
 (*See also* Function words; Nouns;
  Verbs; *specific languages, e.g.,*
  Chinese language; English
  language; Japanese language)
Greek language, versus English, 98*n*,
 103
Greek students (*see* Students,
 individuals, Greek)

Haas, Ken, 138
hanashi kata (Japanese concept),
 162–163
Hartwell, Patrick, 68*n*
Harvey, Paul, 137–138
"have" (verb), in English versus
 Chinese, 120
Hebrew language, versus English,
 162–163
Heidegger, Martin, 153–154
Higher education in America, rhetoric
 in, 177–183
Hinds, John, 167, 170
Hirsch, E. D., Jr., 20, 230
Holt, Virginia, 54, 54*n*

Indirectness (*see* Directness versus
 indirectness)
Induced errors, 5*n*
Instrumental motivation, 131–134
Integrative motivation, 131–134
Interlanguage, 5
 logic of, 67–68
Interpretation and culture, 216–217
 of art, 237–238
  of Matisse's "oriental" paintings,
   37–42
 of readings, 59–64
 (*See also* Perception and culture)
Islamic culture, 28–29, 42–64
 and adaptation to change, 43–44
 and gender roles, 24–25
 and veil for women, 44–47
 (*See also* Students, individuals,
  Islamic)

Japanese culture:
 versus American culture, Japanese
  students on, 161–162
 and argumentation, 169–170, 183–195
 and Chinese culture, 164*n*
 and classroom practices, 163, 167
 group versus individual in, 174
 indirectness in, 164–166
 and Japanese painting, 164–165
 and lexical errors in students'
  writing, 156–158
 Michiru Arai on, 191–195, 246,
  249–254
 and newspaper writing, 166–167
 and rhetorical style, 152–154, 160–171
Japanese language:
 versus English, 154–159
  and ellipsis, 155–156
  and mathematics, 9
  nouns in, 154
  relative pronouns and
   conjunctions in, 155
  word order in, 155
  writing system of, 159–160
Japanese students:
 argumentative writing by, 183–195
 (*See also* Students, individuals,
  Japanese)
Jewish culture and Bernard Malamud's
 "The Magic Barrel," 217–221
Johnson, Mark, 181–182
Journals of ESL students:
 of Albert Youssefi (Iranian), 246–247
 of César Nanzi (Colombian), 248
 of Fatima Tunis (Sierra Leonean), 248
 of Huai-li Luo (Chinese), 248–249
 of Koula Markantonatous (Greek),
  97–98
 of Michiru Arai (Japanese), 245–247,
  249
 reading of, 206–224

Kaplan, Robert, 125, 165
Kingston, Maxine Hong, 207–210, 222
Korean language, versus English,
 211–212
Korean students:
 reading of Western literature by,
  210–213
 (*See also* Students, individuals, Korean)

Lakoff, George, 181–182
Language (*see specific languages, e.g.,*
    Chinese language; English
    language; Japanese language)
Larson, Kay, 37
Lewis, Norman, 6
Literacy, cross-cultural, 20–63
Literature:
  American:
    beginnings of, 235–236
    and re-viewing the literary canon,
      242–244
    in college curriculum, cultural biases
      of, 230–231
    teaching of, to international
      students, 199–228
    (*See also* Readings in classes,
      literary)

Marin, Louis, 59
Markus, H., 101*n*
Mathematics and linguistic differences,
  9
Matisse, Henri, 23, 36–42
Mende culture, 240, 268–269
Metaphors of argumentation,
  181–182
Miller, Roy Andrew, 160
Modals and modal auxiliaries,
  119–120
Motivations of ESL students:
  of Koula Markantonatous (Greek),
    111–112
  of Mimi Soo (Chinese), 114–148
Muted groups, 10–14
My Ántonia (novel, Willa Cather),
  253–254, 270–272

Nakamura, Hajime, 160
Narrative in student writing:
  importance of, 94–95
  (*See also* Autobiography in student
    writing)
Navajo culture, 237
Newspaper writing in Japan,
  166–167
Norinaga, Motoori, 164*n*
Nouns:
  in Chinese versus English, 121–122
  in Japanese versus English, 154

Ohmann, Richard, 112, 180
Ong, Walter J., 172
Oral practice in classroom, 135*n*
Organization of writing by Chinese
    students, 125–129
Orthography (*see* Spelling)
Otani, Yasuteru, 9
Oxbow, The (painting, Thomas Cole),
    238, 239

Paragraphs and American principles of
    rhetoric, 150–151
Passive constructions in writing of
    Oleg Gokhman (Russian), 72–73
Pedagogy:
  composition pedagogy, 94–97
  (*See also* Education; Teachers)
Perception and culture, 216–217
  of art, 237–238
  (*See also* Interpretation and culture)
Performance mistakes, 4*n*
Perl, Jed, 37*n*
Phonemes, in English versus Chinese,
    123–125
Plato and rhetoric, 113
Plurals, in Chinese versus English,
    121–122
Poetry, reading of, 210–216
Pollack, David, 164*n*
Prepositions, in English versus
    Chinese, 121
Present perfect tense, 120
Present tense, 118
Pronouns, in Chinese versus English,
    117
Pronunciation:
  improvement in, over time, 134
  of Korean versus English, 211–212
  of Russian versus English, 71
Provincialism, 13–14
Pueblo Indians (*see* Silko, Leslie
    Marmon)

Queens College:
  American Studies course for ESL
    students at, 229–279
  composition courses at, 3*n*, 21*n*
  Great Works of American Literature
    course at, 26–27
  nonnative speakers of English in, 1*n*

Readings in classes:
  in American Studies course for ESL
      students, 241–257
  for ethnically diverse students, 58
  literary:
      Bernard Malamud's "The Magic
          Barrel," 216–221
      and culture, 202–227
      and religion, 205–206
      and schema theory, 204–206
      John Cheever's "The
          Swimmer," 215
      Leslie Marmon Silko's
          Storyteller, 245–257, 273–279
      Maxine Hong Kingston's *The
          Woman Warrior*, 207–210, 222
      poetry, 210–216
      Robert Browning's "My Last
          Duchess," 210–212
      Salman Rushdie's "Good Advice
          Is Rarer Than Rubies," 30–35,
          59–64
      teaching of, 199–228
      Theodore Roethke's "Elegy for
          Jane," 212–214
      Wallace Stevens's "Thirteen
          Ways of Looking at a
          Blackbird," 216
  and student writing, 96
  (*See also* Culture, and readings in
      classes)
Reichard, Gladys, 237
Reischauer, Edwin O., 160
Relative pronouns and conjunctions,
    in Japanese versus English, 155
Religion, and reading literature,
    205–206
Revision of writing, by Koula
    Markantonatous (Greek), 109–113
Rhetoric:
  American style of, 172–183
      gender-specific bias of, 172–174,
          173n
      guidelines for, 150–151
      in higher education, 177–183
      versus Japanese style, 169–171
  clarity in, 112
  and culture, 6–7, 152–154
      Chinese culture, 11–12, 127–128
      Japanese culture, 152–154

Rhetoric, and culture (*Cont.*):
      versus American culture, 160–171
      in educational practices, 167–168
      (*See also* Directness versus
          indirectness)
  for Plato, 113
  (*See also* Argumentation)
Rhyme and ESL students' reading of
    poetry, 211–212
Rip Van Winkle, 172n
Roethke, Theodore, 212–214
Romance novels, women in, 52–55, 54n
Roque, Oswaldo Rodriguez, 238
Rose, Mike, 176
Rushdie, Salman, 19, 30–35, 58n, 58,
    59–64
Russian language:
  articles lacking in, 75
  versus English:
      pronunciation of, 71
      verbs in, 71–73
Russian student, English articles
    acquired by, 67–92

Sa'adawi, Nawal el, 46–47
Saar, Alison, 241, 269
Said, Edward, 57
Schema theory, 202, 204–206
Schneider, Pierre, 39
Schumann, John, 5n
Secondary education in America,
    writing instruction in, 175n
Self-esteem and second-language
    acquisition, 134
Sentences in writing of Mimi Soo
    (Chinese), 117
Sexism of rhetoric, 172–174, 173n
Shaughnessey, Mina, 183–184
Shollar, Barbara, 254
Silko, Leslie Marmon, 255–257
Soloway, Anita, 14
Spanish language, and Chinese
    speaker, 124–125
Spelling:
  in English versus Chinese, 123–125
  of Oleg Gokhman (Russian), 71
Spivak, Gayatri, 58
Stereotyping of cultural groups, 8n
  and interpretation of students'
      writing, 48

Stevens, Wallace, 216
Students:
  cultural literacy of, 20–64
  experiences, problems, and
    characteristics of, 1–16
  individuals:
    American:
      Kathy Borstock, 208
      Kevin Brown, 208
      Michael Callahan, 210, 217, 220
      Mona Costanza, 215, 219
      Nancy Cohen, 208, 219
      Sheri Grunin, 208, 222
    Chinese:
      Chun-Hsiu Chiang, 121
      Hing-Po Leung, 126–127
      Huai-li Luo, 237, 247–248
      Kelly Chow, 122
      Ko-Ping Chen, 120
      Ku Chien-Chung, 11–13,
        123–124, 128–129, 209–210,
        211, 222–224
      Mei-Ying Tsai, 208–209, 222
      Mimi Soo, 114–148
      S. P. Chan, 126
      Soraya Chang, 119, 124–125
      Su-Chuan Tsai, 119, 215n
      Xiao Tian Qu, 127
      Xuya Chen, 12, 12n
    Colombian:
      César Nanzi, 248
    Ecuadorean:
      Blanca Palacios, 216, 220–221
    Greek:
      Koula Markantonatous, 93–113
    Indian:
      Alka Patel, 219–220
    Iranian:
      Albert Youssefi, 237, 246–247
    Islamic:
      Mohammad Amin (Urdu and
        Uzbeki speaker), 27–29, 42–47
      Najla Afzali (Dari speaker),
        21–26, 47–59
    Japanese:
      Hiroyuki Araseki, 149–152
      Masaaki Ito, 161–162, 185–189
      Michiru Arai, 168–169,
        189–195, 237–238, 245–257,
        249, 250–255, 270–272

Students, cultural literacy of, Japanese
  (Cont.):
    Seiichi Masuda, 154–159
    Tatsuya Suzuki, 160, 161
  Korean:
    Chung-Ae Park, 210, 211, 212,
      217
    Mi-Young Cho, 211, 212, 220
    Sunhi Lee, 212–214, 220
  Pakistani:
    Fauzia Subhani, 62–64
  Peruvian:
    Carmen Cheng (Chinese), 219
  Russian:
    Oleg Gokhman, 68–92
  Sierra Leonean:
    Fatima Tunis (Mende), 234–235,
      239–240, 242–243, 247,
      267–268
  muted groups of, 10–14
  as readers of literature, 201–202
  and rhetoric, cultural variations in,
    6–7
  (See also Errors in students' writing;
    Journals of ESL students;
    Motivations of ESL students;
    Writing by ESL students; specific
    groups of students, e.g., Chinese
    students; Japanese students)
Subjects (grammar), in Chinese versus
  English, 117
Subject-verb agreement in writing of
  Oleg Gokhman (Russian), 71–72
Syllables, in syllable-timed versus
  stress-timed languages, 212

Tanzer, Andrew, 165–167
Teachers:
  in American Studies course for ESL
    students, 242–243
  composition pedagogy of, 94–97
  cross-cultural literacy of, 20–64
  errors made by, 20, 64
  responsibilities of, 1
  on teaching literature, 199–202
Tenses of verbs:
  in Chinese versus English,
    118–121
  in writing of Oleg Gokhman
    (Russian), 73

.oooks:
in American high schools, 175n
on rhetoric, in nineteenth-century
America, 177
Thomas, Michael, 1
Thompson, J. Charles, 118
Thompson, Stith, 256
Time, in Chinese versus English, 118
Transitions in Chinese students'
writing, 125–127
Trollope, Fanny, 172
Tsao, Feng-fu, 126

Van Eyck, Jan, 217
Verbs:
in Chinese versus English,
117–121
tenses of, 118–121
transitive and intransitive, 121
in Japanese versus English,
154–155
modals and modal auxiliaries,
119–120
in writing of Oleg Gokhman
(Russian), 71–72
Vocabulary, and reading literature,
212–215

Whately, Richard, 177
Women:
and gender roles, cultural variations
in, 24–25
in Islamic culture, 44–55
in Japanese culture, Michiru Arai
on, 246, 251, 252
in Leslie Marmon Silko's Storyteller,
255–257
in romance novels, 52–55, 54n
in Western art, 40–41, 41n
writing by, 253
Word order, in Japanese versus
English, 155
Writing by ESL students:
by Albert Youssefi (Iranian),
246–247
autobiography in, importance of,
94–95
by Blanca Palacios (Ecuadorean),
216, 221
by Carmen Cheng (Chinese
Peruvian), 219

Writing by ESL students (Cont.):
by Chinese students, organization
of, 125–129
by Chung-Ae Park (Korean), 217
by Chun-Hsiu Chiang (Chinese), 121
by Fatima Tunis (Sierra Leonean),
240–241, 244, 268–269
by Fauzia Subhani (Pakistani), 62–64
by Hing-Po Leung (Chinese),
126–127
by Hiroyuki Araseki (Japanese),
149–152
by Huai-li Luo (Chinese), 248–249
importance of, in American Studies
course, 233
interpretation of, and stereotyping
of cultural groups, 48
by Kelly Chow (Chinese), 122
by Ko-Ping Chen (Chinese), 120
by Koula Markantonatous (Greek),
97–113
by Ku Chien-Chung (Chinese),
11–13, 123–124, 128–129,
209–210, 222–224
by Masaaki Ito (Japanese), 161–162,
185–189
by Mei-Ying Tsai (Chinese),
208–209, 222
by Michiru Arai (Japanese),
189–195, 245–257, 270–272
by Mimi Soo (Chinese), 114–148
by Mi-Young Cho (Korean), 211
by Mohammad Amin (Urdu and
Uzbeki speaker), 27–29
by Najla Afzali (Dari speaker),
21–23
by Oleg Gokhman (Russian), 69–92
pedagogy for, 94–97
reading aloud of, 96
in response to Leslie Marmon Silko's
Storyteller, 249–255
by S. P. Chan (Chinese), 126
by Soraya Chang (Chinese), 119,
124–125
by Su-Chuan Tsai (Chinese), 119
by Sunhi Lee (Korean), 213, 220
by Xiao Tian Qu (Chinese), 127
(See also Journals of ESL students)
Writing system of Japanese, 159–160